Creating the Big Ten

Creating the Big Ten

Courage, Corruption, and Commercialization

WINTON U. SOLBERG

UNIVERSITY OF ILLINOIS PRESS
Urbana, Chicago, and Springfield

Cataloging-in-Publication Data is available from
the Library of Congress
ISBN 978-0-252-04159-4 (cloth: alk)
ISBN 978-0-252-08324-2 (paper: alk)
ISBN 978-0-252-05025-1 (ebook)

To
Andrew

Contents

Acknowledgments

I am indebted to many for enabling me to bring this story of Big Ten football to a wide audience. Laurie Matheson, the director of the University of Illinois Press, has provided wise counsel, Julianne Rose Laut assisted in putting the manuscript into shape, and an anonymous outside reader made valuable suggestions about the entire enterprise. Daniel M. Nasset has been both a demanding and an encouraging editor of my manuscript at the University of Illinois Press, and I am grateful to him.

In the research for this book I have drawn on the titles listed in my bibliography but, more important, on primary sources in a number of repositories. At the Big Ten Conference Headquarters in Park Ridge, Illinois, Jennifer Heppel, Carol Iwaoka, Kerry Kenny, and Mark Rudner made my visits rewarding. At the Special Collections Research Center in the Regenstein Library at the University of Chicago, Christine Colburn, Julia Gardner, Barbara Gilbert, Leah Richardson, and Rena Schergen were most helpful.

Archivists at the Western Conference (Big Ten) universities were generous in assisting my research. I cheerfully acknowledge William J. Maher and Linda Stahnke at the University of Illinois; Dina Kellems at Indiana University; Denise K. Anderson at the University of Iowa; Karen Jania, Margaret A. Leary, Malgosia Myc, Rachel Dryer, and Julie Piacentine at the Bentley Historical Library at the University of Michigan; Eric Moore at the University of Minnesota; Janet C. Olson at Northwestern University; Kevlin Haire at Ohio State University; David M.

Hovde, Susan Calvert, and Elizabeth Wilkinson at Purdue University; and David Null at the University of Wisconsin.

Archivists in other universities who aided my research include Michelle Sweetser at Marquette University; Joshua D. Caster at the University of Nebraska—Lincoln; William K. Crawley and Peter Lysis at the University of Notre Dame; Marianne Kasica at the University of Pittsburgh; and Judith Ann Schiff at Yale University.

In my research, writing, and manuscript preparation, I encountered technical problems that members of the Library Information Technology office at the University of Illinois helped solve. In this respect I am especially thankful to Lillian Hellman, Drew Kenton, and Rhonda Jurinak. John Paul Goguen was skillful in assembling and preparing for publication the pictures in this book, while Thomas "Tad" Boehmer assisted me in many ways. Dr. Valerie Hotchkiss, director of the Rare Book and Manuscript Library at the University of Illinois, helped expedite the completion of this book.

Creating the Big Ten

.

Prologue

This book is a history of the Big Ten athletic conference in its formative years. It is primarily concerned with the relation between higher education and intercollegiate football in the nation's preeminent athletic conference in the twentieth century. The Big Ten, or the Western Conference as it was known, began with two basic commitments—the amateur athletic code and faculty control of intercollegiate athletics. The two were never well suited to American athletic culture. Americans play to win, not for love of the game, and the coaches made football their domain. Conflict between amateurism and professionalism troubled the Western Conference from its earliest years.

Big Ten athletics—indeed, American intercollegiate athletics—are unique in the world. Physical education is offered in primary and secondary schools everywhere around the globe, but on the Continent and elsewhere in the world athletic sports have little or no place in the university. Students are free to engage in such activities as they wish, but beyond university borders. America is different. For years, academic authorities insisted that college was a place to develop the mind, not the body. Students, however, had their own agenda. They played games and organized athletic associations, and the associations sponsored intercollegiate contests. The college administration, the faculty, and the alumni wanted a voice in the athletic associations. The alumni viewed the success of their school's athletic teams as evidence of the worth of their degree.

In the late nineteenth century, collegiate athletics was shaped by an amateur athletic code imported from England. There, public school sport mandated compulsory games every day, and the public-school sportsmen who went on to Oxford or Cambridge were molded by the cultural context of sport in Victorian England. The universities encouraged energetic outdoor pursuits with a view to producing healthy adolescent boys. Sport was believed to play a central role in the achievement of true masculinity, the harmonious growth of both the physique and the character. Games were regarded as the most powerful means of preventing sexual misconduct and producing "muscular Christians."[1] Through sport, boys acquired the virtues of self-restraint, fairness, honor, praise for another's success, and the ethic of fair competition.[2]

The general philosophy, as sport historian Richard Holt notes, could be summed up in the phrase "fair play." "Fair play was the watchword of the gentlemen amateur." The term "amateur" as applied to athletics meant anyone who did not "play for pay." Originally, Holt points out, "amateurs were gentlemen of the middle and upper classes who played sports that . . . the common people [often enjoyed] . . . but who played these and other games in a special way. Fair play meant not only respecting the written rules of the game, but abiding by what was generally understood to be the spirit of the game."[3]

America went in a different direction. Students at elite eastern colleges proclaimed their allegiance to amateur athletics, but their athletics was riddled with professionalism. Big-time, often commercialized intercollegiate athletics began in the 1880s. Traditionally, college authorities had concerned themselves with the curriculum, not the extra-curriculum. They had neither the time nor the inclination to manage athletics. Students gladly did so.

Since control by individual institutions was inadequate to deal with the problems of intercollegiate athletics, in 1882 President Eliot of Harvard invited other New England college presidents to unite against such evils as professionalism and, for example, the excessive number of baseball matches. "The faculty conferees of Harvard, Yale, and Princeton, along with those of Columbia, Penn, Trinity, Wesleyan, and Williams, met on December 28, 1883, and passed eight resolutions, including the following: no professional athlete should be employed as a coach of any college team; no college team should play against a non-college team; athletes were limited to four years of athletic participation; and each college should set up a faculty committee to approve rules and regulations."[4]

The conferees sent their resolutions to "twenty-one eastern institutions with the condition that when five colleges adopted them [the rules] would become binding."[5] The Harvard faculty adopted them by a 25–5 vote, the Princeton faculty adopted them unanimously, but no other college voted to affirm the resolutions. Students nearly unanimously opposed them. Years later the Big Ten conference passed a number of similar resolutions.

Antagonism to football grew concomitantly with the game. Reputable authorities observed that the leading colleges were becoming training grounds for young gladiators around whom countless spectators roared, and they condemned the game for its professionalism. Among the abuses were the tramp athlete, who played for more than one college without registering in either, the V formation, the flying wedge, and mass momentum plays—strategies that emphasized brutality and violence.

President Eliot of Harvard viewed most college or university athletic sports as worthy in "maintaining healthy . . . bodies in . . . condition for the intellectual and moral life." But, he noted, "with athletics considered as an end in themselves, . . . a college or university has nothing to do." Neither was it appropriate, he said, "for a college or university to provide . . . entertainments for multitudes of people who were not students." According to Eliot, "an unwholesome desire for victory . . . in intercollegiate football has perverted the judgment of the players and the college public," and "eagerness for victory by whatever means has . . . added to the risk of bodily injury incurred by the players."[6]

The evils of intercollegiate sports continued without redress, Eliot observed a year later. "The game of foot-ball grows worse and worse as regards foul and violent play, and the number and gravity of the injuries which players suffer. It has become perfectly clear that the game as now played is unfit for college use."[7]

On football, Yale's Walter Camp differed from Harvard's Eliot in almost every respect, and Camp more than Eliot strongly influenced how Americans viewed the game. Camp was a Yale running back from 1876 to 1882, the head football coach at Yale from 1888 to 1892, and later an executive in and then head of the New Haven Clock Company. For years he was an unofficial but active adviser to the Yale football team. Camp opposed the elimination of mass-momentum plays, but as a member of the football rules committee of the Intercollegiate Football Association he advocated rules changes that transformed rugby into the American game of football.[8]

In the 1890s Camp chaired a committee that included Harvard, Yale, and Princeton members to determine the degree of brutality in football. The committee sent questionnaires to coaches, former players, and school authorities soliciting their views on football. Camp evaluated the responses and was selective in what he published in *Football Facts and Figures* (1894), a book that whitewashed the dark side of football. The Harvard-Yale game that year was the roughest of a series between the two colleges. One Harvard player had his leg broken; another, a collarbone; still another, a nose. "Even the most enthusiastic devotee of football," the *New York Times* wrote, "admitted that the play today will do much to injure the game, and may call for interference by the college authorities."[9]

Camp viewed football from a managerial and technocratic perspective. His approach was like that of his contemporary, Frederick W. Taylor, an engineer who advocated systematic management of a work force in a machine shop. Camp proposed centralized authority in the person of a head coach. Assistant coaches specialized in various aspects of the training, but one man was always in control. Football was work, not play, invaluable preparation for life. It was a team sport; individuals were subordinate to the team. Brains counted more than brawn. Moreover, football was a coaches' affair. The coach had a game plan and managed the players as did a foreman with workers on an assembly line. He demanded obedience. Winning was the primary objective of athletic contests. Real men did not enjoy losing. Football was not merely a game but a spectacle. Camp was thrilled at large crowds and big gate receipts. Camp's athletes were trained in a way that prepared them to take their places in the new American industrial order. Football was the best school for instilling in young men the attributes demanded by business. Camp contributed to accelerating the commercialization and professionalization of intercollegiate football.[10]

A prolific author, Camp spread his views about football and team sports in thirty books and more than two hundred magazine articles. His book, *American Football*, appeared in 1891, and *Walter Camp's Book of College Sports* followed in 1895. Camp selected an All-America football team every year beginning in 1889.[11] As a player, coach, adviser, member of the rules committee, and author, Camp earned a reputation as the father of American football.

At the same time, many others contributed to a national dialogue on college sport. Beginning in 1891, for example, E. L. Godkin wrote powerful editorials critical of collegiate football in the weekly *Nation* magazine. Meanwhile, Caspar Whitney, a prominent sports writer, became a powerful advocate of amateur as opposed to professional athletics. In his view, sport should provide upper-class gentlemen recreation and pleasure. Whitney did not find a receptive audience in the United States.[12]

Manliness and football became twins in the 1890s. The cultural concept of manliness took many forms—the strong gentleman, the muscular Christian, and the master male animal. Competitive intercollegiate sports provided a training ground for all three. Allegedly, football bred in its players courage, endurance, fortitude, quick decision making, and subordination of the individual to the group. An athletic ideology of the time held that a college student had to be a man to play football and that playing football developed character. These notions became indelibly fixed in college football and gained a place in popular culture at the dawn of the twentieth century.[13]

At that time the American people were moving from farms to cities. The Populist movement of the late nineteenth century was an agrarian protest against identified evils, while the Progressive movement of the early twentieth century attempted to lead the new middle class from entrepreneurial to corporate capitalism in order to redeem the promise of American life. Muckrakers denounced trusts, robber barons, adulterated foods, and intercollegiate athletics. They helped create a climate that led to the Sherman Anti-Trust Act (1890) and the Pure Food and Drugs Act (1906).

At the same time, as sport historian S. W. Pope notes, journalists, educators, social reformers, scientists, and politicians created a new athletic ideology. "Organized athletics lent itself to the discourse on the nature of progress" because at "critical . . . junctures political culture and athletic culture overlapped. . . . The ideology of physical culture . . . linked the 'strenuous life' to . . . republican political ideals and the creation of a virtuous citizenry. . . . Hard [physical] training [was] one form of the work ethic." "Play" was viewed as a means of "building character."[14]

The "sporting republic," Pope explains, had "emerged forcefully in the late nineteenth century as the . . . urbanized, industrialized, professionalized middle class became increasingly self-conscious and powerful." As Progressives fashioned a new republicanism to control "economic and political conditions in the new order, the new sporting experts redefined athleticism. Modern sport . . . was a way to preserve competition and channel individual talent into socially efficient action." Theodore Roosevelt was a master of the "sporting sermonette." He and others argued that "the work ethic, innovation, and perseverance were rewarded on the playing field." In team sports the group's needs were uppermost. Sport had moral power. "Architects of the sporting republic," Pope notes, "promised that athletics would preserve America from the selfishness of . . . plutocrats and the labor radicals, . . . and non-republican ideologies. . . . [A]thletics was the essential ingredient in a 'moral education.'" Athletics built character and "promoted healthy democracy by teaching moral principles and a regard for justice." Sport made men moral and prepared them for a wholesome and productive life.[15]

This was the intellectual and moral culture that shaped Amos Alonzo Stagg. He saw something of Horatio Alger in his life story. Born in West Orange, New Jersey, in August 1862, he was the fifth of eight children. His father was a cobbler; the family was poor. Stagg, as he put it, inherited "a stocky, sturdy body."[16] He went to the local public school, worked his way through the Orange High School, joined the Presbyterian Church, and thought of entering the ministry. To prepare for college, he went to Phillips Academy in Exeter, New Hampshire. Here he subsisted on a meager diet while studying Latin, Greek, and mathematics. In 1884 he matriculated at Yale. A mediocre scholar but a natural athlete, he was a standout pitcher who hurled Yale to five championships but refused an offer to become a professional player in a major league. Stagg graduated in 1888 and remained at

At age twenty-six, Amos Alonzo Stagg (on the far left) was the right end on the 1888 Yale football team, then the strongest in the country. Among his teammates were William W. "Pudge" Heffelfinger, named an All-America guard for three years. Source: University of Chicago, Special Collections Research Center.

Yale to study divinity. He was elected as the student secretary of the Yale YMCA and enrolled for some courses, including one in biblical literature taught by the young prodigy, William Rainey Harper.

In the fall of 1888, Stagg, now age twenty-six, won a position as right end on the Yale football team, the strongest in the country. Among Stagg's teammates were William W. "Pudge" Heffelfinger, named an All-America guard for three years, and George W. Woodruff, later the coach at Penn and Illinois. In 1889 Stagg enrolled as a full-time student in the Yale Divinity School. He played football again and was selected as left end on Walter Camp's first All-America team.

In 1889 Stagg withdrew from the divinity school. He "put aside the cloth," as he said, because of an "inability to talk easily on my feet," and went to the International YMCA Training School in Springfield, Massachusetts, first as a student and later as a staff member; it is here that Luther H. Gulick, founding superintendent of the YMCA's physical education department, sold him on the idea of becoming a physical educator.[17] Stagg coached the school's football team, the Christians, for the next two seasons. In 1892 he went to the new University of Chicago, where he remained as head football coach for thirty years.

Athletics in the Big Ten universities, including Chicago, followed a course similar to that in the East. But the schools in the two regions differed. The midwestern universities that formed the Intercollegiate Conference of Faculty Representatives (Big Ten) in 1896 were younger, less elite, and more innovative than their eastern counterparts. Chicago (Baptist) and Northwestern (Methodist) had denominational origins, while the other conference members were public institutions. Several were products of the Morrill Land-Grant Act of 1862.

Some midwestern institutions adopted the graduate coaching system, in which the head football coach was the team captain from the previous year, while athletic missionaries from leading eastern colleges carried the football gospel to the Midwest. By 1890 forty-five former Yale players, thirty-five former Princeton players, and twenty-four former Harvard players had scattered around the country to coach. Many others imported a gridiron hero from the East, considered the breeding ground of the best players.

The University of Michigan had beginnings in 1817 when Catholepistemiad Michigania was founded in Detroit. It relocated to Ann Arbor in 1837. Michigan students first organized to play baseball in 1863. The first student athletic organization became the Baseball Association in 1876. Football began with interclass games in the late 1860s. The Football Association was organized in 1873, and in 1878 the baseball and football clubs merged to form the Athletic Association. In 1879 Michigan played the first intercollegiate football contest in the Midwest with Racine College of Wisconsin at the White Stockings baseball field in Chicago.[18] The team had no coach. In the 1880s and 1890s Michigan played a miscellany of opponents—eastern colleges (Harvard, Yale, Princeton, and Cornell), regional colleges (Albion, Notre Dame, and Purdue), and athletic clubs (Windsor, Detroit, and the Chicago Athletic Association).

At Indiana University, organized athletics began in the 1860s, when returning military veterans introduced baseball. In 1867 students formed the University Baseball Club. The faculty permitted the students to use a campus corner as a baseball diamond but would not allow the team to leave town to play "match" games. On May 2, 1883, Indiana played its first intercollegiate baseball game against Asbury (later DePauw). Meanwhile, the pigskin worked its way westward. A university team under a coach played its first intercollegiate football game against Franklin College in Indianapolis on October 15, 1887. For the next two years, the football team played one neighboring college each year. Ben "Sport" Donnelly, a former Princeton left-end, was the Indiana coach in 1891. For the next several years, two of which were without a coach, Indiana played local colleges and athletic club teams.

At the University of Iowa a football team with no coach played a total of eight games with neighboring colleges between 1889 and 1891. The following year a team with a coach played six games. In 1893 the coach was "Sport" Donnelly. Alden A. Knipe, an All-America halfback, quarterback, and captain of the 1894 Penn team, had served for two years as an assistant coach under Woodruff at Penn while earning a degree in medicine. In 1897 he moved to Iowa City, where he became the Director of Physical Culture, supervised intercollegiate athletics, and was the football coach from 1898 to 1901.

At Wisconsin, young men played intramural baseball and football from the early 1870s. On June 3, 1873, the faculty permitted certain students to visit Beloit College to play a game of baseball—apparently Wisconsin's first intercollegiate athletic contest. John Bascom, president of the University from 1874, did not encourage organized athletics. Although not opposed to recreational sports, "he was impatient at the absurd enthusiasm" with which college officials greeted the "victories of muscles." He doubted whether organized, competitive athletics were likely to promote "symmetrical mastery of the whole man."[19] Young men went their own way, however, and in 1881 they formed the University Athletic Organization. Although slow to develop, intercollegiate football began at Madison in 1889 with three games. Charles Kendall Adams, who became the president of the University in 1892, encouraged athletics, particularly football, as the common denominator of student interest. Parke H. Davis, a former Princeton lineman, was the coach at Wisconsin in 1893. He was the author of the classic history, *Football: The American Intercollegiate Game* (1911).

At Minnesota, freshman and sophomores first played a game of football in 1878. Two years later students formed an association to foster athletics, especially football. A Minnesota football team played a neighboring college twice in 1882, three opponents the following year, and then a series of high school teams. In 1889, a student leader of the football association began to exercise a certain disciplinary force over the players and local residents. Walter W. "Pudge" Heffelfinger, a local boy and a former Yale All-America football player, was the Minnesota coach in 1895.

At Northwestern, students played baseball almost from the day they arrived on the campus. In 1869 they organized a team. The first recorded baseball game with outside competition was in 1871. A trial game of football in February 1876 aroused so much enthusiasm that the students formed a football association. Football was an intramural sport until 1882, when a Northwestern team with no coach played Lake Forest College twice. By 1888 football was sufficiently established to enable Northwestern to play a few games each season, mostly against high school teams and without a coach. Knowlton L. Ames, a Princeton fullback and an All-America choice in 1889, "nicknamed 'Snake' because of his shifty running style,"[20] was the coach at Northwestern in 1891 and 1893.

The University of Illinois opened for instruction in 1868. In the 1870s students enjoyed a primitive version of baseball; the university nine initiated intercollegiate athletics on October 2, 1879, in a game with Illinois College held along with the Intercollegiate Oratorical Contest. Students introduced a primitive version of football in the 1870s. In 1878 they played the game on Thanksgiving Day. Fans put up goal posts on the campus in 1881. Many viewed the sport as rough and brutal; for a time it attracted few. Enthusiasts carried on, however, and they organized a football association. In 1882 the baseball and football associations united to form the Athletic Association, which won faculty approval a year later. Intercollegiate football began in 1890 when a student-led team played three games with neighboring colleges. A year later a Purdue man coached the team, which had six games with colleges in the area. Bowing to the primacy of eastern college football, Illinois hired Fred L. Smith, Princeton '97, a Tiger quarterback, as the coach in 1897 and 1898. Neilson Poe, Princeton '97, replaced him in 1899. Fred Smith returned in 1900, and Edgar G. Holt, Princeton '00, coached in 1901 and 1902. In 1903 George W. Woodruff, who had played football with Stagg at Yale and had coached at Penn, was the Illinois coach.

Athletics at Purdue followed the course traced elsewhere. In 1887 Purdue fielded a football team of "tall, skinny boys who wore spectacles and had the biceps of a sandhill crane."[21] Any student who wished to play made the team by signing up. The coach was a young man who could neither speak nor hear. After a humiliating loss to Butler College in 1887, Purdue played nine football games during the next two seasons, one each with Michigan and Illinois. Both "Snake" Ames and "Sport" Donnelly coached the Purdue eleven in 1891 and 1892. Donnelly also coached at Indiana in 1891.

In 1892, when the University of Chicago opened for instruction, intercollegiate athletics was well established in higher education. Stagg had been President Harper's student at Yale, where he became known as both an athlete and a Christian. He was in Springfield when Harper offered him a position at Chicago as an associate professor and director of the Department of Physical Culture and Athletics and a coach with tenure. "I feel decided," Stagg replied to the offer, "that my life can best be used for my Master's service in the position which you have offered."[22] Stagg's position was the first tenured appointment of a physical education department head and the first tenured appointment of a coach of intercollegiate athletics in an American university.

Stagg brought his national reputation to Chicago, while Harper recognized football's promotional possibilities for a new university. Both men were public evangelists of the gridiron gospel. Stagg asked Harper what his attitude would be toward intercollegiate athletics. Harper replied that he wanted Stagg to "develop teams which we can send around the country and knock out all the colleges. We will give them a palace car and a vacation too."[23] In 1894, when football was widely criticized as brutal and deadly, Harper granted that "limbs were broken and lives lost, . . . but life was . . . attended with risks." The world could easily make similar sacrifices "upon the altar of a vigorous and unsullied manhood. The question of a life or of a score of lives is nothing compared with that of moral purity, human self-restraint, in the interests of which, among college men, outdoor athletics contribute more than all other agencies combined." Athletic sports, Harper believed, "were an important part of college and university life."[24] Stagg professed devotion to the amateur athletic code. Chicago, he promised, would not recruit men or pay their expenses because they were athletes. He promised more than he delivered.

On October 1, 1892, the university opened and the football program began. Stagg coached and played with his team, which met high school and college squads. Chicago also played a Purdue eleven coached by both "Snake" Ames and "Sport" Donnelly. Chicago played two games with Illinois; one in Urbana on Thanksgiving Day. The record for the season was 0-4-3.[25] "The West," Stagg observed, "inevitably was playing inferior football."[26]

In 1893 Chicago played twelve games between October 14 and January 1, the last two indoors. Ten contests were at home. Stagg's 1894 season, which lasted from September 12 to January 4, was designed for show rather than as part of an academic program. The Maroons (the school color was adopted that year) played nineteen games—fourteen in Chicago, a prime place to market football. The highlight of the season was a train trip to the West Coast. During this promotional spectacle Chicago played games in San Francisco (twice), Los Angeles, and Salt Lake City. The Pacific Coast extravaganza advertised Rockefeller's university but had nothing to do with the higher learning. It accelerated the commercialization of intercollegiate football.

It was in this context that William L. Dudley, a professor at Vanderbilt University in Nashville, Tennessee, felt the need to act. In December 1894 he called a meeting in Atlanta at which faculty representatives from seven institutions in Alabama, Georgia, North Carolina, and Tennessee organized the Southern Intercollegiate Athletic Association. When the members met in New Orleans a year later, an additional nineteen institutions from Texas to South Carolina were represented in the new athletic association.

A year later, the most effective response to what was widely recognized as a crisis in football, then the dominant American intercollegiate athletic sport, came out of the Midwest. To that response and the history of intercollegiate football that followed we now turn.

PART ONE

From Disorder to Order

CHAPTER 1

The Beginning of the Big Ten

In January 1895 the presidents of six leading midwestern universities—William Rainey Harper of Chicago, Andrew S. Draper of Illinois, Cyrus K. Northrup of Minnesota, Henry W. Rogers of Northwestern, James H. Smart of Purdue, and Charles K. Adams of Wisconsin—met in Chicago to discuss football. President James B. Angell of the University of Michigan was expected but did not appear. The presidents objected to the alleged brutality of football but did not know how to stop it without abolishing the game, which they did not wish to do. Most of those present hoped to get what was best out of the game by regulating it. In a very long meeting the conferees called upon "all college and university authorities to put forth every practicable effort to prevent professionalism of every form in intercollegiate athletic games and to make every game an honorable contest of athletic skill by excluding from participation all persons not regularly enrolled as students, doing full work as such" and agreed on twelve rules.[1] Only Draper dissented to the adoption of the rules. He considered them too lax to accomplish the desired result.[2]

The Intercollegiate Conference of Faculty Representatives, 1896 to 1905

On February 8, 1896, pursuant to a suggestion from Professor Conway MacMillan of the University of Minnesota, representatives of the athletic committees of seven universities met in Chicago as the presidents had recommended. Chicago was represented by Amos Alonzo Stagg, the only delegate who was both a coach and faculty member. He attended as a faculty member. Those present established the Intercollegiate Conference of Faculty Representatives, known as the Western Conference and later as the Big Ten.

The structure for the government of the conference was set in the beginning. The president of each university was to select a faculty representative to the conference. Presumably the presidents were collectively responsible for the welfare of the conference. The president's appointee was often from the physical education department of the university or, if not, a sports enthusiast from an academic department. The conference members were major universities eager to establish their reputations, and the professional demands on faculty members did not encourage their devotion to intercollegiate athletics. Many faculty representatives to the conference served only briefly, while those who served for many years were able to shape policy. Some veteran faculty representatives favored their university's interests as opposed to the intercollegiate conference's interests.

The purpose of the conference was to make and enforce the rules governing the conduct of intercollegiate sports in the member universities. While endorsing fully "the spirit of the presidents' agreement," the representatives went over it with a free and critical hand, recommending that their universities adopt a certificate of eligibility to participate in sports essentially the same as that required by Harvard. The delegates also prepared "Rules for the Guidance of Athletic Committees" and reformulated the presidents' rules, issuing the "Inter Collegiate Rules Recommended by the Conference, Feb. 8, 1896."[3] With a few significant changes, these rules were in large measure those proposed by the presidents.

The delegates transmitted their handiwork to their institutions for consideration. The responses were varied. Four universities adopted the rules without alteration, while three others adopted them with certain emendations. For one rule, Northwestern proposed a substitute that read, "College teams shall not engage in games with professional teams nor with those representing so-called athletic clubs."[4]

Meeting on November 27, 1896, the faculty representatives went over the twelve rules in light of the responses from the universities. Among other topics raised were athletic training prior to the start of classes and training-table expenses for students living at home. Both items were unrelated to any rule under consideration. The deliberations demonstrated that the delegates supported intercollegiate athletics within a framework of sound academic policy.[5] The "Intercollegiate Rules Recommended by the Conference, November 1896" are essentially the same as the rules adopted earlier in the year.[6] In accordance with conference procedures, the delegates sent the rules to the member schools for consideration.

In early January 1897, before the Western Conference had demonstrated its effectiveness, the presidents of eleven state universities in the North Central region of the country met in Madison, Wisconsin, to deal with intercollegiate athletics.

They believed that intercollegiate athletics, and football in particular, should be subjected to more supervision. A committee appointed "to report such rules as [it] might deem wise" declared that intercollegiate athletics could "be made to subserve the interests of higher education . . . by a systematic reform in three particulars: . . . the organization of boards . . . having control of athletics; . . . uniformity in the adoption of rules determining the eligibility of players; [and] some modification of the rules under which certain games were played." They further recommended that "while ultimate authority" over athletic affairs "should rest with the Faculty, . . . every athletic interest" in a university should have "abundant opportunity" to be "heard and considered."[7] In the past it had been the custom in the North Central states to adopt the rules of the Eastern Association. The committee thought the time had come for the Midwestern universities to supplement these rules with their own rules. The committee recommended that each member of the so-called Madison Conference abide by certain rules that it outlined. These rules largely paralleled the twelve set forth by the presidents and amended by the faculty representatives. The Madison Conference is historically significant as evidence of a deep desire in the Midwest to reform football before the Intercollegiate Conference of Faculty Representatives had demonstrated its capacity in this area.[8]

The delegates also addressed some of the major athletic problems at the time. Foremost was amateurism as opposed to professionalism in college athletics, especially as related to summer baseball. On this matter the delegates declared that "if students employ their summers playing baseball, they will incur suspicion as to their amateur standing, and render their record subject to rigid investigation." The representatives also declared that the conference "unanimously favors such a modification of the rules now governing football as will make the game less rough."[9]

The Western Conference was the pioneer in institutional cooperation in the control of intercollegiate athletics. As noted earlier, several eastern colleges had attempted to cooperate in the control of intercollegiate athletics in 1883–84, but without success. The Presidents' Rules of 1895 and the conference rules of 1896 sought to correct the abuses in intercollegiate athletics.

It is worth noting that the Midwest was not alone in its effort to reform what was widely seen as a problem. In February 1898 a Conference on Intercollegiate Athletics was held at Brown University in Providence, Rhode Island. Faculty, student, and alumni delegates were present from Brown, Columbia, Cornell, Dartmouth, Harvard, Pennsylvania, and Princeton. Yale saw no need for reform and was conspicuously absent. In a lengthy session on the first day, the delegates discussed the objectionable features arising out of intercollegiate contests.

The "Report on Intercollegiate Sports" of the Brown Conference emphasized academic values. The authors wished "to prevent college athletics 'from interfering with the mental and moral training of students,'" and they "did not want college athletes to be tainted by commercialism or professionalism." They subscribed to the amateur ethos in sports. Winning athletic contests was not the prime value to the conferees, although it was to the college athletes and their fans. The report of the committee was an attempt to change the direction of sport in American colleges.[10]

The rules in the Providence Report were similar to those of the Western Conference, but they exhibited no evidence of drawing on the western model. Five rules related to faculty control of athletics. They decreed that each institution should have "an athletic committee with faculty representation"; the athletic committee should "approve all coaches, trainers, captains, and team managers; no athletic competition [should] take place without athletic committee approval; any student participation in more than one sport [should] require athletic committee approval; and the athletic committee [should] ensure that all athletes were bona fide [students]."[11]

Four rules refined student participation in sports: "only students in good academic standing" should be eligible to participate; special or part-time students "could not participate until they had attended college for one year; students deficient in studies in one university department could not participate in athletics if they transferred to another department in the same university; and no student admitted without passing the university entrance examinations, or convincing governing authorities that he was capable of doing a full year's work, would be eligible for athletics."[12]

The Providence Rules included four provisions on eligibility: students should be allowed "no more than four years of eligibility; students transferring from one institution to another could not participate in intercollegiate athletics for one year; only freshman would be allowed to participate on freshman teams; and no freshman could participate on both the freshman and the varsity teams."[13]

The committee made three recommendations on athletic practice and contests: "teams were not to practice during college vacations, except ten days prior to the opening of the fall term . . . ; all athletic contests were to be held on college grounds; and students of the competing colleges were to be given preference in the allotment of seats to contests." Finally, the report denounced professionalism and endorsed the amateur athletic code: "no student could participate in athletics if he had previously played for money" or had "received financial support to play on a college team; no student could participate in athletics if he had ever taught sports for financial gain; and no student would be eligible . . . if he received board free" at a training table "or if he owed money for training table meals."[14]

The Providence Report was admirable in emphasizing academic as opposed to athletic values, but its rules made little impact. At the last meeting of the conferees on May 6, only Brown, Cornell, and Harvard were represented; Columbia, Dartmouth, Pennsylvania, and Princeton did not even send regrets. "As a result of this indifference," wrote Henry Beach Needham, "the death knell of the Conference is sounded. While each college will still have its eligibility rules, there will be no organization to promote the *enforcement* of the rules. The only consolation derivable from this unhappy outcome is the possibility of a close union of *all* the leading Eastern colleges—including Yale—with a council which will have *legislative powers.*"[15] The Providence Conference placed the Western Conference in bold relief. The leading midwestern universities were cooperating to promote athletic sports within a context of academic integrity.

The Western Conference held the promise of imposing order on intercollegiate football in the Midwest, and it set an example in the national reform of intercollegiate athletics. Other colleges were eager to join the circle. In December 1899 Indiana and Iowa became conference members. Both were public universities located within a contiguous geographical area. The faculty representatives agreed that the conference should not exceed nine in number and declared that there be no further expansion of the membership.[16]

In 1901 Notre Dame, Drake, and Nebraska applied for admission. Missionary priests of the Congregation of the Holy Cross (C.S.C.) had founded Notre Dame in South Bend, Indiana, in 1842. In its early years Notre Dame accepted any man or boy who wished to attend. With many Irish-American male students in an isolated location, the school's masculine athletic culture was part of its identity. Notre Dame played its first intercollegiate football game in 1887. In the years to 1901 the Irish battled conference teams from Indiana, Michigan, Northwestern, Purdue, and Wisconsin with few victories.[17] Notre Dame was denied entry to the conference. Whether anti-Catholic prejudice led to the rebuff is impossible to know. Most likely the conference concluded that Notre Dame was not yet ready academically for membership.

Drake, a small college in Des Moines, Iowa, affiliated with the Disciples of Christ denomination, was at the time hardly a serious contender for conference membership.

The University of Nebraska, a land-grant school chartered in 1869, opened for instruction in Lincoln in 1871 and grew slowly in the crisp atmosphere of the western prairie. The school played its first intercollegiate football game in 1890. In 1892 the Cornhuskers defeated the University of Illinois 6–0 at home. In 1898 Fielding Yost was in his second job as the coach at Nebraska. In 1900, when the state of Nebraska spread out over almost 77,000 square miles of prairie and recorded a population of 1,066,300, more than 800,000 of whom were rural residents, the fledgling college became a university under the leadership of E. Benjamin Andrews. Walter C. "Bummy" Booth became the football coach. Nebraska lost to Minnesota 12–20 in a home game that year, initiating what became an annual contest between the Cornhuskers and the Gophers. Nevertheless, Nebraska had a good football season. A year later the school applied for Western Conference membership. The faculty representatives voted that it was inexpedient to enlarge the membership. "We see no reason why we should admit any other colleges to membership," Alfred Pattengill (Michigan) explained. "The conference is simply an advisory body of faculty representatives, who come together voluntarily to see what could be done towards improving the quality of athletics in the West. We have none but the most kindly feeling for the other colleges, and sincerely hope that they will accept the invitation to take part in our meet [a track-and-field meet]."[18] But Pattengill errs. The conference was a legislative body whose members met by schedule. Pattengill was more than a little condescending.

Again in 1902 the faculty committee denied Nebraska and Notre Dame admission. The records shed no light on the reasons for this rebuff. The Rev. Thomas V. Crumley, vice president of Notre Dame and chairman of the school's athletic board, was reportedly "adamant in defense of Notre Dame's standards." Whether he meant athletic or academic standards is unclear. In any case, Notre Dame's academic standards were not then on the level of the conference universities. Crumley said that the battle had been "fought on theological rather than athletic grounds."[19] He may have been correct. Anti-Catholic prejudice was strong in the Midwest, and the faculty representatives may have shared it. Two conference members—Chicago and Northwestern—were identified with Protestant denominations, Baptist and Methodist, respectively. The other conference members were public universities with no religious identity, but many faculty members in these institutions were members of Protestant churches. So the Western Conference tightened its circle.

The White Resolution

Since the Western Conference was a legislative body, the question arose as to what would happen if one or more members did not accept the rules devised by the conference. In November 1900 Henry S. White (Northwestern) recommended that the faculty committees on athletics in the member universities empower their delegates to consent to the measures and rules adopted by the conference on the understanding that each faculty committee reserved the right to reject any measure the conference adopted within sixty days. The conference was to reconsider any measure so rejected at its next session. If the measure then passed by a two-thirds vote, any member university rejecting the measure a second time was to be suspended from the conference.[20] In November 1901 the delegates adopted the White Resolution.[21] It profoundly influenced the conduct of conference affairs.

The WIAAA and the Graduate Committee

Football preoccupied the conference, but track and field had an honorable tradition in the American colleges when the Big Ten was created. The relation between the two types of collegiate athletics was a problem in 1899. Clarence A. Waldo of

Purdue defined the relationship so as to free both types of athletics to go their separate ways. After considerable discussion among the conference colleges and other colleges in the area, the parties involved adopted the "Constitution and By-Laws of the Intercollegiate Conference Athletic Association." Its object was to conduct an annual track and field meet in the Midwest collegiate institutions. The members of the ICAA were the boards in control of athletics in the nine conference universities and such other institutions as might later become members of the conference. The legislative functions of the ICAA remained in the Western Conference. The executive power of the ICAA was vested in a managing committee consisting of the representatives of the members of the ICAA who were alumni of the institutions that they represented, with each association member electing one member. This committee (known variously as the Graduate Committee, the Managing Committee, and the Board of Directors) was to have sole charge of the annual track and field meet, which was to be held on the first Saturday in June. The bylaws laid out in detail the rules for the conduct of the annual meet, including a definition of an amateur athlete.[22] Thus the Western Conference created a separate but closely affiliated body—the Intercollegiate Conference Athletic Association—to administer track and field sports, freeing the conference to devote itself to football.

In 1905 the State of Illinois granted a certificate of incorporation of the Intercollegiate Conference Athletic Association. Its object was "to promote public interest in track and field athletics and other forms of amateur sport and to maintain a high standard of amateurism in athletics, and to conduct and manage athletic contests, exhibitions and meets in furtherance of the purposes above named." The ICAA was to have a capital stock of $1,500, with fifteen shares valued at $100 each. In 1905 all nine stockholders were identified with one of the Big Nine universities. Six men each held two shares and three men each held one share. Records indiscriminately call the stockholders the Graduate Directors, the Graduate Managers, the Graduate Committee, and the Board of Directors. The stockholders were a corporation. They managed an annual track meet and the finances connected with it. As a group they figure prominently in the history of the Western Conference.

The Western Conference and Football

In its early years, the conference enforced its own rules. In 1901, for example, the faculty representatives barred a Minnesota football player from further participation in intercollegiate athletics because he had violated a rule that forbade a student who participated in intercollegiate athletics from using his athletic skill for gain. The athlete had competed in a fat man's race and had accepted $5 as winner of the race.[23]

Since the Western Conference endorsed the amateur athletic code, it created the position of arbitrator to determine questions of eligibility. Clarence A. Waldo (Purdue) was named to the position in 1900. The arbitrator was to define what constituted a college for conference purposes, to evaluate the eligibility to participate in intercollegiate athletics of students who transferred from college to college, and to report to the conference. Waldo was an excellent choice as arbitrator. In 1903, at a meeting of the Association of Colleges and Preparatory Schools of the North Central States, he spoke strongly about the need of "drastic" faculty action against professionalism, declaring "Amateurism or nothing."[24]

Postseason Football Games

In 1890 some Pasadena gentlemen decided to inaugurate a Tournament of Roses, and in 1896 they organized a Tournament of Roses Association. For years the sports events attracted few visitors. People went to Pasadena to see the parade. As football gained a following, the association decided to stage a football game as the major attraction and to make it a national contest between teams from the West and the East. Fielding "Hurry Up" Yost's Michigan team was a powerhouse at the time. In 1901 Michigan tied Wisconsin for the Big Ten championship, whereupon Pasadena promoters invited Michigan to play Stanford in the Tournament of Roses on New Year's Day, 1902. The Michigan players traveled to

A Big Ten team participated in the first Tournament of Roses Game, held in Pasadena on January 1, 1902. On this occasion, the Michigan Wolverines humbled California 49–0. Source: Bentley Historical Library. University of Michigan.

Pasadena by train. The floral association allotted $3,500 for team travel and lodging expenses and $2 a day in meal money. Charles Baird, the Michigan graduate manager of the team, demanded $3 a day so that the men could go comfortably and in reasonable style. The local authorities granted the request, and the Wolverines humbled Stanford 49–0.[25]

In November 1902, when a California floral association invited a conference college to participate in a football game in California under its auspices, the faculty representatives declared that the proposal was not in accordance with the rule that all intercollegiate games were to be played on grounds owned by or under the control of one or both of the participants in the contest and under student or college management. Thus the conference rejected the invitation.[26]

Nevertheless, competition, commercialism, and amateurism were issues before the representatives. At a meeting in December 1905, Pattengill (Michigan) spoke on lessening the intense rivalry that had entered into intercollegiate athletics. He mentioned the abuses he considered it desirable to eliminate. Barton (Illinois) expressed the prevailing sentiment that the high prices for admission to athletic games was the most dangerous evil affecting the purity of college athletics. The receipts from football games had become so large that unless something was done to check the evil, athletics might soon become more important in the public eye than the colleges themselves. Big receipts made a college autocrat of the varsity football player and had a bad effect on the athlete. The large sums of money received as gate receipts had a tendency to magnify the importance of the athletic side of student life. Not more than fifty cents should be charged at any game for any seat, and a lesser sum should be charged when possible.[27] Barton and his colleagues forecast how collegiate athletics would play out. But they were like King Canute trying to hold back the ocean tide.

By late 1905 the clamor for the reform of intercollegiate athletics was widespread. Colleges, athletic conferences, and athletic associations made common cause in the matter. Noteworthy were the Western Conference (later the Big Ten) and the Intercollegiate Athletic Association of the United States (later the National Collegiate Athletic Association or NCAA).

In mid-January 1906, responding to the call for change, President James B. Angell of Michigan called a meeting of conference faculty representatives to discuss athletic problems. "King Football on Trial Today," the *Chicago Tribune* declared on January 19, the day the conference began.

Many of the participants in this meeting were experienced faculty representatives. They included Herbert J. Barton (Illinois), who was elected secretary, Martin W. Sampson (Indiana), Arthur G. Smith (Iowa), Alfred H. Pattengill (Michigan), Frederick S. Jones (Minnesota), Omera F. Long (Northwestern), Thomas F. Moran (Purdue), and Thomas S. Adams (Wisconsin). Others made their conference debut at this time. Harry Pratt Judson, a political scientist, was the interim president of the University of Chicago. Albion Small was head of the Department of Sociology and dean of the College of Liberal Arts and Sciences at Chicago. Frederick Jackson Turner of Wisconsin, the historian of the closing of the American frontier, was a vocal presence. Thomas F. Holgate of Northwestern was the chairman of the meeting.

Early in the session Pattengill read a letter from President Angell to the conference. The general complaint of the public press was the "roughness and the dangerous character" of football, Angell observed, but those who administered universities would agree, that "other objections to the existing mode of carrying on the game [were] as serious as the roughness in the play." First, "the absorbing interest and excitement of students . . . in preparation for the intercollegiate games [made] a damaging invasion into the proper work of the university" at the beginning of the academic year. Moreover, there were too many games. The competition of university classes and departments would "furnish games enough for healthy rivalry." Second, the existing conditions held before the students and the world "false ideals of college life." The students who were featured in newspapers as "the great men of the university [were] the men of brawn rather than the men of brains." Undergraduates and school boys were "filled with aspirations" to emulate the best players, not the best scholars. Third, the university was "looked on as training men for a public spectacle" instead of training them for "useful, intellectual, and moral service." The "intellectual trainers" were "made to appear as of small consequence compared with the football coach [and] trainer." And fourth, "the expenditure of money in the preparation for the game [was] out of all proportion to what a rational provision for exercise and games for students ought to call for." "To preserve the good in the game and to remedy the evils would not be easy," Angell admitted, but university faculties were ready to support measures calculated to diminish or cure the evils.[28]

The delegates voted that their proceedings should not be given to the press until after their deliberations. Barton's minutes are spare, but the press eagerly reported the conflict. With Angell's letter as a reference, each representative commented on the evils to be remedied. Pattengill introduced certain suggestions made by Michigan faculty members concerning changes in football regulations. He represented a faculty that was eager to release Michigan from "the clutch of athletics."[29] Turner said that one evil was brutality, but it was not as bad as in the East, and was a minor matter. Football injured intellectual activity and had a bad effect on the high schools.[30] Prior to the conference, Turner had worked with colleagues at Chicago and Michigan to remove powerful professional football coaches,[31] and he had publicly denounced the influence of football on the intellectual life of the university. The Wisconsin faculty had directed him "to propose public condemnation of the evils of football and a two-year suspension of intercollegiate contests."[32] Judson spoke of the physical evils of football but did not consider them serious. He deemed the moral evil as the greatest, he mentioned the undue exaggeration of interest in intercollegiate games, and he regarded recruiting as a great evil as well.[33] His colleagues instructed him to recommend that, at a minimum, football competition should cease for a term of years.[34] Barton spoke of the intense rivalry and of the desire to win at all hazards as one of the greatest evils to be remedied, and of the moral tone that resulted from this intense rivalry. Other delegates mentioned the brutality of the game, too many games, the large sums of money football generated, the financial support given to able athletes, the deification of the athletic hero, the paying of too high a price for coaching, and the bad influence of football on the student body.[35] After everyone had spoken, the delegates appointed Sampson, Turner, and Moran to draw up a statement of the evils of the situation.

The question of the price charged for admission to intercollegiate games provoked considerable discussion. Many viewed high prices as a hardship on students, while some said that large gate receipts tended unduly to magnify the importance of athletics in student life. A proposal to abolish the system of paid coaches was so contentious that it had to be temporarily postponed. Stagg was a professor as well as a coach, so his position would be secure even if professional coaches were abolished. But if the proposal to eliminate the professional coach passed, said Pattengill, his friend Fielding Yost, the Michigan coach with a contract at $8,500, would not be accepted into the faculty and would not be content to accept the salary paid to faculty members of his rank.[36]

The report of the committee Sampson chaired was unsparingly critical.[37] The condition of affairs "imperatively" demanded change. The choice was either to suspend the game as an intercollegiate sport or to cut away its evils, which fell into two classes. One was the "physical danger and brutality" inherent in the playing rules; the other was the "moral evils attending upon the gradual raising of the game into a thing of absorbing and sometimes hysterical public and collegiate interest." The game had to be "reformed," the "serious degeneration in athletic standards" checked, and "a healthy condition restored." A healthy condition existed not in the playing of a few excellent athletes but in the "active participation in wholesome outdoor exercise by practically the whole student body." The existing system offered an "athletic exhibition of trained performers for the pleasure of spectators." At the root of the difficulties was a "misapprehension . . . of the relation that a form of physical exercise [bore] to the educational life" of a university. Football had come to "offer opportunity for the manifestation of many extreme, nervous and illogical tendencies of modern college life." Among its harmful conditions were "the large number of games played and the length of the season." "The interest of a college, of a whole town, . . . of the entire public is held for a long time at more or less high tension, to the exclusion of far more important interests; and the consequences of prolonged strain are marked in the physical and mental condition of the [players], and in the scholarly efficiency of the students in general. This heightened excitement, occasionally artificially induced by various devices for arousing 'enthusiasm,'" the committee's statement continues, "involves unreal ideals of university manhood, exaltation of the athlete above the student, bitter rivalry with friendly institutions, unfair judgments of these institutions, suspicions of underhand treatment, and the employment of methods either illegal or barely within the letter of the law,—the result being to create a feeling that the main matter of importance in the autumn semester is to turn out, at all hazards, a winning football team."

Professional coaching, they asserted, was another abnormal condition. "Much good has resulted from the instruction given by expert athletes of high, sportsmanlike ideals," but the pressure on a coach "to develop a winning team or lose prestige [or perhaps] his position was an incessant temptation to secure players in all sorts of ways, and to instruct them to utilize, in playing, various means to defeat the spirit of the rules of the game." They continued: "Along with this is the zeal of many alumni who . . . raise or contribute money to pay the expenses of athletes in college, thus professionalizing them and corrupting the student sentiment." Also wrong, they said, were the "recruiting of students by coaches, managers, alumni, and others for essentially athletic purposes," emphasizing that

> the excess of severe and prolonged training, the moral evils frequently following the abrupt breaking of training at the end of the season, the hardship upon students, who are called to give undue time and money to intercollegiate games, the notion that a championship must be contended for, the too great publicity given to minor details of practice, . . . the adoption by the high schools of distorted notions of college ideas and college customs, and the excesses—such as betting—attendant upon all contests, that are especially pronounced when the public interest is as great as it is in football.

The conference therefore desired to "eliminate from the general conduct of the game certain wholly unnecessary evils—extravagance in salaries and the purchase of supplies, the over-long season, the too-frequent games, the centering of the interest in the team as distinguished from the general participation of students in athletics, and the wholly false emphasis that is laid upon what cannot be regarded as anything other than an incident in college life."[38]

On the next day, the conference returned to the controversial question of the professional coach. A resolution declaring that the conference recommended that there should be no coaching of football teams except by their own members after October 1, 1907, was discussed but failed adoption. Then it was moved "that inter-collegiate football be suspended for two years by the institutions represented in this Conference." Turner, Small, and Adams supported the motion, while Pattengill, Sampson, Moran, Long, Smith, and Barton thought it was desirable if possible to find conditions under which the game could be saved as an intercollegiate sport.[39] This motion was allowed to lie on the table, whereupon the conference adopted the following recommendations to be made to the colleges: that "football as played at present be abolished as an intercollegiate and collegiate sport in the conference colleges; that the Conference awaits from the Rules Committee such modification of the playing rules as will free the game from brutality and unnecessary danger; that in the event of such alteration not being sufficient the Conference will delegate a committee of its own to draw up rules; and that if a satisfactory game can thus be established, the restrictions recommended by the conference shall apply to its conduct and management."[40] In case these recommendations were not accepted, the conference proposed as the only alternative the suspension of intercollegiate football for at least two years.[41]

The conference declared that if a satisfactory game of football could be established, its recommendations should apply to the conduct of the game. These were as follows:[42]

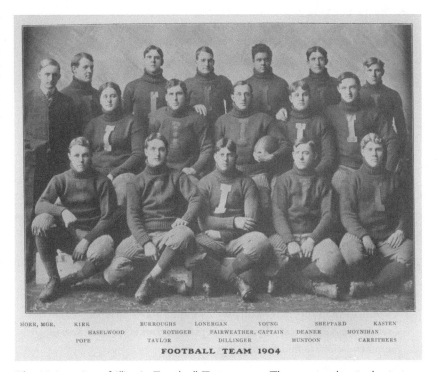

HORR, MGR.	KIRK		BURROUGHS	LONERGAN	YOUNG		SHEPPARD	KASTEN
		HASELWOOD		ROTHGEB	FAIRWEATHER, CAPTAIN	DEANER		MOYNIHAN
		POPE		TAYLOR	DILLINGER		HUNTOON	CARRITHERS

FOOTBALL TEAM 1904

The University of Illinois Football Team, 1904. These sturdy students are ready to give all for Alma Mater. Source: University of Illinois Archives, *Illio* '06, 301, tif 7555.

1. The "freshman rule:" A residence requirement of one year and one full year of credit in addition to meeting the entrance requirements of the college of liberal arts or its equivalent in order to participate in intercollegiate athletics.

2. The "three-year rule:" No student was to participate in intercollegiate athletics for more than three years in the aggregate, and participation was confined to undergraduates.

3. No team consisting in whole or in part of college students was to play with teams representing high schools, academies, or independent professional schools.

4. No more than five intercollegiate games of football should be played by any team in each season.

5. Eliminate the rule that did not count the first three football games in each season.

6. Freshmen teams and second elevens were to play only with teams from their own institutions.

7. The price of admission to intercollegiate contests for members of the university was to be not more than fifty cents, including reserved seats.

8. No training table was to be maintained.

9. The chairman of the board of athletic control in each college should state in his certificate of each player's eligibility that the student had passed all entrance requirements, that all intervening work had been passed; and that he was pursuing a full course of studies.

10. There was to be no coaching except by regular members of the instructional staff, appointed by the trustees on recommendation of the faculty, and salaries should be no more than those paid to other faculty members of the same rank.

11. No preliminary training period prior to the beginning of instruction was permitted.

12. The football season should end on the second Saturday before Thanksgiving.

13. Because the amount of money received at athletic contests was too large, steps should be taken to reduce the receipts and expenditures resulting from intercollegiate contests.

14. The athletic surplus should be devoted to permanent university improvements, and the financial management of athletics should be entirely within the control of the faculty, which should publish a report of the receipts and expenses.[43] The faculty representatives agreed on these recommendations in mid-January.

After the meeting, the conferees made public a statement that was not among their recommendations. The intense spirit to win, they declared, which was not

The Illinois-Wisconsin football game, November 10, 1906. In the game played on Illinois Field, Wisconsin trounced Illinois 16–6. Source: University of Illinois Archives RS 39/2/20, box 44, folder "1905–1907."

in accordance with university ideals, had been one of the worst evils attendant on the game. Thus the delegates urged the adoption of football schedules that would prevent the naming of a champion at the close of the season. Presumably each university team would play only one "big" game each season.[44]

This meeting was a high point in the history of the Western Conference. Angell had clearly defined the gravity of the problem. The conferees courageously considered suspending football for two years if not abolishing the game. In the end, they decided on measures to reform football.

Fielding Yost was not present in Chicago, but the position of the professional coach figured prominently in the meeting. Yost was born in 1871 in a rural community in West Virginia. He attended a normal school in Fairmount, West Virginia, and Ohio Normal, a Methodist institution, in Adair, Ohio. As a student he played football for two years. In 1895 he entered the University of West Virginia law school, graduating in 1897 with a business career in mind. But he decided to try coaching. He was the football coach for one year at both Ohio Wesleyan and the University of Nebraska, where his men beat the University of Colorado 23–10, and despite a faculty order not to play the Denver Athletic Club, "a gang of pros," they played the suspected pros and won 11–10.[45] Yost went the next year to the University of Kansas, and then to Stanford for a year. He applied to the University of Illinois for a coaching position, but Illinois had no vacancy. Charles Baird, the Michigan athletic director, offered Yost a job, and in 1902 he went to

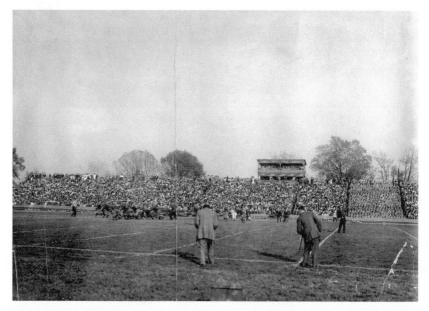

Chicago, coached by Amos A. Stagg, played Illinois, which employed the graduate coaching system, on Illinois Field in Urbana, October 15, 1910. Illinois won 3–0, with a 45-yard dropkick by Otto Seiler. Source: University of Illinois Archives RS 39/2/20, box 44, folder "Ath 2–3. October 15, 1910."

Ann Arbor with a salary of $2,300 plus living expenses to coach for ten weeks during the football season. Not a faculty member, he devoted the remainder of the year to business enterprises, in particular the extraction of oil and natural resources in Tennessee and other border states. For years a tremendous success as the head football coach of the Wolverines, Yost brought financial stability to the Michigan program and instilled the "Michigan spirit." His salary was increased by $450 after his first year, and in 1908 and 1909 he was paid $4,000 for the football season. Yost's salary was much greater than that of a full professor, and his imperious nature did not endear him to the faculty.[46]

The Intercollegiate Athletic Association of the United States

Delegates representing sixty-two colleges from all parts of the country, but mainly from New England and the Middle States, met in New York on December 28, 1905, and organized the Intercollegiate Athletic Association of the United States with a view to reforming football. Captain Palmer E. Pierce of the U.S. Military Academy was instrumental in the creation of the organization, and he served as its president for many years. The association created a new football rules committee and drafted a constitution and bylaws.[47]

The first annual convention of the ICAAUS was held in New York in December 1906. The accredited delegates of twenty-eight colleges and universities and eleven visitors attended. Most of the members were Eastern institutions. The delegates adopted a constitution and bylaws designed to regulate and supervise amateur athletic sports in the nation's colleges and universities in order to maintain them on "an ethical plane in keeping with the dignity and high purpose of education . . . and incidentally to support representative rules committees." From its beginning the ICAAUS proposed to "accomplish the work of collegiate athletic reform" by becoming a "clearing house of athletic ideas for the whole country and by operating a "central bureau of propaganda and publication concerning college athletics." Stagg, a visitor, advocated "a national organization to regulate athletic sports . . . [by] exerting a salutary ethical influence." He avowedly "stood for the highest standard in this respect and would not allow professionalism to creep into college sports." He expected that the University of Chicago would join the association.[48]

An extract of a letter from James E. Sullivan, the president of the Amateur Athletic Union, was read. Sullivan wrote that the AAU must look to the colleges for cooperation in forming "alliances with athletic associations at home and throughout the entire world." "From an athletic standpoint," Sullivan added, "the colleges lack organization." He noted that there was "too much desire on the part of each college to go it alone."[49] Born in 1860, Sullivan had been active in the amateur sports community in New York when "the line between professional and amateur in athletics [was] indistinct." He deplored what he saw as a failure to define and regulate amateurism. As president of the AAU from 1889 to 1914 he was inflexible in enforcing a strict definition of amateurism. Although the AAU claimed jurisdiction over twenty-three different sports, it was primarily interested in controlling amateur athletics and did so by making it impossible for athletes to participate in athletic events that it sponsored without registering with the AAU.[50]

The ICAAUS grew slowly in its early years. Most of the member colleges were located in New England and the Middle States. The organization made headway in the Western Conference, but slowly. Minnesota was a charter member. At the 1906 annual meeting, Dr. Harry L. Williams was the accredited Minnesota delegate. He had played football with Stagg at Yale. After graduating from Yale he had studied medicine at the University of Pennsylvania and had done graduate work in Berlin and Vienna. In 1900 he became the football coach at Minnesota.[51] Chicago joined the ICAAUS in 1907. Stagg was an accredited convention delegate that year. He made an effort to secure the cooperation of the conference universities, he reported, because he would be doing his "greatest work for that particular section of the country, and also add greater prestige to the Intercollegiate Athletic

Association of the United States." He was eager to attract new members to the conference. Iowa and Northwestern voted to join the association. Chicago and Minnesota were already members.[52] In 1909 Harvard, Columbia, and Indiana University joined the association. The need for it was being recognized.[53] In 1910 eight more institutions, including Wisconsin, became members, bringing the total to seventy-six. Now, granted its national character and to secure a more distinctive title, the ICAAUS renamed itself the National Collegiate Athletic Association (NCAA).[54]

Palmer E. Pierce was the president of the NCAA until 1912.[55] During his presidency he addressed every annual convention of the association. He often rehearsed the formation and early history of the association and then turned to substantive matters. While the NCAA was not a muckraker, he avowed, it did encourage investigation into collegiate athletics to find a remedy for the evils. The association had a Committee on Amateurism, and its Football Rules Committee, chaired by Harry L. Williams, outlined the steps by which the amalgamated old American Rules Committee and the new American Intercollegiate Rules Committee had legislated harmoniously for the entire United States. The NCAA emphasized the necessity of faculty control of collegiate athletics. According to Pierce, college teams should play only college teams and avoid contests under rules different from those of the NCAA.[56]

The Western Conference regularly named a faculty representative as a delegate to the annual NCAA convention. These meetings served as a forum for the exchange of ideas about intercollegiate athletics.

The number of intercollegiate athletic contests permitted each season was an issue in the Western Conference. The faculty representatives disputed the number of football games to allow each season. At the 1907 NCAA convention, Paul C. Phillips, MD, of Amherst College, spoke on the length of athletic schedules from the standpoint of all those involved in intercollegiate sports. He thought it wise to have a limit to the number of games allowed in each sport. Certain principles were fundamental in determining their length. First, athletes should not be treated as a special class. The favoritism shown the athletic class in some cases had been the bête noire of the whole athletic structure. Second, schedules should not be approved that required on the part of the team a greater number of absences than allowed to all students. Third, the physical effect of the exercise was another determining factor in the limitation of schedules. This applied with great force to football. Nine games of intercollegiate football per season was the extreme; a reduction to seven would be far better. He noted that the Western Conference allowed but five games.[57]

Clarence A. Waldo, formerly the conference arbitrator, was a faculty member at Washington University in St. Louis in 1909 when he addressed the annual convention of the ICAAUS (the NCAA). By "their very nature, college athletic sports are organized," Waldo noted, "and therefore some one is in control." The authorities who attempted to regulate college athletics included the trustees, the president, the faculty, the coaches, and the alumni. Waldo advocated faculty control, which meant control by committee, a condition towards which all faculty action gravitated. He characterized eleven kinds of faculty members who "drifted" into athletic leadership in colleges and helped to "destroy true college ideals." "Too often," he said, "they take their opinions" from the athletic director, "whose continuance in office" depended on his popularity with "the sporting element" in college life. The wrong kind of control sought space in the newspapers to gratify noncollege people and built "immense stadia" so that "young gladiators" could bring in "vast revenues." He concluded: "True control mean[s] cutting away ex-crescences which are college ideals."[58]

The reform meeting called by President Angell in 1906 was a high point in conference history. University authorities courageously confronted the evils of intercollegiate football and reaffirmed academic values. Moreover, the NCAA was gaining strength and working along similar lines. It remained to be seen how the reform would develop over time.

Perspective

Looking at the long sweep of history, one is vividly aware that America was still a very young nation when a number of aspiring individuals combined to better the condition of their group by creating both the Western Conference (Big Ten) and the National Collegiate Athletic Association (NCAA). Their achievement can be seen in wider perspective by noting that while these two organizations were taking national shape, a number of individuals and groups joined force be-cause they believed that the national government ought not control educational affairs but that some oversight was necessary. Hugh Hawkins has described how the following five associations banded together to promote higher education: the National Association of State Universities (NASU), founded in 1895; the As-sociation of American Universities (AAU), founded in 1900; the Association of American Colleges (AAC), founded in 1915; the American Council on Education (ACE), founded in 1918; and the Association of American Land-Grant Colleges (1920–25), which became the Association of Land-Grant Colleges and Universi-ties (ALGCU), 1926–55. The Western Conference and the NCAA pursued similar strategies to promote different goals.[59]

CHAPTER 2

Michigan Withdraws
from the Conference

When the dark side of intercollegiate football required corrective action, President Angell called on the faculty representatives to reform the game. In January 1906 the conference took constructive measures, but the news of their handiwork startled the member institutions.[1] At Illinois, the senate adopted a recommendation that football be abolished as an intercollegiate sport in the conference colleges. Evarts B. Greene, a history professor and dean of the liberal arts college, responding to a proposal to wait for the Rules Committee to modify the playing rules, moved as a substitute: "It is the sense of the Senate that the game of intercollegiate football be suspended for two years and that this action be taken independently of the action of the other institutions represented in the conference." After discussion, Greene's substitute motion lost.[2]

Because the changes recommended caused such a stir, President Angell suggested that the faculty representatives meet again to confirm or reject their proposal. At a special session in March, the delegates reaffirmed most of the recommendations and announced when each one was to take effect. The conference divided recommendation 2. The first part stated that no student was to participate in intercollegiate athletics for more than three years in the aggregate. This rule was to be effective September 1, 1906, except for students who participated in athletics in the academic year 1905–06; for these it was to be effective December 1, 1906 (that is, after the 1906 football season). The second part ruled that participation was to be confined to students who had not graduated from any department of a college or university. This part was to be effective September 1, 1906. The delegates amended recommendation 8, which said, "No training table was to be maintained," to read "There shall be no training table or training quarters for any athletic team." The conferees amended recommendation 12 to say that the football season was to end the Saturday before Thanksgiving.[3]

The delegates later took up recommendation 10 on coaching. Newspapers reported four hours of stormy debate. Pattengill, Yost's friend, tried to repeal the professional coach clause. As amended, recommendation 10 read, "No coach be appointed except by University governing bodies on the recommendation of the Faculty, or President, in the regular way, and at a moderate salary. This recommendation to become operative as soon as existing contracts in several institutions permit." Thus Yost could be retained for three more years. The special session directed that its recommendations be referred to a regular conference session for adoption.[4]

The next day the delegates recommended that each athletic board adopt the recommendations made by the conference the previous day. Before adjourning, the delegates adopted a resolution declaring that all athletic contracts made in the conference institutions contain clauses making such contracts binding only in so far as they were not in conflict with existing or future legislation by state legislatures or boards of regents of the several universities or by the Intercollegiate Athletic Conference.[5]

In early April, Acting President Holgate explained that Northwestern had suspended intercollegiate football games for five years with a view to relieving "the present unhealthy conditions," a substantial debt, and giving the new athletic director sufficient time "to develop local student enterprises."[6]

In June, the Illinois faculty senate returned to the matter of athletic coaching. Herbert Barton moved to instruct the Board of Athletic Control to make no further contact with institutions that had not adopted the rule on coaching recommended by the conference. The motion lost, 11–18.[7] By this action the Illinois senate opened the way for the highly paid professional athletic coach.

Despite the apparent harmony, when the faculty representatives met after the football season, Victor H. Lane (Michigan) asked for modifications of the reform measures. The conference agreed to allow seven football games each season instead of five, at least two to be non-conference games. The conference set September 20 as a uniform date for the beginning of football practice, ruled that the price of admission to intercollegiate contests should not be more than fifty cents to any university member, and decreed that the rules on the period of participation in intercollegiate athletics should apply only to football, baseball, and track athletics. A motion that the rule limiting participation in intercollegiate contests to three years in the aggregate was not to apply to students who entered their university prior to September 1, 1906, carried. The motion was vital to Michigan because making the rule retroactive would deprive the Michigan football team of its best players. Chicago, Illinois, Indiana, Iowa, and Michigan favored these measures.[8] In modifying certain reforms at Michigan's request, the conference was apparently trying to mollify a conference member. It was neither a courageous nor an admirable act.

The Chicago and Michigan football teams were the strongest in the conference, and both recognized Minnesota and Wisconsin as competitors. These four allegedly considered scheduling games only among themselves. Stagg tried to persuade Michigan to play the Maroons in the city of Chicago, the most lucrative football market in the Midwest. The teams were to agree to abide by conference rules when playing each other but not when playing nonconference teams. Michigan was reluctant to adopt the plan because it sought athletic opportunity elsewhere. It scheduled games with Eastern nonconference colleges to be played under nonconference rules.[9]

Although the preceding recommendations met a largely favorable reception, Wisconsin refused to allow seven football games each season, to allow men to play four years instead of three, and to allow freshmen to take part in intercollegiate athletics except football, baseball, and track.[10] Illinois agreed that the rule limiting the time a student could engage in intercollegiate athletics to three years in the aggregate should not apply to students who entered the University prior to 1906. Illinois rejected the proposal to increase to seven the number of football games in a season, approved the recommendation that the price of admission to intercollegiate contests should be fifty cents to any spectator, endorsed the proposal to permit no football practice before September 20, and approved of the rule that the duration of participation in intercollegiate athletics should apply only to football, baseball, and track.[11]

In January 1907 the faculty representatives met in Chicago to deal with the responses of the conference members. All of the faculties had approved of making September 20 a uniform date for beginning football practice, but the faculty of several institutions had rejected three of the recommendations made the previous December. According to the White Resolution, each of these rules now required a two-thirds vote to pass. The recommendation to increase the number of football games from five to seven now lost. The minutes of the meeting do not record the tally, but the press reported that Chicago, Michigan, and Iowa voted for the measure. The proposal to reaffirm the recommendation making conference rules regarding the period of participation in intercollegiate athletics applicable only to football, baseball, and track lost. Purdue, Northwestern, Wisconsin, and Minnesota voted against it. A proposal to make the three-year eligibility rule inapplicable to students who entered college before September 1, 1906, lost. Purdue, Northwestern, Wisconsin, and Minnesota voted against it.[12]

Michigan Out

When news of the January conference reached Ann Arbor, some students and some alumni inaugurated a campaign to withdraw Michigan from the conference. From 1901 to 1905 Yost's football teams had played from ten to thirteen games each season and had won or tied for the conference championship four times. A shortened season, loss of the training table, and the retroactive clause of the three-year eligibility rule threatened Michigan's gridiron glory. Frank B. Fletcher, a student leader, enlisted his father, Regent Frank W. Fletcher, who directed the action of the regents in athletic matters, and the regents recommended withdrawal from the conference to the Athletic Board in Control. The student members of the board hoped to win control of the board, but the board referred the question to the university senate. Thus the question was whether the senate, which represented the faculty, or the regents would control Michigan athletic policy.[13] Meanwhile, Michigan went its own way in football. For two years the Wolverines cut off games with Chicago and all but one conference school.

People at Michigan differed as to whether the university would be better or worse off by withdrawing from the conference. Stagg informed Baird, the Michigan director of athletics, that he was deeply impressed with the seriousness of the situation at Ann Arbor. Michigan would make a mistake in withdrawing, and in doing so would harm intercollegiate athletics in the Midwest.[14]

In mid-February the Michigan faculty senate declared that it recognized the ultimate authority of the Board of Regents in matters of policy but expressed the hope that the regents would leave the regulation of student athletics with the senate and the Board in Control of Athletics. Two weeks later the regents declared that Michigan should not withdraw from the conference. The board favored repeal of the retroactive feature of the three-year rule and allowing seven rather than five football games a season; therefore, it authorized games with nonconference colleges during 1907 under conference rules with the exception of the two additional games. In 1907 Michigan played six games, including one with Penn in Ann Arbor.[15]

In mid-March, Victor Lane (Michigan) declared to Albion Small (Chicago) that the question as to whether athletics at Michigan should continue to be under faculty control was still serious. The situation was aggravated by the fact that the Michigan student body seemed to have determined that relationship in the conference was no longer desirable. The Board in Control of Athletics had resolved that Michigan retain membership in the conference, but when playing other than conference teams should be governed by all conference rules except the three-year rule, insofar as it applied retroactively, and the five-game rule. Michigan would not expect to play any conference team when playing a schedule that provided for seven games in football.

The board thought that Michigan could not play Chicago in the fall by reason of its contract with Pennsylvania and the inability to arrange that game unless it came on a Saturday immediately preceding or immediately succeeding the date for that game. This would leave Michigan with no conference game in 1907. The board took this action because they believed that it might still the troubled waters and retain faculty control. "If we are entitled to any consideration under the circumstances," Lane concluded, "we will be glad of it."[16]

Days later Henry M. Bates of the Michigan law faculty asked Small's coopera-tion in securing a special meeting of the conference on April 13. The decision of the conference to make the three-year rule retroactive and the failure to increase the number of football games from five to seven had aroused widespread opposi-tion in the Michigan student body and the alumni, Bates wrote, and pressure was brought to bear on the board of regents to compel Michigan's withdrawal from the conference. Bates described the reasons for opposition to the retroactive feature of the three-year rule and the objectionable features of the five-game limit. Bates asked Small to cooperate with the board in obtaining a special conference meet-ing to reconsider the retroactive feature of the three-year rule and the five-game limit in football.[17]

In reply to Bates, Small wrote that the conference had decided in 1905–06 that the influence of intercollegiate athletics upon academic life had become excessive and that faculties had a duty to reduce athletic activities to saner proportions. That two trifles, five games or seven and the eligibility of certain undergraduates, distracted the attention of so many in nine universities demonstrated the point. Small believed, as did many at Chicago and at Michigan, that the ends which the conference aimed to reach could be gained if the rules in the two particulars noted were made less stringent. Nevertheless, "inability calmly to accept the de-cisions of the conference upon such details, even when the decision appeared from our standpoint ill advised," Small wrote, "seems to me to afford cumulative evidence of that athletic paranoia which it is our aim to cure. The whole idea of the conference is that correctives of student over enthusiasm must be found in conditions that will be set by more experienced men, and men not in a single university, but in cooperating universities." A composite judgment was likely to be better than "the prejudices of our several situations. The fact that some confer-ence members that put Michigan and Chicago in the minority on these questions have less intense athletic interests than Michigan and Chicago have developed should make us pause and consider whether their opinion was not on the whole saner than ours. Instead of resenting the right of judgment of other members of the conference, we should thank them for exerting a salutary influence."[18]

The conference, Small added, represented the primacy of academic standards as against athletic standards. Michigan undergraduates had made the main issue, "Shall the representatives of our academic standards set the limits of our athletes, or shall the athletes dictate the limits for academic activities?" It would be "the most obvious self stultification" for the conference to reconvene for the purpose suggested. To consent to meet in extraordinary session to discuss whether it will recede from its position in order to conciliate a body of students who prefer to control it if they can or to defy the verdict if they can't was unthinkable. Small spoke only for himself, but he was among the men in the Chicago faculty who had always been most interested in athletics. If he had to choose between such a conference as Bates suggested and adopting the Wisconsin proposal of complete suspension of intercollegiate athletics for at least two years, Small favored the latter. Most of the Chicago faculty would consider the interruption of athletic contests less unfortunate than Small did. If the proposed conference were held, Small would vote for instructions to reverse Chicago's vote on the two "obnoxious details," his reason being that it would be demoralizing to even discuss amending the conference decision in response to the kind of pressure that has resulted in Michigan's call for reconsideration.[19]

Small had reread the Michigan board's statement four times. He had never read a document of the kind the essential spirit of which impressed him more favorably. "Its candor seems to be a sight draft upon the sympathetic treatment which it requests." And yet Small concluded that the wisest course for the conference was to accept in good faith Michigan's assurance of a desire to remain in the conference, to overlook Michigan's temporary inability to act under the rules of the conference, to await Michigan's notification of ability to resume cooperation under the rules, and, whenever assurance was received from Michigan that it could conform to the conference code, to terminate the non-intercourse to which Michigan's action would force the conference colleges. Concluding, Small said that he had written to Bates as freely as he would talk with Chicago colleagues. If the Chicago faculty looked at the case as Small thought probable, it would turn out to be the most effective means of cooperation with Michigan. "The noise makers will of course interpret it at first the other way."[20]

The controversy deepened. Chicago would not grant Michigan the right to play more than five football games in 1907 or the right not to observe conference rules in nonconference games. Practically the only concession Chicago would make was to give Ann Arbor the site of the next Chicago-Michigan game. In a telegraph poll of the conference members regarding the other conference colleges playing Michigan, the conference assumed responsibility for disciplining Michigan.

Athletic relations between Chicago and Michigan remained difficult. Stagg scheduled as many home games as possible because Chicago attracted big crowds and brought big gate receipts. Ann Arbor authorities charged that Chicago was seeking its own advantage and was unfair to Michigan. Michigan was ready to break up the Big Four coalition in order to regain athletic heights, while Chicago was willing to leave Michigan out if it would not abide by conference rules. The Big Four would then become the Big Three—Chicago, Minnesota, and Wisconsin.[21]

The proposed special session was held in Chicago on April 13, 1907. Among those present were Stagg and Small for Chicago and Lane and Bates for Michigan. The purpose of the meeting was to deal with Michigan's expressed intent to disregard two conference rules when playing with nonconference institutions. Asked to state the attitude of Michigan toward conference rules, Lane replied that it was the same as submitted in a communication from Michigan to other conference institutions on March 22 (Bates's letter to Small of that date).[22]

An editorial in the *Chicago Tribune* observed that the bitterness engendered by athletic rivalry in the Big Nine had not disappeared with better football rules. University senates spent their time squabbling over petty details of intercollegiate athletic relationships. Many were ready to conclude that intercollegiate athletic contests should be abandoned if they continued to cause irritation among schools that should be friendly with one another.[23]

As events unfolded, the Michigan regents revised the control of athletics in the university. In October 1907 they abolished the Board in Control of Athletics and established a new board of eight members, to be organized by December 1. In November the regents stated that the athletic board should be responsible to the teaching force of the university, and that faculty control should be preserved by means of a majority representation of faculty members on the board. As constituted, the new board contained four faculty members nominated by the deans and approved by the president, two students, and one nominee of the alumni association.[24]

The Intercollegiate Conference unanimously adopted a resolution declaring it the sense of the body that membership in the conference could not be retained by an institution that did not have full and complete faculty control of athletics. As a concession, the delegates allowed Michigan to retain membership and voting power temporarily, although the school's games with conference colleges were canceled. Paige (Minnesota) again moved that the number of football games to be played in any one season be increased to seven. His motion was laid on the table by a vote of 6 to 2, Michigan not voting. Insistent, Paige then moved to recommend to the athletic boards of the conference universities that the number of football games to be played in any one season be increased to seven. His motion, an end run to achieve his objective, unanimously carried.[25] Paige was trying to make possible a game between Minnesota and Michigan. It promised a rich reward.

Confronting a crisis, the member universities considered the recent conference recommendations. On the recommendation to increase the number of football games to seven in any season, the conference courageously voted to continue its policy of five games.[26]

In late December Stagg learned that Michigan was going to make a strong effort to get the conference to change the retroactive clause of the three-year rule and the rule against the training table and to increase the number of games to seven. Stagg favored seven games, and he believed that the Chicago faculty would have favored seven except for the Michigan situation. Stagg had talked with the president and the leading men at Chicago and was satisfied that their opposition to the seven-game measure was based on the belief that there should not be a single change in the rules until Michigan decided one way or the other.[27]

At the conference meeting on January 4, the faculty representatives faced the impending crisis over Michigan's status in the conference. Patterson of Michigan described Michigan's athletic situation, whereupon the delegates informed him that the White Resolution would go into effect unless Michigan informed the president of the conference on or before February 1, 1908, that by a vote of its Board in Control, Michigan would conform to the conference rules. At this session Paige's motion to increase the number of football games to seven in each season was carried 5–4. The chairman authorized a sealed vote in case it became necessary to consider the measure a second time.[28]

The athletic authorities at Ann Arbor did not relent. So on February 1, 1908, Michigan ceased to be a member of the conference. Michigan students were "convinced that Michigan would be better off 'on the outside looking in than on the inside looking out.'" At Ann Arbor, people praised the members of the Board in Control who refused to back down on the board's decision that "Michigan could play its four-year men in games with nonconference colleges, and could schedule as many games as were desired with such institutions."[29]

Later in February, Clarence A. Waldo, a former Purdue faculty representative, described the Michigan athletic situation. Cutting to the bone, he wrote:

> There are two factions at Mich. whose ideals are now sharply opposed. The one faction is for commercial success and athletic glory. To them the good of the student and in the long run the good of the institution are secondary. The other faction wishes to administer athletics for the good of the student and make it as it ever must be in college under normal conditions secondary to scholarship.
>
> The first faction is made up of Baird, Yost, the regents, the sporting alumni and a minority of the athletic association. The second includes the faculty, almost to a man, I believe, and all of the thinking students. The first faction is still in power and dies hard. But it is on its last legs.[30]

A perceptive analyst, Waldo identifies the factions at Michigan and at most conference universities. On the one hand are the coaches and athletic directors, the governing board, alumni, and members of the athletic community. Waldo does not include the president, the faculty representative, or student athletic boosters as he might have. On the other hand are faculty members and students who are devoted to the university as an academic enterprise not a commercialized sports and entertainment center.

The Conference Carries On

The seven-game issue precipitated a lively controversy in the member universities, avidly reported in the press. Michigan, Minnesota, Northwestern, Indiana, and Iowa favored seven games, the press reported, while Chicago, Illinois, Purdue, and Wisconsin opposed that number. Under conference procedures, if any faculty protested the seven-game recommendation, the conference would take up the matter again, and six votes would be necessary to secure adoption. The change of one vote would permit a seven-game schedule.

The Illinois students favored more football games, and at their request President James called a mass meeting in January to hear arguments in favor of a seven-game schedule. Most undergraduate men and "a liberal sprinkling" of women attended. James explained the reason for giving final control of athletics to the senate instead of the Athletic Board of Control, and six students chosen as representative by various student groups presented students' views on the subject.[31]

In light of these representations, James asked the senate to reconsider its action. While not always winning, especially in football, Illinois had maintained "a clean record for honesty and fairness and sportsman-like conduct" and "a faithful observance of the agreements made with other institutions."[32]

In February the senate again considered the recommendations of the conference. After considerable discussion of the proposal to increase the number of football games in any season from six to seven, the senate voted 21 to 20 in favor of seven games, two of which were to be minor games. A substitute motion proposed that the university's faculty representative should vote for seven games only in case the representatives from Wisconsin and Chicago joined in this action. The motion lost, 13 to 16. The main motion then passed 21 to 20.[33]

When the faculty representatives met again in June, they took up the matter of the two sealed votes. One exempted certain minor sports from the one-year residence rule. The other was to increase to seven the number of games in one season. The six affirmatives were Chicago, Illinois, Indiana, Iowa, Minnesota, and Purdue, while the two negatives were Wisconsin and Northwestern. With a two-thirds vote, the measure passed. But Chicago, Illinois, and Purdue were affirmative only for the 1908 season. They were negative for a seven-game series in 1909. The schedule would revert to five games in 1909 unless changed by further legislation.[34]

Michigan and Minnesota made a football alliance despite Michigan's withdrawal from the conference, and early in 1909 the athletic authorities at these schools scheduled a football game for November 1909. The deal prompted the Graduate Committee of the Intercollegiate Athletic Association to call a meeting with a conference committee in Chicago in February 1909. Members of the Graduate Committee representing Chicago, Illinois, Iowa, Minnesota, Northwestern, and Wisconsin were present, along with the faculty representatives of the member universities. Also present at the invitation of the Graduate Committee were W. D. McKenzie, the former Michigan representative on the Graduate Committee, and George W. Patterson. William Scott Bond (Chicago), the chair of the meeting, explained why it had been called and outlined its purposes. Patterson explained what he considered to be the leading causes of Michigan's decision to withdraw. One was the retroactive clause of the reform rules that prevented some good athletes from playing their fourth year. Another was the canceling of the Chicago game that was to be played in Ann Arbor. Still another was "the abolishment of the training table." Two members of the board of regents, Patterson added, had had boys in the university who had worked on their fathers and helped influence the regents in favor of student as against faculty sentiment on the question of withdrawal from the conference.[35]

After the 1906 conference meeting that adopted the reform rules, Stagg explained, he and Pattengill had agreed that there should be no games played between Michigan, Chicago, and Wisconsin until the football rivalries subsided. Chicago was carrying out the agreement with the concurrence of Pattengill, who was then chairman of the Michigan Board in Control of Athletics. Had Pattengill not died soon after 1906, Patterson added, Michigan would never have withdrawn from the conference. As it was, Michigan thought that Chicago had acted unfairly.[36]

Patterson noted the similarity of the Michigan and the conference rules except for the training-table rule. He seemed to think that securing food in Ann Arbor differed from securing food in other conference sites. It was commonly thought, said Patterson, that all of the conference universities had training tables in spite of the rule against them. The faculty representatives denied the charge. Further, the Illinois, Indiana, Iowa, and Wisconsin representatives believed that it would be impossible for the quality of the food furnished by Ann Arbor boarding tables to be worse than that furnished by boardinghouses in their university towns. Conference members were unanimous in their desire that Michigan return to the conference, if Michigan fully adopted the conference rules.[37]

With the exception of the training table, Patterson declared, the difference between the eligibility rules of Michigan and the conference were rather trivial. There would be no trouble in getting Michigan to waive these differences in favor of the conference rules, with the exception of the training-table rule.[38]

With this matter pending, plans to implement a controversial Minnesota-Michigan alliance were initiated. In November 1909 the Wolverines beat the Gophers in Minneapolis 15–6. Then in November 1910 Michigan beat Minnesota 6–0 in Ann Arbor. In early December, Paige and Stagg met at Paige's request to talk over the difficulties growing out of the Minnesota-Michigan alliance. To Stagg, it was apparent that the Minnesota athletic board had instructed Paige to try to secure the approval of the conference to continue the Minnesota-Michigan football contract. Paige's purpose in conferring with Stagg was to see if Chicago would back up Minnesota. Stagg told him that was impossible. Paige met Stagg again to see if Chicago would back up Minnesota in asking for a single game with Michigan for 1911. Failing that, he was to secure a rule forbidding football games between the East and the West so that the University of Chicago could not have the advantage growing out of their location. The people at Minnesota realized they could not secure alliances with eastern teams and did not wish Chicago to have any. Failing to secure conference consent to games with Michigan, Paige was to propose either that the conference would not maintain athletic relations with any University which, having been a member of the conference, withdrew therefrom, until said University was reinstated, or that the conference would maintain athletic relations only with universities in the Middle West, and that all athletic relations be within the conference.[39] Stagg avowed that Chicago would be willing to give up the school's games with Cornell after the contract for 1911 had been fulfilled. For the conference, it was wise to have an interchange of football games between all conference members so far as possible. This could not easily be done because at the time neither Wisconsin nor Northwestern was allowed to play more than five games of football. Stagg proposed that conference members play at least four games of football with one another.[40]

The Paige-Stagg exchange reveals sharp tensions and avid self-seeking, not a commitment to the welfare of the conference.

The Conference Meeting of December 1911

This meeting was enormously important. On Michigan's relation to the conference, there were three possibilities. One was that Michigan would return to the conference and abide by the rules. Another was that Minnesota would repudiate conference dictation of the school's athletic policy, thereby making it unnecessary for Michigan to return to the conference in order to continue relations with Minnesota. Still another was that Minnesota would decline to defy the conference in regard to games between Michigan and Minnesota, leaving Michigan without any western games of importance. As to the first, no possibility existed of Michigan returning to the conference. Undergraduate sentiment was opposed to return, alumni opinion was divided, but the most vociferous group opposed the "sacrifice of a single Michigan ideal." The attitude of the new Board in Control of Athletics was doubtful and would be until it met for organization in about two weeks. But the board had only four faculty members out of a total of eleven. In any case, the Michigan regents dictated athletic policy, and the Board in Control was its creature. Michigan flouted the basic conference principle, faculty control of athletics. As for the second possibility, if Minnesota refused to submit to conference dictation in the matter of schedule-making, it would cement relations between Minnesota and Michigan. The two institutions would be former conference members who needed each other in making a suitable football schedule and in working together to disintegrate the conference and effect an intercollegiate reorganization. It seemed improbable that Minnesota would resent the reprimand openly delivered during the past week. Athletics at Minnesota was allegedly in the hands of a board in control composed of five students and two alumni; the faculty had no voice. In fact, however, the ultimate power was vested in a board composed of five faculty members who had absolute power to veto anything done by the student board. Thus, the third possibility seemed likely to be adopted. If Minnesota remained in the conference and met Michigan, Minnesota would be denied games by Chicago, Wisconsin, and Illinois. So the virtual ostracizing of Minnesota would be almost as severe a blow as expulsion from the conference itself: Minnesota would remain in the conference, but without the games with Michigan.

The delegates reaffirmed the conference position on the main issues of athletic reform by regulations adopted unanimously. First, members of the conference were "not to hold athletic relations with universities or colleges that have been members of the conference and have withdrawn," or, being members, should withdraw, until reinstated. Second, members of the conference should "maintain athletic relations in football and baseball" only with universities and colleges in the Midwest, "except as to existing contracts." Third, each member of the conference should schedule "not less than four football games with other members of the conference," and should "endeavor . . . to rotate its games from year to year, so as to play all the members of the conference." In addition, the conference agreed that no one should participate in any intercollegiate sport unless he was a "bona fide matriculated student doing full work in courses leading to a degree."[41] The regulations made it impossible for Minnesota to schedule games with Michigan until Michigan was reinstated in the conference.

Shortly before the December meeting, Chicago newspapers published reports from Ann Arbor reflecting on the good faith of Stagg and the University of Chicago in conference matters. The wide publicity given the statements led Stagg to reply in a letter in which he described Michigan's connection with the conference, declared that Chicago had at all times been friendly toward Michigan, and had tried in every way to hold Michigan in the conference.[42]

In late November, Small asked Stagg to come to his home. President George E. Vincent of Minnesota was to be there as well. Stagg went, and Vincent took up various points on which he wished to be informed, amateurism in particular. Vincent also asked what could be done to get Michigan back into the conference, since the students and alumni of the University of Minnesota and practically the whole state were united in demanding a game between Minnesota and Michigan; he had brought up this matter earlier when he and Stagg had met on November 4. At that time Vincent had said that it put him in a bad position to stand out against the idea of the Minnesota-Michigan game when the whole state was so insistent. At that time and again on the present occasion Vincent suggested the possibility of granting Michigan the privilege of having a training table for the evening meal, following practice. The conference might be willing to yield on this matter, Stagg said, providing the men arranged for their board and that no money be contributed from the athletic fund except for the extra trouble to which the boardinghouse keepers were put by reason of the late meal, and that publicity be given the financial arrangement which was made in each place.

The Vincent-Stagg discussion illustrates the pressure placed on the president of a public university by a public eager for more games, and it helps to understand why a university president would appoint a faculty member sympathetic to intercollegiate athletics as the faculty representative to the conference. Vincent was not the only university president who found it expedient to placate the great god football.

Vincent went on to another point he wished to discuss with Stagg as a friend. There was a feeling in the conference that Chicago had an undue advantage because of Stagg's status as a faculty representative and a coach. Stagg would do a great thing for himself and for Chicago if he would resign. He was perfectly willing to resign, Stagg replied, if he thought that by doing so he could do more good out than in the conference, "that it would not be any sacrifice for me to make, inasmuch as my purpose in life was to do as much good as I could." Stagg wondered whether the feeling against him was not largely confined to Minnesota in and Michigan outside the conference. He also wondered whether the feeling were not an outgrowth of petty jealousy. Stagg was sure that no faculty representative who had worked with him over the years would have such a feeling. He had never stood for anything that would be to Chicago's advantage and not for the general good of the conference. Harry Williams had twice suggested that Chicago had an advantage because Stagg was in the conference, "but in light of my knowledge of Harry Williams' selfishness and his general disregard of ethical standards in athletics," Stagg said, "I could not help feel that it was entirely petty jealousy." Vincent added that many of Stagg's faculty friends felt as Vincent did. When Stagg expressed surprise at that, Vincent stated that his motive for presenting the matter to him was the request of President Judson. Stagg thought it strange that Judson had not talked the matter over with him. The request was unusual in that Stagg was the director of the department of physical culture and athletics, and

the tendency was to have such directors represent the universities in the conference. Albion Small, the host for the occasion, said that he had heard expressions
from Chicago faculty members on the advisability of Stagg not representing the
University in the conference. Small thought it would be a good thing for Stagg
to resign as a faculty representative. Stagg was not ready to do so immediately;
he thought it was his duty to attend the forthcoming meeting, since he knew
there was going to be a big fight then. "This was no time for the promotion of
peace and harmony, but rather a time for a determined fight against the spirit of
Minnesota in regard to the Conference and a number of the rules, as well as their
purpose of breaking down the Conference rules in order that Minnesota might
play Michigan." Stagg had proposed a Purity Code and at the same time he fought
to protect the interests of the University of Chicago rather than the conference.
Petty jealousy trumped ennobling spirit.[43]

In the annual conference meeting on December 2, 1911, the members discussed
the Michigan-Minnesota alliance. According to Stagg, Baird—Michigan's athletic
director—had made that agreement for political reasons. He had been an enemy
of the conference for years and was particularly jealous of Chicago's apparent
power in the conference. In addition, Michigan's wretched showing in athletics,
particularly football, in which they had been beaten by Pennsylvania, defeated
by Syracuse, and had made poor showings against minor teams, together with
the irritation on the part of the students over the poor schedule and their miser-
able showing, placed great pressure on the Michigan athletic management by
the graduates, faculty, and part of the student body for competition with their
"natural Western rivals," which meant a return to the conference. Baird's success
in securing the Michigan-Minnesota agreement was regarded with glee in Ann
Arbor as a rare feat in putting one over on Stagg. Baird was aided in this scheme
by Minnesota alumni who were members of the Minnesota Athletic Board, particularly George Belden, who worked with Baird. Undoubtedly the alumni and
students on the board supported the plan for good reason. At Minnesota it was
generally felt that the game would be a cinch for Minnesota. The commercial in-
stincts of Minnesota had always been especially strong, and a big game promised
enormous gate receipts. Moreover, Minnesota would gain in prestige by making
a better showing against Michigan than Michigan had against Pennsylvania. In
the event, Michigan defeated Minnesota, 15–6.[44]

Michigan's Relations with the Conference

After Michigan ceased to be a conference member, the Ann Arbor athletic community weighed the advantages and disadvantages of being outside the circle. In
November 1910 the board of regents created a new board in control of athletics
consisting of eleven members: four faculty members, three students, three alumni,

and the athletic director. The faculty members were outnumbered. According to the conference, faculty control of intercollegiate athletics was essential. A majority of the board favored staying out of the conference, although opposition to this policy was growing among alumni and students. Moreover, the football games Michigan played with Pennsylvania, Vanderbilt, and Syracuse failed to arouse interest among Michigan fans.[45]

On April 19, 1912, the Michigan Board in Control of Athletics made a defining statement of policy. While recognizing the value of the conference in the past, the board added that the conference "impaired its usefulness" by legislation on individual cases instead of on general principles. Michigan authorities should deal entirely with maintenance of a training table and matters of eligibility. The athletic board had no intention of returning to the conference and wished this point understood by all.[46]

As the controversy grew, conference members proclaimed that they would welcome Michigan back if the Wolverines would accept the conference requirements and the Michigan alumni in Chicago voted to rejoin the Big Nine.[47] But the board of regents justified the university's position on withdrawal. In May, the board adopted the following three resolutions of its Committee on Athletics:

1. It is inconsistent with the dignity of any university to surrender to any other authority its rights to prescribe and maintain its own rules and regulations.

2. A university can best meet its responsibilities by reserving full power over the activities of the students under its control except where that power is expressly delegated to others under specific limitations.

3. This board believes that an agreement can be reached upon rules heretofore adopted by the Western Conference, and that these rules, and all subsequent rules, before enforcement and adoption respectively, should be approved unanimously by the members of the Conference; that under these conditions this Board would welcome a resumption by the University of Michigan of membership in the Conference.[48]

On July 18, 1913, the board of regents directed its secretary to transmit a copy of the resolutions to the governing boards of each of the universities in the Western Conference.

The Michigan regents, observed President Vincent, were requesting intervention in the affairs of the conference. From good authority he had learned that a further request would be made for a meeting of the governing boards of the universities in the conference. He had substantive reason to believe that this movement came from "that group at Michigan that was responsible for removing the control of athletics from the faculty and turning it over to a committee of students and alumni responsible directly to the Board of Regents." "What is your attitude toward this proposal?" Vincent asked President James of Illinois. "And what action will you advise your board to take?" James would not approve any action that ignored the faculty in this matter, and Vincent would stand to the end for the control of athletics through the faculty and not through a board of students and alumni directly responsible to the regents. Some Michigan alumni in Detroit had been working with at least one member of the Minnesota board, Vincent added. "A certain group at Detroit belong to the faction that brought about alumni and student control at Michigan. It is the same group that has been opposing the return of Michigan to the conference." It would be disastrous, Vincent added, if the regents of the conference universities were to take athletic control out of the hands of the faculty and assume direct responsibility.[49]

In early September the Minnesota regents voted to refer the Michigan resolutions to the university senate, an action that intimated to the Michigan regents that Minnesota proposed to maintain control of athletics through the faculty. Vincent had reason to believe that the next move by the Michigan regents would be to bring about a conference of the governing boards of the conference institutions with a view to reaching some agreement that might be forced on the faculties of the conference universities, and, if possible, to bring about in the conference institutions the reorganization of athletic control on the Michigan plan. Vincent was unalterably opposed to the plan, which was "thoroughly demoralizing." He would do everything in his power to withstand any attempt to foist the Michigan policy on Minnesota. Vincent communicated his views to the presidents of the conference universities.[50]

David Kinley, vice president of the University of Illinois, responded on behalf of James. He was sure that Illinois would stand stiffly for retention of faculty control, and he offered to start a counter influence.[51] Vincent replied that the information he had concerning the plans of the Michigan regents came from personal sources. He had seen an announcement that the "college editors" were to hold a meeting in Chicago, and that the outcome might be a request to the regents of the conference institutions to hold a meeting with a view to settling the difficulties and restoring Michigan to membership.[52]

The Committee on Intercollegiate Athletics at Minnesota, whose chairman was James Paige, issued a report on September 20 regarding the Michigan resolutions it recommended that the board of regents adopt. The committee was in hearty accord with the spirit of the first Michigan resolution but did not consider a delegation of authority, subject to revocation at pleasure, as a surrender of authority. The committee was in complete sympathy with the second Michigan resolution, which expressed the status quo in the Western Conference. The committee did not feel that any real progress could be made in the conference if all changes depended on a unanimous vote, since the third Michigan resolution would practically establish minority control in the conference. Minnesota hoped Michigan might soon find it possible to re-enter the Western Conference. It pledged its support in securing that result, "so far as possible without sacrificing the fundamental principles underlying the organization of the Conference."[53] Vincent informed all the presidents of the conference colleges about the action taken by Minnesota.[54]

In early October President James understood that the editors of college newspapers in the various universities had gotten up a sort of arrangement among themselves by which they would launch a vigorous campaign "in support of the Michigan heresy." He wrote Vincent and Judson suggesting that if they could persuade their boys "to stay out of the ring," it would have a very good effect. He was trying to use his own influence with the Illinois students.[55] Vincent replied by telegram: "Our editors have made no promise [that they] will not start agitation. I hear that the campaign has been postponed one week."[56] Judson replied that he had taken up the matter among their students and did not believe that the movement in question would make any headway. He was certain as to the action of his board of trustees.[57]

President James laid the Michigan resolutions before his board of trustees in early October with a recommendation that they be referred to the senate with power to act.[58] After full discussion, George Huff, the director of athletics, presented a response that the senate adopted. The senate agreed with the first resolution but failed to see wherein Michigan had surrendered to any other authority any right to prescribe and maintain its own rules and regulations, because any authority delegated to the Western Conference was subject to revocation at pleasure, and therefore had not been surrendered. The senate fully agreed with the second resolution, which it understood to be the status quo in the Western Conference. With reference to the third resolution, the senate could not subscribe to the proposition that action upon rules heretofore adopted by the Western Conference and upon all subsequent rules must be unanimous, because such a regulation would practically establish minority control in the conference. The senate expressed the hope that Michigan would soon resume relations with its sister institutions in the conference, and pledged its support in securing Michigan's re-entrance on condition that Michigan would seek to resume membership under the regulations and leave for future discussion the prevailing difference of opinion.[59]

In early October President Winthrop E. Stone of Purdue sent to the presidents of all conference institutions a copy of the resolutions adopted by his board of trustees. The board believed that the actions of the conference had been efficacious in eliminating many abuses from intercollegiate athletics. It regarded the work of the conference as of great value in correcting and developing intercollegiate sport and had entire confidence in the conference to continue to occupy wise positions in these matters in the future. The board believed that matters relating to the government and instruction of students should be left in the hands of the faculty, subject to the approval of the governing board, and it expressed the wish that Michigan might speedily readjust its differences with the conference through the adoption and recognition of approved regulations governing intercollegiate athletics and be restored to its former membership in the conference.[60]

Two days after Stone wrote, James sent a copy of the Illinois senate's resolutions to the presidents of the other conference universities. President Van Hise replied that the only action yet taken by Wisconsin in reference to the Michigan resolutions was referring them to the university faculty for their consent. Chicago's Judson was much gratified by the attitude of Illinois in the matter.[61] Vincent wrote to James, thanking him for the resolutions and saying that "our editor tells me" that he had had a telegram from the *Michigan Daily* editor indicating that the campaign had been called off and that the newspaper would therefore begin a demand for the university to secure reinstatement in the conference, presumably on the basis of the existing organization. Vincent hoped that faculty control would be restored at Ann Arbor and that Michigan would return to "comradeship" with the conference.[62]

In mid-October Judson sent James the resolutions adopted by the Chicago board of trustees regarding the Michigan resolutions. First, any university should retain final control over rules and regulations in the government of its own students. Second, the regulations relating to the engagement of students in intercollegiate contests should be left in the hands of the appropriate faculty, subject to the final authority of the board of trustees. Third, because intercollegiate contests involve more than one institution, regulations relating to such contests must be based on mutual agreement: in conferences involving so large a number of institutions as are in the Western Intercollegiate Conference the principle of unanimity was inadvisable. The board of trustees would be gratified if Michigan could see its way to resuming membership in the conference.[63]

Reviewing this tangled affair, it is clear that the conference acted to reform the game of football in order to save it. The Ann Arbor athletic authorities arrogantly and adamantly resisted reforms they viewed as a threat to Michigan's football preeminence. The conference stood its ground, whereupon Michigan withdrew from the conference. The Michigan-Minnesota alliance troubled matters. The conference united in opposition to Paige's efforts on behalf of Minnesota and the obstructionism of Ann Arbor. Michigan did not return to the conference until 1918. In dealing with the crisis Michigan precipitated, the Western Conference had perhaps its finest moment. It stood for academic values as opposed to athletic interests, proved its usefulness, and gained significantly in stature.

CHAPTER 3

The Crisis over Amateurism

Professionalism was the norm for most public athletic competitions in early nineteenth century America, but amateurism—sport for the sake of sport—emerged at Oxford and Cambridge in the late nineteenth century. The Amateur Athletic Club in London popularized it, and upper-class Englishmen proclaimed the gospel as a means of excluding their social inferiors.[1]

The amateur athletic code spread to America in the late nineteenth century. Although it was an invented "tradition," apologists made the case for it. Caspar Whitney, a sports writer for *Harper's Weekly, Outing Magazine*, and other periodicals, championed the elitist English idea of amateur sport and was "contemptuous of working-class athletes." James Sullivan, the New York-born son of Irish immigrants, competed in different sports and began writing about and publishing on them at an early age. A key figure in the creation of the Amateur Athletic Union, Sullivan was the most important "sport bureaucrat" in America until his death in 1914. He wanted athletics for the masses while also enforcing a strict definition of amateurism.[2]

American colleges publicly proclaimed amateurism at the turn of the century, and the rules of the Western Conference were designed to enforce amateurism, but often it was difficult to distinguish between the amateur and the professional athlete. Summer baseball was the nub of the problem. Illinois was known as a baseball school. George Huff, the athletic director and a baseball coach, defended the practice of allowing college athletes to play baseball during the summer for pay. With the Illinois scholastic standing as strict as it was, there was "absolutely no danger if the bars of professionalism are thrown down to the college man." A student should be allowed to "earn as much money in the summer time as his ability [would] allow . . . and still be eligible for intercollegiate athletic and debating teams." Huff opposed a college man's going into professional baseball. A college graduate, he said, had "greater opportunities . . . in his chosen profession than in baseball."[3]

Herbert J. Barton of Illinois endorsed the freshman rule and the scholarship rule but found "not a single valid argument" for the regulation on summer baseball. Belief in an amateur team, he declared, was "an iridescent dream." "Such a team would be found at the end of a rainbow and nowhere else," he said. Barton would "allow any student to play ball whenever he has a chance to earn a dollar."[4]

At the Western Conference meeting in December 1911, when the faculty representatives were asked to deal with a rule that prohibited a student from using his athletic skill for gain or taking part in an intercollegiate contest in which a money prize was offered, they evaded the issue by laying it on the table to be taken up at a special meeting in January.[5]

Huff thought it was time to abolish the only law the conference had never been able to enforce. "George Huff knows the human student better than the preceptors of college laws do," a *Chicago Tribune* columnist wrote, "and he says that college professors who do not admit that the rule in question is not more honored in the breach than the observance are either stupid or deliberately stringing themselves."[6] Stagg, however, opposed professionalism in collegiate athletics. The conference colleges were not immune, he admitted, but the situation was not as bad as it was painted. Nor was summer baseball a necessity because so many players wanted it.[7]

The problem of professionalism in summer baseball agitated the conference for years. No one knew how to deal with it satisfactorily. With the passage of time, however, football became the dominant intercollegiate athletic sport and the baseball problem became less urgent.

Eligibility

Eligibility was inseparably related to amateurism, and it was a prime conference concern. According to a rule, "No student shall participate in any intercollegiate contest who has ever used, or is using, his knowledge of athletics or his athletic or gymnastic skill for gain; or who has taken part in any athletic contest in which a money prize was offered, regardless of the disposition of the same." George Goodenough, the Illinois faculty representative, proposed to amend the rule to read that no student should be compensated "while his University was in session." In January 1912 the faculty representatives took up this matter. The vote to endorse the amendment was 3 ayes (Illinois, Indiana, and Minnesota) and 5 nays (Chicago, Iowa, Northwestern, Purdue, and Wisconsin), so the motion lost.[8]

In late January a committee appointed to consider eligibility questions recommended some changes in the rules intended to settle problems that defied easy solution. Students from conference colleges had engaged in athletic competition as representatives of the Chicago Athletic Club and the Illinois Athletic Club. A new rule forbade the practice. Moreover, a new rule allowed a student to play on any baseball team that was not in a league provided he received no compensation. The wrangling over these and related eligibility problems was long and intense. Both the issues and the personalities inflamed the tempers of the faculty representatives. H. W. Johnston, the Indiana delegate, seized the occasion to deal a blow to George Huff. He moved "that this Conference deprecates the employment in its athletics of any persons who are securing pay from professional baseball clubs for services in any capacity."[9] The motion carried. Huff was known to be a scout for professional baseball teams and as having recently gone east to manage the Boston Red Sox. Moreover, his opposition to the amateur standard in intercollegiate athletics, which the other conference colleges endorsed, counted against him.

In closing, two delegates moved that the sentiment of the conference "in regard to the present situation in athletics" be stated as follows: "We should endeavor to establish and uphold a high amateur standard in all college sports (a) By securing the cooperation of the student body through an educational campaign that shall explain the meaning of and necessity for such a standard; (b) By securing the cooperation of the faculty and alumni by an educational campaign that will emphasize the moral and ethical importance of Amateur Athletics in an educational system."[10] The statement was a useless gesture. It may have allowed its authors to believe that they had done their duty.

The Call for a Presidents' Conference

On January 27, the faculty representatives asked their respective presidents to meet with them to consider athletic matters. In February some ICAA members endorsed the proposal. The final arrangements were for a meeting of the conference presidents, after which a joint session with the ICAA men might be desirable.

James asked his council of administration what position the university should take at the meeting. In March he called a special meeting of the faculty senate to consider the crisis in intercollegiate athletics over the so-called amateur rule, which he said set up a purely financial test, whereas the only proper test was whether the student was in college for the sake of sport or sport was a mere incident in his college activity. The amateur rule seemed to promote lying—by athletes and by parents and sponsors. The conference had to give up all pretense and enforce the rule, which "the better element in American athletics" favored retaining. Many who wished to retain the rule admitted that it could not be enforced. James insisted that the university hold high the standards of true sport so as to move the high schools and the public in the proper direction. Intercollegiate athletics had very decided value, he added. They promoted intramural athletics, brought the students together, encouraged good fellowship among the conference colleges, had a positive effect in raising athletic standards, and stimulated public interest in the work of universities. James wanted to preserve the Western Conference.[11]

At the senate meeting, James introduced three students to give their view of the subject. They were critical of the existing situation and thought that "it would be well to consider withdrawing from the Conference." Fourteen faculty members were invited to discuss the crisis. Several opined that the amateur rule would not work because it represented a high ideal—sport for the sake of sport—that was out of touch with American realities. To exclude money from sports was un-American. The evidence showed that student athletes in all conference universities were professionals. The athletes lied about their status because they thought that the eligibility rule violated their rights and that lying was negligible. At many conference schools, but not Illinois, athletes participated in not one but three sports (football, baseball, and track), which did not violate the amateur code but made them more like professional athletes than students. It was impossible to find students who would use athletics to benefit rather than injure themselves as scholars. The faculty endorsed the amateur rule, believed that 80 percent of the public considered it unjust, and concluded that the rule could not and ought not be enforced. However, some senators declared that intercollegiate athletics itself was the source of the problems. The enforcement of the rules had not advanced with the stringency of the rules. The greatest objection to the rule was the encouragement it gave athletes to lie. Either change the rule and enforce it, or abolish it. The university could not continue to allow deceit.[12] The senators who described intercollegiate athletics itself as the problem were right on target, but it was a minority view and would have to struggle to make itself heard.

After hearing the range of opinion, William A. Noyes, a professor of chemistry, moved that in view of the impossibility of enforcing the amateur rule, it should be dropped and an experiment made of preserving simply the one-year residence and the so-called scholarship rule. Charles W. Rolfe, a professor of geology, moved as a substitute, "that the question of baseball be referred to a special committee, to be appointed by the president, with a view to seeing whether an acceptable formulation of an amateur rule can be found." The senate adopted this measure.[13]

On the day after the senate met, James asked all male students in the university to meet to discuss the athletic situation. Some two thousand men attended the mass meeting (about 72 percent of the 2,766 male undergraduates enrolled). The university band stirred up the crowd and then James welcomed those present. He spoke of harmonious student-faculty relations at Illinois and declared that every student should participate in athletics provided that athletics were secondary to scholastic improvement. He did not favor breaking up the conference.[14]

In March, *Illinois Magazine* published a symposium on "Illinois and the Western Conference." Goodenough defended the conference. Its primary purpose, he wrote, was to regulate competition, not to provide it. The conference had only two restrictive rules: one forbade competition with colleges that had withdrawn from the conference; the other required each conference college to play at least four football games each season with other conference colleges. The contention that the conference should include "only institutions with strong teams" failed to recognize "shifting conditions." Stagg did not dominate the conference, as often charged. "The present strained relations," Goodenough said, were over "the so-called amateur rule," but the question was really "amateurism in fact versus amateurism by definition." "The scholarship test furnishes a . . . more rational basis for [a definition] than the money test. . . . The differences in the conference are perhaps so radical," he concluded, that it "may be forced to dissolve or split." Such an outcome "would be deplorable" because the conference had been "instrumental in raising athletic standards throughout the country." "We feel," Chester C. Roberts, a varsity football student declared, "that the conference as existing today is absolutely valueless and more or less of a sham; that rather than promoting cooperation among the universities of the Big Eight, it develops bitter and strained relations." Unless the conference revised and enforced its rules, the western colleges would be better off without it. But a conference that would effectively govern was desirable.[15]

The Presidents' Conference

As proposed earlier, the presidents of the Big Eight universities met in Chicago on March 19 and 20, 1912. Judson (Chicago) moved three resolutions, which the assembly adopted: "intercollegiate athletics has educational advantages which should be retained; the conference was essential and should be maintained; and the amateur basis and spirit for intercollegiate athletics should be sustained." W. E. Stone (Purdue) offered four conditions that should prevail in the conference universities. First, the Intercollegiate Conference was an indispensable means of bringing college athletics into "reasonable and sane relations to the aims and purposes of higher education." Second, the amateur spirit must prevail in college life, and its establishment must be sought by enacting and enforcing athletic rules and by a program of education. Third, to restrain "existing tendencies toward undue exaggeration in college athletics," the Intercollegiate Conference should place "reasonable limitations upon too great expenditure of time and money on intercollegiate contests," should promote intramural games, establish the letter and spirit of amateurism, and eliminate from college circles professional influences in coaching, playing, and the management of contests. Fourth, the faculties of the conference colleges had a duty to be intimately informed on athletic matters and to regard their rational control "as a legitimate and important responsibility upon the governing body." Stone's points rehearsed the fundamental principles of the conference. They were adopted.[16]

President Van Hise (Wisconsin) submitted several resolutions. One was that the presidents recommend to their respective faculties or councils that the conference rules be amended so that each institution would be represented by two members of the faculty, at least one of whom was to have no connection with the Department of Physical Training. Another was that the presidents recommend to their faculties or councils that the sole business of the next conference meeting center on the constitution of the conference on the basis recommended by the presidents. Apparently, Van Hise did not know that the conference had no constitution. Van Hise also moved that the presidents recommend to their faculties that the rules governing intercollegiate games be made by their own conference. He submitted additional information on the subject. The rules governing the game of football were made by a rules committee of fourteen members (in other words, the Rules Committee of the NCAA), seven of whom were relics of the history of football legislation and were self-perpetuating, and seven of whom were elected by the NCAA. He went on to describe and comment on the changes made by the rules committee.[17]

The Intercollegiate Conference Athletic Association had joined in the call for the conference. The Western Conference had established the ICAA in 1901 to sponsor an annual track and field day for conference colleges and other colleges. The directors of the ICAA were to be graduates of the members of the Western Conference, men who were identified with athletics during their college years. They were known variously as the Graduate Committee, the Graduate Directors, the Management Committee, and the Board of Directors. The embryo of the ICAA had existed as early as 1896. The ICAA sponsored its first annual field day in 1900. At one time each faculty representative to the conference owned one-and-two-thirds shares of stock in the ICAA. In 1912 Macy S. Good, a Purdue graduate, was the president of the organization. Warren D. Howe, an Indiana alumnus and the secretary-treasurer, maintained the ICAA office in Chicago; George R. Carr, Illinois '01, a member, was a former manager of the Illinois football team and later the vice president and general manager of the Dearborn Drug and Chemical Works in Chicago.

At a luncheon on March 20, the Graduate Directors presented a memorandum and made a statement to the presidents of the Big Eight universities. For years, they declared, the Western Conference had been trying to establish the amateur standard in intercollegiate athletic competition, but now it was being swept away by the demand for professionalism. One of the principal arguments for professionalism was that some men needed to make a living, which they could best do in athletics. Another argument was that the rules led men to perjure themselves, so the rules should be abolished. It was possible, the directors thought, for universities to enforce the rules and to cultivate the amateur spirit among alumni and the student body. The great question was whether intercollegiate athletics should be based on amateur competition or commercialism. The games should be played for the sake of the games or not at all. According to the Graduate Directors, it would be better to abolish intercollegiate athletics than to maintain them on a professional basis. Seemingly radical, the proposal deserved serious consideration.[18]

After the Graduate Directors had made their presentation, the presidents adopted three resolutions based on Stone's memorandum: intercollegiate athletics had educational values that should be retained, the conference was essential and should be maintained, and the amateur basis and spirit for intercollegiate athletics should be sustained. The presidents also adopted the three resolutions introduced by Van Hise.[19]

The Illinois Report on Amateurism

The Western Conference endorsed the amateur athletic code, but Illinois questioned it. James named David Kinley as chair of a committee to discover what the university should or should not do on this and related questions. On May 1 Kinley's committee reported to the senate and to James. James prefaced its release to the public with a statement on the university's attitude toward eligibility in intercollegiate athletics. According to the conference rule, James wrote, an amateur is an athlete who never has directly or indirectly received any money, either as pay or as a prize, for playing in any athletic contest; has never taken part in a game in which any professional player has engaged, nor in a game on, or with, a team on which any member has been a professional. A student who violates any of these rules, with or without his knowledge, is declared to be not an amateur and is not permitted to represent his institution in intercollegiate games. Since each institution interpreted the rules for itself, different standards of interpretation and administration of the rules were possible, and students of some institutions had questioned the fairness of the faculties of other universities in refusing to disqualify protested players. It seemed desirable to clarify the situation by adopting new rules or some better method of administering the old rules.[20]

According to the Kinley report, which Kinley sent to members of the senate and President James, answers to the question of what was the essence of amateurism in sport were conflicting because of differences of opinion as to what constituted amateurism and because eight universities each had an interpretation of the rule. The Western Conference had made the essence of the distinction between amateurism and professionalism the receipt of money as pay for playing, or as prize money. But the receipt of money was not of itself accepted as a universal or sufficient test of the distinction between an amateur and a professional for all sports. "At bottom amateurism is a question of the spirit in which sport is entered upon. It refers fundamentally to the players' state of mind or heart."[21] Therefore it was difficult to establish an external standard of determination. Under the present rule, no college in the conference had had an amateur baseball team for years. The rule that left the determination of amateur standing to the institution in which the players themselves were concerned led to difference of standards and of strictness in enforcing the rules. On the merits of the question, participation by a college student "in an occasional game for which he himself or others on the team may receive pay, or for which a money or other prize is received by the team as a whole, or by an individual; or participation in a game as a member of a team some other members of which receive pay, does not itself destroy the amateur spirit of the individual college student; is not necessarily demoralizing, and does not necessarily tend to the promotion of professionalism." What everyone aimed at was to make physical training and athletic contests part of the education that universities offered, and to keep students away from the professional spirit and practice. The main purposes of a university were the intellectual and moral development of young people, purposes promoted by establishing and maintaining athletics and physical training. The committee approved of intercollegiate athletics because it believed that the contests promoted friendliness, gave a broader outlook to the contestants and a wider interest in sport among the members of the competing institutions, and helped to set a common standard of college sport, which was beneficial to all concerned. Intercollegiate contests could be permitted, however, only if the colleges themselves insist that all participants "meet the requirements of amateurism according to some definition." For students, participation in intercollegiate contests was not a right but a privilege, a privilege hedged about by conditions that universities might change from time to time, and if they did, no individual would have just cause for complaint.[22]

Kinley sent a copy of the report or a related document to President Vincent (Minnesota), who was convinced that something must be done promptly if the conference was to be preserved and do the work that it might legitimately undertake. A year's experience had convinced him that the amateur standard as interpreted at the time could not be enforced. He was not sure if the modifications

Kinley's committee proposed would solve the problem. His chief fear was that the proposed Committee on Eligibility would find itself in a difficult dilemma. Unless it passed all athletes, it would be charged with favoritism. One of the chief drawbacks was the suspicion that one institution entertained for another. People at Minnesota were convinced that there was no baseball nine in the conference that had lived up to the rules strictly. The Kinley report confirmed this view. Vincent hoped that Illinois and other institutions might soon discuss the situation. Minnesota was holding to the conference not because it believed in the existing standard of eligibility but because it was not willing to withdraw until it was convinced that no really workable system could be adopted. Vincent trusted that Illinois would insist on pushing this to some kind of settlement.[23]

The report's attempt to change the definition of amateurism as related to intercollegiate athletics went nowhere. Kinley and others at Illinois thought it desirable that some action be taken that would define amateurism in a way that would be more satisfactory to conference members and would meet the conditions of play more reasonably. Accordingly, Kinley composed a letter that James then sent to the presidents of the conference institutions inviting them to send a delegate to a meeting in Urbana on April 25–26 where the principal subjects would be the definition of amateurism and the means of enforcing the intercollegiate rules on amateurism.[24]

Vincent thought that something like stability had been reached. He hesitated to reopen the question because he had little faith that doing so would achieve any satisfactory compromise. President Judson thought it was not desirable to take up the eligibility question again, but if a meeting was held, Chicago would be represented. The other conference presidents apparently shared this view, and the proposed meeting was not held.[25]

The amateur athletic code was deeply rooted in American collegiate culture, though it was constantly undermined. The Illinois report challenged the code, but the problem persisted because it was insoluble.

Orderly Athletics

Originally the Big Seven, the conference became the Big Nine in 1899 with the admission of Indiana and Iowa. After Michigan withdrew in 1908, the conference became the Big Eight. Membership was highly coveted. The faculty representatives, loath to admit new members, strove to impose order on Western Conference athletics.

Ohio State was eager to join the Western Conference, which provided a higher level of athletic competition than Ohio State enjoyed as a member of the Ohio Conference, where its competitors, except for Michigan, were Ohio colleges. But to qualify for membership, Ohio State would have to demonstrate that it adhered to the amateur athletic code and that the faculty controlled intercollegiate athletics. The school's athletic board was a large, unwieldy body. In December 1911 the faculty, students, and alumni had proposed to reconstitute it with five student members, two faculty, and two alumni. At a special meeting on December 18 the faculty refused to ratify the change. So in January the authorities began to inquire about the athletic situation on the campus and elsewhere. On January 22 the board agreed to petition the conference for admission, and days later OSU made its presentation. In mid-January H. W. Johnston (Indiana), president of the conference, visited Ohio State and spoke favorably of its chances for admission. Meanwhile, a faculty committee—Alonzo H. Tuttle, Thomas E. French, and J. A. Leighton—went to work. Tuttle and Leighton visited Chicago, Northwestern, and Illinois to see how they ran their athletics; Thomas E. French visited Michigan. The report of the committee, which the faculty adopted on February 14 and the trustees ratified a week later, went into effect on March 5. It vested control of intercollegiate athletics in an athletic board of control of nine members—five from the faculty and two each representing the alumni and the students. The faculty members, to be appointed annually by the president, were to constitute the faculty committee on athletics and eligibility. The alumni members were to be chosen annually by the alumni association, and the two student members were to be elected annually by the members of the athletic association. This done, on April 6 the faculty committee admitted Ohio State to the Western Conference, which again became the Big Nine.[26]

In December 1913 Nebraska, Marquette, and Notre Dame applied for admission to the conference. Both Nebraska and Notre Dame had applied for membership in 1901 without success. The conference appointed a committee to consider the applications and proceeded with other business.

Football was enormously popular at the University of Nebraska and throughout the state. Nebraska dominated the Missouri Valley Conference, of which it had been a member since 1906. From 1907 to 1910, under Coach W. G. "King" Cole, the Cornhuskers' record was 25-3-8. From 1911 to 1916, under Coach Ewald O. Stiehm, the Stiehm Rollers compiled a record of 35-3-2. In the early twentieth century Nebraska battled many conference teams. From 1904 to 1913 they played Minnesota every year, invariably losing. In this same period the Cornhuskers engaged Iowa five times, losing four and winning one game. Nebraska fought Michigan twice, winning 31–0 in 1905 and tying 6–6 in 1911. Based on ability, Nebraska could make a strong case for a conference berth. The committee appointed to consider the matter made no recommendation, the stated reason being that the members were not fully decided as to whether the conference should be enlarged.[27]

Marquette University effectively began operations in Milwaukee, Wisconsin, in 1881. By the early twentieth century football had replaced baseball as the most popular college sport at Marquette. In 1905 the university hired a football coach, but during that season Wisconsin defeated the Milwaukee players 29–0. Two years later the Marquette eleven defeated all the Wisconsin college teams they engaged. A year later, under Coach William Juneau, the squad sought stronger competition. In 1908 Marquette played another Western Conference team, Illinois, to a 6–6 tie. Wisconsin defeated Marquette 9–6 that season, and on Thanksgiving Day Marquette held Notre Dame to one touchdown before fifty-five hundred spectators. For the next three years Juneau's men demonstrated their gridiron prowess. Wisconsin refused to schedule a return match. High hope for its athletic future inspired Marquette to seek membership in the Big Nine. But in 1912 most of the team's veterans graduated, Juneau went to Madison to coach the Badgers, and Marquette football declined.[28]

Notre Dame, in an isolated location with a male student body, developed a unique culture of athleticism. The school channeled most of its students into athletic sports, and once its athletic prowess became well known, Notre Dame attracted athletically minded students. In the early twentieth century, Notre Dame played twenty-nine games with conference colleges. With Notre Dame, the conference colleges won sixteen, lost nine, and tied four contests. Most of these games were played well before 1913, when Notre Dame applied for membership in the conference. Between 1898 and 1910, Michigan State, not a conference member, and Notre Dame played eight games. Michigan State lost seven games. Notre Dame scored 177 points to 17 for Michigan State. Notre Dame played no games with conference colleges between 1909 and 1913. Judged by competitiveness alone, Notre Dame was a serious candidate for conference membership. After considerable discussion about Notre Dame and Marquette, however, the faculty committee, using a familiar formula, declared it "the sense of the Conference that it is inexpedient to enlarge the membership at this time."[29]

Albion Small (Chicago) attended the meeting that considered these applications. Writing to Stagg that evening, he said, "The Conference came and went today without racking up much dust. Nebraska was turned down by the surprisingly close vote of 5 to 4. (Minn., Iowa, Ill. and Ohio being the four.) Notre Dame and Marquette were rejected unanimously."[30] Small's letter revealed that Chicago, Indiana, Northwestern, Purdue, and Wisconsin turned down Nebraska. The reasons for the rejection are not part of the record. We do not know whether or to what extent religious prejudice influenced the decision on Notre Dame. America was predominantly Protestant; antipathy toward Catholics was wide and deep, especially in Indiana. Indiana and Purdue universities, both in the state of Indiana, may not have wanted neighboring Notre Dame as a competitor.

Coach Amos A. Stagg of the University of Chicago with three football players at a game on November 25, 1916. On this occasion, Minnesota defeated Chicago 49–0. Source: University of Chicago, Special Collections Research Center.

About this time William T. Foster published an indictment of intercollegiate football in an article for an influential monthly magazine. A Harvard graduate, Foster set out his conception of the ideal college in the concluding chapter of his 1911 doctoral dissertation at Teachers College, Columbia University, which led to his appointment as the first president of Reed College. There Foster rejected intercollegiate sports and fostered close intellectual collaboration between faculty and students. He was one of the leading pre-Keynesian economists, but on intercollegiate football he was a voice crying in the wilderness.[31]

On June 9, 1917, after the University of Michigan regents delegated the control of athletic affairs to the faculty, the conference invited Michigan to resume membership. Michigan re-entered the conference on November 20, making the conference the Big Ten. Ralph W. Aigler, who attended the conference session of December 9 as the Michigan representative, quickly became a leading architect of conference policy.[32]

In December 1917 Notre Dame repeated its bid for membership at a time when the school was gaining a strong reputation in football. The faculty representatives invited Rev. Mathew J. Walsh to make a statement. We do not know what Father Walsh said, and the minutes merely record that the application was denied.[33]

Persistent, Notre Dame applied again in 1919. Jesse Harper, the football coach, was eager for the Catholic college to belong to the Western Conference. At the morning session on December 6, Professor William E. Farrell spoke to the faculty representatives. The secretary of the faculty board in control of athletics, Ferrell made a statement in support of Notre Dame's application. After he spoke, the faculty committee adjourned to meet with the committee of graduate directors. In the afternoon the conference adopted a resolution that repeated the familiar formula: "it is not expedient at this time to enlarge the membership."[34]

We are left to speculate as to the attitude of the members. Perhaps size alone governed the decision. Michigan had rejoined the conference. Ten, a round number, facilitated athletic scheduling. But other reasons may have been at work. Notre Dame was a Catholic institution. Religious prejudice probably mattered. The conference consisted of public universities with no religious affiliation except for Chicago, which had Baptist roots, and Northwestern, with a Methodist heritage. Anxiety about a strong football team might also have counted. Notre Dame attracted Catholic athletes from around the country, which worked to the school's advantage. Notre Dame football teams were becoming powerful. Academic standards may also have been a factor. Notre Dame was not yet strong academically.

So the Big Ten pursued its destiny with no new members. It was not only the premier athletic conference in the Midwest but also the premier intercollegiate athletic conference in the nation. And it was a decade senior to the National Collegiate Athletic Association. The Big Ten and the NCAA shared many of the same goals. The Big Ten routinely delegated one of its members to attend the annual meeting of the NCAA. Faculty representatives presented papers at the NCAA annual conventions, and faculty members from conference institutions held offices in the NCAA and served on its committees.

The Work of the Conference

The Western Conference was designed to ensure faculty control of intercollegiate athletics in the member universities. The conference minutes provide at best a spare record of its actions. The faculty representatives transacted much of their work by committees. As a result, the conference moved at a glacial pace. The standing committees—on eligibility, colleges, and officials—were the workhorses of the conference. The eligibility of a student to participate in intercollegiate athletics as an amateur was a prime concern. In the early days an arbitrator investigated and reported on cases of eligibility. Later, a committee on eligibility took over the task.[35]

In November 1912 George A. Goodenough (Illinois), chair of the eligibility committee, informed the conference that he had made a report showing the inducement and payment of athletes in each conference institution. The report is not available, but the committee made the following recommendations. First, athletic and other university authorities should not concentrate attention on a few "star" athletes in high schools and "rush" them for possibly a year or more before graduation. Second, while it was not possible or desirable to prevent alumni from taking an active part in the recruiting of athletes from high schools, it was the committee's opinion that athletic directors, coaches, and all persons connected directly with the university should remain entirely passive. Directors and coaches should not initiate correspondence or interviews with high school athletes. Third, no concessions under the control of the athletic authorities should be awarded to students. The conference adopted these resolutions.[36] No doubt these lofty statements enabled the faculty representatives to believe that they were exercising faculty control over intercollegiate athletics. In fact, however, the recommendations were like putting one's finger into a dike. In December 1914 the conference called the attention of the athletic directors to the conference rule prohibiting directors, coaches, and others directly connected with the university from initiating correspondence with high school athletes with a view to influencing them to attend their respective institutions.[37]

The Committee on Colleges was established to define four-year institutions by type and to decide which of them should be classified as colleges for conference purposes. The list was instrumental in determining which college athletic teams could play the freshman athletic teams of the conference universities. For example, the committee's classifications enabled the conference to take Wabash College and De Pauw University, both located in Indiana, from the list of institutions that were obliged to exclude first-year men from their team when playing conference universities.[38] As American higher education matured, this committee became increasingly less important.

In addition to the standing committees, the conference appointed others as needed. The Committee on Football Officials was responsible for seeing that the game officials were properly qualified. Officials could not work professional games as well as college games. This committee became increasingly important over time. The Committee on Athletic Schedules ruled on the number of intercollegiate contests that conference teams could play each season. The members appointed a committee to consult the managers of teams and the athletic directors about schedule difficulties and to report to the conference. The Committee on Preliminary Training investigated the problem of when football practice should begin in the fall and tried to make sure that the member schools observed the agreed-upon date.

The Governance of Football

The faculty representatives made the rules and tried to enforce them. A variety of such matters required attention. In May 1912 the conference reaffirmed by a vote of 7 to 1 a ruling "that all students, during their first year of residence, shall compete in athletics only against members of their own institutions." Harold W. Johnston (Indiana) objected, declaring that the conference had no jurisdiction over games between college teams and teams representing high schools.[39]

The faculty committee devoted considerable attention to football, the dominant intercollegiate sport. In 1912 the conference passed a resolution providing for a committee of football experts to consider football rules and make recommendations to the conference. On reconsideration, the delegates rescinded the action. What prompted this decision? Perhaps the conference was wedded to the status quo, or perhaps the members wanted a game with few rules.[40]

In a June 1913 meeting in Madison, Wisconsin, the faculty representatives considered a rule that required each conference member to play at least four games of football with other conference members each season. The rule insured a minimum degree of cohesion among the member universities, but cohesion was not the goal of the conference members with the strongest football teams. They wanted to play games with each other before large crowds that brought big gate receipts.[41]

The faculty representatives recognized that some (many?) college men were more interested in sports than studies. To promote learning, in December 1913 the faculty committee resolved that in any one college year no student be permitted to engage in intercollegiate contests in more than one of the following sports: football, baseball, basketball, track, and swimming. The rule was to become effective in September 1915. The delegates sent a resolution on the subject to the conference members for report. Apparently, no disapproval was forthcoming because the conference passed the resolution. At some point, however, Ohio State rejected the so-called "Two Sport Resolution." So on December 5 the measure was put upon its passage a second time and was rejected by a vote of 7 to 2.[42] The decision gave students a green light to compete in two and even three varsity sports a year. Many did, making them quasi-professional athletes.

In the early days of intercollegiate athletics, a student player was the captain of an athletic team. With the advent of the professional coach, a problem arose if a coach directed the play from the sidelines. To prevent such action, in June 1914 the conference declared that participation by coaches in directing athletic contests was undesirable. It requested that the athletic directors suggest regulations to eliminate this participation in the case of each particular sport.[43]

Secret football practice was also a concern. In June 1914 the conference voted to ask the athletic directors whether secret practice was necessary or desirable. We do not know if the faculty representatives heard from the directors. In June 1915 the conference passed a resolution that said "secret practice in football [should] be confined to two days a week." Since three conference members objected, in December 1915 the measure was placed on its second passage and lost by a vote of 6 to 3. The faculty committee then passed a resolution: "There shall be open practice in football at least one day in each week."[44]

When in the academic year was football practice permitted to begin? In December 1913 the delegates appointed a committee to investigate such practice before September 20 and referred to it a resolution saying that in those institutions that opened later than September 20, football practice between the date of opening and September 20 was not to begin earlier than 3 P.M.[45]

The problem persisted. The pressure came from coaches, athletic directors, student fans, alumni boosters, and perhaps university presidents. It was unrelenting. The faculty committee had a nagging suspicion that football consumed too much of the players' time. In December 1915 the delegates appointed a special committee to investigate and report on football practice prior to September 20. Reporting the following June, the committee offered some rules on the subject. Candidates for football teams might engage in individual practice prior to September 20, but there could be no collective practice. The coaches were to have nothing to do with the men's movements either on or off the field before September 20. The athletic department could give out suits and footballs for the men to use, but the department had to withhold tackling dummies and other paraphernalia until September 20. It was not permissible for the captain or anyone else to conduct signal practice, tackling, or any other form of organized practice. Meetings for "chalk talks" or other forms of instruction could not be held before September 20. This session included a reading of a communication from the conference directors and coaches about when football practice was to begin. Then Thomas French (Purdue) introduced a resolution that would move the date for the opening of football practice from September 20 to September 15 but would not provide facilities for practice prior to that date. The resolution unanimously carried.[46]

A recurrent issue was the number of football games each season. At one time five games per season were allowed. Later, the number went to seven. In 1918 a motion to permit eight games was defeated by a vote of 6 to 3. In December 1920 Pyre (Wisconsin) returned to a continuing problem when he introduced a resolution asking that a committee investigate "the football routine of the several Conference institutions" and report with a view to possible regulation of the time consumed in football training.[47]

The subject of postseason and championship games was a continuing concern. In December 1919 the conference declared on a motion by Albion Small (Chicago) "that arrangements of schedules, rules, and understandings designed to further the determination of the Conference championship in any branch of sport are deemed by the Conference to be undesirable." In 1920 the conference adopted a resolution that "the Conference reaffirms its judgment that post-season games, in all branches of sport, are undesirable." Granted the pressures at work, this decision risked not being sufficiently strong. Accordingly, in June 1921 the conference declared that its "disapproval" of postseason games was to have the force of a conference rule.[48] This declaration is a watershed in conference history. Previously, the conference team that won the most games was the conference champion. Now, despite pressure for postseason games, the faculty committee courageously resisted the rising tide.

In early conference history, football players wore no identifying mark on their uniforms. The result was confusion and worse. Thugs could operate undetected, referees could not identify evildoers, and fans could not spot their heroes. To remedy the problem, some teams began to wear digits on their jerseys. In 1914 the conference recommended the numbering of players in football games but did not consider it advisable to pass a regulation on the matter. In December 1920 Aigler (Michigan) moved that players on conference football teams wear numbers not less than eight inches high, the color being such as to show the numbers distinctly. Contesting teams were to exchange lists of eligible players together with the numbers to be worn by such players, at least one week before the game. The resolution passed.[49]

When the conference began, some faculty representatives insisted that the price of football tickets be kept low for students because the game was primarily for them. Later, the price of tickets to "migrants"—that is, students who followed their team to distant sites—became an issue. In December 1919 the subject of "the abuse of student admission to foreign games" prompted the conference to rule "that the fifty cent rate, insofar as it applies to students of the institution represented by the visiting team, be withdrawn." Wisconsin challenged the fifty-cent rate, so the ruling was modified by substituting the phrase "shall not be obligatory" for the words "be withdrawn." The matter was placed on passage under the White Resolution and carried.[50]

"Just at the close of the session," Albion Small (Chicago) confided to Stagg after the December 19 meeting, "Paige [Minnesota] sprung his old chestnut about its being time to bury the hatchet and rescind the 'boycott rule' against Michigan. Pyre of Wis. at once blurted out—'Has [Minnesota coach Harry] Williams got his telegram to Yost all written?' and Paige couldn't even get a second to his motion. I am sure that his vote in favor of Nebraska was on the ground that the larger the conference gets the easier it will be to get a vote for the games with Michigan, and he cares more about them than about the Conference."

CHAPTER 4

The Conference and the War

The war that engulfed the nation in April 1917 transformed intercollegiate athletics. College athletes along with other students rushed off in large numbers to the battle, while the colleges devoted their energies to winning the war. In June, shortly after the United States declared war on Germany, E. P. Harding (Minnesota) introduced in the conference a resolution of his university's senate "that intercollegiate athletics be suspended until after the war." Albion Small (Chicago) countered that the conference should accept the recommendation of the president of the United States with reference to the continuance of athletic sports, and that this action not be construed as mandatory on the individual institutions. The substitute carried by a vote of 7 to 2.[1]

In December the conference agreed that there be no change in conference rules as applied to college games but that the several conference colleges be allowed individual discretion in scheduling games with military organizations.[2] The following June, at Michigan's request, the conference amended the resolution by inserting the phrase "during the period of the war." Because the Michigan faculty objected to the preceding resolution, it was put on its second passage under the White Resolution. Eight faculty representatives voted yes, Iowa was absent, and Michigan voted no. So the resolution of December 1917 was declared to be in force.[3]

During the 1917 football season, the total number of games played by conference colleges ranged from five to ten: Minnesota (five); Chicago (six); Indiana, Northwestern, Purdue, and Wisconsin (seven); Illinois and Iowa (eight); Ohio

State (nine); and Michigan (ten). The number of conference games ranged from one to five: Michigan (one); Indiana and Iowa (three); Minnesota, Ohio State, and Purdue (four); and Chicago, Illinois, Northwestern, and Wisconsin (five). Several Big Ten football players enlisted or were called into military service, and during the season three conference college teams played games with military teams that included former college athletes. They were as follows: Illinois with Camp Funston, which was part of Ft. Riley in Kansas; Iowa with the Great Lakes Naval Training Station, near North Chicago; and Ohio State with Camp Sherman, near Chillicothe, Ohio.

The Western Conference called a special meeting in September 1918 to consider the relation of the conference to the U. S. War Department and the Student Army Training Corps. After each faculty representative described the situation at his institution, a motion that the conference abdicate all its functions for the period of the war was introduced. A substitute motion prompted discussion and led to the adoption of a resolution stating that since "virtually all the student body of each of the Conference institutions [was] to be under military jurisdiction and that the rules and regulations of the conference [were therefore] superseded by the rules of the War Department," the Western Conference would "suspend its activities as a controlling body during the period of the emergency . . . to be resumed at the end of that time." The conference "tender[ed] to the War Department its services in carrying on athletic activities . . . in and among its members." The conference and the Graduate Committee of the ICAA would send delegates "to confer with the War Department to tender the service of the Conference and to obtain a clearer understanding as to how the wishes of the War Department" might be implemented. A reporter for the *Chicago Tribune* reported that "the resolutions were adopted after the [faculty committee] had held an informal meeting with members of the graduate committee." The Western Conference appointed Thomas E. French (Ohio State) and the ICAA appointed Avery Brundage "to go to Washington . . . to secure rulings which may solve complex situations." Until Washington issued orders, the military "commandants at the various Big Ten universities" were to have "complete control of athletics." "It seemed feasible," said the colonel in charge of the SATC, "to allow all men in the corps to participate in all athletic contests," a ruling that made freshmen eligible to play on varsity teams for the first time since 1905.[4]

The SATC posed a special problem for the Western Conference. On June 29, 1918, the army had announced that an SATC unit would be established at all "arts and sciences colleges . . . enrolling one hundred or more 'able-bodied' male students" over age eighteen. The SATC was to utilize the colleges "to select and train officer-candidates." All male students who entered qualifying institutions in the fall of 1918 who were physically fit and eighteen or over would become privates on duty in the army. They would wear uniforms, live in barracks (college facilities), eat in a mess hall, receive a monthly allowance, and be subject to military discipline. An army officer would take charge of the military aspects of the program.[5]

Many college and university presidents had long favored military training in the nation's institutions of higher education, and they enthusiastically supported the SATC. President James of the University of Illinois, who strongly supported military training in universities, appeared before the House Committee on Military Affairs and outlined his views of the steps to be taken in reorganizing this important resource. First, the War Department should detail more officers "for the work of supervision and instruction." Second, the Federal Government "should furnish the same kind and amount of supplies and equipment for the use of . . . cadet regiments as for the National Guard." James also "advocated the establishment by the Government of military scholarships of $250 a year, but on condition that the candidate after graduation from the University should enter the army as a second lieutenant for one year, with a lieutenant's pay. . . . Such a plan would involve the establishment in the best of the land-grant colleges of a course in military science adequate to qualify the student to enter the army on almost equal footing with graduates of West Point."[6]

Among its other dimensions, the SATC offered a solution to the problem of declining college enrollments in time of war. At Minnesota, for example, 3,120 student-soldiers were registered in the program; at Wisconsin, 2,250; at Columbia, considerably more than 2,000.[7] But the SATC was a response to the war, not a permanent program.

Now, in early October, French reported on his talks with the Washington authorities. A digest of the points French submitted pertained mainly to football without mention of that game. All members of the SATC were to be eligible for competition. The athletic departments of the universities were to have charge of intercollegiate games. Two trips in November were allowed. Games with other army organizations might be played, and SATC men were not prohibited from playing with or against men not in the SATC. Eight games were allowed. The season was to end no later than November 30.[8]

Governed by these guidelines, the 1918 season proceeded. The Big Ten universities played a total of sixty-one games, including twenty-five conference games as follows: Chicago (5), Illinois (4), Iowa (3), Michigan (2), Minnesota (2), Northwestern (2), Ohio State (3), Purdue (1), and Wisconsin (3). Conference colleges also competed against thirteen "soldier factories" located in close proximity to the schools. In addition, the Big Ten colleges faced twenty-three non-conference colleges on the gridiron. Since the conference had turned down Nebraska and Notre Dame when they applied for membership shortly before the war began, it is worth noting that during the war years Iowa engaged Nebraska and Purdue met Notre Dame. "The caliber of football played by the conference teams was far below that of former years," wrote Walter Eckersall, because many of the best college players were on the Army and Navy teams.[9]

Shortly after the Armistice and the 1918 football season, the War Department demobilized the SATC. The emergency had passed, the faculty representatives declared in December 1918, and conference regulations were again in effect. The army had allowed universities eight football games a season. As soon as military rule ended, a motion was made to extend the conference football schedule to eight games a season instead of seven. The motion was defeated by a vote of 6 to 3.[10]

On June 9, 1918, before the Armistice, the faculty representatives discussed the question of the eligibility of players in military training camps. A resolution that expressed the sense of the conference said that men who had severed their connection with their respective universities by entering the service of the United States were ineligible for participation in intercollegiate athletics. The conference Committee on Eligibility was to administer the rule.[11] After the Armistice, the faculty representatives took a different view of the matter. Meeting in Chicago in December, they unanimously agreed that "in determining future questions of eligibility under Conference rules, no account shall be taken of athletic or scholastic records during military service or of interruptions by reason of the same." Moreover, "absences from the university on account of military service shall not render a student ineligible under Rule 12." This rule declared that a student who had "been in attendance less than one college half-year" would not be allowed "to play in any intercollegiate contest thereafter" until he had "been in attendance six consecutive calendar months."[12]

During the war the SATC (Safe at the College, some called it), exercised a lasting influence on intercollegiate athletics. The military regime required all male students, not just varsity players, to participate in athletic sports. Moreover, freshmen were eligible for varsity teams, while coaches and athletic directors learned to curb their profligate ways. It was not necessary, the commandant ruled, to take an athletic team to a visiting venue one or two days before a contest, as was the custom. Just as good results were obtained, and at a great saving, when a team arrived on the morning of a game. In addition, war regulations undermined the belief that a training table was essential, and they placed other features in the conference on a "sane basis."[13]

American participation in the war helped to transform the role of sport in the nation. Newton D. Baker, the secretary of war, promoted physical education. As part of the war effort, the War Department and the Navy Department each created a Commission on Training Camp Activities chaired by Raymond B. Fosdick. Joseph E. Raycroft, a professor of physical education at Princeton, headed the army's athletic program, while Walter Camp chaired the navy's offering. Fosdick brought forward a tentative plan, he said, "to invite the cooperation" of various organizations "to help in providing an adequate leisure-time program for the troops in the training camps." The YMCA, the Knights of Columbus, the Jewish Welfare Board, the American Library Association, and the Playground and Recreation Association of America (later called the War Camp Community Service) responded to his call. Fosdick's commission borrowed from the British Army the idea of appointing an athletic director in every training camp. The British, Fosdick said, "understood [better than did the Americans] the relaxing and therapeutic effect of vigorous games." Thirty-five Army camps and about half as many Navy stations sprang up. In them competent men offered instruction and competition in every kind of sport. Never before in the history of the country had so large a number of young men been engaged in organized and competitive athletics.[14]

When the fighting ended, the American military command needed to maintain high morale in the Army of Occupation. They could keep the men busy with military drill or involve them in athletics. Relying on British example, Fosdick recommended limited military drill to keep the men physically fit, with the remainder of the time given to athletic sports and educational activities.[15]

Elwood S. Brown, the director of the athletic department of the YMCA, proposed a program of athletic competition at the company and brigade levels that would culminate in an American Expeditionary Force Championship. With a choice between sports or military duties, the troops became massively involved in athletic activities. Brown also proposed, and Army officials approved, a plan for the Inter-Allied Games, a sports festival for superior athletes from the nations that had been allied in the war effort. The games were held in Paris in July 1919 in a hastily constructed facility, Pershing Stadium. As a result of all this athletic activity, two million men were going to carry back home a lively notion of good, clean sport.[16]

When the war began, medical examiners had found that from one-third to one-half of the men called up for military service were physically unfit. Moreover, 30 percent were rejected by their draft boards, while others were turned back at the camps. According to General Leonard Wood, the remedy for this alarming plight was twofold—"physical supervision" of the nation's children "in the schools" and "universal training for national service."[17] Alarmed at the situation, many states passed laws requiring that physical education be taught in the public schools, and the content of physical education changed from calisthenics to sport.

With the end of the war, the conference authorities had to decide whether to revive the old intercollegiate athletic system or "to build a bigger, better, and more enduring one." "Habit, vested interest, sentiment, and a certain timid lethargy of imagination all argue for a mere restoration of the old," James R. Angell, a dean at the University of Chicago, told the annual convention of the NCAA in 1918, "but foresight, ambition, vision, faith, and courage plead for something better."[18]

According to Angell, "three fairly distinct views regarding the . . . reconstruction policy of collegiate athletics" were evident. One was the "athletic standpatter" who insisted that the prewar system "was in all essentials satisfactory." The standpatters, he said, were perhaps not a very large group, but they had a "shrill voice and [were] decidedly influential." Another was the "mild progressive," who believed that "the faults of the old system" could be patiently eradicated and that the conference could make improvements as it proceeded. Numerically large, the mild progressives probably comprised most college alumni. A third view was that of the "radical reformer," who maintained that "the old system was the child of Beelzebub and that no amount . . . of superficial reform [would] alter that fact [or] change its inner character." The radical reformers, a small group, included "some cranks [but] also . . . some prophets with real brains."[19]

The analysis was acute, but historical development follows its own idiosyncratic and unpredictable ways. Standpatters, progressives, and radical reformers all competed for mastery in the 1920s. They had to contend with each other and with new forces at work when the nation returned to "normalcy."

Closing Out the Decade

Early in 1919 the athletic directors and coaches of the Western Conference schools began to prepare for the coming football season. In March the Big Ten football coaches held their annual meeting in Chicago to select officials for the fall games. Unlike former years, they classified the officials as referees, umpires, field judges, and head linesmen for the seven games scheduled from October 11 to November 22. The coaches also decided to instruct field judges, who kept time in all games where there were four officials, to take time out for penalties following incomplete forward passes.[20]

When fall practice began as scheduled on September 15, coaches in conference colleges were flooded with "a wealth of material, including from fourteen to twenty-three lettermen." "Most conference teams have slated four games with conference rivals," the *Tribune* reported, which would make it "possible to determine the conference championship at the end of the season."[21]

At the request of Wisconsin, a special meeting of the conference was called for October 1919 to deal with the status of members of the Northwestern football team who had entered the University from the Great Lakes Naval Station in the second quarter of the college year. It seemed desirable for the conference to have a more definite understanding in regard to some of the conference regulations "under the unusual conditions of the present football season." Four members of the Great Lakes football team had entered Northwestern when discharged from the Navy. J. F. A. Pyre (Wisconsin) asserted that the conference rule which required a full year's residence was not met by the Northwestern players who had entered the college during the second quarter. Omera F. Long (Northwestern) stated the interpretation upon which Northwestern had considered these players to have gained the year's residence. The question hinged upon the character of the 1919 summer session at Northwestern. Faced with the problem, the conference concluded that Northwestern had acted upon the assumption that attendance upon the summer session of 1919 should be counted as part of a year's residence, and it did not object to the Northwestern interpretation.[22]

In June 1920, after the dust of war had settled, the conference interpreted an action it had taken in December 1918. In determining future questions of eligibility, that action held, no account was to be taken of athletic or scholastic records during military service or of interruptions in those records. The conference now declared that a student whose participation in a particular sport had been interrupted by military service should be entitled to three years' participation in the sport involved, provided that actual residence not be extended beyond four academic years.[23]

A conference rule held each of the conference colleges to a schedule of seven football games, and another rule decreed that each team in the conference was to play at least four contests each year with other Big Ten members. In 1919 Illinois played seven games with conference colleges, defeating six opponents, losing only to Wisconsin, and capturing the Big Ten championship. "Illinois is one of the gamest elevens which has appeared on a western gridiron in years," Walter Eckersall wrote in the *Tribune*. "Some of the players were hurt in the early part of the year, but few of them were laid off long enough to recover entirely. They were sent into the game when they should have been in the stands. They did not complain or protest. They simply did what they were told, no matter how painful, and this accounts for the championship." The season, Eckersall exulted, was "the most successful football year since the adoption of the forward pass and the ten-yard rule thirteen years ago."[24]

With Illinois as an example and the 1919 football season as the high point in the history of the conference, one could understand that other coaches in the conference wanted to schedule more than four conference games. Who could doubt that athletic directors, coaches, and fans would demand more than seven games a year?

Reformed football was not nearly as brutal as the pre-reformed game. "Development of the open style of play to supplant the smashing game" of the late nineteenth century accounted for the "decreasing number of fatalities," a *Tribune* sportswriter noted in late 1919. But football was still the roughest of American outdoor sports, which went far to explain why fans loved the game. The number of fatalities of high school and college football players was sixteen in 1915, eighteen in 1916, twelve in 1917, ten in 1918, and five in 1919.[25]

With the war over, the future of the Intercollegiate Conference or Big Ten seemed bright. In 1919 Harvard, Yale, and Princeton, the "Big Three" in football, agreed to curb excesses in promoting the game. The Big Ten was the nation's premier athletic conference, intercollegiate football was enormously popular, and the Western Conference had reduced disorder to order in collegiate football. Nevertheless, a specter loomed on the horizon. That specter was professional football.[26]

PART TWO

From Order to Disorder

CHAPTER 5

The Big Ten in the
Golden Age of Sports

The cultural context of the 1920s shaped intercollegiate athletics. The war emergency had, according to Reed College president William T. Foster, "justified anew the most persistent of the many charges brought against intercollegiate athletics" during the previous decade. The nation, he said in an address to the National Education Association, had been "annually graduating a few men of extraordinary athletic ability and many men of undeveloped intellectual power. In athletics a few only are highly trained; the majority not at all." The customary "policy of vicarious athletics" meant that there were not enough available intercollegiate athletes to meet 20 percent of "the need for men with minds and bodies disciplined by physical training." Moreover, in preparing for conflict, medical examiners had rejected 29 percent of the young men called up as physically unfit for unlimited service and had classified an additional 18 percent as fit only for limited service.[1] After the war, voices called for corrective measures. Some suggested that the state had a duty to conserve the nation's manhood by means of universal military service, while others urged the schools and colleges to inaugurate comprehensive programs of physical education and competitive athletics. In this climate of opinion, intercollegiate athletics flourished.

After a brief spell of economic hardship, the decade was seemingly one of prosperity. Many Americans were hard pressed, but most people viewed the good times as their birthright.

The 1920s were characterized by the advent of mass culture, mass advertising, a consumption culture, and new attitudes toward work. People abandoned the Progressive commitment to social reform and its athletic ideology. They viewed sport as entertainment, an "escape from the rigid routine of the machine."[2] In this climate of opinion, intercollegiate athletics flourished.

The decade was one of ballyhoo and nonsense. The tabloids accentuated the eccentric and the bizarre, while the mainstream press glorified sports luminaries. The passion for sports spawned both Gee Whiz journalists like Grantland Rice, who celebrated athletic heroes, and Aw Nuts journalists like Westbrook Pegler, who had no illusions about any of them. Neither praising nor damning collegiate athletics was John R. Tunis, who understood them in the context of the nation's intellectual, cultural, and moral life.[3]

The newspapers had made the average American a football fan before the war. After the war the press fed the appetite it had created with increased attention to football. In the early 1920s, newspaper circulation increased dramatically. Football was an essentially American game played by Americans for Americans. Sports writers dared not say that football was anything but great. So the press celebrated the game and its heroes.[4]

The Big Ten was the nation's premier intercollegiate athletic conference. In addition to a multitude of small state and regional organizations, several strong regional conferences dotted the landscape. The Big Three—Harvard, Yale, and Princeton—less prominent than they had been earlier, became part of the Ivy League in 1954. Meanwhile, several other conferences arose, notably the Southern Intercollegiate Athletic Association, a year older than the Western Conference; the Southwest Conference, formed in 1914; and the Pacific Coast Conference, organized in 1915.

Football Ascendant

Football was the dominant intercollegiate sport, and the Midwest was challenging the East for national supremacy on the gridiron. Several coaches in the Western Conference were making their mark. With a concentration of coaching talent unequaled at any one time in any one section of the nation, the conference made itself felt. Walter Camp traveled west in 1920 to watch the Ohio State–Wisconsin game, after which he declared it the most exciting one he had seen in years. A year later Howard Jones and his Iowa Hawkeyes took the Big Ten crown, the first for Iowa since 1900. Later that season the Hawkeyes boasted a 10–7 victory over Rockne's Notre Dame.[5]

The Big Ten remained committed to amateur athletics, which it found difficult to maintain. Summer baseball remained a problem. The conference was on record as opposed to it, but the athletic directors were divided on the subject.

In its 1920 Homecoming Game, Illinois defeated Minnesota 17–7. On this occasion, Art Carney caught a forward pass and raced 40 yards for a touchdown. Carney was an All-America end. Source: University of Illinois Archives RS 39/2/20, box 44, folder "Ath 2–3, . . . 1920."

Several favored allowing students to play baseball for pay during the summer.[6] Professional football was also a problem. In December 1920 the conference struck a blow against it. Purdue had objected to a resolution that held that anyone who participated as player or official in a professional football game should be disqualified for all employment in connection with college athletics. As a result, the matter was taken up again. Put on passage a second time, it passed.[7]

In December 1919 the conference had declared that championship games were undesirable, and in June 1920 it decreed the same regarding postseason games in all branches of sport. Both decisions aimed at preventing athletics from overshadowing scholarship. By 1920 the Tournament of Roses football game was immensely popular. In that year the undefeated national champion Harvard team representing the East went to Pasadena to play an Oregon team representing the West. Two hundred thousand people witnessed the parade and thirty thousand watched a hard-fought game, with Harvard as victor. During the 1920 football season, the University of California "Wonder Team" was unbeaten. Selecting a competitor for 1921 was difficult. Both Harvard and Princeton were eligible, but college authorities opposed their teams making the trip. After considering other possibilities, tournament officials invited the Ohio State team coached by John W. Wilce, the Big Ten champion in three recent years, to take part. In a conference session on the eve of the scheduled contest, a resolution "that the recent action of the Conference in sanctioning the Ohio State trip to California shall not be considered as a precedent" carried. On January 1, 1921, California's "Wonder Team" walloped Ohio State 28–0 before 41,500 spectators in Tournament Park (the Rose Bowl had not yet been built). On June 4 the faculty representatives declared that the disapproval of postseason games previously classified as an expression of opinion was to have the force of a conference rule.[8]

Late in 1921, tournament officials tried to identify the next team to represent the East against California in the New Year's Day spectacle. The Hawkeyes won the Big Ten conference football championship that year. At a conference session in December the Iowa representative requested a ruling on the matter, and the delegates replied by affirming that "the game at Pasadena proposed by the Tournament of Roses constituted a 'post-season game' and would therefore be in violation of the rule adopted by the conference in June 1921."[9]

The conference professed to believe that intercollegiate athletics promoted good relations among the participants. In fact, however, athletic competition was keen, the rules were violated, and contention resulted. In June 1921 the conference appointed a committee to report at a future meeting "as to the disposition to be made by the Conference of the University of Ohio's protest concerning certain published expressions of opinion on the part of Coach Richards of the University of Wisconsin."[10] John R. Richards, the former athletic director and football coach at Ohio State, had resigned after the 1912 football season to become the Wisconsin football coach. John W. Wilce followed Richards at Ohio State. Wisconsin and Ohio State had played each other every year from 1914 to 1920, alternating the site of the game. Under Wilce, the Buckeyes had won the conference championship three times by 1920. When the Western Conference fixed its football schedule for 1921, no Ohio State–Wisconsin game was scheduled. Richards blamed Wilce for the break: "For Wilce to take the attitude he maintained today is beyond understanding," said Richards when he learned about the new schedule. "We played at Columbus this year, and it is only fair for Ohio State to come to Madison next year. I can only say that no Wisconsin eleven coached by me will ever meet an Ohio State team again."[11] Richards added a stronger utterance that was published in the *Daily Cardinal* and given nation-wide publicity.[12]

As a result of the feeling that developed, William O. Thompson, the president of Ohio State, wrote Edward A. Birge, his counterpart at Wisconsin, that there was likely to be some unfortunate action in the Western Conference through a report. To maintain the good feeling between the student bodies of the two institutions, Thompson wanted Birge to work with him in dealing with the matter. Since he could not leave Columbus, Thompson sent Thomas E. French (Ohio State) to Madison, with the hope that the two might "bring about a better understanding and possibly a way of escape from an annoying and probably unfortunate experience with the Western Conference Board." After the dust settled, Thompson hoped that in the future as in the past the athletic relations of the two schools would be those of friendly rivalry.[13]

Schools for the Training of Coaches

The growing prominence of intramural sports and intercollegiate athletics in schools, colleges, and universities created a need for trained coaches. Meeting in June 1921, the faculty representatives raised a question about the relationship of a School for the Training of Coaches to intercollegiate athletics. The school at Illinois prompted the question: What is the relation between an academic program and an athletic program? The delegates named Thomas Moran (Purdue) as chairman of a committee to investigate and recommend a course of action.[14]

The University of Illinois school began in the 1914 summer session when George Huff, the director of physical training for men, alert to the increasing demand for trained individuals to direct high school athletics, introduced courses in coaching baseball, football, basketball, and track taught by the varsity coaches for each of these sports. The program was entirely separate from physical education courses; it was repeated in the summer sessions from 1915 through 1919. The attendance was 193 in 1915, 56 in 1917 (the nation was at war), and 199 in 1919, when athletic coaches from twenty-eight states attended the six-week course.[15]

George Huff, University of Illinois Athletic Director, ca. 1910. Huff's passion was college baseball, but as athletic director he was exemplary in safeguarding the integrity of intercollegiate football in the Big Ten Conference. Source: University of Illinois Archives RS 39/2/24, folder 121.

The University of Illinois record in the major sports was excellent. In 1914–15, Illinois athletic teams were the undisputed champions of the Big Ten in football, baseball, basketball, and track and field. The record was without parallel in Western Conference intercollegiate athletics. It bolstered the belief that Illinois was well qualified to offer a school for coaches. In the spring of 1916 Huff urged the University to introduce a four-year curriculum in coaching, but President James was not prepared to proceed.[16] Later, the senate's Committee on Educational Policy studied Huff's proposal, and on April 7, 1919, it recommended the approval of a four-year program in coaching and physical education. Its purpose was "to enable male students to fill positions as athletic directors, coaches, and gymnasium instructors, or any combination of [such] positions." On April 12 the trustees approved of the recommendation.[17]

In 1919–20 the university introduced its curriculum in academic coaching—forty-four hours, equally divided between theory and practice. "Track and field, boxing, wrestling, football, baseball, basketball, swimming, gymnastics, games, playground instruction, anthropometry, the physiology of exercise and kinesiology, orthopedics, training, and first aid" occupied twenty-four courses. Educational psychology, technique of teaching, organization and administration of physical education, coaching, and three hours of electives occupied another twenty hours. The other thirty hours of prescribed subjects were physiology, anatomy, hygiene, psychology, public speaking, rhetoric, and military.[18] The program started well. In the first semester it enrolled 65 men, and in 1921–22 the curriculum attracted a total of 197.[19]

Schools for coaches were becoming popular. The University of Chicago and the School of Physical Education in Ithaca, New York, offered such courses.[20] Rockne began his coaching schools in the early 1920s. By 1925 he had set up seven; more than a thousand student coaches were enrolled. In addition to his football schools, Rockne went into partnership with the University of Wisconsin basketball coach to run coaching schools for football and basketball.[21]

At a conference session in December 1921, Moran reported that the conference had only one well-developed School for Athletic Coaches—Illinois, which had a four-year course leading to a degree. Several institutions had established certain courses that could develop into such schools. Chicago, Iowa, Minnesota, Northwestern, and Purdue had no such school and did not contemplate the establishment of one.[22] Indiana offered certain courses in athletic coaching in the summer session. Ohio State offered an elective in coaching in the College of Education. Wisconsin had a physical education major in the School of Education. Michigan had started a school for athletic coaches in the fall of 1921; its course of study had been worked out only for the first semester. These courses might develop into schools for coaches, so the problem was one that the conference should consider for all the conference universities.[23]

Based on Moran's survey, the conference reached the following conclusions:

A student who specialized in athletics throughout a four-year course in a school for coaches was, in reality, although not technically, a professional athlete. Competition between men who were preparing for athletics as a profession and men who were studying liberal arts, law, engineering, or medicine, with athletics incidental, was unfair and unequal. A course made up, in large part, of training in athletic coaching could not have the educational value and would not involve the inherent difficulties of a standard college course; as a consequence the scholastic requirements for athletic competition under the conference rules would be, in part at least, nullified by such schools. In case candidates for football teams could enter summer courses in football coaching, the conference rule prohibiting football coaching prior to September 15 would go by the boards.[24]

The committee reported that "it was unable to recommend . . . any definite line of action," but the matter was "too important, too delicate, and with too many ramifications to be disposed of hastily." Further, "the conference might say that men enrolled in Schools for Coaching "should not be eligible for intercollegiate competition, or that men in such schools should play only against men in similar schools, or that varsity candidates should not be eligible for summer courses in football coaching, or the conference might require certain academic standards in Schools for Coaching as a condition for eligibility for conference athletics." And yet "each of these possibilities was open to obvious objections, some to very serious objections." The committee recommended that the conference take time to discuss the report, that copies of it be given to conference members, and that the report be taken up again at the next meeting with a view to action. After prolonged discussion, the conference added Aigler (Michigan) to the committee and instructed it to submit to the conference on the next day "a resolution embodying the opinion of the conference upon the subject."[25]

The next day Moran recommended an addition to Rule 1, which decreed that "in order to participate in intercollegiate sport one must be a bona fide matriculated student regularly enrolled as a candidate for a degree and doing full work." The addition declared that to be eligible to compete in athletics "students taking courses in physical education or athletic coaching must carry a minimum of fourteen hours of regular academic or scholastic work in addition to their courses in physical education and athletic coaching." After discussion the conference agreed that the matter be referred back to the committee and that its members meet representatives of the University of Illinois and report back to the conference in June.[26]

In June, Moran reported. He had visited Illinois and discussed with the authorities the work being done in the school for athletic coaches. He was convinced "that very earnest work and work of no trifling character" was being done in the school. About 100 of the 136 hours required for graduation consisted of academic work.

The percentage of failure, he said, "was rather higher than in other departments." Men taking this course "had some advantage on athletic teams over men enrolled in other schools of the University," Moran concluded, "but not so marked . . . as at first appeared." Because the members had not consulted among themselves, Moran's committee had no recommendation to present. Perhaps it was too early to act, inasmuch as several other conference institutions were considering or had already taken steps to establish such schools.[27] G. A. Young (Purdue) presented Moran's report to the faculty committee. After prolonged discussion, the conference adopted the following resolution:

> No student in a school for coaches, athletic directors, physical education or any other similar technical courses, shall be eligible unless he shall have carried and passed and be at the time carrying a minimum of 14 hours per semester of regular academic or scholastic work as distinguished from courses in the theory, art, or practice of athletics or physical education; and in the case of students enrolled in other schools, work in such courses in the theory, or practice of athletics or physical education may not be counted in making up full work as required for eligibility.[28]

With this resolution the conference established a standard designed to ensure that college athletes and aspiring coaches met academic requirements. Football players could retain academic eligibility while devoting much of their time to sports.

The AAUP Report

Thomas Moran investigated the relation of intercollegiate athletics to academic programs as a member of the American Association of University Professors. Faculty members in elite universities had founded the AAUP in 1915 to promote scholarship, stimulate the intellectual interests of college students, and defend the academic freedom of faculty members. By 1925 the AAUP had 5,520 members in 217 institutions in the United States and Canada, 5,357 of whom were in American institutions, including 987 scattered among the Big Ten universities. The AAUP advanced its goals by means of committees, whose reports were presented at an annual meeting and published in the AAUP *Bulletin*.

Moran chaired the Committee on College Athletics. At the annual AAUP meeting in December 1924 he made a statement regarding intercollegiate athletics and presented a list of topics prepared by his committee as a basis for discussion. The statement observed that the average college student was not "in sympathy with our athletic eligibility requirements." Students did not appreciate the importance of eligibility rules and the need to distinguish between the amateur and the professional in college athletics. From such a background students derived their "chaotic and perverted notions in regard to the regulation of athletics." The need was to coordinate students, alumni, and athletic experts with the right attitudes toward intercollegiate athletics and to convince students that the rules were "for the best interests of their school and of intercollegiate athletics."[29]

The alumni presented a more difficult problem. Moran reported that "while most organized alumni had a correct attitude toward the regulation of intercollegiate athletics, many individuals were doing all they could to debauch the athletic situation. Most difficult was the man who saw "nothing wrong in subsidizing athletes, and only in exceptional cases did a board of control know the facts about such matters." Rules of eligibility were inadequate, but "the pressure of a wholesome alumni public opinion" could be "effective in removing the rather widespread evil" of subsidizing athletes.[30]

"Since competition in intercollegiate athletics had become so tense," Moran observed, "associations of business and professional men" in many university communities had "interest[ed] themselves in athletic affairs. Outside pressure was sometimes brought to bear upon matters of eligibility, schedule making, and ... methods of coaching and training. The intentions of 'boosters' was sometimes good, sometimes indifferent, and sometimes vicious. Many of these men were not college graduates and did not see the need to preserve amateurism and honesty in college sports. Others were sordid enough to spend their money to bring great crowds to town to stimulate trade." Most of these men, he said, "could be made to see the situation in its true light if the matter was presented to them properly." The most pressing need of the athletic situation, Moran concluded, was for "the cultivation of a vigorous and enlightened public opinion among those persons and groups most vitally interested in college athletics."[31]

Moran offered several points for discussion, which those present pursued vigorously. Most important was the influence of the alumni upon intercollegiate athletics. It was desirable to put intercollegiate athletics under the control of the faculty and to enlist the support of alumni for the intellectual rather than the athletic activities of the college. To advance this objective the AAUP should cooperate with organizations representing college administrations through the American Council of Education. Speakers deplored "the influence of commercial clubs and other outside organizations upon intercollegiate athletics" and noted the "danger of commercialism in intercollegiate athletics." Discussion focused on the negative influence of intercollegiate athletics upon scholastic attainment. "The consequences of prolonged absences from college work for members of athletic teams and large bodies of students attending distant games were disastrous"; so too was "the effect of undue pressure on capable students to devote so much time to athletics that they fell far short of their possible achievement in scholarship." The observers did not overlook the "favorable effect of athletics within reasonable limits."[32]

By the mid-1920s, as Moran's report and the discussion of it demonstrated, progressives were highly critical of intercollegiate athletics. Neither standpatters nor radicals, they viewed intercollegiate athletics as incompatible with the academic integrity of universities.

Closing out the Decade

The 1920s were reputedly the Golden Age of sports. In 1923 receipts at Western Conference football games totaled more than $1 million. At the University of Michigan, football receipts for 1923 were $291,500.

"Real sport is playing simply for the love of the game," John R. Tunis observed, but sports writers had built up a fiction, "The Great Sports Myth." It held that competitive sports instilled moral values and "nobility of character." The evidence showed that "the strain of competition and the glare of publicity" actually tended to "wear down and destroy character." The myth also held that "sport teaches self-control." The reverse was the case. Finally, the myth contended that competition strengthened the ties between nations and individuals. This did not happen. Tunis cited the nasty Harvard-Princeton rupture over football in 1926 to illustrate his point.[33]

The 1920s had begun with great expectations, but the decade ended with a bang and a whimper. During the 1929 football season, five hundred thousand spectators viewed the college game in various parts of the country. Then, on October 29, the stock market crashed.

The Threat of Professional Football

Professional football notably took shape in several places in the late nineteenth century. One was the athletic clubs in urban centers from coast to coast. These clubs were avowedly committed to amateur athletics, but in practice they were a cradle of professional football. "Chicago's first big professional team," wrote Harry A. Marsh, "masqueraded for two or three seasons as an amateur, the Chicago Athletic Club under the direction of Harry Cornish."[34] The facts refine the story. In 1890 a number of upper-class gentlemen incorporated the Chicago Athletic Association. In 1892 the founders, devoted to amateur athletics, organized a football team that competed against athletic club teams and college teams in the East and the Midwest. Among the members of the team were Ben "Sport" Donnelly, a former Princeton end, Knowlton L. "Snake" Ames, an All-America Princeton fullback, and William W. "Pudge" Heffelfinger, a Yale gridiron great. In 1895, wanting a stronger team, CAA authorities sent Cornish to scout out players in colleges and universities in the Northwest. Some club members feared that Cornish would offer them money to play. Caspar Whitney, the apostle of amateurism, wrote that "men are bought and sold like cattle to play . . . on 'strictly amateur' college elevens." Whitney charged that Roger Shearman, the Michigan football manager, had offered a Michigan student who was playing on the CAA team $600 to fin- ish the season with Michigan, whereupon the CAA players raised $600 to keep him.[35] William Hale "Big Bill" Thompson (later the mayor of Chicago) became captain of the CAA football team in 1895. He engaged men who had played for Yale, Princeton, Pennsylvania, Michigan, Purdue, Illinois, and Wisconsin. For a time Heffelfinger was one of his assistant coaches. Club members devoted to amateur athletics charged Thompson with paying players. When they gained control, Thompson withdrew and founded the Illinois Athletic Club.

Meanwhile, professional football gained a foothold in western Pennsylvania. In October 1892 the Pittsburgh Athletic Club met the Allegheny Athletic Club before a crowd of three thousand on the PAC's home field. The teams split $1,200 in gate receipts, and the game established the sport's popularity in western Pennsylvania.[36]

A second contest between these two teams was set for November 12. AAC backers secretly bet on their club, while PAC supporters waited to see the game- day rosters. On that day, Pudge Heffelfinger and Sport Donnelly entered the field with the Allegheny club, whereupon the PAC refused to play unless all bets were canceled. When the game was finally played, the AAC won 4–0. The AAC paid Heffelfinger $500 and both Heffelfinger and Donnelly $25 in traveling expenses. After paying Heffelfinger and the PAC its guarantee, the AAC realized a profit of more than $600.[37]

Thus professional football established itself in Pittsburgh and the western Pennsylvania towns of Allegheny, Latrobe, and Greensburg. It is early days only an "outstanding ringer" was paid, and later a small town could afford to pay only $20 or $10 a game. Entirely professional teams emerged in 1896, briefly with the Allegheny Athletic Association, and in 1897 with Latrobe and Greensburg. By the early 1900s such teams paid their players by dividing whatever profits they had earned. For Latrobe, this came to an average of $3.50 per player for each of the nine games played.[38]

Professional football emerged more slowly in the eastern United States, where it was overshadowed by the football powers of Yale, Harvard, Princeton, and Pennsylvania. In the late 1890s the major eastern colleges progressively withdrew from competition with athletic clubs. Thus these teams had to turn to each other for competition. At the same time, the Orange (New Jersey) Athletic Club and the Crescent Athletic Club of Brooklyn witnessed to the presence of professional teams in the area. Upstate New York also laid a foundation for professionalism in the 1890s. Syracuse, Watertown, Rochester, and Buffalo fielded professional football teams with varying degrees of alacrity.[39]

Independent football, the predecessor of professional football, began in the steel and coal towns of southwestern Pennsylvania and northeastern Ohio in the late nineteenth century. With no real management, these teams drew on local talent, men lacking any college affiliation who played for love of the game and shared gate receipts, if any. Particularly popular in medium-sized factory centers, this kind of football quickly spread across the Midwest. It included many towns in Ohio, several in Indiana, and one or more in Michigan, Illinois, Wisconsin, and Minnesota.[40]

Professional football is said to have begun in 1903 with the battle between the Canton Bulldogs and the Massillon Tigers for the season's honors. One of the teams imported paid "ringers" to insure victory. The two teams remained fierce rivals. Eager to enlist top players, both teams were willing to pay their recruits, many of whom were former college players. Thus, strong community rivalries sparked the change from independent to professional football.[41]

Professional football differed from the college game in several respects. Pro football was played on Sunday rather than Saturday because it appealed to workers who were not college educated and whose only free day was Sunday. The game never penetrated the South, where people sanctified the Lord's Day. Many players on pro football teams had been associated with a college in the Northeast or the Midwest; others were identified with a Big Ten university. The number of athletes who played on a pro team from 1915 to 1917 and are identified with a Big Ten university are as follows: Indiana, 18; Ohio State, 18; Michigan, 13; Chicago, 11; Wisconsin, 12; Purdue, 9; Minnesota, 6; Illinois, 5; Iowa, 1; and Northwestern, 1.[42]

The experience of two athletes in their progression from college football to pro football may be illustrative of the times. Eugene Schobinger of Morgan Park, Illinois, graduated from the University of Illinois in 1915 with a bachelor's degree in municipal and sanitary engineering. A fullback, he was named to the 1914 All Big-Ten and All-Western teams. He was also a leading pole vaulter, a member of the varsity water polo team, and a member of Delta Kappa Epsilon fraternity.[43] Shortly after graduating, he began his professional football career. On October 3, 1915, his Illinois All-Stars lost 34–0 to the Evanston North Ends in Mason Park in Evanston before a crowd of twenty-five hundred. A year later Schobinger played with the Evanston North Ends, the perennial independent Illinois football champions and reputedly one of the best teams in the country. During October the team engaged the Milwaukee Maple Leafs on DePaul field in Evanston. Then they met the Davenport Athletic Club at Three-I Park in Davenport, Iowa. And later they encountered the Racine Regulars, said to be one of the best Wisconsin teams, in a scoreless tie. Hence, Schobinger launched his professional gridiron career.

Franklin Bartlett "Bart" Macomber, whom Robert Zuppke had coached at the Oak Park, Illinois, High School, entered the University of Illinois in 1913. He majored in commerce, was active in several prominent student organizations, a member of Phi Kappa Psi fraternity, and one of the most popular men on the campus. On the gridiron he distinguished himself as a halfback and the team's kicker. In 1914 he helped lead Illinois to a conference championship. In the game with Ohio State at Columbus, Macomber made a goal in the closing minutes of play that staved off defeat. Walter Camp selected Macomber, "one of the stars of the Middle West," as a halfback on his 1915 All America team.[44] He was captain of the 1916 football team, which defeated Minnesota 14–0 in one of the great upsets of all time. Macomber then cast in his lot with pro football. During the 1916 season he was a quarterback with the Pine Village Athletic Club. The following spring Macomber was the star in a vaudeville show which he put across in "true bigtime manner" at the Orpheum Theater in Champaign.[45] In October 1917, having made a name for himself as an entertainer, Macomber signed a contract to play professional football with the Youngstown (Ohio) Patricians.[46] Macomber never graduated from the university.[47]

College men and noncollege men had been playing professional football for some time, and on August 20, 1920, representatives from four professional football teams created the American Professional Football Conference. In 1922 it was renamed the National Football League.

The rise of professional football in the athletic clubs and the municipal elevens was not lost on the Big Ten guardians of amateur athletics. At a conference session in December 1916, Albion Small (Chicago) introduced the subject of professional football, and the conference unanimously set its face against the perceived danger by adopting a resolution with two clauses: first, all employees of college athletic departments who take part in professional football games should be suspended from their employment; and second, members of teams participating in professional contests before graduation were to forfeit their letter and to be recommended to their faculties for further discipline.[48] A year later the conference amended the resolution by banning a "player or official" rather than "all employees" of college athletic departments from taking part in professional football games, and they prohibited members of teams from "participating or officiating" in professional contests.[49] Since the University of Iowa objected to the second part of the resolution, in June 1917 the matter was put on its passage a second time under the White Resolution and was passed.[50]

Returning to the subject in December 1919, Small secured adoption of a resolution that said, first, "participation either as player or official in a professional football game shall disqualify for all employment or connection with athletics," and second, violators of the rule of December 1916 relating to coaches and the June 1917 ruling relating to players were likewise disqualified.[51] In addition, the faculty committee recommended to the conference colleges the adoption of a rule that in the future any student, having received his letter, would forfeit the same if he engaged in professional football subsequent to graduation. Small introduced these resolutions at Coach Alonzo Stagg's suggestion.[52]

Repeated opposition to professionalism came in a motion made in June 1919 to restate Rule 5 (b) so that it read, "No person who receives a regular annual or monthly compensation from the university for services rendered shall be eligible to play on any team." The motion was laid on the table until December, when it was adopted and submitted to the faculties for consideration.[53] At the conference session in June 1920 the members learned that Purdue had objected to the resolution. Since Thomas F. Moran (Purdue) was absent, the conference deferred action.[54] In December 1920 the resolution was placed upon its passage under the White Resolution and passed: participation either as a player or official in a professional football game disqualified one for all employment in connection with athletics.[55]

The Taylorville-Carlinville Game

According to some, the football season of 1921 aroused unparalleled interest in the history of the sport. Professional football gained a decided impetus, drawing at least marginal gate receipts and paying the players for their performance. In November a professional football game between two Illinois towns involved both big money and conference college athletes. Carlinville, with about five thousand inhabitants, and Taylorville, twice as large, both southeast of Springfield, were bitter rivals in football. In 1920 Carlinville had beaten Taylorville 10–7 in a home game, whereupon Taylorville boasted that in 1921 the outcome on their home ground would be different. A group of Carlinville residents thought otherwise. A Notre Dame reserve athlete from Carlinville approached seven of his teammates about playing for Carlinville during the Thanksgiving break for $200 each plus expenses. They accepted, knowing that college players had preceded them in playing for pay. With victory thus assured, Carlinville residents bet what was said to be close to $50,000 on the outcome of the game. When the news leaked out, Taylorville retaliated in kind, hiring nine Illinois athletes, and locals bet on the outcome. The game was played to a large and enthusiastic crowd on November 27, the Sunday after Thanksgiving Day. In the first half Taylorville used its home town team, while in the second half Taylorville trotted out its Illinois players and beat Carlinville 16–7. Residents of the two towns allegedly had bet as much as $100,000 on the outcome of the contest.

Early in 1922 the press exposed the Carlinville-Taylorville debacle, demonstrating the dark side of collegiate athletics. Grover Hoover, the coach of the Taylorville team, taking the part of the college players, declared that the colleges were unfair to their men. "Representatives of the University of Illinois procured professional players for its teams," he charged, "and then 'fired them when they play for someone else.'" An Illinois representative had come to Taylorville, Hoover alleged, had seen local boy Roy L. "Dope" Simpson play, and then, knowing that Simpson was playing professional ball, "offer[ed] him inducements to enter the University." Dick Simpson, manager of the team and "Dope's" brother, confirmed Hoover's charges.[56] "It is a lie," snorted George Huff, when told about Hoover's statement. Illinois had never employed a scout to judge or recruit players, and the university had never offered financial inducements.[57] Hoover then boiled over and exposed more about intercollegiate athletics. "Why are not Aubrey Devine and Gordon Locke, football stars at Iowa, protested by Illinois?" he asked. "I'll tell you why; because Illinois men have played semi-professional baseball against them, and would suffer themselves, if they squealed. Why are there no protests against Wisconsin athletes who have played professional ball?" Hoover then asked. "I don't have to name them; let them investigate up at Madison." Hoover charged that a great percentage of Illinois baseball players competed in semi-professional games through the summers. Rockne, he added, had been told a month before that his players were on the Carlinville team that played Taylorville. Rockne knew the practice, having participated in it. Apparently, Rockne had expected the whole thing to blow over.[58]

Both universities involved punished their players for participating in the notorious game. Eight Notre Dame athletes, including two All-America football players, confessed that they had played at Taylorville, whereupon school officials disqualified them for athletic competition. The Illinois student newspaper commended Notre Dame for setting a fine example.[59] At Illinois, the faculty eligibility committee investigated the participation of Illinois players and declared the nine men ineligible for competition on athletic teams representing the university in athletic contests.[60] Four of the sanctioned men had been on the 1921 varsity football team. One, a senior who graduated in 1922, had been the captain of the varsity team. Three of the players were enrolled in the program in athletic coaching. One of the players had not been enrolled in the university in the fall of 1921 and had not attended until the summer session of 1922.

Robert Zuppke, the Illinois football coach, viewed the scandal as a good thing. He hoped it would start a thorough cleanup. Zuppke was committed to a tough, competitive, collegiate game. Other conference football teams played professional athletes, Zuppke added, men who came to college as amateurs but could not stand the temptation of a few dollars. It was better to have the coaches themselves clean up than to have outsiders step in. Accusations from outside caused unfriendliness.[61]

The penalized Illinois athletes "knew they were breaking a rule," according to a *Chicago Tribune* editorial, which viewed the rule as "more than questionable." "If the young men now in bad at Illinois were attending [the] school for its educational advantages [and] engaged in college athletics for the love of it ... , why should they not play football or anything else for money?" The *Tribune* could see "an educational injury in allowing college boys to run around the country playing as semi-professionals in school months, but that could be corrected without declaring . . . that any college athlete who ever received money for his athletic proficiency could not continue in college sports." "This purely conventional idea of amateurism," the editorial continued, had "its roots in the English caste system." The rule was "in its worst form" when it "prohibited college baseball players from playing semi-professional ball in the summer." "We do not want college sports commercialized," the writer added, "but there is a difference between getting professionals in a college to make records in sports and declaring a boy a professional in college sports because he has used his skill to make money outside of college sports."[62] No doubt many endorsed the *Tribune's* point of view. But there was no reason to believe that the men were playing football for love rather than money.

The Reaction to Professionalism

The exposure of professionalism in college athletics created a great stir. For the first time, declared Stagg, some Big Ten athletic directors realized that intercollegiate athletics could not exist except upon the amateur principle. This was the rock on which the conference found its mooring. All of the sports were involved; no exception could be made for baseball, as had been the case for a time. The presidents of the conference universities conferred and agreed that each would talk with his athletic director, charging him to counter the developing situation.[63]

In light of the scandal, some athletic directors changed their views on amateur athletics. Now they all favored rigidly enforcing the rules. Huff had advocated as the standard of eligibility only the one-year-residence rule and the scholarship rule. While not changing his point of view, he was willing to enforce a new rule to the limit. Nelson Kellogg (Purdue) now saw that it was impossible to allow privileges to the baseball players unavailable to those in football and basketball. Tom Jones (Wisconsin) now wanted to stiffen a rule that would ban summer baseball. The directors agreed on a new rule: no student would be eligible for intercollegiate competition who, as a representative of any athletic organization not connected with his college, whether during term time or vacation, took part in any contest where admission was charged or a collection was taken. Certain recognized athletic meets, such as national Amateur Athletic Union meets, were to be excepted, provided that the student secured permission in advance. On the motion to adopt this rule, Illinois and Ohio voted no, Northwestern was absent, and the other directors voted yes. Northwestern later voted yes. This rule was to begin at the end of the 1921–22 academic year.[64]

At this mid-March meeting, the directors recommended that a committee of three be appointed "to devise constructive methods of setting forth the amateur principles for which we stand, to plan methods of publicity and distribution of ideas, and to devise ways and means of enforcing this rule. The reports of the committee were to be submitted at each meeting of the directors." The directors appointed Fielding Yost as chairman of the committee.[65] Stagg later admitted that he made the motion that a permanent committee be appointed, adding that he recommended Yost as chairman in order "to tie him particularly and Michigan strongly up to the amateur idea because they were in a position of considerable power."[66]

At an opportune moment, when all the directors were in "a contrite and conscientious frame of mind," Stagg made a brief but earnest talk in favor of starting out anew, and the directors pledged themselves to enforce their eligibility rules. He followed his talk by asking each of the directors to sign the following pledge:

> We, the Athletic Directors of the Intercollegiate Conference of Faculty Representatives, hereby pledge ourselves to take over the enforcement of the amateur rules and to exchange freely all information and rumors of any violation of these rules which may come to our attention. We furthermore agree that all such information shall be held strictly confidential.

All ten directors signed and submitted the motions they had adopted to the faculty representatives. According to Stagg, the March session was the most satisfactory meeting the directors had ever had.[67] But the directors who signed were like alcoholics pledging abstinence. Some, if not all, could not resist when tempted.

When the directors met again in Chicago in June 1922, they agreed to hold meetings on the first Saturday in December, March, and June, and special meetings as might be called. Then Yost moved and Huff seconded a motion that the directors appoint a commissioner "to assist in the enforcement of the amateur rules, to aid and assist in the promotion of the amateur spirit, and to carry on research study in intercollegiate athletic problems." The motion carried. The directors were no doubt influenced by the American League and the National League baseball magnates. Shaken by the Black Sox scandal and players throwing games in 1920, they had appointed a commissioner, Kenesaw Mountain Landis, to bring order into baseball. A commissioner was needed to bring order into football.

The directors agreed to prorate the expenses of the commissioner among the conference schools based on the gross football receipts less guarantees paid visiting teams, and to appropriate $10,000 for salary and expenses for the ensuing year, with the understanding that this sum continue for two years, with a possible figure of $25,000 for the two years. The directors then discussed the men available for the position and then agreed to invite "Mr. Berry of the Springfield Training

School"—the YMCA enterprise in Massachusetts with which Amos Alonzo Stagg had been affiliated—to meet with a committee consisting of Yost (Michigan), Jones (Wisconsin), and St. John (Ohio State). The directors empowered the committee to make Berry, a coach at the YMCA college, a tentative offer.[68]

We do not know why Berry was dropped. He had published works on athletics and may have been considered too bookish. We do know that the need for someone to bring order into Big Ten affairs was urgent. The record of further negotiations is somewhat muddled. On July 24 Jones asked the athletic directors to approve or disapprove of the committee's recommendation that John L. Griffith be appointed as commissioner of athletics for the Western Conference at a salary of $6,000 plus travel expenses, to be paid monthly. The office of the commissioner was to be located in Chicago, the appointment for two years (beginning August 1, 1922). To finance the office of the commissioner, each member university was to pay $100 for five months (July through November), with a final pay adjustment at the December meeting. Directors Evans and Stagg were to audit and authorize all expenditures.[69]

Everything was now in order for the arrival of the Big Ten commissioner.   ·

CHAPTER 6

The Commissioner
and the Conference

John L. Griffith, the new Big Ten Conference commissioner, was at the University of Illinois at the time of his appointment. Born on August 20, 1875, in Mt. Carroll, Illinois, he prepared in the local high school and the Warren Academy and attended Beloit College, where he studied history and economics, made an enviable record as an all-around athlete, and graduated AB in 1902. He coached athletics at Yankton College in South Dakota from 1902 to 1905, at Morningside College in Sioux City, Iowa, from 1905 to 1908, and then at Drake University in Des Moines, Iowa, where he was an athletic coach and the first director of athletics. His record as football coach from 1908 was not impressive; he resigned the position in 1915. He was the basketball coach in 1909–10. Griffith made his name at Drake in track athletics. In April 1910 he founded and managed a track-and-field meet, the Drake Relays, which became an annual event that gained national prominence. In 1913 Griffith became the dean of men at Drake. During an internal struggle over the executive power in the college, the president went to New York on business, naming Griffith as acting regent or president in his absence.[1]

Griffith entered the army at some time in 1917. In December he was the athletic director at Camp Dodge, Iowa, and later served in the same capacity at Camp Gordon in Georgia and at Camp Pike in Arkansas. Training camps were new when America entered the war, as Griffith wrote, and no plan was ready for them. The camps were modeled after the Aldershot plan so successfully employed by Great Britain. The camps revealed that many men of military age were rejected as physically unfit. They also demonstrated that group games and mass athletics were valuable in teaching men to act as groups, that personal contact games are the best in developing aggressiveness and in improving the fighting spirit, and that team athletics are valuable in developing morale.[2] On January 11, 1919, Griffith was ordered to Washington, D.C., where he served as the executive officer of the Athletic Division of the Commission on Training Camp Activities in the War Department.[3]

On January 31, 1919, George Huff, the Illinois athletic director, wrote asking Griffith for the name of a specialist in physical education whom he might wish to appoint. Griffith sent two names and added that if the work was anything he could do, he would be interested. Griffith and Huff met in March, after which Griffith wrote Huff about how to organize the physical education work at Illinois. In mid-April Griffith submitted an application, and on June 10 the trustees authorized his appointment as assistant professor of athletic coaching and physical education in the Department of Physical Education. He was to be in charge of a program in high school physical education and an instructor in athletic coaching courses.[4]

An army captain when appointed at Illinois, Griffith was a member of the Department of Physical Education and the manager of the athletic coaching program from 1919 to 1922.[5] Huff knew Griffith and may have been instrumental in securing his appointment.[6]

Griffith founded the *Athletic Journal* in March 1921 to focus on the world of sports.[7] A national publication aimed at athletes and coaches, the weekly carried articles on all sports by authors from around the country. Griffith wrote many of the articles, and he contributed one or more editorials each week. Along with the journal, Griffith and George "Potsy" Clark, a former Illinois athlete who became a coach, founded the Griffith-Clark Physical Education Service Company. It sold pamphlets on plays in various athletic games and the major sports.

Griffith set up his office at 116 South Michigan Avenue and moved the *Athletic Journal* to Chicago. His editorials shed light on his frame of mind. The nation's future fighting force was under the influence of the coaches, he declared, and they were responsible for seeing that male students were physically fit. The combat games were best for developing physical fitness and the spirit of aggressiveness, courage, and the ability to take punishment. To discontinue the work of coaches and inter-school competition "would strike at the very heart of the nation."[8]

Griffith viewed athletics as part of an educational whole. The main function of the colleges was to promote citizenship. Coaches had a better opportunity than faculty members to teach loyalty, morality, cooperation, unselfishness, devotion to a cause, and willingness to play according to the rules. In the postwar years, when strikes and the specter of Bolshevism spread fear in the nation, Griffith declared that America "was not made great through syndicalism, communism, or I.W.W.-ism," the International Workers of the World. Every coach and college athlete had "a duty to combat foreign propaganda." The nation had "no finer body of men" than "the school and college athletic coaching fraternity."[9] Yet a good coach with losses would forfeit his position, while a mediocre faculty member could hold his position for years and retire with a pension, thanks to the American Association of University Professors. Griffith was ever ready to praise coaches and disparage faculty members.

Before settling into office, Griffith discovered that the amateur athletic code had been violated in the Big Ten. In January 1922, Illinois officials had barred from further competition nine of their football players who had participated in the Carlinville-Taylorville game. And in September, when George Huff learned that Don Murry, a Wisconsin tackle, had played in the Taylorville game, Huff informed Wisconsin and the conference Committee on Eligibility of his findings but said nothing to the press. Wisconsin had played Murry in all its games during the season. On November 2, the eligibility committee removed Murry from the Badger team, whereupon John Richards, the Wisconsin coach, issued a statement charging five Illinois men with professionalism and giving their names to the chair of the eligibility committee. Huff questioned the accused men and cleared all of them except Allison "Bill" Augur, who admitted playing in the Taylorville-Danville game a week preceding the Carlinville contest. Huff barred Augur from athletic competition and regarded it as unfair to Illinois that Wisconsin had played Murry, who had been reported as ineligible, in all its games during the season.[10]

Writing to George Goodenough (Illinois), the chair of the conference eligibility committee, Edward A. Birge, president of the University of Wisconsin, explained that the Wisconsin athletic council believed, on the face of the facts in its possession, that Murry had not violated any conference rule during the period when he was not a student in any institution, but in view of the scandalous notoriety attached to the conduct of numerous student players in the game in which he took part, the council was unwilling to accept the sole responsibility of deciding his status. Therefore, it referred the case to the conference eligibility committee. But before doing so, the council asked Commissioner Griffith to test the validity of the evidence by further investigation. After some delay, Griffith reported that he could not investigate the case. Why is not known. He may have wished to avoid making a decision that would alienate one of the contending parties. It was clear, Birge added, that Murry should not have been allowed to take part in games before his status had been finally settled by the conference eligibility committee. As to the ill-advised remarks of the Wisconsin football coach (Richards) on conference procedures, Birge observed that Richards had become conscious of their impropriety, and if he were to remain with the university he would be "more circumspect in matters of publicity than he has sometimes been in the past."[11]

In September 1922 Stagg described Richards in a memorandum for the record. Earl Huntington, who had played football at Chicago and was the freshman football coach under Stagg from 1918 to 1927, had told him, "Coach Richards does not care a hang whether his men are professionals or not." When Huntington spoke to Richards when Stagg was looking up the amateur standing of a player named Hinkle, Richards had said, "Why is Old Man Stagg such a dam fool as to try to find out whether Hinkle plays professionally or not? You never catch me doing a thing like that. I don't give a dam whether my men play professionally or not and I would never try to find out if they did."[12]

When the conference met in December, the faculty committee adopted a resolution regarding Wisconsin and the enforcement of the conference rules. The resolution related that Donald F. Murry was permitted by Wisconsin to participate in intercollegiate games, although he was known at the time to have participated in the Taylorville-Carlinville game the previous season. Wisconsin was informed of this fact by another conference athletic official. The case was submitted to the Committee on Eligibility, which declared Murry ineligible. The decision of the committee was followed by a tirade on the part of Richards against the conference institution that called attention to the infraction of the rules, and against six other members of this body as well. Allegedly, seven of the conference institutions were not enforcing the rules. It was also charged that several football players in one of the conference institutions were not eligible to participate in athletics. These charges were made in an ill-tempered manner in the columns of the daily press, and not in the way prescribed by the rules and regulations of the conference. It was this same coach who, more than a year ago, let loose a storm of abuse against the athletic officials of one of the institutional members of this body.[13] In view of these facts, the conference asked the president of the University of Wisconsin what steps, if any, his institution contemplated in looking to a more rigorous enforcement of the conference rules than the handling of the Murry case would indicate, "and to the prevention of such unseemly outbursts on the part of his football coach in the columns of the daily papers." The faculty committee requested that copies of President Birge's reply be sent to the several conference representatives.[14] Richards's day had come. In 1923 Jack Ryan replaced him as the Wisconsin football coach.[15]

Griffith and His Agenda

Griffith assumed his position as commissioner in 1922 and served in that capacity until his death in 1945. He confronted a tremendous challenge. As many as seventy-five thousand football spectators gathered in more than one college stadium for a game, and specialization had created "a veritable athletic Frankenstein." The trouble with college athletics, Walter Camp, the "father" of American football, charged, was too much athletics and too few athletes. A few men trained to the last notch but thousands of students did not share in the benefit. The Frankenstein was sprawled out all over college life. Football was the mainstay of the athletic finance of the college. The heart of the problem was over-organization and the resulting expense through concentration of the college interest on big teams and big games. College football was well systematized and highly organized. The old college spirit was left to trained cheerleaders.[16]

In 1922 the chairman of the faculty committee on athletics and faculty advisor on the student board of athletic control in an unidentified small college probably in the Midwest, published a devastating account of the method of attracting athletes in college communities, the faculty attitude toward intercollegiate athletics, and the attitude of the administration toward intercollegiate athletics, explained in part as the reflection of community and alumni sentiment.[17] The author helped define the challenge that awaited Griffith.

Griffith's powers, ill-defined at the time of appointment, grew gradually by experience and accumulation and also by some sort of understanding with the faculty representatives, athletic directors, and football coaches. His paramount concern was the defense of amateur athletics. This led him to mount an educational campaign on behalf of the amateur code and to battle the recruitment and inducement of high school athletes. His office was a clearinghouse for reports of violations of conference rules and an agency for investigating cases. He kept in close touch with the athletic directors, he met with the faculty representatives on invitation, and he reached a large audience by talks to athletic, civic, and school groups.

Griffith identified three classes of people who decried the efforts of the colleges to conduct their athletics on an amateur basis—commercial interests that profited from professional athletics, college men who wished to avoid the amateur rule either because it was difficult to administer or because of selfish motives, and those who were ignorant concerning the underlying principles of amateur athletics. Griffith suggested that conference members conduct an educational campaign on behalf of amateurism by articles in the alumni magazines, talks at student convocations and mass meetings, debates in coaching school classes, and articles in student papers.[18]

As Griffith knew, undergraduates, athletes, and alumni induced athletes to help their university build strong athletic teams. Alumni associations employed field agents to do this work. The states that were home to conference members could furnish the Big Ten's needs for football players, as the population figures showed.[19]

Griffith made a study of the geographical origins of the football players in each Big Ten university from 1924 to 1929. His study showed that both the location and the football reputation of a school influenced where athletes sought opportunity. Another study of the number of athletes in each Big Ten university who came from Chicago and vicinity revealed that the University of Illinois led with sixty, followed by Northwestern with fifty, Wisconsin twenty-two, Purdue seventeen, Michigan nine, Indiana four, Iowa two, Ohio State one, and Minnesota zero.[20]

These studies shed light on the dynamics of recruitment and inducements. When the faculty representatives met in June 1923, Omera Long (Northwestern) presented some resolutions on "football inducements" drafted by the athletic committee of the Northwestern General Alumni Association. According to the resolutions, numerous alumni of the universities in the Western Conference believed that many students who participated in intercollegiate athletics were induced to enter their respective institutions by financial aid they received from interested alumni or others who, except for their desire to advance the athletics of their respective institutions, would not give such assistance. In several institutions, it was understood, valuable scholarships were annually awarded to students largely on account of their athletic ability, without regard to scholastic attainment. If such practices continued, there was danger that intercollegiate athletics would become "so commercialized as to eventually defeat such sports and to cause the respective universities to prohibit such contests." Signs of commercialism, evident in intercollegiate athletics since the late nineteenth century and apparent in the secondary schools, were "decidedly demoralizing" and tended to unduly emphasize athletic attainment as a part of university life. Apparently, the conference rules were either not sufficiently broad in scope or had not been properly enforced to correct the situation. The Northwestern Alumni Association recommended taking steps to amend or clarify the conference rules so as "to prohibit students from engaging in intercollegiate athletics who are receiving substantial financial assistance from alumni or from others who, except for furthering the cause of athletics at their respective institutions, would not give such assistance." The association's athletic committee sent its views to the Northwestern faculty representative, the Northwestern athletic director, Commissioner Griffith, and the alumni associations of the conference universities. "Several directors" were in sympathy with some plan furthering the sentiment of the resolutions. The conference referred the resolutions to a special committee that was instructed to report in December, particularly on the feasibility of requiring from participants in athletics a statement as to their financial sources.[21] In December Long reported for the special committee that the practice at representative Eastern institutions was "indicated," presumably meaning that there was evidence of the practice.[22]

In June 1924 Long's special committee asked whether existing conference regulations on the subject were adequate or whether the alleged practice of subsidizing athletes was so widespread that action was required. According to the committee, the intent of the faculty representatives was expressed in the existing regulations. The athletic directors had stated what they considered permissible and impermissible under existing regulations. The special committee considered their statement satisfactory. The alumni remained the most important consideration. The committee was convinced that any new legislation should have the backing of alumni sentiment. To get at the facts, Long had asked the presidents of the Big Ten schools to send one or more alumni to meet with the committee. More than twenty men met on March 14. They appointed a committee to sift out recommendations and present suggestions that might be adopted and given to the special conference committee with a pledge of alumni backing. When the alumni report had been redrafted and adopted by the representatives, Long's committee would report to the conference.[23]

When the faculty representatives met in December 1925, Long referred to the report he had made the previous year and added that through lack of agreement in the alumni committee there was no proposal to recommend to the conference. It was suggested that the Alumni Directors (of the Intercollegiate Conference Athletic Association) in their new advisory relation could be of great assistance in this difficult problem. So the special committee was discharged.[24] The mountain had labored and given birth to a mouse.

Griffith was preoccupied with recruitment and subsidization (in other words, inducement). On this matter, he insisted, conditions were infinitely better than fifteen or twenty years earlier—a self-serving statement for which he had no evidence. And yet the conference was not making progress in discouraging illegitimate recruiting. Certain individuals in some conference universities attempted to secure an unfair advantage by hiring athletes. It might be that conference rules should have been more explicit, but more educational work was needed to let the alumni know what was considered illegitimate recruiting and that the directors did not want to hire athletes, provided that this was the case. The directors should discuss conducting an educational campaign with students and alumni on these topics, and on what was desirable in paying the expenses of athletes to visit institutions in order to decide whether they might wish to attend a particular school. Griffith was convinced that the alumni in more than one of the conference universities were contributing to a fund to be used for athletic help. He may have known the identity of these alumni, but if so, he was not going to reveal their names.

Early in 1924 the conference athletic directors agreed to adhere to a common recruiting rule. If one or two schools cheated, others would soon know it. Then they would break the rules, explaining that others were doing it. The directors were the only hope in the matter of recruiting. If they would insist that they did not want the alumni to raise funds and to hire athletes, few alumni would claim an unsportsmanlike advantage for their university. If the conference did not handle this situation, it would be an admission of weakness on its part.[25]

To battle the criticisms of college athletics, Griffith proposed an educational campaign that would state the purpose and value of intercollegiate athletics and show that the profits of the football season were used not only to finance intercollegiate athletics but also to promote intramural athletics "and the required work" (did he mean academic work?). The articles should also show that the directors were honestly and fearlessly enforcing the rule against professionalism.[26]

Griffith suggested that the directors agree on what was desirable in paying the expenses of athletes for exploratory visits to decide whether they might wish to attend the institution.[27] Was it permissible, he asked, for athletic associations to hire tutors for delinquent athletes?[28]

Along with efforts to promote amateur athletics in the Big Ten, Griffith conducted studies designed to promote the reputation of the conference. One showed that some fifteen hundred conference lettermen had served in the armed forces during the war. Another showed that intercollegiate sports had a moral purpose: they emphasized cooperation, courage, courtesy, honesty, persistence, and unselfishness. And a social purpose: the code of sportsmanship was the most advanced social code recognized by the American people.[29] Griffith compiled some useful data, but his reports were often fanciful. Defensive, he felt compelled to promote his product. He offered bromides about the moral and social value of intercollegiate athletics when he knew about illegitimate recruiting and athletic directors who cut corners.

Moreover, Griffith lacked clean hands. In 1922, when Michigan was making a run for the Big Ten football title, some Lansing businessmen proposed to give Harry Kipke, a Lansing man and Michigan's star player, a new Oldsmobile at the halftime of the Michigan-Wisconsin game. Asked if there would be any objection to the gift, Griffith replied that in his judgment "such a thing was perfectly all right." Fielding Yost, Kipke's coach, demurred. Acceptance of an automobile would not prejudice Kipke's eligibility, said Yost, but would lead people to conclude that the gift had something to do with the recruitment of Kipke to attend Michigan.[30]

Griffith was attentive to the cultural context of intercollegiate athletics. He knew that many were critical of the whole enterprise. The crux of their charge was that collegiate athletics (in other words, football) threatened the integrity of higher education. No charge could be more serious. He catalogued the attacks in order to rebut them. A few star athletes were too well developed while the physical fitness of other students was neglected? The athletic director imbued with the idea of serving others would do what he could for all students. Men who excelled in athletics were injured physically? Studies did not bear out the charge, although there were exceptions. Athletes did not graduate with as high scholarship as others? In most institutions athletes as a class did not rank as high scholastically as other groups picked at random, but if the sole purpose of the college man was academic success, colleges erred in inculcating aesthetic, physical, and moral qualities in youth. Schemes to promote academics by making athletics less popular were foolish. Athletics were becoming highly commercialized? The solution was to teach athletes to play by the underlying principles of the game rather than by mercenary motives.[31]

Most interesting is President David Kinley of the University of Illinois, who defended intercollegiate athletics along lines similar to those of Griffith. First, he asserted intercollegiate athletics, especially football, stimulated "the interest of all the students in certain general university matters." Second, a failed student ambition to get on the varsity team helped to develop intramural sports. Third, intercollegiate athletics "promoted a better acquaintance and a friendlier spirit towards other institutions." Fourth, intercollegiate athletics helped strengthen academic standards because "the man who wants to [make] the team must meet those standards." Fifth, intercollegiate athletics helped to "retain the interest of the alumni and the public." And sixth, the advertising of intercollegiate games helped to eliminate sectionalism. Kinley did note the price paid for the benefits. "The betting, the gambling, the professionalism, [and] the distraction of students from their studies" were bad. The intercollegiate conferences set standards against professionalism, but they were broken because university officers did not enforce them or failed to insist that alumni observe them.[32] Sad to say, Kinley's apologia for intercollegiate football was a weak and regrettable performance for a university president.

By the mid-1920s Griffith viewed professional football as a threat to the college game. The sports editor of the *Chicago Tribune* boosted both professional and collegiate football, Griffith observed, although the former had not gone well "in this section." The conference directors had decided that it was best not to give professional football any publicity by discussing it in public, and yet "we" are doing certain things to discourage the development of the game. "We refuse to employ in a conference university athletic department any man who has been engaged in professional football, and we advise our athletes not to go into professional football after graduation." The athletic directors should do everything possible "to prevent the growth of this menace. That professional football is a menace no one can deny." The conference had had no problem with professional football thus far, but, Griffith said, "if professional football grows we will have just as much trouble with this game as we have with baseball." If collegiate football continued to hold the attention of the public, professional football would not pay, and if it was not financially successful, it would cease to be a menace. "Nothing could be more foolish than to suggest that professional football should be encouraged for the purpose of attracting the general public away from the college game."[33] In sum, an evil did not exist if one did not recognize it.

In February 1924 Griffith called the athletic directors' attention to a report "made public recently" in which President James R. Angell of Yale said:

> Every university within reach of a large population conducts through the autumn months what is practically a great programme of public entertainment, for which relatively high prices of admission are charged and from which accrues tremendous income for the purpose of the sport and for the promotion of the general academic programme. That the ease with which this money is gained tends to stimulate expenditure in the conduct of our collegiate athletics upon a plane wholly disproportionate to the manner in which the remaining work of the institution is conducted can hardly be questioned.

The inevitable distraction from college work which the excitement of these week-end occasions, accompanied as they often are by social entertaining on a large scale, has to be reckoned with. It is to be hoped that the good which flows from it all is more than offset for any evils dependent upon it, but the situation, as such, is one which no thoughtful observers of American education can view without some misgivings, and we must be prepared to deal with it in a vigorous manner, if it appears that the primary business of the university is really being substantially interfered with.[34]

Since Angell publicly confessed his faith in athletic matters, antagonism to athletics could not have been at issue.[35]

In transmitting Angell's remarks to the directors, Griffith said nothing about Angell's charge that athletics substantially interfered with the primary business of the university. Instead, he raised a peripheral issue. Since so much alarm was being manifested regarding the fact that athletics were being conducted on a large scale and that large sums of money were being handled, would it not be wise if the conference schools made a study to show how these monies were used and a statement giving the returns representing the conference as a whole rather than the individual institutions? Griffith was willing to make such a study.[36]

In fact, however, the issue may not have been peripheral. If the athletic interests in the conference schools did not want to shut down college athletics but to protect them in some way from all the criticism, then accounting for the expenditures in the hopes of showing some benefit to the university as a whole was in fact central to their purpose.

Griffith also sent the directors adverse comments on intercollegiate athletics from other spokesmen. He cited the Association of American Colleges, which had declared its disapproval of the evident tendency to overemphasize the spectacular features of intercollegiate athletic sports. The intense rivalries and the excessive demands of the public, the AAC added, laid upon the colleges a strain to which they ought not be subjected. He cited Harry Pratt Judson, the former president of the University of Chicago, who asked whether we were to conduct an institution of higher learning as an amusement park.[37]

He also cited James Bryce, a distinguished jurist, historian, and statesman who was the British ambassador to the United States from 1907 to 1913. According to Griffith, Bryce "knew America better perhaps than any American." In commenting on intercollegiate athletics, Bryce said, "This is a strange inversion of what might be expected in a high civilization, and a strange perversion of the true spirit of university life. It is not an encouraging symptom." The American athletic situation reminded Bryce of "the inordinate passion for the sports of the amphitheatre, ... especially for chariot racing, which grew more and more intense with the decadence of art and literature and national spirit in the Roman Empire." "What does civilization mean," Bryce asked, "except that we realize more and more the superiority of the mind over the body."[38]

About the same time, Alexander Meiklejohn, a former president of Amherst College who, when fired by the trustees, became a faculty member at the University of Wisconsin, entered the fray. According to Meiklejohn, college sport was made of two motives—one, "a desire of the players and the undergraduate community . . . for the sheer joy of competition," and two, "the desire of players and communities for victory in the games." But, he asks, "What are [the] motives [of the college authorities] in relation to college sport? The answer is that victories are supposed to win for the college the favor of men who without them would be indifferent or antagonistic. . . . [T]he college needs the favor and support of [such] men" and therefore "appeal[s] to them on other grounds." This appeal is especially made to the "public," people who "do not know the college in other ways," and the "athletic alumni . . . graduates and nongraduates who value athletic victories very highly." Meiklejohn points out that "for these men a college is an athletic club," and coaches were outsiders running the game for selfish purposes. Naturally Griffith demurred. He defended the paid coach, adding that athletics were invaluable in an educational program.[39]

Confronted by this chorus of criticism, Griffith wondered about the proper path forward. Robert Angell, writing for the *Michigan Alumnus* (in his third and final report) asserted, "Complete abolition of inter-collegiate athletics suggests itself as the quickest solution," yet he said it seemed "unlikely that large universities would be acting wisely in . . . overturning the system in one blow." "A better plan," he said, "appears to be to undertake a gradual lessening of interest in athletics. . . . Those seeking to better conditions find the present coaching system particularly objectionable." There was no hope, he said, of "coping with the evils of professionalism and of the unhealthy overgrowth of college athletics" without removing the cause "at its foundation." Mieklejohn's take on the coaches: "[The coaches], demanding for ten weeks' work salaries twice those paid to our best professors for a year, these outsiders make the rules of the game, dominate the play, and substitute for our games annual contests between themselves." Meiklejohn favored the abolition of the athletic board of control. Such boards had enlarged "the scope of athletic management." They had "built Stadiums, Coliseums, and Bowls [and had] brought the gate receipts of a team for a season into the hundreds of thousands of dollars. In a word, [the athletic boards have] over-managed our college games." The system had given the boards "the money and the public place from which every other type of exaggeration" flowed.[40]

Angell's report continues:

> Since a single institution could not well act alone in a matter of this sort, a conference of executives, members of governing boards, and faculty representatives

of all the universities in the Western Conference might well be called to agree upon a joint plan of action. . . . Other suggestions worth considering on such an occasion were leaving the teams completely under the direction of the captains during their annual games, the abolition of all freshman teams, and building up intramural competition to the point where candidates for varsity positions were picked from the best players on class, fraternity, and club teams. . . . [A conference determined] to better conditions should go on record as opposing any enlargement of plants designed to accommodate more spectators. Finally, it seems no more than just for a university to pay those who were engaged to train the mind. [That is, the faculty.] . . . Enormous [coaching] salaries are due to the competition between schools in developing championship teams.[41]

Such ruminations were not in line with Griffith's character. He was by nature a booster, not a critical thinker, and the requirements of his job reinforced his native bent. His questioning of the situation he encountered is revealing. Devoted to amateur athletics, he confronted a complex situation and seemingly did not know which way to turn.[42]

Griffith would have found comfort from L. W. St. John, the Ohio State athletic director, who on the whole agreed with President Angell but took issue with Meiklejohn. According to St. John, the Intercollegiate Conference had largely eliminated many of the things Meiklejohn identified. In stating his case, St. John dealt first with evils. Proselyting of students because of their athletic prowess was the hardest to meet. The solution lay in better moral education of students, alumni, and the general public. Professionalism was being better handled as time went on. The members of the Western Conference were each represented by an athletic director who was a member of the university faculty. They realized that the feeling of professors was one of growing hostility toward intercollegiate athletics. The "win at any cost" policy had to be countered. The extravagant use of intercollegiate funds was a growing abuse. Another source of evil was undesirable publicity. It led one to believe that sport was conducted primarily for the public instead of for the players and the student body.

St. John proceeded to describe the benefits of intercollegiate sport. First, they made an educational contribution, as authorities including Meiklejohn had said. Second, intercollegiate sports had been the means of financing the college intramural program. Third, intercollegiate sports rounded out the whole scheme of physical education. To limit sport to the bounds of one institution was to take from it all that gave it power and steam. St. John believed in the administration of intercollegiate sports directly responsible to the president of the institution.

The use of large gate receipts was inseparably related to the intercollegiate sport enterprise. According to St. John, the unwise use included the support of training quarters and table, the employing of coaches to scout the secondary schools and small colleges for promising athletes, and the payment of excessively large salaries for coaching. The wise use of receipts included equipment and "necessary support of the athletic teams," spectator accommodations, a vast array of intramural facilities, facilities for faculty recreation, a fund for research in physical education, various permanent university improvements, and wholesome publicity.[43]

In 1924 the conference renewed Griffith's contract and authorized $12,500 for the expense of the commissioner's office for 1924–25. The payment was to be prorated among the conference universities based on football receipts for the 1924 season.

Table 6.1 shows the receipts and the prorated share of each of the conference universities.

They employed the same formula in prorating the expenses of the commissioner's office for 1925, as shown in Table 6.2. The tables show the relation between

L. W. St. John, Ohio State athletic director.
Source: Ohio State University Archives.

Table 6.1.   1924 Season

University	Net Football Receipts	Percentage	Share
Michigan	$ 333,507.02	19.75	$460.75
Chicago	233,577.97	13.84	730.00
Illinois	227,367.03	13.47	683.75
Ohio State	186,010.11	11.01	1,376.25
Wisconsin	170,566.26	10.10	1,262.50
Minnesota	160,886.28	9.53	1,191.25
Iowa	139,834.59	8.28	1,035.00
Northwestern	109,494.88	6.49	811.25
Purdue	65,607.01	3.89	486.25
Indiana	61,499.30	3.64	455.00
Total	**$ 1,688,350.45**	**100.00**	**$12,500.00**

Note: "Statement Showing Proration of Expense of the Office of the Commissioner [1924]," Stagg Papers, box 85, folder 1.

a successful football season and gate receipts. Michigan had the largest receipts in both years. In 1924 the Wolverines had a record of 6-2-0. A year later, under Fielding Yost's leadership, the record was 7-1-0 and the receipts were larger. Illinois vaulted from third place in 1924, when the team's record was 6-1-1, to second place in 1925, when the record was 5-3-0. Harold "Red" Grange excited a frenzy in 1924, and fans filled the stadium a year later. Chicago slipped from second place in 1924, when its record was 4-1-3, to third place in 1925 at 3-4-1. Even so, Chicago's gate receipts were larger in 1925 than in 1924 because of the popularity of college football in a time of prosperity.

As the two tables illustrate, Ohio State's increase in receipts mirrored its win-loss record. In 1924 it was 2-3-3, and in 1925 it was 4-3-1. Wisconsin had a win-loss record of 2-3-3 in 1924. Its receipts declined a year later, though its record that year was 6-1-1. The figures confirmed a lesson: winning paid.

Table 6.2.   1925 Season

University	Net Football Receipts	Percentage	Share
Michigan	$372,484.88	17.99	$ 2,238.10
Illinois	348,030.16	16.73	2,091.18
Chicago	345,001.47	6.58	2,072.96
Ohio State	260,246.34	12.51	1,563.70
Minnesota	220,346.07	10.59	1,323.96
Iowa	168,252.08	8.09	1,010.95
Wisconsin	135,089.40	6.49	811.89
Northwestern	120,851.00	5.81	726.14
Purdue	65,803.59	3.16	395.39
Indiana	44,262.05	2.13	265.95
Total	**2,080,367.03**	**100.00**	**$12,500.00**

Note:"Statement Showing Proration of Expense of the Office of the Commissioner [1925]," Stagg Papers, box 85, folder 2.

CHAPTER 7

The Big Ten Stadiums

The stadium as a structure to accommodate spectators assembled to watch events of various types has a history extending back to ancient Greece. The most famous example of the type is the Coliseum, which had a capacity of over fifty thousand and was a symbol of ancient Rome. The modern equivalent is the football stadium, the college version of which became iconic in America.[1]

When college football began in the 1870s, the Harvard, Yale, and Princeton teams played in New York City, Hoboken, New Jersey, and Springfield, Massachusetts, before they relocated to college grounds. For a time Harvard played to fans on wooden bleachers, but a stadium seating thirty-five thousand was completed in 1903 at a cost of $300,000. The Harvard class of 1879 gave a $100,000 anniversary gift to build the structure. Another $33,000 came from gate receipts. Harvard University did not contribute to the cost of the structure, but even so opponents denounced the stadium as a glorification of the evil side of athletics.[2]

In 1908 Yale proposed to build a bowl with an embankment on which to erect the stands with an estimated capacity of seventy thousand. The Yale Bowl was completed in 1914 at a cost of $700,000. Princeton joined the march the next year with a stadium built at a cost of about $300,000, the generosity of Edgar Palmer, Princeton '03. Palmer Stadium seated more than forty thousand and provided space for track-and-field events as well as football. Syracuse University built a football stadium with a gift of $500,000. The Archbold Stadium had a seating capacity of twenty thousand.[3]

In the early days of midwestern football, spectators stood along the sidelines to watch the game; later, wooden stands were built to accommodate the fans, and when crowds promised large gate receipts, reinforced structures replaced the wooden stands.

The next stage in the evolution of playing fields and spectators' stands was similar in all Big Ten schools. In 1893 the playing field at the University of Chicago was a plot north of the campus donated by Marshall Field and named after him. In 1894 students and faculty raised $1,200 and contributed labor to complete a two-thousand seat grandstand two days before a Thanksgiving Day game against Michigan. A new west stand brought the seating capacity to 13,500. In 1913 additional bleachers made it possible to accommodate twenty-five thousand fans, and the *Chicago Tribune* campaigned to name the field in honor of Amos Alonzo Stagg.

For years the Wisconsin Badgers played football on the site of a camp used for training Union soldiers during the Civil War. The state donated the land to the university, and the university erected a facility first used for football in 1895. Camp Randall Stadium with wooden bleachers was built in 1915. Part of it collapsed that year, and a new stadium with concrete bleachers seating ten thousand was ready for use in 1917.

At Ohio State, athletic sports took place on an area north of the campus, remote from the city of Columbus. By 1908, with improvements, Ohio Field had a seating capacity of sixty-one hundred. In 1909 a crowd of seven thousand attended a football game there; a year later new bleachers were built. With OSU's admission to the Big Ten conference in 1912, football soon outgrew Ohio Field.

At Illinois, in 1892 the students' Athletic Association petitioned for a sports area. The trustees provided $350 to develop part of the north campus, and the Athletic Association raised the balance needed to create Illinois Field. Bleachers were erected on the east side in 1904 and on the west side in 1906. When the Illini won the Big Ten football championship in 1914, fans agitated for new stands. On the eve of the world war, James M. White, the university's supervising architect, drew plans for a concrete stadium on the southwestern campus.[4]

In the 1920s the country was seemingly prosperous, college football was popular, the game was profitable, and colleges clamored to construct a stadium. Joining the stampede were the University of Washington and Oklahoma State (1920); California (Berkeley), Southern California, and Kansas (1921); California (Los Angeles) and Vanderbilt (1922); Michigan State and Nebraska (1923); Louisiana State, Texas, and the U. S. Military Academy (1924); Oklahoma and Pittsburgh (1925); Missouri, Oregon, and North Carolina (1926); Texas A & M and Utah (1927); Arizona (1928); Alabama and Texas Christian (1929); and Notre Dame (1930).[5]

The Big Ten Stadiums

By 1920 the Western Conference had solidified its reputation as the nation's leading intercollegiate athletic conference by means of its excellent football teams. It could not be left behind in the rush to erect imposing physical facilities for the game. Several Big Ten stadiums were designed as memorials to students and faculty members who had given their lives in the recent war. Most but not all of these structures were designed solely for football. College stadiums became America's most revered playing fields. Few of the people responsible for building the stadiums asked what relation, if any, the stadiums had to higher education.[6]

Ohio State was the first conference member to erect a football temple. In 1917 the school's athletic board discussed the matter. Thomas E. French, chair of both the athletic board and the engineering department, as well as the faculty representative to the conference, drew plans. Two years later the trustees learned of a proposal to finance the construction by the sale of bonds, and they resolved to develop recreational facilities on the campus, adding that gifts would be accepted for a stadium. In 1920, a campaign to build Ohio Stadium brought in nearly $1 million by subscription and football receipts. William O. Thompson, president of Ohio State, called the stadium "the largest single enterprise which the University has ever undertaken." As the campaign progressed, the trustees declared that the university would assume no legal liability for any debt incurred in erecting the stadium. The athletic board agreed to assume responsibility for financing, if necessary. In the spring of 1921 the trustees approved the architect's and engineer's plans. The board defeated a proposal to use brick and stone for the structure rather than reinforced concrete and to reduce the seating capacity from sixty-three thousand to forty-five thousand. The stadium campaign brought the campus considerable publicity, which led to the establishment of a university news bureau underwritten by the athletic department. In the dedication game on October 21, 1922, Michigan beat Ohio State 19–0.[7] The treasurer's final report put the cost of the stadium at $1,548,634. In 1924 the stadium brought in gate receipts of $275,723.75.[8]

Illinois was next to join what was a seemingly irresistible cause. In the early 1920s four options vied for favor in a university building program—a student union building, a war memorial, a Gregory memorial (John Milton Gregory was the first regent or president of the university), and an athletic stadium. Students, athletic officials, and alumni campaigned for a stadium. Illinois, with its lumberyard bleachers, lagged behind its rivals, they argued; football produced the revenue needed to pay the salaries of the coaching staff, and the time was approaching when other Big Ten teams would refuse to play on Illinois Field. Put to a vote in which a third of the students participated, 1,353 favored a stadium, while 637 favored a union building.

The Ohio State University football stadium. Source: Ohio State University Archives.

In December 1920 athletic director George Huff asked the board of trustees to give the athletic association authority to undertake a campaign to raise funds for the stadium. The board approved.[9] Three Illinois students visited Ohio State to confer with student leaders of their stadium campaign, and headquarters for the Illinois drive were established in the Administration Building. W. Elmer Ekblaw (AB '10, AM '12), the "father" of Homecoming, an autumn ritual Illinois introduced to higher education, was named the executive secretary of the stadium campaign. He viewed the drive to raise $1,500,000 as a quasi-religious crusade. Until students and alumni recognized the heavy debt they owed their alma mater, he declared, they would be neither loyal nor true. The stadium movement would initiate a finer esprit de corps among Illinois men and women and organize them into a devoted, loyal, partisan body. "You have never done anything directly for Illinois," Ekblaw told students and alumni. "You have made no sacrifice for her. You have not acknowledged your obligation to her. Now you and all the rest of the Illini are called upon to respond to this appeal for direct service and support. We are going to raise every cent, every dollar of the fund necessary for this project, without asking the help of the legislature or of the state funds. Now come across."[10] Samson Raphaelson, Illinois '17, a Hollywood scriptwriter and author of the story that became *The Jazz Singer*, was named publicity manager for the stadium drive. Students were to be organized in groups of ten, each with a captain. There was to be a chairman for every county in Illinois and every state in the nation. Students began work with enthusiasm.[11]

In March the Campus Plan Commission recommended and the board of trustees resolved "that the proposed Stadium be built on University property between First Street and the right-of-way of the Illinois Central Railroad."[12] The site was southwest of the campus. The leadership of the drive now passed from students to alumni and athletic officials. The presidents of Illinois alumni clubs from New York to Denver, along with members of the executive committee of the Illinois American Legion, met in Urbana. They organized a council that included Huff, Zuppke, and Ekblaw, and set a goal of $350,000 for students to raise.

In June, on recommendation of the athletic association, the board of trustees designated the Chicago firm Holabird and Roche as the stadium architects. Several members of the architecture faculty had drawn up plans and submitted a bill for their work, but their efforts came to naught.[13] In August, however, the board of trustees declared that since the proposed stadium was "to be erected with money subscribed by alumni and friends of the University," and since a committee representing the donors had asked President Kinley to approve their selection of Holabird and Roche, it was "the right and privilege" of the donors to select an architect. The board accepted the firm selected by the committee,[14] which included Huff, Zuppke, Avery Brundage, and Robert Carr.[15]

In November 1921 Huff assembled a group of "active and interested Illini" in Chicago. Among the twenty-two men present were President Kinley, Huff, Zuppke, and Ekblaw. Huff presented the request of the Illinois Department of the American Legion that the recreation field and the stadium be made a state memorial and that the memorial features be included in the stadium. The men discussed the campaign for funds and the construction of the stadium.[16]

The athletic association and the board of trustees jointly advanced the project. The pledge drive began in the autumn of 1921, and by February 1922 pledges had been secured amounting to $1,776,535, of which $219,264 had been paid in. The board authorized the athletic association to act as its agent in the construction of the stadium and to appoint a committee of alumni and others acceptable to the board to conduct the business connected with the erection of the stadium. This committee was to be the board's agent in connection with the location and erection of the stadium.[17]

In March the trustees adopted a procedure to govern expenditures from the stadium fund and to review the stadium plans presented by the Stadium Executive Committee. The committee proposed that the stadium be used not only for intercollegiate games but also for intramural athletics and should therefore be located close to the center of student population, give accessibility to the public attending the "so-called big games," and be located east of First Street and north of Maple Street in Champaign.[18]

Meanwhile, plans for the stadium proceeded. In April 1922, the Stadium Executive Committee informed the appropriate authorities that they wished to combine the alumni desire to have a distinctive part in some University enterprise and the need of better athletic facilities with the desire to provide a memorial of University sons who gave their lives in the war. Pledges would be for a memorial stadium. Pledges then amounted to $1,852,355; payment of $251,235 had been made. The athletic association owned twenty acres in the designated area. In late April Athletic Director Huff purchased the Stoolman Tract, an adjoining eighteen acres, for $81,000.

In May 1922 John Holabird presented plans and a model of the stadium. The board approved the plans and asked Holabird to make a further study of certain features. To find some method for dealing with two hundred columns in the structure was a challenge. Holabird went to New York to consult Charles A. Platt, a distinguished landscape architect. He suggested a colonnade.

Memorial columns were erected to honor the 183 men and one woman who had given their lives for their country. Donors could pledge to a Memorial Stadium Fund for the purpose. The names of those honored were to be inscribed on the columns, with the names of donors listed on a plaque. The pillar on the extreme southwest end of the structure honored Curtis G. Redden, an Illinois native and all-around athlete who graduated from the University of Michigan law school in June 1903 and was elected captain of the Wolverines football team that year. During the war Redden had commanded Battery F, 149th Artillery, a unit of Illinois men. Fielding Yost, the Michigan football coach, and men from Redden's battery donated the funds for the pillar.[19]

Memorial Stadium, with a capacity of sixty-one thousand, consisted of tiered stands on its east and west sides. The stadium was initiated in 1923, a season in which Illinois won all its eight games and tied Michigan for the Big Ten title. Five games were at home. The stadium dedication was held in the east stand on October 17, 1924. The band led a parade from the campus to the site. Huff presented the stadium to the chairman of the board of trustees on behalf of twenty-one thousand students, alumni, and other university friends (those who had pledged). William L. Noble, the chairman of the board of trustees, accepted the stadium on behalf of the board. In his address, President Kinley viewed the dedication as a consecration. "We cannot hallow this structure," he said, echoing Lincoln's Gettysburg Address. "They made it holy by dying for the principles and ideals in which they believed. It is for us to keep it hallowed by living those principles and ideals." The dedication meant that members of the university "pledge themselves to maintain . . . that immortal spirit of service and self-sacrifice which made these boys and this girl of ours walk up to the face of death."[20] The solemn rite resembled a worship service.

The next day was Homecoming. Zuppke's Illini and Yost's Wolverines were meeting for a game. After the flag was raised and the band played the "Star-Spangled Banner," the teams entered the stadium. Moments later Red Grange won fame as the Galloping Ghost.

The University of Illinois football stadium was dedicated on Homecoming Day, October 18, 1924. President Kinley drew on Lincoln's Gettysburg Address in his dedication remarks. In the football game on this day, Illinois defeated Michigan 39–14. Source: University of Illinois Archives RS 39/2/20, box 85, folder "Stadium Dedication."

At the end of November, stadium subscriptions were $2,166,617, and collections stood at $1,273,719. The number of subscribers was 21,111, including 9,258 alumni and citizens and 11,853 students. Three years later the subscriptions were $2,164,765, and the collections were $1,652,532. The number of subscribers was 21,243, including 9,345 alumni and citizens and 11,895 students. Classes were suspended for a mass meeting to solicit subscriptions. It was easy to pledge, hard to pay.

While Illinois built its stadium, other Big Ten universities either updated existing facilities or built new ones. In Minnesota, university officials working with the alumni association after the armistice proposed a memorial auditorium to commemorate the war. This plan met initial opposition, but it was revitalized in 1921 with the focus on a stadium to be used for football games, convocations, and class gatherings. It was to honor Minnesota servicemen who had given their lives in the war.[21]

The alumni association formed the Greater University Corporation to receive gifts to the memorial fund. A one-hundred-member campaign committee representing every county in the state headed the operation. Its fundraising campaign was to take place among faculty and students in the fall of 1922 and nationwide among alumni and university friends the following spring. The campus drive, highly organized, was considered a success. The alumni magazine described the second stage as "the most pretentious thing of its kind ever staged at Minnesota."[22] Eight football coaches of the Western Conference were present to show their support.[23] But Joseph M. Artman, a Minnesota alumnus who was a member of the University of Chicago theology department, was a dissenter. "I feel that our colleges, in allowing our alumni practically to own the stadiums," he wrote, "are opening the way for insidious control of the universities in the most unwhole-some fashion." Some looked upon Artman as "a knocker," but he added, "I frankly feel that our colleges and universities instead of controlling athletics are allowing athletics to control them."[24]

Minnesota's collection of pledges ran relatively smoothly, certainly more so than that of Illinois. Work on the stadium began in April 1924. By mid-June alumni and friends had made good on 86 percent of their pledges, and the faculty registered at 83 percent. Total costs for the stadium were estimated at $700,000. Completed forty days ahead of schedule, the first football game was played there on October 14, 1924.[25]

Minnesota's Memorial Stadium was the home of Gopher teams until the Hubert H. Humphrey Metrodome opened years later. Football returned to the Minneapolis campus in 2009 in the TCF Bank Stadium, a project costing $288.5 million that enlisted community and state support, university backing, and corporate sponsorship. The curved wall of the stadium, known as the Veteran's Tribute, honored all Minnesota veterans.[26]

Purdue established Stuart Field as its site for football games in 1892. But new times required new responses. David Ross, who graduated from Purdue in 1893 with a degree in mechanical engineering, conceived the idea for a stadium and selected the site on the outskirts of West Lafayette. Ross had invented and patented designs for a gear that controlled the steering of automobiles. The gear made him rich. In 1921 Purdue alumni secured passage of a law that enabled the governor to appoint three people to the board of trustees on recommendation of the alumni. Ross was the first trustee under this arrangement. Alumni, dissatisfied with the Purdue record in football, expected him to promote athletics. He did not give athletics much importance, however, but he conceded that successful teams might add to Purdue's prestige and keep the alumni interested. So he enlisted George Ade in his plan.[27] Ade had graduated from Purdue in 1877 and had become a writer for a Chicago newspaper. He won a literary reputation as a great humorist with fables about the American character. Ade wrote the first American play about football and college life, "The College Widow," which opened in New York to great acclaim on September 20, 1904. Ade's publications made him rich.[28] Ross showed Ade a sixty-five-acre tract north of the campus. The two men bought it in 1922 for a little under $40,000 and deeded it to the university. The Ross-Ade Foundation, controlled by the university, was formed to issue bonds. The design of the athletic facility was intended to seat 32,000. Construction began in June 1924, and Ross-Ade Stadium was dedicated in November. Its seating capacity was 13,500, with standing room for an additional 15,000. Expansions brought the capacity to 23,074 in 1930, and to 69,000 by 1970.

In the mid-1920s Stagg and his cohort at Chicago pushed the idea of a new stadium, while President Judson informed the trustees that the construction of a great stadium would serve notice that educational ideas were of secondary importance. The authorities were willing to increase the size of Stagg Field rather than build a new facility. With gate receipts and subscriptions the seating capacity was increased to fifty thousand. Nevertheless, Stagg and some alumni pressed for a new stadium south of the Midway costing $3 million. Years of financial success due to Maroon victories fed the desire. Nevertheless, university officials wanted the alumni to support an educational program, not a stadium. In the late 1920s the Maroons began a losing streak, and Stagg Field remained the home of Chicago football.[29]

Wisconsin had made do with Camp Randall as the site for football since 1917, but in the new intercollegiate football climate the authorities considered it inadequate. By 1924, with additional construction, the capacity of the bowl-shaped structure was thirty-three thousand. As money became available from the legislature and gate receipts, Camp Randall Stadium eventually was able to accommodate 76,129 spectators.

At the turn of the century Indiana's Jordan Field housed athletic sports. It remained in use for years and seemed to be entirely satisfactory. The Indiana football team played its last game there on November 24, 1923. In the new intellectual climate, some alumni called for a football stadium as a memorial to university alumni who had fought in four wars before 1920. William J. Moenkhaus (AB, 1894; AM, 1895), the faculty representative to the Big Ten Conference, and Ulysses S. Hanna (AB, 1895) were closely associated with plans for the structure. In April 1923 the university's board of trustees sent Moenkhaus and Hanna to Illinois, Iowa, and other universities to secure information about building a new facility. In midsummer, Indiana began construction of a concrete gridiron temple, but in March cracks were discovered in the structure. The faulty building was demolished and a new one completed a year later. Meanwhile, the Indiana football team played all its 1924 games either in Indianapolis or on the freshman field. The first Indiana football game in Memorial Stadium, with a capacity of twenty-two thousand, was against Purdue in November 1925. The Hoosiers played football in that facility through the 1959 season. In 1960 a new Memorial Stadium opened with a seating capacity of 52,354.

Northwestern had several football venues in its early history. The first was Deering Meadow. In 1891 the university built Sheppard Field on the site of the present fraternity quads. It soon became inadequate. William A. Dyche, who graduated from Northwestern in 1882 and received an MA in 1888, was the force behind Northwestern stadium building. In 1903 he saw the need for new athletic grounds and within two years arranged for the construction of Northwestern Field. Its wooden stands, with a capacity of ten thousand spectators, served for two decades. Dyche later became a trustee, the business manager of Northwestern, and president of the alumni association. In 1924, at his urging, the trustees appointed a committee to work with architect James Gamble Rogers on plans for a new facility. As designed, the stadium could be built for an estimated $975,000. A nonprofit stadium corporation was formed to issue bonds valued at $1.25 million, to be retired over fifteen years. Named in honor of Dyche, the stadium, with a seating capacity of forty-seven thousand, hosted its inaugural game before nineteen thousand spectators in October 1926. The stadium was dedicated on November 13, 1926. Additions brought the seating capacity to 49,246 and later to fifty-five thousand.[30]

Fielding Yost made Michigan a dominant force in intercollegiate football. From 1906 to 1926 the Wolverines' home ground was Ferry Field on the Ann Arbor campus. It had an official capacity of 41,240. The Wolverines were so successful that students, alumni, and the public clamored for tickets. Yost wanted a new stadium. In 1923, on a trip to the West Coast, he scouted out the Los Angeles Coliseum and the University of California-Berkeley stadium. What he saw fired his imagination. By late 1924 Yost began to work on a new stadium. After choosing the site, he sent an engineering construction company blueprints and pictures of other stadiums and proposed the financing of a stadium estimated to cost $1.25 million that would draw on the $250,000 available from the 1925 and 1926 football seasons and raise $1 million by an ingenious scheme of selling bonds tied to ticket privileges for each game; it would cost the Michigan taxpayers nothing and would avoid the experience of other Big Ten schools in trying to collect the pledges that had been made to construct a stadium. In late March Yost presented his report to the athletic board, which approved it by a unanimous vote and requested the board of regents to reconsider their 1923 recommendation that the stadium remain on Ferry Field. The board of regents was not scheduled to meet again until late April.

During the 1920s, with criticism of intercollegiate football widespread, Yost's plans aroused faculty opposition at Michigan. One reason for it was the structure of the board in control of athletics. In addition to Yost, the board had three student members, three alumni members, and four faculty members. Yost's faction could outvote the faculty members. Robert C. Angell, an assistant professor of sociology and the grandson of James Burrill Angell, the president of the Univer-

"Sure - we won the Game!
We outplayed them you know!."
F.M.Yost.

Fielding Yost made his reputation as the Michigan football coach. Later, as the athletic director at Michigan, he built the Michigan football stadium. Source: University of Michigan, Bentley Historical Library.

sity of Michigan from 1871 to 1909, was the spokesman for the faculty discontent. Angell's article, "Increasing the Intellectual Interests of Students," took a broad view of the subject.[31] "Inter-collegiate athletics offer the most serious problem of all," he concluded. "Complete abolition of inter-collegiate athletics suggests itself as the quickest solution of the problem."[32] Writing in the *Ann Arbor News*, Angell described those who had no true interest in intellectual matters as a menace to the tone of the university. Complete abolition of intercollegiate athletics was the quickest solution to the problem. Since Michigan could not act alone in the matter, Angell asked for a conference of all the universities in the Western Conference to agree on a joint plan of action. "As a seat of learning and culture," Angell asserted, "Michigan has no interest in winning athletic titles." John Griffith, the Big Ten commissioner, came to Yost's aid with an interview in the *Ann Arbor News* in which he rehearsed some of his standard bromides. He rejected the idea that football was not an appropriate pursuit for universities. It did not follow, he added, "that students would be in the library Saturday afternoons" if the game were terminated.[33]

The dispute led in late April to a debate on the proposition that intercollegiate athletics in their present form was objectionable and should be materially modified. Debate on the subject was a rare event! In May the faculty senate voted to study rather than endorse Yost's report, and it requested the acting university president to appoint a committee to investigate university athletics and report to the faculty senate. The acting president appointed the committee. H. G. Salsinger, a sports reporter, opposed the stadium proposal in the *Detroit News*, and the regents agreed to reconsider their 1923 stadium resolution. Thus, they opened the question to further consideration by those involved.

The *Michigan Daily* now became an advocate of a stadium, while faculty members differed on the matter. Allen Sherzer of the mechanical engineering department rebutted Professor Robert Angell, while William W. Sleator, a professor of physics, defined the academic nature of the controversy. The university could never fail by not enlarging the stadium, Sleator observed, and it could not fail by abolishing competitive athletics altogether. If there was any profit in enlarging the stadium, the university should be ashamed to take it. Scholarship, teaching, and investigations justified the university, not football.

While the debate excited interest, Yost resumed his battle for the stadium. Alumni groups reinforced his plea by appealing to the regents. In January 1926, following the report of the Day Committee, the faculty senate voted to favor a new stadium seating at least sixty thousand. The report also increased faculty representation on the athletic board to a total of eight. The regents adopted the report with some modifications and approved of seating for seventy-two thousand. They also reconstituted the Board in Control of Intercollegiate Athletics, which was to include two students, three alumni, and nine faculty members, two of whom were to be the president of the university and Yost as his adviser. With the approval needed, Yost had the footings of the stadium constructed so that its capacity could later be increased. Michigan Stadium opened in 1927 with a seating capacity of 84,500.[34] After relatively simple renovations the stadium held 102,501. Knute Rockne had little regard for Fielding Yost, but he respected Yost's architectural sense and business acumen. The Notre Dame stadium, completed in 1930, was a virtual clone of its Michigan predecessor.[35]

In October 1928 Paul Belting, the athletic director at Iowa, announced plans for the construction of a new stadium. The following March the state board of education approved the plans, construction proceeded at a swift pace, and in September 1929 the edifice was declared complete. The cost of the project, which could accommodate more than sixty thousand fans, was $500,000, which was funded largely by bonds. In 1972 the facility was named Kinnick Stadium in honor of Nile Kinnick, an All-America halfback and Phi Beta Kappa student at Iowa.

The Meanings of the Stadiums

The Big Ten stadiums were Western Conference icons, the most identifiable structure on each campus. Many were larger than the Rome Coliseum. They were built at a time when automobiles and good hard roads enabled fans to travel to the games. The stadiums were filled because sports writers told fans that college football was a great game. These structures were the setting for show business, a mass entertainment with a marching band, a drum major, majorettes, and a mascot. The stadium brought students and alumni together to sing the college song and celebrate Alma Mater. Local entrepreneurs viewed the crowds that packed the stadiums as a source of profit. Above all, football was a coaches' game. Coaches were paid from gate receipts, gate receipts depended on winning teams, winning teams required good athletes, and good athletes tempted coaches to recruit and subsidize.[36]

To percipient observers, the stadiums diverted the universities from their proper purpose—the education of young Americans. The stadiums identified the conference with big-time football and the commercialization of intercollegiate athletics. With the stadiums, the Big Ten crossed the Rubicon. There would be no turning back.

CHAPTER 8

Red Grange and the Lure of Professional Football

John Griffith and Big Ten officials were professedly committed to amateurism in intercollegiate athletics. They viewed professional football as a threat to the college game. But pro football had been establishing roots since the turn of the century, and the link between intercollegiate and professional football was tightened in the mid-1920s by the career of Harold "Red" Grange.

He made a name for himself as a college football player who became a professional football player. Grange and professional football were born twins.

Red Grange was born in Forksville, Pennsylvania, in 1903, where his father was a foreman in a lumber camp. He was six years old, and his mother had just died when the family removed to Wheaton, thirty miles west of Chicago. His father became a policeman and later the Wheaton chief of police. Harold acquired a nickname, the "Wheaton Iceman," because he carried big blocks of ice to people's houses every summer, a task that hardened his legs and strengthened his arms and shoulders. A skinny, well-coordinated athlete, Grange was on both the track team and the football team in high school.

At his father's insistence, "Red," another nickname, went to the University of Illinois in 1922. It was the cheapest place he could get a college education, and most of the Wheaton kids he knew also went to the university in Urbana. A freshman with a good high school record, Grange registered in the General Business Curriculum and joined the Zeta Psi fraternity. His fraternity brothers insisted that he go out for football. Though he weighed only 166 pounds, he gained a berth on the freshman squad. Academically, he was a marginal student in his first semester but did somewhat better the second semester. His best grades were in physical education and in infantry drill and tactics. As a sophomore he registered in the College of Liberal Arts and Sciences and joined Zuppke's football team. His academic standing was average, but he won distinction in football. On November 3, 1923, at the opening of Memorial Stadium, Illinois played Chicago to a capacity crowd of sixty-one thousand fans. In seventeen plays Grange gained 173 yards. Illinois won 7–0, and Walter Camp named Grange as the left halfback on his All-America team.[1]

In the fall of 1924 Grange, a twenty-one-year-old junior, carried five courses with a C average in the first semester. In the second semester, he took six courses, with an average between C and D. On October 17 Memorial Stadium was dedicated. On the following day, with sixty-seven thousand spectators in the stands and an estimated twenty thousand unable to get in, Illinois met Michigan on the gridiron. In the first twelve minutes of play, Grange ran for four touchdowns. One after another, they were for ninety-five, sixty-seven, fifty-six, and forty-five yards. Grange later covered another forty yards for a total of 303 yards. Spectators went wild as Illinois beat Michigan 39–14. The nation's newspapers celebrated Grange's exploit. Grantland Rice named Grange the Galloping Ghost, and Walter Camp selected him for his All-America team.[2]

Grange had ninety-two academic credits as he began his senior year, two more than needed to proceed to graduation at a regular pace. The eyes of the nation were

Red Grange races for the goal line in a game with Michigan in 1924. Illinois won, 39–14. Source: University of Illinois Archives RS 39/2/2, box 45, folder "Ath 2–3 . . . Red Grange, 1924–1929."

upon him. During the 1925 football season the Fighting Illini—the name had only recently come into use—under Captain Grange played eight games. Grange made his only collegiate appearance outside the Midwest against Pennsylvania in Philadelphia. The East was the cradle of intercollegiate football, and Penn had a strong team. People knew about Grange, and sixty-two thousand fans crowded into Franklin Field, on which Grange carried the ball thirty-six times for a total of 363 yards. He led Illinois to a 24–2 victory over the previously unbeaten Quakers. Sportswriter Damon Runyan described Grange as "three or four men and a horse rolled into one for football purposes. . . . He is melody, and symphony, on the football field."[3] The Penn game became Grange's second foundation for fame.[4] Returning to Urbana, the Illini fought a hard match with the Chicago Maroons, winning 13–6. At this point, two more games remained in the season. One was with Wabash College, and the other with Ohio State in Columbus on November 21.

During Grange's senior year Charles C. Pyle, "a notorious money hungry promoter"[5] known as "Cash and Carry" Pyle, got in touch with him. Pyle owned the Virginia and the Park theaters in Champaign. One night in 1925 an usher told Grange, who was seated in the Virginia, that Mr. Pyle wanted to see him. Grange went to Pyle's office, opened the door, and before he could sit down, Pyle said, "Red, how'd you like to make a hundred thousand dollars?" He would like that, Grange replied; who wouldn't?[6]

Pyle described what he had in mind. He wanted Grange to join a pro team, the Chicago Bears, and tour the country. George Halas and Ed "Dutch" Sternaman, former Illinois football players, were the owners of the Bears. If Grange were interested, Pyle would work it out with them. Pyle would be Grange's manager and handle all the details. The owners of the Bears would split their profits 50-50 with Pyle, and Pyle would split 60-40 with Grange, in Grange's favor. Pyle would also arrange exhibition games in the East that would feature Grange. The two men agreed on these arrangements but decided to sign nothing until after Grange's last football game of the season. Rumors about Grange becoming a professional circulated widely, but Grange denied that he had signed with a pro team.[7]

David Kinley, the president of the university, kept a watchful eye on Grange. On November 14, Kinley wrote him the following avuncular letter:

> I fear from what I hear that I may not have made myself entirely clear to you in our talk the other day about your cutting classes. I asked you to adjust your absences and to get back into your classes. I understood you to say that you would do the latter and get excuses, for which you told me you had good cause, for your recent absences. In order that there may be no misunderstanding, I am dropping this note to say that it is imperative that you get back into your classes at once in order to avoid being dropped for cutting.
>
> Please do this Monday morning. I am informed that, *any* further cutting by

you will put you on probation at once. As I think you and I agreed, you do not want to finish the season, even if you could be allowed to do so, with a 'handicap' against your opponents in the way of neglecting your own studies while they were committed to keep up with theirs.

As for your future plans, I am deeply interested in having a good career open up for you and hope I may be able to help in this matter in the near future. I think, however, as I said to you, that in my opinion, as in that of all your friends with whom I have talked, you will make a mistake if you do not go on with your college work this year and finish up. I hope we can talk the matter over before long.[8]

Kinley offered wise counsel, but the situation was out of his hands. As the *New York Times* reported variously that third week in November, "Excused from football practice for two days, ... Grange went to Wheaton" to talk with his father, "who hoped that Harold had not accepted a contract but thought that he was entitled to cash in on his gridiron fame." Zuppke told Grange to "turn in his suit if he was a pro." According to the press, President Kinley urged Grange not to accept any offers to play pro football.[9]

Red Grange and Coach Robert Zuppke, ca. 1925. Zuppke was disappointed with Grange when his famous player turned professional. Source: University of Illinois Archives RS 39/2/10, box 45, folder "Ath 2–3 . . . Red Grange, 1924–1929."

On Saturday, November 21, Illinois played Ohio State in Columbus before 85,500 spectators, one of the largest crowds ever assembled anywhere up to that time for a football contest. Illinois defeated Ohio State 14–9. After the game, Grange announced his intention to play with the Chicago Bears. He went to Chicago that night, signed a contract the next day. "Cash and Carry" Pyle would manage his affairs.[10] Grange had turned pro and had an agent.

Grange's unceremonious departure from the university sparked mixed reactions. Grantland Rice wrote that "becoming a professional probably was the wise choice for Grange, who could expect a quick and large reward," but it would be better for almost all other college players "to complete their educations." Rice also wrote that "modern civilization was not so concerned with sportsmanship or standards as with results," but "Grange on the football field met both tests." "There could be no complaint," Rice said, "with any decision he makes." "Scarcity is what made radium worth more than gold."[11]

The public applauded Grange for seizing an opportunity to make a fortune honestly in a short time. President Kinley had no intention of making a public statement on the Grange football hysteria. He said, "If Mr. Grange, having considered the matter fully, decided that this was the proper course of action for him, that is his affair, not mine."[12]

Some viewed Grange as "a fallen idol." No one could blame him for wishing to capitalize on his fame or for playing professional football, an Illinois newspaper wrote, but by waiting until he had completed his college course, Grange would have signified that he was in college for an education. Instead, he had indicated that he went to the university to play football, and by so doing would cause thousands of "plastic student minds" to place greater emphasis on college athletics than on education.[13]

In late October 1925, John R. Tunis wrote a profile of Grange. During a week in Urbana, the sportswriter had observed many big-city reporters in the vicinity of the Zeta Psi house. They assured Tunis that Grange was colorless off the football field. Alas, only too true! The publicity director for the athletic association described Grange as "better than the average student, although . . . not a highbrow by any means." Tunis cited Grange's academic record of the last semester: in five courses Grange had a B, a C, two Ds, and an E. The B was in Geography 3, which was rated around the campus "as something less than the hardest course in the university." But Grange had done something for his college. He brought crowds of seventy thousand people to Champaign three or four times a year for football. At $3 a head that meant over $200,000 a game. There was no lurid "story" in this "quiet, simple, modest, unassuming Mr. Grange. But there is perhaps, just a touch of tragedy. There is in every football star that same touch." Viewing all this, Tunis wrote, "a well-groomed, modest young chap may wonder to himself, in odd moment, just what it is all about."[14]

Grange's new career stimulated interest in the relation between college football and professional football. Pro football had "made remarkable strides" in the early 1920s, the press reported, and was now an established sport. It was obvious from the moment Grange became a national hero, John Griffith said, that a pro team would seek him. By 1925, the Professional Football League, formed in 1920 to put the pro game on a sound basis, had twenty teams in a score of cities. The league took steps to prevent a team from employing a player who was still an amateur. Backers of the pro game predicted that it would improve rather than harm the college game. The pro game was "post-graduate football." Many football fans were not college men and could not get tickets for the big college games. The pro game was played on Sundays and holidays when working-class fans could attend.[15]

Commissioner Griffith, however, refused to join the pro football chorus. He admitted that professionalism was "making deep inroads" into college football. He could not blame Grange, he said, but was sorry that he had joined with the professionals, an action that would "hurt the amateur sport [and] help the professional game." Griffith wished that Grange had taken Huff's advice and finished school. "Then he could have capitalized on his athletic ability or . . . followed well-founded business proposition." Griffith predicted that Grange "would cut loose in the professional ranks [as he had] while a college grid star."[16]

Pyle arranged two exhibition tours for Grange. The first one involved a brutal schedule of ten games in just over two weeks. Grange began his pro career with the Chicago Bears on November 26. He went on with the Bears to play in Chicago on November 29, in St. Louis on December 2, in Philadelphia on December 5, and the next day with the New York Giants in the Polo Grounds. At this point Grange and his teammates showed the fatigue and the physical effects of the wear and tear of their bruising schedule.[17]

Grange and Pyle stayed in New York for a few days to transact business. While there, Pyle presented Grange a check for $50,000, and Pyle collected an estimated $125,000 for Grange's endorsement of consumer products. The two men signed a contract for Grange to appear in a movie. For signing the contract, they received "a few thousand dollars and the promise of about $5,000 per week while making a picture."[18]

Resuming their schedule, the Bears played in Washington, D.C., on December 8. While in the nation's capital, Senator William B. McKinley of Illinois took Grange and George Halas to meet President Calvin Coolidge. The senator introduced his guest as "Red Grange, who plays with the Bears." President Coolidge shook Grange's hand and said, "Nice to meet you, young man. I've always liked animal acts."[19]

The next day the Bears engaged the Providence Steam Rollers in Boston, and on December 10 the Pyle-Halas Bears lost to the Pittsburgh All-Stars. On December 12, without the fatigued and injured Grange, the Bears lost to the Detroit

Panthers. Returning to Chicago on December 13, the Bears met the New York Giants on Wrigley Field before some eighteen thousand fans. At this point Grange had played in nine games in eighteen days and had earned about $50,000.

Pyle arranged a second tour for the Bears with Grange as the featured attraction. This show business, for which the impresario provided the players a Pullman car and a porter, consisted of nine games in more than a month. The venture began on Christmas Day in Coral Gables, Florida, went on to Tampa on New Year's Day, and then Jacksonville. In their private railroad car the Bears proceeded to New Orleans, and then to Los Angeles, where Grange was introduced to a number of movie stars, and the team won 17–7 before some eighty thousand fans in the Los Angeles Coliseum. The Bears next journeyed to San Diego, then proceeded to San Francisco, then Portland, after which they ended the exhibition tour in Seattle on 31 January. Grange and Pyle pocketed about $150,000 from gate receipts, bringing their total for the two tours to $250,000. Pyle gave Grange a second check for $50,000. Counting the money he had made weekly, Grange noted: "I had earned nearly $125,000 in my first season as a professional football player. Now I thought I could go on to make it a million."[20]

As the winter tour began, the *Literary Digest* wrote that praise and blame, admiration and envy, amusement and scorn, mingled in about equal measure in the flood of comment occasioned by Red Grange's plunge into professional football. His sudden abandonment of his academic career to launch into commercial football linked to the gold mine of "movie" and advertising sidelines had brought the football controversy to the boiling point. Many critics pointed to Grange's defection from his disconsolate alma mater as a shocking example of gridiron demoralization. His daily grind of football games had fatigued and discouraged him. Admittedly, he had made a great deal of money, perhaps $150,000 so far, and Pyle was on his way west to arrange a $300,000 cinema contract. But it was not as easy as he had thought. To his critics, Grange said, "Why shouldn't I play football for money?" But he could not keep up the pace. He was going back to finish college. Grange was a fellow who needed a friend. He was "bobbing about helplessly in a sea of greed and cunning and idiotic publicity" that he was "too inexperienced to navigate." In all of this Grange was merely the victim of "get-rich-quick promoters" who prostituted him to their ends. "They [wrecked] him as an athlete by scheduling him to play a series of games that no human frame [could] stand.... Neither nature, nor his home, nor his college had given him the education or the character to withstand the temptations that were put in his way." Grange would have had to have an experience of life beyond anything that was possible in his case in order to understand the kind of "frothy popularity" he had or the "seamy commercialism" that was out to use him. "You would suppose," the author added, "that somewhere in the University of Illinois there would have been someone who could have gone to him and made him see what he was getting into." There should have been someone on the faculty or perhaps the president of the university himself who had "sense enough and backbone enough" to take Grange in hand before he was swallowed into the mess and prove to a skeptical public that "the universities know how to prepare men to meet the realities of life."[21]

After the tiring tour, Grange went to Hollywood to work for the Film Booking Office (FBO), owned by the magnate Joseph P. Kennedy of Boston. Kennedy had asked his young boys, Joe Junior and Jack (the future president), if they would like to see Grange in a movie. The boys liked the idea, so Kennedy made Grange the star in *One Minute to Play*, about a halfback who foils some gamblers by winning a game in the last minute. It was a critical and financial success. Kennedy also featured Grange in *Racing Romeo* (1927), which allowed him to enjoy some stunt driving. Pyle arranged for Grange to appear in a serial action film called *The Galloping Ghost*.[22]

In early 1926, shortly after Grange turned pro, George Huff and Robert Zuppke told George Hallas that he had not offended football league rules by signing Red Grange the day after his last college game, but behind the rules was the desire for college athletes not to leave college before they graduated. The debate over Grange dropping out without his degree, the two men added, had intensified collegiate ill-will toward professional football.[23]

Grange had signed with the Bears for only two tours. Pyle organized a new pro team, the New York Yankees, and Grange played for Pyle's Yankees in Yankee Stadium. Grange badly hurt his knee while playing with the Yankees against the Chicago Bears and was out of football for a year. When he returned to the gridiron, he played at about 70 percent of his former capacity. He retired from football in 1934.[24]

Grange's barnstorming tour had raised questions about the relation between the college game and the pro game. In 1926 some twenty million spectators were expected to pay $50 million to watch college football, but Pyle was confident that the public would take to pro football. Some four million football players graduated from college every year, he noted, and most of them wanted to keep on playing. Would pro football have a chance with rival leagues grappling for popularity? Professional football should find a niche for itself, a sportswriter observed, but it would never approach the interest given the college game. Tradition (in other words, traditional rivalries) and the heart interest (fans) were the leading elements in the game many millions followed and loved.[25]

Shortly after Grange turned pro, an Illinois alumnus wrote to President Kinley suggesting that a life-size statue of Grange, in football uniform and possibly holding a football under one arm, be made and placed in some conspicuous place at the university, possibly near the stadium. "After careful consideration of this suggestion," Kinley replied, "it seems to me that it would not be a good thing to do."[26]

Years later, in conjunction with the renovation of Memorial Stadium, at the suggestion of the Division of Intercollegiate Athletics, donors pledged funds to construct a statue dedicated to the famous athlete. Decades after President Kinley had turned down the idea, a larger-than-life- size statue of Red Grange, in football uniform with a football in his arm, was erected on the west side of Memorial Stadium.[27]

Despite allegations to the contrary, Grange did not go to college to become a pro football player. He went to the university to get an education. His natural talent enabled him to become a celebrated athlete, and he capitalized on his gridiron glory. He was a product of the athletic culture of his time. Zuppke "consider[ed] Grange his masterpiece." Shortly after Grange defected to the Bears, he declared, "Grange has no right to capitalize upon his athletic fame; his fame belongs to Illinois, not to him."[28] Grange also ignited controversy over the relation of pro football to the intercollegiate game. Grange's fame and fortune in pro football most likely influenced many young athletes to go to college not for an education but for a career in professional football.[29] In all of this, as John R. Tunis wrote, there was perhaps "just a touch of tragedy."

Griffith continued to view professional football as a threat to the collegiate game. Most sportswriters, he noted, went out of their way to help promote the professional game, and yet some pro games played in Chicago attracted small numbers of spectators. The conference directors had decided that it was best not to give professional football any publicity by discussing it in public. In various ways, the directors discouraged the development of the pro game. They refused to employ as a coach or official in an athletic department any man who had been engaged in professional football, and they advised their athletes not to go into professional football. Griffith urged the directors to do everything possible to prevent the growth of this menace. "That professional football is a menace no one can deny." If the college games continued to hold the attention of the public, professional football would not pay, Griffith predicted, and if it was not financially successful, it would cease to be a menace.[30]

Tunis sought to understand the place of sports in American culture. To the American sports follower, he wrote, football was more than a game, it was a religion, "almost our national religion." It had its dogmas. Only through "college spirit" could a man be saved. The ritual had pervaded the game so gradually that it had become a part of college life. The colleges realized that they had on their hands an octopus that was strangling many of the legitimate pursuits of educational institutions. "Some college presidents," he noted, "were as completely hypnotized by the effects of football as the most fervent undergraduates. But the majority undoubtedly feel it to be harmful . . . because it gives both to students and the public . . . an entirely wrong idea of the purpose of a great educational institution." "The greatest objection of the educators," he concluded, was that "the religion of football . . . teaches the most ephemeral of values." It set up "false gods" before a student learned "to distinguish between things of enduring worth and the things that were not."[31]

In most American colleges there were two factions. The football faction was "well organized, powerful, articulate, embrac[ed] most of the students, the athletic directors, their staffs, many influential graduates and members of the Board of Trustees, and occasionally the president himself." The anti-football faction was "smaller, less powerful, vastly less noisy, but growing rapidly." It would like to change football or do away with it, but it has been powerless. A college president who made "a gesture against football" would find many forces arranged against him. The president could do little to change the fundamental nature of intercollegiate football. "So the average college president," Tunis wrote, "let ill enough alone." But he could monitor the propaganda that emanated from his own institution. Tunis cited a biography of Red Grange sent out by the University of Illinois publicity department and asked why such stuff should come from an educational institution supposedly devoted to sound learning.

Tunis was skeptical about college authorities who charged that the public was responsible for the football mania. Someday football might cease to be a religion and become merely a sport. For football was a game that ought not die out. "Why not take football for what is: The Great American Game? And let it go at that."[32]

Red Grange and Pro Football

Red Grange is the classic example of the athlete who capitalized on his college gridiron fame to become a professional football player. And yet Grange is best understood as a stage, admittedly an important stage, in the development of professional football in America. As we saw in Chapter 5, pro football had its origins in the athletic clubs in Chicago and elsewhere in the late nineteenth century and in the municipal elevens in southwestern Pennsylvania and northeastern Ohio in the early twentieth century. Here pickup teams played football on Sundays for love of the game, and some of the players were paid.

Big Ten guardians of amateur athletics were alert to the rise of professional football. In 1916, Albion Small (Chicago) had persuaded the Western Conference to adopt a resolution declaring that employees of athletic departments who participated in professional football games should be suspended from their employment and that members of teams participating in professional contests before graduation were to suffer certain penalties. Returning to the subject in December 1919, Small secured adoption of a resolution saying that participation in a professional football game would disqualify the participant for all employment or connection with athletics in a conference university. Moreover, the faculty representatives recommended to the conference colleges the adoption of a rule that in the future any student, having received his letter, would forfeit the same if he engaged in professional football subsequent to graduation. Albion Small had introduced these resolutions at the suggestion of Coach Amos Alonzo Stagg.

The career of Red Grange marked the beginning of a new era in Big Ten football. After Grange, professional football became increasingly popular and attracted increasingly large audiences. Talented college football players often aspired to join the professional ranks. Commissioner Griffith advised conference members to ignore pro football and concentrate on the college game.

Nevertheless, pro football continued to find an increasingly large place in America. The first professional football game at Soldier Field in Chicago was on November 11, 1926, between the Chicago Bears and the Chicago Cardinals. The game was for charity. The Bears, originally the Decatur (Illinois) Staleys, sponsored by the A. E. Staley Company (Decatur), became the Chicago Staleys in 1921 when they moved their home games to Wrigley Field in Chicago. In 1922 the Staleys became the Bears (Wrigley Field had been the Bears' home for decades); the team moved to Soldier Field in 1970. Both the Bears and the Cardinals were charter members of the National Football League (NFL), which had been formed in 1920 as the American Professional Football Association and was renamed the National Football League in 1922. The Cardinals played another regular season game at Soldier Field later in November 1926. The most noteworthy professional game of the year came on December 26, 1926, when the Bears met the Green Bay Packers for the first time at Soldier Field. In 1971 the Chicago Bears became the principal tenants of Soldier Field on a short-term lease, and in 1980 George Halas signed a twenty-year lease for the Bears to play there.[33]

CHAPTER 9

The Conference at Work

Big Ten football gained a large and zealous following in the 1920s not only among the students, faculty, and alumni of the member universities but also among the public in the Midwest and in the nation at large. In all likelihood, fans knew little and cared less about the structure and operating procedures of the parent organization, the Intercollegiate Conference, which had no constitution but did have operating procedures. The chairman of each session of the faculty representatives was chosen by rotation, while the members elected the secretary. Those present legislated, but under the White Resolution their decisions often had to be put to a second vote. Things moved slowly. Veteran representatives had an advantage in shaping policy. The faculty representatives, athletic directors, and coaches were engaged in a common enterprise, but each had its own interests. On occasion the faculty men invited the directors and the commissioner to present their views to the assembled faculty representatives, answer questions, and then withdraw.[1] Some athletic directors chafed at the arrangement.

Football dominated intercollegiate athletics in the 1920s. Its management was the conference's prime concern. The number of games in a season and the scheduling of them were recurring issues. Since 1908 the conference had allowed seven games in a season. Customarily, the athletic directors met at the end of the football season and agreed upon a schedule for future years. With the increasing popularity of football, it became more and more difficult to make football schedules to satisfy everyone. Some schools preferred to play teams with which they were on friendly terms, and some had a history of meeting regularly with the same opponent. For example, Minnesota and Wisconsin had met thirty-four times, Chicago and Illinois thirty-one times, and Indiana and Purdue twenty-eight times.

In December 1920 a motion to increase the number of games each season from seven to eight met with little favor.[2] The desire for more games persisted, and resistance finally gave way. In December 1922 Stagg, on behalf of the athletic directors, suggested changes in the rule limiting football schedules and the number of men that might be carried on trips at the expense of the athletic management. After discussion, the conference revised the rule restricting the number of football games to seven: "A football game may be scheduled on every Saturday of October and on every Saturday of November up to and including the Saturday preceding Thanksgiving Day and on no other day, provided that preliminary practice shall begin not more than two weeks before the first Saturday in October." Although the revised statement did not explicitly allow eight games in a season, that was the intent. The rule restricting travel expenditures remained unchanged.[3]

Three faculties challenged the change, so in March 1923 a special meeting was held to consider the matter. Under the White Resolution, the proposal was put to its second passage and lost. The faculty committee then considered a motion to allow eight rather than seven football games in a season. The motion carried 7–3, with Illinois, Northwestern, and Wisconsin voting no.[4] When the faculty committee met in Ann Arbor on June 1, the question of increasing the number of football games in a season from seven to eight was again posed; it carried by 7–2, with Illinois and Wisconsin voting no. Indiana later telegraphed approval.[5] The more-games forces had won. During the 1923 season all but three conference colleges played eight football games. Indiana, Minnesota, and Wisconsin each played seven games.

Fielding Yost was director of athletics at Michigan in 1925 when he assessed the status of intercollegiate athletics. Athletics should "become an integral part of an educative program," he wrote, but athletics faced many "detracting influences." Among them were too many games. Not more than four important games of football should be scheduled; three or four games of lesser importance might be played. No boy should absent himself from class for athletic practice. Post-season games between teams in different parts of the country set a bad precedent. Intersectional games were unwise. No attempt should be made to determine any so-called national championship. Inequality of competition was unfair. Amateurism must be the basis of intercollegiate athletics. Proselyting and recruiting of high school athletes or offering them inducements was perhaps the most serious problem to contend with. Betting on intercollegiate games was a commercializing influence that detracted from the spirit of play.[6]

In a special meeting in March 1925, Paige (Minnesota) described the difficulties under the existing system of making football schedules. Since it was the sense of the faculty representatives that each member institution was entitled to at least four or five conference games, the chairman of the session appointed a committee to consider the matter and to devise machinery for effecting the result.[7]

In June, Paige submitted several drafts of a rule on the subject. After considerable discussion the delegates adopted a rule that declared, "Each Conference college shall be entitled to at least four football games each year with Conference colleges. The Athletic Directors are requested to observe this provision in making the football schedules." Chicago and Illinois rejected the new rule. An informal poll showed that a majority of the colleges were not in favor of a rotating football schedule, one in which each conference college played every other conference college over time. Nevertheless, the faculty representatives appointed a committee to confer with the directors and make a further study of rotating schedules.[8] Since Chicago and Illinois had rejected the rule relating to a four-game schedule passed in June, reaffirmation of the rule was put to a vote under the White Resolution in December 1925. It carried by eight to two.[9] Presumably Chicago and Illinois voted no.

A four-game schedule differed from a rotating schedule. The former required each conference member to play at least four conference games each season. The most powerful teams and those in the best football markets could engage each other and reap rich rewards. A rotating schedule required each conference member to play every other conference member over a given period. It appealed to the conference members with the less-powerful teams and those located in the less-attractive football markets.

Efforts to deal with the number and the scheduling of games were recurring. The faculty representatives were told that an AAUP committee concerned with scholarship and athletics would probably soon recommend that colleges and universities reduce the number of intercollegiate football games to four, or that intercollegiate competition for an athlete be reduced to one or two years. At a conference meeting in March 1926 Pyre (Wisconsin) proposed that the conference permit nine intercollegiate football games each year as follows: four between teams composed exclusively of college seniors, three between teams composed of juniors, and two between teams composed of sophomores. Pyre also suggested limiting coaching and eliminating scouting. He moved the appointment of a committee to consider proposals from the presidents of the conference universities and from the floor and to report at a future meeting. Pyre was named as chairman of the committee.[10]

In May 1926 Long (Northwestern) moved that a committee be appointed to confer with the directors on the feasibility of making football schedules in September rather than December. The motion carried. At the same time, Skinner (Indiana) moved that the conference make an effort "to change football games, making it less personal and sensational." The motion carried.[11] Who would dare to be on record in opposition? Fans loved football because it was personal and sensational. The rougher the better.

Omera Long, professor of classics, was for many years the Northwestern faculty representative to the Big Ten Conference. Source: Northwestern Archives.

At a conference session in November, Messrs. Witting and McCree representing the Big Ten Alumni Association presented a plan for making football schedules by a rotating principle. Long reported progress for the special committee on earlier schedules. Griffith and the athletic directors appeared late in the meeting for a joint session, and Griffith announced football schedules as arranged for the following year. Recent communications from certain university presidents regarding football schedules, recruiting, and other problems were reported and discussed. It was the unanimous feeling of the faculty representatives that the commissioner should immediately collect special data on the points at issue and bring them before a meeting to which the presidents, the chairman of the board of trustees, the faculty representatives, the athletic directors, the coaches, and one representative of each alumni body should be heard. The suggestion led to the Committee of Sixty, which is discussed below.[12]

The athletic directors tried to make up schedules on a four-year basis, and in January 1927 they tentatively agreed on four-year contracts.[13] The following May they recommended that intercollegiate football games not be played on more than eight Saturdays and not more than two games on any Saturday, and that freshmen teams play with teams of their own institutions. Aigler (Michigan) moved that the recommendation read, "No conference institution shall play intercollegiate football on more than eight days in any year." The faculty committee adopted the motion eight to two, with Northwestern and Purdue negative.[14] The annual meeting in December 1927 learned that Illinois, Purdue, and Northwestern had objected to the rule passed in May. A motion to reaffirm under the White Resolution carried seven to three, with Illinois, Purdue, and Northwestern negative.[15]

At a conference meeting in May 1929 a committee (Huff, Stagg, and Griffith) reported that the directors had postponed the making of a four-year schedule because of the growing practice of recruiting and proselyting. The action arose out of the directors' conviction that the proselyting of the best prep school athletes by various colleges made it impossible to know the quality of the team one would be playing. Those present expressed the belief that the time had come for "drastic action." The committee asked that the directors be permitted to postpone the making of long-time schedules.[16] Scheduling was obviously an insoluble problem.

At the May 1928 conference session the delegates informally discussed a proposed football game with the U. S. Military Academy. Notre Dame had played both the Army and Navy academy teams and had showed that such games were profitable. However, conference regulations prohibited such contests. An unnamed faculty representative proposed to change the rules to allow a conference team to compete with a nonconference institution under conference rules of eligibility. But a rule that allowed conference teams to play only with teams representing educational institutions was then invoked, and army posts were not regarded as such. Ohio and Wisconsin objected to the decision. In due time the changes were reaffirmed under the White Resolution. After the conference debated the matter, two army officers appeared and argued against banning the game with the military academy team.[17]

After further debate, the proposal to prevent the game was put to the members. The vote was 5–5, with Illinois, Michigan, Minnesota, Ohio, and Wisconsin in opposition. The chairman declared the motion lost. Pyre (Wisconsin) then moved that the previous decision be reaffirmed with the proviso that it should not apply to the Military Academy at West Point or the Naval Academy at Annapolis. Upon a poll, the motion carried unanimously.[18]

The members were not yet done with the subject. In May 1930 Aigler (Michigan) raised a question about the exemption clause in one of the regulations. After considerable discussion, he moved that the proviso exempting the U.S. Military Academy and the U. S. Naval Academy from the operation of the rule be stricken out. The motion carried unanimously.[19]

This maneuvering around the rules enabled Big Ten teams to play with the service academies. On November 9, 1929, Illinois defeated West Point 17–7 before sixty-eight thousand spectators in Memorial Stadium in Urbana. And on November 8, 1930 West Point scored 13–0 over Illinois before more than seventy thousand spectators in Yankee Stadium in New York City. At the conference session in May 1929 Goodenough (Illinois) reported that the request of Ohio State

Illinois scheduled some football games with glamorous nonconference opponents. In the Illinois-Army game on November 9, 1929, Illinois defeated Army 17–7. Source: University of Illinois Archives RS 39/2/20, box 45, folder "Ath 2-3, Football 1928–1929."

to shift the Navy–Ohio State game from November 16 to November 30, 1929, had been put to a mail vote and carried. In the event, on November 8, 1930, Ohio State humbled Navy 27–0 before forty-five thousand spectators in the Municipal Stadium in Baltimore. And on November 7, 1931, the Buckeyes defeated the Naval Academy 20–0 in the Ohio State Stadium before 60,649 spectators, the largest crowd of the season.

Gate receipts had the sweet smell of success. They tempted the faculty representatives to become businessmen who sold a valuable product. In the May 25, 1929, session, Paige presented a resolution from the Minnesota Athletic Board protesting the scheduled football game in Grant Park in Chicago on October 19, 1929, between Wisconsin and Notre Dame. Paige and F. W. Luehring, the Minnesota athletic director, were among the six signers of the resolution. Grant Park was a large area located directly north of Soldier Field and the Field Museum. Minnesota and Northwestern, said the resolution, were scheduled to play at the same hour and day at Evanston. Playing the game at Grant Park by Wisconsin and Notre Dame was said to be contrary to conference rule 12, but that rule does not seem to be pertinent.[20] Playing the game at Grant Park would materially affect the receipts from the Minnesota and Northwestern game as well as the receipts in all other conference games near Chicago. The Grant Park game was not scheduled until after the Minnesota-Northwestern game had been scheduled. There was no need to schedule the Wisconsin game with Notre Dame at Grant Park inasmuch as it could be played at either Madison or South Bend. Paige moved that it be the sense of the conference that the game ought not to be played at the stated place and that a solution be proposed by Pyre (Wisconsin), Long (Northwestern), and Paige (Minnesota), the interested parties.[21] As things fell out, on October 19, 1929, Notre Dame defeated Wisconsin 19–0 before ninety thousand specta-tors in Soldier Field,[22] while Minnesota beat Northwestern 26–14 before twelve thousand fans in Evanston's Dyche Stadium.

At the December 1930 session, Chairman William J. Moenkhaus (Indiana) reported that a vote taken at the request of Northwestern to transfer its football game with Notre Dame on November 22, 1930, to Chicago had been negative, with the contest eventually played in Dyche Stadium with Notre Dame a 14–0

Bronislau "Bronko" Nagurski was born in Canada of Polish-Ukrainian de-scent, and he grew up working on the family farm in International Falls, Minnesota. Clarence Spears, the Minnesota football coach, discovered him. Nagurski was a standout football player at Minnesota from 1927 to 1929. He turned professional to play for the Chicago Bears from 1930 to 1937. Source: Chicago History Museum.

Clarence W. "Doc" Spears, an All-America guard at Dartmouth in 1914–15, coached the Minnesota football team from 1925 to 1929 and the Wisconsin eleven from 1932 to 1935. His career college football record was 148-83-14. While coaching, Spears studied medicine, and following his football career he maintained a medical practice for many years. Source: University of Minnesota Archives.

winner before forty-eight thousand spectators. Moenkhaus also reported a vote to ascertain the wishes of the conference regarding Northwestern's request to shift the 1931 Notre Dame game to Chicago in favor of postponing the decision to the present meeting. After considerable discussion, nine votes favored granting the request. Illinois voted no. Moenkhaus observed that the result was not due to lack of appreciation of the worthiness of the proposed move, but rather that yielding would lead to a flood of requests "for equally meritorious objectives that would involve departures from regulations more serious in their consequence." In granting the request for 1931, the conference wished to make it clear that it would "not entertain applications for permission to extend the football playing season beyond the last Saturday before Thanksgiving," nor would it "consent to increasing the number of permitted games." "The rules governing these matters were adopted as a result of a conviction that college athletics must be kept within a certain relationship to the fundamental purposes of colleges, namely, education. . . . Moreover, it should be noted that our athletic teams . . . are not aggregations of hired performers whose services are available when, where and as we may choose."[23] A noble declaration, but a bit hollow in light of the pursuit of monetary gain that characterized the negotiations. On October 10, 1931, Northwestern and Notre Dame played to a 0–0 tie before sixty-five thousand fans in Soldier Field.

Scouting was one of the tools coaches used in their passionate desire to win, but the conference was concerned about excessive scouting. At its December 5,

1925, meeting the secretary was instructed to call the athletic directors' attention to an abuse seen in the large number of scouts employed and to suggest that in the conference's opinion this assignment should be limited to one man.[24] Perhaps the suggestion was insufficient. At any rate, in May 1927 the conference decided that not more than one scout be sent to any particular game, except that two might be sent when both contestants had been scheduled by the scouting institution[25]—that is, when a team would be playing both contestants later in that season. Both Chicago and Purdue objected to the ruling, so a motion to reaffirm was put to a vote under the White Resolution. It carried by 7–3, with Chicago, Ohio, and Purdue in opposition.[26] There the matter rested until 1930, when Paige (Minnesota) moved to amend the existing rule so as to eliminate the scouting of an opponent by any institution at more than one game during the season.

In the 1890s the tramp athlete (one who played for several colleges in one season without registering in any of them) was a problem, and in reformed football the migrant athlete was a problem as well. In June 1923 Goodenough presented a resolution from the Illinois faculty senate, saying that "no migrant student who has competed in intercollegiate sports be allowed to compete as the representative of a conference institution." The resolution carried by 6–3.[27] When the conference met in December, the secretary reported that Chicago, Michigan, Minnesota, and Northwestern had objected to the resolution. So it was placed on its second passage and lost 6–4.[28]

The migrant athlete remained a concern. In late 1925 John A. Skinner (Purdue) urged that consideration be given to rules on proselyting and proposals affecting migrants and the limits of participation.[29] In May 1929 the chairman of a session presented a recommendation from the athletic directors to bar the migrant athlete from participation. The recommendation was referred to a committee for further report.[30] In December the migrant rule as passed in May, which had been rejected by Michigan and Northwestern, was put upon its passage a second time under the White Resolution and failed by a vote of 5–5. (The minutes of the meeting do not record the passage of a rule.)[31] Despite the lack of clarity on this matter, it appears that migrant athletes were given a green light.

Migrating students who attended games at other schools as spectators were also a problem. Good roads, frequent trains, and the football craze prompted collegians to follow their team afield. In 1924, when Michigan was scheduled to play Illinois in Urbana, students, alumni, and fans from Michigan made a beeline for Urbana. A special train accommodated more than one hundred Michigan women with chaperons, while several chartered trains were to leave Ann Arbor on nonstop runs to Urbana-Champaign at half-hour intervals. Twenty-one trains averaging thirteen cars each left Chicago for the Twin Cities. The Michigan Band, seventy-seven musicians, made the trip with financial assistance from the Ann Arbor Chamber of Commerce. Michigan had a return engagement with Illinois in 1925.

Railroad officials stated that the crowd being transported to Urbana-Champaign would break all records. Twenty-nine special trains would be chartered for the event, coming from Ann Arbor, Detroit, St. Louis, Kansas City, and Chicago.[32]

At a meeting in May 1926 Pyre (Wisconsin) said that after extensive correspondence with conference authorities it was concluded that as a first step the athletic directors should be asked to begin with the current year to curb the evils of migrating student attendance at games. The conference referred the proposal to the athletic directors with the suggestion that effective control might be reached through the manner of allotting tickets and by eliminating the visiting band.[33]

The conference also deliberated on the size of the entourage that was to travel. In a December 1924 joint session of faculty representatives and athletic directors, Fielding Yost reported the directors' unanimous recommendation that the permissible number of men carried to football games be changed from thirty-five to forty. The faculty representatives agreed to allow forty men, and the conference reaffirmed the change the following March.[34] As embodied in a 1925 document, only eligible players, coaches, trainers, and managers, not to exceed a total of forty persons, could be carried at the expense of the athletic administration to any single event.[35] In December 1926 the athletic directors recommended the carrying of thirty-five additional men on one trip during a season. Put to a vote, it lost.[36]

The Conference Committees

Much of the conference work was done by committees. The Committee on Eligibility was of prime importance. Chaired by Goodenough (Illinois), it sought to maintain the amateur athletic code. In June 1921, for example, the committee ruled that eighteen Indiana freshmen who had gone to the Culver Military Academy to play football, even though the athletic authorities were blameless in the matter, had used up one year of participation and should be eligible subsequently for no more than two years of competition.[37]

In 1927 Goodenough raised some questions about which the conference expressed its informal opinion. Participation in the so-called "East-West" game (between Eastern and Western college teams) constituted competition, and any student of a conference institution who participated therein would lose his amateur standing. Students officiating without pay in high-school games in which other officials might receive pay did not lose their eligibility, nor did students who participated in strictly amateur games during vacation or during the Christmas or Easter recess.[38] After Goodenough died, Thomas French (Ohio State) chaired the committee. Aigler (Michigan) and Long (Northwestern) were the other members. The choice of three veteran representatives testified to the importance of the committee.

The Committee on Colleges was charged with recommending the names of institutions that should be considered colleges for conference purposes. Iden-

George A. Goodenough, professor of mechanical engineering, was the chairman of the athletic committee of the university senate and the Illinois faculty representative to the Big Ten Conference. Source: University of Illinois Archives. RS 39/2/20, box 130, folder "Fac-4, Gao."

tifying institutions in and beyond the conference's geographical area that fit the description was challenging. In 1920 the approved list of colleges in the states where conference members were located included 106 institutions as follows: Illinois (28), Indiana (12), Iowa (19), Michigan (11), Minnesota (7), Ohio (23), and Wisconsin (6).[39] When the conference met in December 1921, Moran (Purdue), the chairman, reported that there was still room for some normalization in the list with a view to securing a more equal standard. He also raised the question of the status of normal schools.[40]

In 1922 Moran observed that the area of the conference had so increased as to suggest the adoption of a new policy with respect to the list of colleges for conference purposes. The conference requested the committee to formulate a definition on the subject, and Moran presented a statement that said a "college" for conference purposes was to consist of "any college, university, normal school, or other institution in advance of the high school grade which did scholastic work generally recognized as being of college grade and which supported a team in football, baseball, basketball, or track, playing a schedule or schedules in whole or in part against teams of college rank." Whenever any conference member proposed to play a man who had previously competed in any form of intercollegiate athletics, without counting this previous participation, such intention, with complete information regarding the facts in the particular case, was to be communicated

143

to the Committee on Colleges not less than six months prior to such intended participation, and no student was to participate without committee approval. This statement was to become effective on June 1, 1923.[41]

The list and definition had a purpose, as evident in a December 1924 meeting. Huff asked whether the College List in the Digest was an exact guide.[42] Moran replied that the list was exact as published for given states after September 1923, and that under the present procedure a transfer student was not automatically out if his name was not at once submitted to the committee. Moran's committee had dealt with three cases submitted by Illinois. In one case the committee decided that an athlete who had competed for three years on teams of the Oklahoma State Teachers College was ineligible for further conference participation. In another case the committee ruled that three athletes who had competed for three years each on the teams of the Southwestern Texas Teachers College in San Marcos, Texas, were ineligible for further conference participation. As for a man who had played for three years at the Missouri Wesleyan College, the committee decided that competition at this institution should not be counted for conference purposes.[43]

The Committee on Officials selected and assigned the referees, umpires, and head linesmen for conference college football games. Often it appointed officials to serve in games between conference and nonconference institutions. Football was a type of combat; competent officials were vital to good sportsmanship. Arthur Smith (Iowa), William V. Pooley (Northwestern), and H. G. Prentiss (Iowa), who served at various times as chairman of the committee, reported at the annual meeting. In 1911 Smith asked the athletic directors for confidential statements on the work done by officials during the season.[44] In 1919 the conference decided that football officials were to receive $50 per game.[45] For a time H. G. Prentiss (Iowa) acted solely as the Committee on Officials. In the early 1920s Ralph Aigler (Michigan) replaced him.[46] In December 1923, the conference added Byron Lambert (Iowa) to the committee and decreed that the committee, with Griffith's assistance, was to appoint officials for all games in which conference colleges participated. Nothing, Aigler declared, was more important to the preservation of friendly relations in intercollegiate athletics than competent officiating.[47]

A year later Aigler reported a new procedure in assigning football officials. A rating by coaches was to be the basis for constituting a list of the most capable officials. Provision was made for checking their work, the conduct of coaches, and the sportsmanship of the crowds. Some thirty approved officials met in October and approved of the plan.[48] The conference had no right, Aigler observed, to use as an official any man who had at any time officiated in professional games. Griffith thought that this attitude might complicate things. When the committee did not assign games to some twelve to fifteen men who had worked some professional games, a number of them appealed to the conference for reinstatement.[49]

In September 1925, meeting in Chicago, conference football officials and coaches considered matters relative to the technique and procedure of officiating and adopted certain interpretations of the rules that were to be applied to all conference games. Griffith's *Athletic Journal* published the results of the meeting.[50] In December, officials, directors, and a majority of the coaches strongly favored the system of assigning officials from an approved list.[51]

Nevertheless, allowing coaches to rate football officials presented problems. So in November 1926 Aigler recommended that his committee appoint football officials without regard to the coaches' black list. The conference adopted the recommendation.

Early in 1927 Griffith was swamped with letters from men who wanted to work conference football games.[52] When the faculty representatives met in May, the directors recommended that Griffith be authorized to select and appoint football officials. After consideration, the conference decided that the Committee on Football Officials was to consist of the current and preceding conference chairmen together with Griffith, except for 1927, when it was to consist of Moran, Aigler, and Griffith.[53] In December, Aigler suggested fine tuning of this arrangement, and the conference agreed that the committee as constituted by the action in May should function from the current date to one year thereafter.[54] Days later Griffith asked the conference coaches to grade the conference football officials. He made a list of men who in the mind of some coach should be cut off the conference list. He ended with twenty-six approved names.[55]

Since the conference regularly elected a chairman of the Committee on Officials to serve for one year, and since Griffith was the continuing member of the committee of three, he had an advantage in selecting football officials. The conference minutes contain no hint as to whether the faculty representatives knew how officials for football games were selected. Long (Northwestern) served on the officials committee by virtue of the rotating feature in the personnel of the committee. He believed that since a conference committee together with Griffith made the appointments, and since the membership of the committee rotated, any suspicion of favoritism was avoided.[56]

In fact, however, the selection of game officials worked to private advantage. Athletic directors and coaches routinely urged newspapermen for the assignment. "Football journalists [obtained] the most lucrative refereeing jobs," and they were paid for "promoting in the press" the games they officiated. "The real villains," according to the sportswriter Paul Gallico, "were the publishers who paid journalists poorly" and printed promotional "swill" in their pages. Rockne had quid pro quo arrangements in the selection of game officials with prominent journalists, including Walter Eckersall, the *Chicago Tribune's* football expert, and Harry Costello of the *Detroit News*, who "pushed himself for the Army–Notre Dame assignment by promising to put in a good word with Walter Camp for Rockne's All-America team candidates."[57]

Griffith collaborated with Rockne in the assignment of officials. On February 6, 1925, he wrote to his friend Rock regarding officials for a game on October 3. When he was out of the office a day earlier, Griffith related, Aigler and Long had assigned Gardner to the Chicago-Kentucky game, Kearns to the Michigan–Michigan Aggie game, and Young to the Wisconsin–Iowa State game. "If I had been here," Griffith added, "possibly I could have saved these three men and will put up a fight for it still if you wish. However, since this is an unimportant game possibly there are other men you would just as soon use. If these men had promised to hold this date open for you I can get around it by suggesting that we slipped up by not checking our records." Griffith went on to name the officials for four games in October and November, including two that involved conference members: Notre Dame–Minnesota and Notre Dame–Northwestern. Aigler, Griffith added, insisted on using Eldridge as the referee of the Chicago-Wisconsin game (on November 21), "and unless you have an agreement with Eldridge it will be hard to change this because of the connection between the two men. . . . I am writing you confidentially, Rock, about this whole matter and think it would be well for you to destroy this letter. If any of these changes are not satisfactory, let me know and I will do my best to fix things the way you would like to have them. Frankly, this whole committee plan is not very satisfactory from my standpoint."[58]

Rockne left "this officiating thing" in Griffith's hands, but "if Professors Long and Aigler have been doing any assigning," he wrote, "I shall object immediately and strenuously." Notre Dame was playing Northwestern, and Rockne did not see why Long (Northwestern) should pick "our officials." Rockne added that Whyte was not satisfactory for the Minnesota game and Knight was not satisfactory for the Northwestern game. Rockne authorized Griffith to show his letter to Long and Aigler and tell them "that if they insist on appointing officials for our Minnesota and Northwestern games, that I will cancel both games and contracts and via the Christy Walsh Syndicate will let the world from coast to coast know just why. I thought that this year these two men would let you do the picking as an absolutely fair, impartial neutral. I know this would be absolutely satisfactory to everybody, but Professors Long and Aigler 'No' with much vehemence." Rockne assured Griffith that for the present at least everything was confidential.[59]

Writing to Griffith about questions of eligibility, Rockne said that he had his own opinions regarding the people in charge of athletics at Michigan and was very glad that Notre Dame was not competing against them in any sport. "Personally,

Yost and Griffith. Source: Chicago History Museum.

I am inclined to think that Yost is not a bit more honest now than he was twenty years ago. Evidently a leopard's spots do not change."[60]

In September 1925 Griffith told Rockne that he would be glad to work his Penn State game if Rockne desired. He would be with Rockne for the coming Baylor game, and the arrangements made by Rockne for Griffith on October 3 were satisfactory. Griffith would be glad to have an article on a football strategy for the *Athletic Journal* that Rockne had suggested. Two weeks later Griffith was "just mean enough" to remind Rockne of his offer to contribute the article.[61] Clearly, Griffith made ethically questionable deals.

The selection of officials challenged the nation's athletic authorities. As Murray Sperber notes in *Shake Down the Thunder*, the NCAA Rules Committee tried to gain control of officiating rather than allowing coaches to hire their "journalist and other friends." The Rules Committee, Sperber writes, planned to "send the schools a list of approved men and, for each game, the opposing coaches would agree on four." "Rockne decided to fight the Rules Committee. . . . He realized that coaches at nonconference schools . . . did not have to accept the committee's selections and could negotiate their choice of officials. . . . [H]e maneuvered the Rules Committee into sending him lists" with the names of Eckersall, Costello, and "most of his other personal favorites." Rockne "never lost control of his game-officiating correspondents." "[H]e liked to keep the big games for sportswriters because they would publicize the events and provide excellent coverage." Eckersall and Costello promoted Rockne's career, and Rockne selected them as game officials. Griffith was amenable to Rockne's requests concerning his games with conference opponents, and he agreed to Rockne's use of regular Big Ten officials, especially his journalist friends, for other Notre Dame contests. In addition to Eckersall, Rockne hired other friends on the Big Ten list, including Milton Ghee of the *Chicago American*. Notre Dame's football success gave Rockne great leverage with game officials.[62]

On October 23, 1926, Notre Dame and Northwestern played a hard-fought game of brute force and strategy before forty thousand fans in Evanston. During the hotly disputed contest some Northwestern freshmen seated in front of Griffith hollered several times, "Kill the dirty Irish."[63] Notre Dame managed to defeat Northwestern 6–0, but Rockne was infuriated at what he viewed as bad officiating. Meyer Morton, the referee, whom he considered partial to Northwestern, had called Northwestern off-side once when it didn't hurt, Rockne complained, but Northwestern had been off-side just about as often as was Notre Dame. At the end of the game Rockne said to Morton, "It looks to me like a Big Ten suckhole."[64]

On October 25 Rockne wrote to Griffith regarding Morton, who had been assigned to officiate at the Notre Dame–Indiana game on November 6. After Morton's exhibition at Evanston the previous Saturday, Rockne did not think it wise to bring him to South Bend. Morton impressed Rockne as a man who was seeking his own interests rather than the interests of football. In the last ten years, Rockne added, he had never mentioned anything about officials to Griffith, "but Morton is absolutely impossible." Griffith replied that the "combative spirit in our games this fall is keener" than he had ever seen it. He got it all the time from different conference universities. Those who had the "interest of the game at heart would have to hold our students, alumni, and rabid sports writers in check or the Midwest would be comparable to Europe on the eve of the war." Griffith relieved Morton of the assignment to work the Notre Dame–Indiana game and sought to still the animosities. "I have always felt that you have done more than your share in trying to get along with the other fellows even at times when you have had a lot of provocation," he wrote to Rockne, "and I want you to know that I am for you all the way." A few days later, following a conversation they had, Griffith boosted Rockne's spirit by assuring him that the petty annoyances he had were all trivial; he was at the top of the football profession and was recognized throughout the country for his ability and character. Regarding the Morton incident, it might be helpful for Griffith to have a statement from Rockne regarding what happened and what Rockne said to Morton on the field. Thus far we have only his side of it.[65]

A Trustee's Observations

In American higher education, boards of trustees are legally vested with authority over their institutions. They delegate their power to committees, the college president, the faculty, and others. Evidence abounds as to how boards function in their corporate capacity, but few trustees have left accounts of institutional governance. David E. Ross was a trustee of Purdue University for ten years. In 1931 in an address on "Athletics" to the Association of Governing Boards of State Universities and Allied Institutions, Ross had much to say about intercollegiate athletics.

Football was the problem in intercollegiate athletics, Ross said, because it was the great producer of money. The game required a tremendous investment for physical plant and equipment. The modern stadium represented "the most ineffective expenditure of money for practical purposes," and the competitive effort for supremacy required expensive coaches, trainers, and other agencies charged with producing successful teams.[66]

As to the effect of intercollegiate and intramural athletics on the student body, nothing was equal to intercollegiate athletics "for giving character and unity to the spirit of an institution." However, with the migration of students to other campuses to attend games, universities lost the control they had on their own campuses. Coaches were a necessity, but the trained coach brought professionalism. Under no condition should coaches or athletic directors be allowed to arrange the schedules for their teams. They would look to gate receipts, which

David Ross was closely identified with Purdue University as a former student, co-founder of the football stadium, and member of the Purdue Board of Trustees. Source: Purdue University.

professionalizes the contest. University presidents should arrange the schedules, perhaps laying them out for years in a rotating manner.[67]

Admitting that many faculty members viewed interest in athletic contests with alarm and dismay because it deflected students from academic pursuits, Ross said the wise faculty man realizes that the student showing enthusiasm for athletics has his mind diverted by clean, healthful exercise and away from dissipation and vicious tendencies. So on the whole the average faculty member would look upon the athletic situation with favor.[68]

The average alumnus looks with pride on his school's outstanding athletic teams and stadium as the acme of perfection in their alma mater. Rarely, however, have faculties, presidents, and boards of control attempted to interest outstanding alumni in the serious side of the university. To do so would realize a powerful alumni force for the development of the more serious purposes of the university.[69]

Boards of control are responsible for financing intercollegiate athletics, but any board that permitted the financing to be based on the athletic earning ability of a group of adolescents was making a serious mistake. The purpose of college athletics for the undergraduate was not to furnish a spectacle or the commercializing of earning ability in order to pay interest and principle of debts created for the purpose. Gate receipts should be incidental to further sportsmanship and sports as a whole. "We must never forget," Ross added, "that the colleges have a profound influence on the high schools. These schools try to ape the physical investments, coaches, and equipment of the colleges."[70]

The general public unduly emphasizes the advertising value of a winning team. It tends to demand victory whatever the cost. Gambling, ever present, has ruined the sport in the public's estimation. Since we are training college students for citizenship, we must inculcate in them ideas of fairness, sportsmanship, and integrity. The day we surrender to the professional player and his backer begins the disintegration of the athletic contest. Ross recommended two things. First, a material reduction in the price of tickets for football games. Second, a pooling of athletic contest funds within conferences, knowing the difficulties where vast debts on athletic plants were yet to be paid.[71]

Ross was a thoughtful trustee. He deserved to be taken seriously by those concerned with the nation's welfare. But his comments no doubt antagonized coaches, athletic directors, trustees, and Big Ten university presidents. We know that L. W. St. John, the OSU athletic director, labeled the proposal to pool conference athletic funds a wild idea and utterly foolish. That idea, combined with the rotating schedules plan, St. John declared, "border[ed] somewhat on rank communism of a dangerous type."[72]

CHAPTER 10

The True Spirit of the University

By 1925 the Big Ten had decades of experience in intercollegiate athletics. Although committed to amateur athletics, the conference found it difficult to maintain the amateur code. Football brought large gate receipts; few were willing to criticize a game that reputedly built character and united the college crowd. And yet a saving remnant voiced concern about the damaging influence of collegiate athletics on academic values.

Ernest H. Wilkins, dean of the Colleges of Arts, Literature, and Science at the University of Chicago, broached the issue of football reform. A Harvard PhD (1910) and an authority on Italian language and literature, Wilkins joined the Chicago faculty in 1912 and became a dean in 1923. He investigated Stagg's football team when it was winning championships, and in November 1925 he voiced his concern to Max Mason, the president of the university: "Many phases of the football problem have become so acute here," Wilkins wrote, "that we can no longer rightly defer a frank and courageous study of the problem." However, Mason and Harold H. Swift, the president of the board of trustees, were not ready to act. Mason was a former Wisconsin football player, and Swift actively recruited athletes for the Maroon team. Wilkins's memorandum was an indictment of football at Chicago written "from the perspective of what was best for student-players." His survey of the academic grades of the 1923 and 1924 players indicated that either the football men were "mentally of low grade, or that the conditions under which they lived during the football quarter . . . prevent them from doing their work properly." To Wilkins, "the situation call[ed] for drastic and extensive reform, but not the abolition of football." His reform measures, Wilkins warned, were "the only possible means of saving intercollegiate football from abolition which it would incur if allowed to continue in its present course."[1]

Wilkins was the chairman from 1922 to 1926 of a committee of the American Association of University Professors known as the Committee on Methods of Increasing the Intellectual Interest and Raising the Intellectual Standards of Undergraduates. In late 1925 Wilkins delivered an address, "The Relation of Intercollegiate Football to the Purpose of the American College," to the annual convention of the NCAA.[2] The address foreshadowed the AAUP committee report issued in April 1926.[3]

The purpose of the report was to present "an account of football conditions" in American higher education and to suggest means of limitation and control. Following a long bibliography on the subject,[4] the report discussed the advantages and disadvantages of the game for four discrete groups. For the undergraduates, football afforded "absorbing recreation," created a "strong sense of common interest" and a "bond of loyalty," and made for a "clean and interesting topic of conversation" during the football season. The greatest disadvantages were the "over-excitement about football which prevails through the autumn, and the consequent distortion of values that prevails continuously." Such over-excitement led inevitably to the "neglect of college work" and to the time taken for other excesses. "The other major disadvantage," the report noted, was "a distortion in the student mind of the normal scale of the values of college work and of life. The over-excitement lasts through the football season; the distortion of values lasts throughout the college course, if not through life. This distortion is . . . the chief count in a reasoned indictment of football in its present state. . . . [T]he tendency is to exalt football prowess above all other kinds of excellence." Spectacular athletic ability excited admiration. Such "distortion of values" was "greatly increased by newspaper publicity" and "excited interest in football on the part of the alumni and the general public. The enormous financial outlay involved in the maintenance of football creates in the undergraduate mind a false sense of its importance." The result of the distortion of values was that other types of excellence sank in the "relative scale of student estimation," and the "student standard of values" lost touch with the "fundamental purposes of college education." Thus, "the sense of the need for intellectual training and the incentive to win intellectual distinction in college are diminished. . . . [M]any students who might really become leaders in human society fail to attain . . . the development of their potential leadership."[5]

The report continued to line out other disadvantages of football, such as "its tendency to give occasion for drinking, its encouragement of betting, and its provocation of dishonesty." Drinking was "aggravated by over-excitement of any sort, . . . and too often brings to the fraternity house alumni out for . . . rejuvenation with . . . plentiful moistening." Football games led to betting on the part of undergraduates, alumni, and the general public, and "the crudest form of dishonesty in the indirect hiring of athletes—usually by alumni . . . and without the connivance of college authorities." "The football ticket situation" afforded a "temptation to dishonesty," as when students who buy tickets and sign an agreement not to sell them for a higher price yet do sell their tickets.[6]

For the few members of the varsity team, football provided training in discipline and cooperation. The report pointed out that "the character and personal influence of the coach may be . . . the greatest advantage of all. The chief disadvantages of the game for the players were "the same as those for the undergraduate body—over-excitement and the distortion of values." The team members were subjected to the abnormal strain of playing before thousands of wildly excited spectators. "The distortion of values . . . operates in a particularly virulent form with the players themselves; for it tends to establish the conviction that athletic prowess was of primary public significance." As well, "the actual loss of time and energy on the part of football men often resulted in . . . interference with, or complete wreckage of, their college work."[7]

For the faculty, the football situation "seriously impaired" its morale. While football had "recreative advantages" for the faculty as for the students, its chief disadvantage was the "distortion of values caused by the football situation among undergraduates, alumni, and the general public." A "specific source of discontent in some cases" was the employment of nonfaculty coaches at salaries disproportionately higher than professorial salaries, which set the institutional seal of approval on "the predominant importance of football."[8]

As for the alumni, football kept them in touch with a form of college interest, which was beneficial, but all too often the attitude of the alumni to football reflected a distortion of values dating from student days. Alumni were frequently more interested in football than in any other phase of college activity. This distortion of values re-enforced the distortion of values among the student body and led to a misconception of the central purpose of the college. Gifts by alumni conditioned upon an athletic development that might be regarded by the college as excessive were likely to do more harm than good, even though they might be made in the utmost good faith and in a sincere spirit of loyalty.[9]

As for the public, colleges needed and desired the interest of the public, but it was "undesirable and injurious" that this interest "should be primarily athletic." The public, "fed on newspaper publicity," was "likely to fail to understand [the] real purpose and nature of higher education" and likely to fail to give colleges and universities the moral and financial support they deserved.[10]

Having demonstrated that the root of the trouble with intercollegiate football was its "excessive prominence . . . in the range of college and public values," the report went on to explain a means by which to "reduce football to its proper place" in higher education and "avoid the mutual reenforcing of over-excitement and publicity and their many undesirable consequences." One proposal to this end was to limit participation in football to one year for any one player. The effect would lower the standard of play without changing the relative strength of the teams, and it would maintain "the influence of football as a builder of college spirit and the stimulus of alumni enthusiasm." Among the resulting values, "there would be interference with the academic work of a given student but one of four years," and the student body would have "a number of men with varsity experience who could share in the coaching." Alumni or others would "scarcely pay an athlete's expenses in order to give him a chance to play but one season." As well, the "extravagant publicity for individual players" would be minimized, and the "lowered standard of play might reduce the number of college athletes entering professional football."[11]

While insisting that the primary purpose of the American college was "the training of the mind," the report viewed athletics as "subordinate to this purpose" but valuable "because they encourage friendship between colleges and foster unity within institutions." But football had "taken such a hold on undergraduates, alumni, and the public" that it overshadowed academic purpose. This situation could be "largely obviated," the report said, "by the colleges scheduling only four games each season, each game with a team in its own class and in its own vicinity." Such a schedule would "render impossible the choice of mythical national and even sectional championships." Thus the press would give the game less publicity, "the public imagination would not be whetted," and the fever of undergraduate interest would not be raised. The need for spring and early-season training would be eliminated, and the attention to football would be diminished by shortening the season. "Colleges playing teams only in their own class and vicinity would minimize the commercial aspect of schedule making; and no small college teams would be called upon to sacrifice themselves in order to make money for their institutions—as at present. This altruistic motive given for these set-up games, the making of money to support other sports, is in no sense a defense for football." The plan proposed that "graduate coaching systems be instituted, and that no coach be paid a salary beyond that of a professor." The report asserted that adoption of the plan would "improve the general situation," but it did not agree with the proposed graduate coaching system. Instead, it favored a faculty coaching system.[12]

The report declared, "The responsibility for the educational welfare of our college students lies primarily with our faculties," and it recommended the faculty take action in this matter. "Administrative officers on whom pressure in behalf of football is being brought from outside sources would presumably welcome faculty reinforcement. . . . The ideal course of action would be that each group of colleges should, through a joint committee [of teachers and administrators], decide upon a plan to be submitted . . . for adoption to the individual faculties of that group of colleges." The Wilkins committee recommended that "each faculty, after informal conference with its president," request that the president "negotiate with presidents of related institutions for the appointment of such a joint committee. Officers of the local chapters of the AAUP should "take the initiative in arranging for such informal conferences." If the cooperative procedure proposed "did not prove feasible," the committee recommended that "the faculty or faculties concerned should individually adopt the plan of reform."[13]

Wilkins offered a compelling critique of football in American higher education. Griffith responded to it by assembling editorials from around the country that supported his outlook.[14] According to the *Des Moines Register*, "Football is by no means the main business of college, but in attacking the over-emphasis on it there must be regard for the fact that it stands for something other than itself." The *New York Times* declared that the report failed to recognize that football did good things because "it appealed powerfully to the undergraduate's emotional nature." The *Syracuse Standard* noted that football led to a "distortion of values that damaged higher education" and went on to say that the proposal to limit student participation in intercollegiate athletics to one year was "a drastic remedy." The *New York Mirror* ridiculed the report. The professors say that collegiate football leads to dishonesty, neglect of work, and drinking: "Isn't that too bad!"[15]

In 1926 S. V. Sanford, a dean at the University of Georgia, replied to Wilkins in an address to the NCAA convention. Sanford thought it strange that 8 percent of the Wilkins report was devoted to the advantages of football and 92 percent to its disadvantages. Football was not the only thing that caused the college student to be filled with overexcitement or to have a distortion of true values. Abolish football and something worse would take its place. Sanford called on college faculties to have the moral courage to announce an educational policy in matters athletic (which the Wilkins report did). Until American universities reached some uniform agreement (on what, Sanford does not say), a college professor here and there would continue to magnify the evil and minimize the good in intercollegiate football.[16]

The Committee of Sixty

Although conference rules prohibited the recruitment of high school athletes to attend a particular university, many believed that the practice was fairly widespread. Observers accused certain universities and alumni associations of employing illegal methods to induce athletes to enroll in designated institutions, and nearly every year some prep-school athletes confessed that they had entered a named college because they were offered attractive inducements. Some said that they were paid to attend certain schools. The athletic authorities viewed recruiting and inducement as a threat to the integrity of the Big Ten.

The Committee of Sixty, so named because it included six men from each of the ten conference universities, met in January 1927 in Chicago. The presidents who attended were from Chicago, Indiana, Iowa, Michigan, Minnesota, Northwestern, Purdue, and Wisconsin. The president of Ohio State did not attend. Illinois was represented by its provost. The purpose of the meeting was to establish closer harmony between the athletic and academic departments, wrote Walter Eckersall, who characterized the event as "the most pretentious meeting in the history of American intercollegiate athletics."[17] Eckersall was right on target.

James Paige (Minnesota), who chaired the agenda committee, was known for holding inflexible opinions and as a partisan of his university rather than for the welfare of the conference. The committee's report included several items high on his agenda: increasing the number of intraconference football games, adopting a rotating schedule (as opposed to a four years' schedule) of football games, and recruiting, proselyting, and kindred topics.

In a long morning session, the committee agreed on the following: give more men the benefits of intercollegiate competition, correct the evils of undergraduate migration to out-of-town football games, enable coaches to train more coaches, and take the emphasis from a few games and distribute it throughout the season. These proposals were no more than rhetorical flourishes. When President Clarence E. Little (Michigan) moved that anything tending to give more students the benefits of participation in intercollegiate athletics be considered as desirable, he was ruled out of order. Later, he moved that the assembly go on record as favoring greater participation by undergraduates in intercollegiate athletics and as not favoring excessive migration on the part of undergraduates during the football season. His motions carried.[18]

Finally, those present considered "recruiting, proselyting, and kindred topics," presumably the reason for the meeting. Griffith presented a confidential report on recruiting made by the athletic directors. The Committee of Sixty then took up the items in the report seriatim. After some amendments, the delegates adopted them unanimously as follows.

1. Universities were not to award scholarships, loans, or remissions of tuition on the basis of athletic skill.
2. Athletic directors and coaches should not endeavor to recruit athletes actively.
3. Alumni and students should follow the rule of conduct governing financial assistance set forth in number 1 and do all in their power to prevent its violation by others.

James Paige was a professor of law and the Minnesota faculty representative to the Big Ten Conference. He often placed the interest of his university above that of the conference. Source: University of Minnesota Archives, http://umedia.lib.umn.edu/node/957994.

4. Secretaries of alumni associations should refrain from improper recruiting activities.
5. Prospective athletes should not be promised employment in or by the athletic department of a university. After matriculation, athletes might be employed by the athletic department to do necessary work, but they should be paid according to a regular and reasonable scale and should be required to give full service in return.[19]

After adopting the report, the Committee of Sixty concluded their deliberations with several resolutions. One was to print the resolutions on recruiting and send them to officers and alumni of the conference universities with the request that they present to Griffith any information they had as to the violation of the spirit of the resolutions. Another was that everyone who heard rumors or had information regarding illegitimate recruiting should report the same to the commissioner of athletics. (Many would find the line between legitimate and illegitimate recruiting imperceptible.) A third was to recommend to the conference the resolutions passed for enactment by the necessary rules and regulations. The committee also requested that the conference pass legislation to enforce the spirit of the resolutions they had adopted. (How could this be done?) President Edward C. Elliott (Purdue) moved that after September 1 no student should be permitted to participate in intercollegiate contests until he had successfully completed two years of study in the institution. The motion lost 9–1, and the meeting adjourned.[20]

The Committee of Sixty revealed widespread unease over athletic conditions, but it contributed little to remediating matters. Clarence Little introduced an idea that he had announced in his inaugural address as president of the University of Michigan in 1925—namely, to give more students the benefits of participation in collegiate athletics.[21] However, he was ruled out of order. The presidents could not afford to be bold (as Vincent of Minnesota had admitted in his conversation with Stagg). They were beholden to a variety of interests: a state legislature, a board of trustees, an alumni association, athletic directors and coaches, and an army of boosters. J. Frank Lindsey, an Indiana alumnus and a Chicago realtor who was present in Chicago, saw in the meeting an unwillingness of the chiefs to speak truth on proselyting. It would have been better, he said, if spades had been called spades. One or two of the sixty people were willing to submit information that would have been interesting, but there was a rigid reserve toward stirring up matters.[22] The resolutions that advised athletic directors, coaches, students, and alumni to discourage "questionable" or "improper" recruiting activities were vague and pusillanimous.

College presidents and the Committee of Sixty now intimated that intercollegiate football was no longer an amateur sport; it was semi-professional. But they lacked the courage to admit it outright. They were fully aware of the official and unofficial subsidy of athletes. The code they adopted would be toothless.[23]

As the presidents had suggested, the athletic directors drew up Big Ten football schedules for the next four years in three secret meetings, the third of which was held in Chicago when the Committee of Sixty met. The presidents thought that long-time contracts would overcome some of the difficulties of schedule making. The directors believed that the schedule would satisfy most Big Ten fans, and that having it ready four years in advance would promote good will and friendly relations within the conference. The schedule retained old rivalries. Chicago would keep its time-honored matches—Illinois, Purdue, and Wisconsin—for four years. Illinois would continue to play its natural foes—Chicago, Ohio State, and Michigan—and also Purdue. Michigan would meet Illinois and Ohio State annually for the next four years, but Wisconsin only twice. Indiana would continue to meet Purdue and Northwestern. Purdue would meet Indiana and Wisconsin for four years and Northwestern for three years.[24]

The Membership of the Conference

The enlargement of the conference was by no means a dead issue. Notre Dame had applied for admission and had been rebuffed several times, most recently in 1919. In early 1926 Rev. Matthew J. Walsh, the president of Notre Dame, decided to apply again. Membership in a conference known for its reforms would help silence the criticism of Rockne's football program at Notre Dame. Jesse Harper, the Notre Dame coach who had been active in the school's previous applications, suggested a plan for winning approval. As implemented, Rockne made a good-will tour of the conference schools to speak with coaches and athletic directors, and James E. McCarthy, the secretary of the faculty athletic board, visited the faculty representatives. Presumably, McCarthy, the young dean of commerce and a graduate of Columbia University with business experience, could speak their language and possibly overcome prejudices against Catholic higher education. Rockne's tour went well except for Michigan, which was evidently against Notre Dame; Chicago and Illinois were doubtful. McCarthy returned to South Bend believing that Big Ten hostility to and jealousy of Rockne were the principle obstacles to Notre Dame's admission to the conference. Walsh and McCarthy went to Purdue to persuade Moran, the senior faculty representative in the conference, to champion their cause. Walsh's involvement demonstrated the seriousness of Notre Dame. But Chicago and Michigan had lobbied against Notre Dame, so instead of applying in May, Walsh decided on a different strategy.[25]

When the conference met in May, a communication from Notre Dame was read asking the representatives to appoint a committee to investigate Notre Dame's athletic and academic standards with a view to a petition for membership. The faculty committee also heard Dean McCarthy, the secretary of the board in control of athletics at Notre Dame. He replied to various questions. Later, Aigler moved the time-honored formula, "It is the sense of this Conference that it is inadvisable to enlarge the Conference at the present time." The motion carried unanimously.[26] This action came immediately after McCarthy's appearance, with no time for deliberating. Aigler was friendly with Yost, and Yost was hostile to Rockne, which may explain how things fell out.

This rebuff did not end Notre Dame's efforts to join the club. Walsh pleaded Notre Dame's acceptability to the presidents of Michigan and Chicago, known as the principal opponents of Notre Dame's application. They were noncommittal, reluctant to override their athletic directors, Yost and Stagg, who were critics of Rockne and Notre Dame. Perhaps the presidents envied Rock's celebrity status and economic success. Both presidents advised Walsh to submit a formal application for admission when the conference met in December. Rockne "was not optimistic" about the prospects, believing that there was "some political intriguing in the Big Ten we don't understand and possibly could not overcome." There was also intrigue at Notre Dame. McCarthy told important Notre Dame alumni that "Big Ten hostility to Rockne was the main obstacle to conference admission."[27] Rockne's penchant for embarrassing the university by thoughtless statements and actions was preventing Notre Dame from achieving the type of public recognition that would win conference membership. Alumni groups were displeased with McCarthy's arguments. They complained to Walsh that McCarthy considered dropping Rockne from the staff. Dismissing Rockne was unacceptable. He had been too successful as a coach and was too great a national celebrity to be replaced.

During the summer and fall both Rockne and Notre Dame were on their best athletic behavior, trying to strengthen the school's quest for admission at the forthcoming conference session. The faculty athletic board asked Griffith's advice about certain matters of athletic competition for its freshman and varsity reserve squads. Griffith and Rockne collaborated in choosing officials for football games. To Fielding Yost, Rockne's blast against the referee in the 1926 Notre Dame–Northwestern game confirmed his low opinion of Rockne and hardened Michigan's opposition to Notre Dame's bid for membership. Hostility to the admission of Notre Dame appeared in the press, and Notre Dame did not apply for membership.[28]

What explains the rejection of Notre Dame? No doubt opposition to Rockne and his football program weighed heavily in the result. Yost strongly disliked Rockne and was jealous of his accomplishments. Aigler was close to Yost and influential in the conference. Both Yost and Stagg believed that Notre Dame's "requirement for academic good standing and collegiate eligibility was below Western Conference standards."[29] In 1923, after a Notre Dame–Iowa football game, which Iowa won, Iowa president Walter A. Jessup had declared that "from an advertising standpoint a win over Notre Dame meant more to the University of Iowa than defeating any other team on its schedule," but "from the perspective of the quality of the football played, winning or losing meant absolutely nothing ... because Notre Dame players were not required to pass their examinations or have any certain number of credits to be able to play and that [athletes] could stay on and play five or six years. In order to play on the first team, Iowa players had to earn many more credits than was required at Notre Dame."[30]

Notre Dame was a national Catholic football school with a tradition and a reputation. It attracted the best athletes from Catholic schools around the country and was formidable on the gridiron. Did religious identity or religious prejudice shape the outcome of the application? Rockne interpreted the rejection of Notre Dame as a triumph for Yost's religious prejudices. He described Yost as "a hillbilly from Tennessee and hence very narrow in religion."[31] All of the conference universities were public institutions except Chicago, which had Baptist roots, and Northwestern, which had Methodist ties. We know little about the religious affiliation of the faculty representatives in the conference, but we do know the intellectual and cultural climate that shaped them. America was historically a Protestant nation. The influx of Roman Catholics beginning in the 1840s consisted largely of European peasant and working-class stock, and the Vatican's suppression of modernism in 1908 had had a chilling effect upon both research and speculative thought among Catholics. In fact, American Catholics had failed "to pursue intellectual activity and achieve distinction in scholarship and science."

Notre Dame lacked a doctoral program and was not of the academic caliber of the conference universities. George Shuster, a Catholic layman and briefly the head of the Notre Dame English department, described the problem of Roman Catholicism in America in two articles—"Have We Any Scholars?" published in the Jesuit weekly *America* on August 13, 1925, and "Insulated Catholics," published in *Commonweal* on August 19, 1925.[32] Years passed before American Catholic intellectuals organized to improve their situation, as Patrick J. Hayes described in *A Catholic Brain Trust: The History of the Catholic Commission on Intellectual and Cultural Affairs, 1945–1965*.[33] We cannot be certain what the faculty representatives thought about the Notre Dame application, but it would be rash to assign a religious prejudice of anti-Catholicism alone to their action.

Football Receipts

During the 1920s, college football attracted more and more fans and brought in larger and larger gate receipts. The record for each of the conference universities from 1923 to 1929 and the total for each conference university in these years is shown in table 10.1.[34]

As the data show, the rising tide did not lift conference boats equally. Receipts were a product of such things as location, rotating schedules, win and loss records, a coach's reputation, and an athlete's fame. The total for all Big Ten universities from 1923 through 1929 was $20,817,106. Michigan, with $563,062.08 in 1927, had the largest receipts of all the conference universities in the years under review. By way of comparison, in 1928 Notre Dame had $723,692 in gate receipts and a profit of $500,000.[35]

Alumni Associations and Recruiting

The belief that individual alumni and alumni associations were recruiters was pervasive. In April 1927 the Big Ten Alumni Committee met in Chicago to discuss ways for more effective alumni cooperation with conference regulations affecting athletic recruiting and proselyting and to make helpful suggestions. All ten conference members were represented.

To promote more effective regulation of illegitimate recruiting and proselyting, the alumni committee offered to the faculty representatives, through the conference presidents, certain regulations that they believed would receive the official endorsement of the alumni organizations. To save sports from harmful attacks from public and educational investigating bodies, the committee made a number of recommendations that were embodied in a report written by J. Frank Lindsey of Indiana. An enthusiast of Indiana sports, Lindsey's recommendations were as follows: First, the alumni group agreed with the report of the Committee of Sixty

Table 10.1. Football Receipts of the Conference Universities, 1923–1929

University	1923	1924	1925	1926	1927	1928	1929
Chicago	$248,367.13	$233,577.97	$345,001.49	$393,661.43	$389,661.17	$328,381.91	$159,092.12
Illinois	182,508.31	227,367.03	348,030.16	266,337.22	321,632.60	327,353,04	351,544.61
Indiana	35,086.99	61,499.30	44,262.05	67,508.25	103,996.35	114,075.80	129,095.70
Iowa	95,640.89	139,839.59	168,252.08	153,360.53	136,689.85	185,555.74	217,459.45
Michigan	194,193.04	333,507.02	372,484.88	338,907.94	563,062.08	421,979.77	508,756.30
Minnesota	128,986.75	160,886.28	220,346.07	252,320.50	315,031.95	247,680.50	266,717.50
Northwestern	74,141.48	109,494.88	120,851.00	192,653.04	248,173.49	292,919.84	306,289.00
Ohio State	190,416.35	186,010.11	266,246.34	251,237.42	373,355.11	324,063.46	374,109.54
Purdue	47,713.26	65,607.01	65,863.58	108,278.51	108,141.57	128,897.71	124,680.70
Wisconsin	123,266.91	170,508,26	135,089.40	204,878.49	217,886.20	242,972.33	272,869.58
Total	1,320,821.11	1,688,292.45	2,080,367.03	2,229,143.33	2,777,600.37	2,663,880.10	2,710,614.97

on recruiting and aid to athletes with an amendment that said: "Faculty directors should examine into the source of funds of each athlete in considerable detail to make sure that the athlete understands thoroughly the import of amateur rules." Second, believing that many matters relating to recruiting and proselyting were "grossly misunderstood," the alumni recommended that coaches and athletic directors refrain from attending interscholastic tournaments for the purpose of establishing contacts with "athletic material." Third, to relieve the pressure put on coaches and alumni engaged in proselyting activities, the committee thought it was vital to carry out a miscellaneous regulation passed by the conference in 1906 that said, "Steps shall be taken to reduce the receipts and expenses of athletic contests." Fourth, members of the Western Conference should refrain from employing coaches from other conference schools without first obtaining permission to negotiate from the employers of such coaches. Fifth, prominent athletes should not accept pay for writing on subjects dealing with athletics. Sixth, athletes should not lend their names for a consideration in any form of commercial advertising. Seventh, the committee agreed, individually and severally, to use their influence through word of mouth, alumni papers, and other news mediums in furthering within their respective alumni the "Big Ten Alumni Code of Honor." The code celebrated the excellence in amateur athletics in the Big Ten. The signers would look with disfavor upon anyone who, from "a lust for victory," loaned or gave money to conference athletes on the basis of athletic skill, thereby jeopardizing the athlete's amateur standing.[36]

Lindsey sent Griffith a copy of the letter he had written to the conference presidents. Griffith found it interesting to note that Lindsey suggested in his letter that the alumni were the chief source of evil in recruiting, and that the purpose of the meeting had been to get the alumni to cooperate to eliminate recruiting. At their meeting, however, the alumni apparently felt that the coaches and the athletic directors were to blame for all the ills in athletics; therefore, they recommended legislation affecting the game or the men who administer it. Griffith was very disappointed. He had hoped that the alumni would initiate some movement that would result in "the alumni playing the game with us." Instead, they proposed to go over the heads of the athletic men to the presidents and to suggest the presidents see that the directors and coaches are "hedged in with more legislation."[37] Replying directly to Lindsey, Griffith took issue with him at great length. He was not trying to find fault but was stating some thoughts that Lindsey's recommendations provoked.[38]

Reed Harris had observed American higher education from his years on the college newspaper at Columbia University. In 1932 he published a book on how football vulgarized the American colleges. The book included a chapter titled "50,000 Alumni Can Be Wrong."[39]

CHAPTER 11

The Carnegie Report

Andrew Carnegie established the Carnegie Foundation for the Advancement of Teaching in 1905. Henry S. Pritchett, the foundation's president, made it a valuable agency for the improvement of American education. Pritchett cared for sports pursued for fun, and as president of the Massachusetts Institute for Technology he had impressed his views on sportsmanship on an institution of higher learning. He was struck by the exaggerated importance attached to sports in the American college, especially football, and under his direction the foundation published a series of studies of athletics.[1]

In 1925 Pritchett observed that "mass athletics" was costly. It was the reason football "must be a paying venture." The desire to win at all costs was deeply rooted in American sports culture. "Athletic sports and games can be made a beneficent force in American education," Pritchett wrote, "but not by continuing their commercialization or by permitting them longer to retain their pre-eminence in our distorted scale of academic values." Faculties should "consist of specialists in scholarship and education, not in the financing of athletics." "The panacea of 'faculty control of athletics,'" he wrote, was not the "remedy that some had supposed it to be." The wisdom of giving alumni large control in the matter was "dubious." The townsman who profited from a winning season was becoming a "sinister figure." It should be possible, he said, to awaken students, faculty, and alumni to their athletic responsibilities. For this "the initiative must rest with the . . . college or university president." The president must strive mightily over years to accomplish in athletics results that might have been achieved quickly "thirty or even ten years ago." In this respect the college president "has been a leader who has not led."[2]

Pritchett wanted the subject studied more. In January 1926, in compliance with a request from the NCAA and others, the foundation authorized an investigation of school, college, and university athletics in the United States and Canada. Pritchett chose Howard J. Savage, a staff member, to conduct the study. Savage, an alumnus of Tufts University with a Harvard PhD in literature, had taught at Bryn Mawr College. His assistants were Harold W. Bentley, an instructor at Columbia University; John T. McGovern, and Dean F. Smiley, a Cornell MD. The staff identified topics of inquiry and visited 130 schools, colleges, and universities to investigate athletic conditions. The results of their work appear in bulletin 23 of *American College Athletics* (1929).[3]

In the preface, Pritchett noted the unique character of American higher education. What relation did athletics have to a university, and how did students find the time and money to support such a costly activity? The Carnegie inquiry answered those questions in two ways. First, in the United States the university was an "intellectual agency," but also "a social, commercial, and athletic agency." These activities, Pritchett wrote, "overshadowed the intellectual life for which the university is assumed to exist." Second, football was no longer a student's game but a highly commercialized enterprise. The process by which football was transformed into a professional enterprise was inseparable from the transformation of the American college into the American university, which was not merely an agency for training students to think but a place where young people could acquire elementary vocational skills. How far could an intellectual agency go in the development of other causes without danger to its primary purpose? Noting that the game of football spurred the growth of professionalism in college games, Pritchett described the unfavorable results that followed. He deplored the fact that American newspapers used the college athlete for publicity purposes. The weakness of the American university was its "lack of intellectual sincerity."[4] The development in the colleges of commercialized sports resulted from "the tendencies of the time, the growing luxury, the keen inter-collegiate competition, the influence of well-meaning, but unwise, alumni, the acquiescence in newspaper publicity, the reluctance of the authorities of the university or the college to take an unpopular stand." The responsibility and the authority for correcting the situation lay with the president and the faculty.[5]

The Carnegie Report describes the growth of college athletics, the development of amateurism, and the Western Conference in national perspective. As for faculty control, "although the regulations of the Intercollegiate Conference stipulate for complete faculty control and provide for an operating body of faculty representatives, the actual control often appears to rest with the directors or the coaches."[6] The regulation of athletics must rest with faculty members. "One or two universities (Iowa, Minnesota) fix such authority in their presidents; in final decisions and in the execution of policies little regard appears to be paid to representatives of the faculty."[7]

About 63 percent of undergraduates in the institutions studied take part in athletics regularly or intermittently, the report notes, most of them in intramural athletics, while in intercollegiate competition football includes from 5 to 6 percent of registrants. As for the coaching school and an intensive, year-round study of football, the report noted that "it is doubtful if in any other department of the American college curriculum a single subject receives more thoroughgoing attention. . . . The ethical aspects of using on supposedly amateur college teams men who are essentially professional in their attitude toward the game, not to mention men who, however 'legitimately,' receive university scholarships for studying football as a part of the college curriculum, do not appear to have been seriously scrutinized."[8] The investigators made no attempt to measure "the moral qualities participation in college athletics is widely supposed to engender—courage, obedience, unselfishness, persistence, and the rest," but their study of the recruiting and subsidizing of college athletes "affords much direct evidence that college athletics can breed, and in fact, have bred, among athletes, coaches, directors, and even in some instances among college administrative officers, equivocation and dishonesty, which actual participation has not removed or prevented. The impairment of moral stamina that such practices imply is the darkest blot upon American college athletics."[9] As for the academic achievement of athletes as compared to non-athletes, "on the one hand, we have youths well endowed physically and mentally who should outdistance their fellows in the race of life; on the other, we find no evidence that the best places in this race have been won by these men, whose tastes and training have led them into intercollegiate athletics."[10]

As for the college athletics coach, the report identifies Northwestern as a school where the coach owed his job to alumni groups. In an ideal university, the report asserts, "professional coaching would find no place."[11]

In America, the college looks to its alumni as a source of funds, and the alumni who manifest interest in their university are likely to be passionately interested in athletics, particularly football. Some alumni devote themselves to recruiting and subsidizing college athletes. In describing forty-two voluntary regional intercollegiate athletic associations, Savage writes that "one or two, notably the Intercollegiate Conference [Big Ten], have gone further than others in engaging a commissioner and a paid executive staff."[12]

The investigators amassed considerable data on the recruiting and subsidizing of athletes. These evils, they assert, had diminished over the previous two decades but were still going on. The Intercollegiate Conference, "regarded by many as the most thoroughly controlled of all conference bodies,"[13] repeatedly called recruiting and subsidizing its most serious problem. The varieties of recruiting ranged from "rare and casual contacts" made by an individual to an intensively organized system. Michigan, Northwestern, and Wisconsin were examples.[14] Professional recruiting usually involved head coaches, members of the athletic staff, the alumni secretary, or academic appointees. Some evidence led to the conclusion that at a few institutions, including Michigan, Ohio State, Purdue, and Wisconsin, coaches, managers, athletes, and even university officials combined in a "broad but intensive approach to . . . schoolboy athletes."[15] Recruiting was conducted by alumni at only about one-third of the schools visited. In some cases alumni had practically forced fraternities to entertain prospective athletes. The alumni athletic committee of Purdue invited all alumni to contribute $25 from each local group and $10 a year from individuals to dispense hospitality and employ a field secretary. "It was once the custom of an individual alumnus to operate a kind of recruiting excursion—several special Pullman cars hired at his own expense to take athletes from the city of his residence to the campus of his university (Indiana)."[16] Fraternity chapters competed to support athletic stars hoping to shed luster on the house. As examples the report cites Purdue and Wisconsin. Subsidizing was found to exist at eighty-one of the 112 institutions studied. At twenty-eight institutions, including Chicago and Illinois, the inquiry found no evidence that athletes were subsidized by any group or individual. However, alumni, businessmen, and others frequently aided athletes at the other Big Ten schools—Michigan, Minnesota, Northwestern, Purdue, Ohio State, Wisconsin (often), and Iowa (on occasion). At Northwestern there were sixteen beneficiaries of an alumni "slush fund."[17]

In America, newspapers stimulate and then feed an appetite for sports, magnifying the importance of the college athlete and college athletics.[18] In sports writing, sensationalism almost always originated in a deliberate appeal to the less intelligent reader. Accounts of college football suffered most from the use of battlefield terms. "The corruption of the vocabulary of many sports reporters . . . is one of the most astonishing results of sensational journalism."[19]

The report indicted eight Big Ten institutions for infractions of conference rules, especially the recruitment and subsidizing of athletes. It gave Chicago and Illinois a pass, though Stagg was a zealous recruiter. In closing, the report weighed the good versus the bad in collegiate athletics. Among the former were the salutary physical effects upon the nation and their socializing influences in school and after. Among the latter were the widespread belief among alumni that the value of an institution depended on successful athletic teams, the evil effects of recruiting and subsidizing, commercialization of collegiate athletics, the "lack of intellectual challenge to the young and alert mind," and the failure of athletics to contribute appreciably to morals and conduct.

The report does not view the athletic situation as hopeless. The prime needs of American college athletics were twofold. First, a change of values: diminish commercialism and esteem college sport for the opportunities it offers to "exercise the body and mind and to foster habits of bodily health and character." Second, "challenge the best intellectual capabilities of the undergraduate." The "granting of opportunity for the fulfillment of intellectual promise need not impair the socializing qualities of college sport."[20]

The Carnegie Report was published on October 23, 1929. It aroused a storm of controversy. On October 24 the *New York Times* ran a page-one headline, "College Sports Tainted by Bounties, Carnegie Finds in Wide Study." A survey of 130 schools showed that one in seven athletes was subsidized. The *Chicago Tribune* published six articles under catchy headlines. One was "Carnegie Report Hits 8 Big Ten Schools; Griffith Calls Carnegie Report Unfair to Big 10 Cites Condemnation of Wisconsin, Minnesota." Another, "Excerpts from Carnegie Report," described charges against Big Ten schools in subsidizing and recruiting by alumni officers. Still another declared that "N.U. and Michigan Deny 'Unethical Sports' Charges; Other Big Ten Schools Add Refutations."[21] A day later, under the headline "Carnegie Probe Seems to Be a Waste of Time," Westbrook Pegler wrote that the report described conditions that had long been taken for granted. Pegler had a penchant for telling the truth.[22]

Some Big Ten worthies found nothing good in the report. Griffith responded in the *Athletic Journal* in November 1929. The report was based on the British and European idea that the university is an intellectual agency, he charged, rather than the American idea that the university is a socializing agency. If the sole purpose of the university is developing scholarship and teaching men and women to think, it may be that intercollegiate contests have no place in the educational scheme. But if the American university is a socializing agency, it is difficult to understand how athletic contests, spectacles, and pageants might not have a place in the life of the educational institution. Much that the report said regarding recruiting and subsidizing was true, but since it was impossible for the investigators in limited time to learn the true conditions on these practices, much fault would be found in the report. Certain universities were trying to eliminate from their teams men who had been illegitimately recruited or subsidized. There was no reason to believe that college athletics were tottering on their foundation. Athletics had been showing steady improvement in recent years, and in years to come college athletics would have a more secure place in the educational scheme and a firmer place in the minds of the American people.[23]

Griffith's comments reveal his prejudices and priorities. His view of American higher education is flawed. From colonial days to about 1820, the American college drew on an English model. Then a reform movement designed to make the colleges more practical and more democratic in content and constituency began. It gathered force in the 1840s and culminated in the Morrill Land-Grant Act in 1862. In the late nineteenth century the university replaced the college as the paradigm of higher education, and the American university drew on the German model of a university devoted to research. Both the college and the university aimed at the intellectual and moral development of students. Socializing was incidental

November 9, 1929: with Army on their own 15-yard line, Arnie Wolgast, Illinois right end, intercepted a pass and raced 85 yards for a touchdown, giving Illinois the victory, 17–7. Source: University of Illinois Archives *Illio* '32, p. 215, tif 7554.

to higher education. Moreover, Griffith, an incorrigible booster, declares that intercollegiate athletics are getting better and better when he knows that the Big Ten confronts corruption within its own ranks.[24]

The NCAA held its annual convention in New York in early January 1930. The athletic directors of seven conference universities, Griffith, and Long (Northwestern) were present. [25] Howard J. Savage began his convention address by asking whether bulletin 23 was a "constructive report." His remarks were a response to Griffith that never mentioned him by name. In his report Savage had tried to show that in every institution studied athletics were worth bettering. "Constructive reports" are often whitewashing. True leaders welcome efforts to improve our educational structure, whereas the educational demagogue welcomes the whitewashing document. The bulletin did not state all the disagreeable facts substantiated by the investigators. They had not been apprised of any inaccuracy in the study as printed. Savage also discussed the question of responsibility for the conduct of college athletics. Once a legislative body vested corporate powers in a board of trustees, the trustees are on their own. They delegate their powers. The ultimate legal responsibilities for college athletics devolve upon the trustees, but the immediate responsibility rests with the president and the faculty. The quality of sport at an institution of higher education reflects the interest of the presiding officer—that is, a concern with the relations of the inherent values of college sport to the function of the college or university. There is confusion over the relation of college sport to what some refer to as "educational democracy." More than one writer asserts that to eliminate athletic subsidies would be disastrous to those democratic qualities of American education that are dear to us. This attitude is used to justify the pursuit of college athletics for gain by young men who should devote their major efforts to training their intellectual faculties. The term "educational democracy" is a catchword of the educational demagogue. The truth is that the recruiting and subsidizing of athletes is unworthy of an institution of higher learning. In closing, Savage declared that the defense of the intellectual integrity of the American college lies with its president and faculty, and with them also rests the authority of both its present and its future.[26]

In an address to Delta Theta Epsilon (an honorary athletic coaching fraternity) in Urbana, Illinois, in mid-January, Harry Kipke, the Michigan football coach, said there was "no need to worry about the future of athletics." "All the attacks of all the learned professors in the country can't check the popularity of football." Kipke portrayed the Western Conference as "the cleanest collegiate athletic group to be found anywhere." The Carnegie Report, he added, "was concerned with abuses which were two and three years old, . . . and which had for the most part been cleaned up."[27]

In mid-January the Carnegie Foundation published a bulletin that surveyed the literature of American school and college athletics. In a foreword, Pritchett noted certain contrasts between the theory and the practice of college athletics. Faculty control of college athletics was a favorite formula for "athletic righteousness." As a "panacea for the ills of college sport," it was widely adopted. But in fact some institutions that had "most completely adopted the doctrine of faculty control" had been doing the most to "impair the status of the amateur, the foundation of true sportsmanship." "Many of the advantages claimed for present-day sport," Pritchett added, "represent the desires and hopes of the proponents rather than demonstrated results."[28]

Days later, Aigler (Michigan) charged that the Carnegie Report was "wild, disappointing and disheartening," was "almost vicious." The investigator had employed the methods of the prosecutor rather than those of an impartial investigator searching for the truth. It seemed as if the investigator was writing muckraking articles on which to hang serious charges. Savage had "no intention of being fair and accurate." Moreover, the report reflected an Eastern bias.[29] Aigler's tirade did little credit to the judgment of a law professor. In fact, it revealed him as unable to see clearly the situation in the Big Ten.

Returning to the matter in April 1930, Griffith said that Savage did not present a true report because he dealt almost entirely with the defects of college athletics and devoted little space to the merits. Moreover, Pritchett judged American higher education by British and German standards, and his conclusions regarding athletics were not based on the findings of the investigators.[30]

Griffith viewed with apprehension an attempt to cast intercollegiate athletics into a common mold. "If we are to develop incentive, originality, and responsibility in this country," he said, "our people should not be subjected to the dictates of those men, no matter how worthy their motives may be, who in the last analysis impose their will on others."[31]

The subject of college athletics haunted Pritchett in retirement. "One of the worst features of American football," he wrote in 1934, was "the fact that the players were

Ralph W. Aigler served for many years as the Michigan faculty representative to the Big Ten Conference. In this capacity he made valuable contributions to the conference, but he zealously defended Michigan's interests. Source: University of Michigan, Bentley Historical Library.

put under the supervision of a trainer who was not, as a rule, a cultivated man, but who had such chances to influence them and mold their character as no professor can expect to have." Two years later Pritchett wondered "whether college games had been so saturated with the professional spirit that they could not be rescued from their present low state." He would like to see a "moratorium declared on football by all the better American colleges for a few years, during which the game might be got back into the hands of boys to be played for pleasure. . . . I believe there is no greater obligation today on college presidents than to reform the situation."[32]

The Carnegie Report delineated the state of intercollegiate athletics in the 1920s. Some colleges admitted that the charges were well founded, but in identifying the evils the report was like a pin prick on the hide of an elephant. The Flexner Report on medical education had stimulated the reform of medical education in America. The Savage Report made no similar impact. Years later many felt that the college athletic situation was worse than ever. In November 1936 the National Association of State Universities unanimously asked the Carnegie Foundation to "undertake a supplementary study of intercollegiate athletics." When the matter was put to the executive committee of the foundation, the meeting turned "into a sort of confessional for the college presidents," a number of whom were in attendance. "The college presidents made it plain that the thing is too big for them," noted Frank Vanderlip, treasurer of the Carnegie Foundation's board.[33] Pritchett had imposed on college presidents an obligation to reform the situation, but the presidents showed no willingness to accept the obligation.

CHAPTER 12

The Big Ten Censures Iowa

College football became enormously popular during the 1920s, and the career of Red Grange riveted attention on the Big Ten. Commissioner Griffith admitted to problems in conference athletics, but he was a booster, and people loved boosters. At the same time, a saving remnant called attention to the need to reconcile football with higher education. They went unheard. This was the context in which dramatic events in the conference played out.

On May 25, 1929, the Big Ten severed athletic relations with the University of Iowa, its most drastic action yet taken. The severance was epochal in Midwestern athletics because it imputed bad faith, double dealing, and athletic dishonesty to the highest educational institution of a great state whose citizens naturally look to that institution for good faith, square dealing, and high ideals.[1]

The conference acted because the faculty representatives had instructed the athletic directors to arrange football schedules in advance, and a committee (Huff, Stagg, and Griffith) had reported on the difficulty of making a four-year schedule "because of the growing practice of recruiting and proselyting and the belief was expressed that the time had come for drastic action." In the following discussion, Huff asked where the authority lay to enforce a general regulation that said, "Members of the Conference shall sever athletic relations with any member that does not conform in full to the Conference rules." Griffith had evidence that three conference institutions had violated conference rules and regulations; the evidence seemed conclusive against Iowa. Stagg urged action. Griffith observed that all the information in his office on violation of conference regulations was at the disposal of the conference.[2]

Amos Alonzo Stagg, cen-
ter, with Walter S. Kennedy
(left), 1898 football team captain, and John J. Kelly (right)
1929 team captain, at the
Chicago-Wisconsin game,
November 9, 1929. Source:
University of Chicago, Special Collections Research
Center.

After the directors withdrew, the faculty representatives appointed a committee headed by Paige (Minnesota) to receive the report of the athletic directors. Then Huff, Stagg, and Griffith placed before them the evidence they had
collected indicating a violation of conference rules by Iowa. After "most careful
consideration" the committee declared that Iowa had violated the rule that said,
"No scholarships, loans, or remissions of tuition shall be awarded on the basis
of athletic skill, and no financial aid shall be given to students by individuals or
organizations, alumni or otherwise, with the purpose of subsidizing them as
athletes or of promoting the athletic success of a particular University,"[3] as well
as a general regulation that defined the legitimate expenses for various purposes
that athletic associations might incur.[4] Accordingly, the committee recommended
that the conference sever athletic relations with the University of Iowa, effective
January 1, 1930. The ruling would not interfere with the 1929 football season, the
schedule for which was already fixed.[5]

The act of censure shed light not only on perfidious Iowa but also on other
conference members. The imposition of the penalty was the culmination of a
long chain of events in and beyond Iowa City. To understand what happened, we
must review the developments that led to the crisis at Iowa and in the Western
Conference.

In 1929 Walter A. Jessup was the president of the university. He wielded the
reins with an ever-vigilant eye on the legislature and maintained tight control
over the administration as he oversaw a period of unprecedented growth in the

institution. He expected his faculty to cede the running of the university to him. The university had long endorsed the principle of faculty control of athletic programs, but as the historian Stow Persons noted, so-called faculty control "simply demonstrated that university faculties acquiesced in practices of recruitment, certification, subsidization, and intensive training which set the athletes in the major sports apart from the student body and resulted in the elaboration of athletic programs grotesquely at odds with the ostensible purposes of the universities." The athletic council, a standing board of the university senate, was appointed by the president and given governing powers over the athletic program. In 1923, with a view to incorporating athletics within the academic structure of the university, Jessup proposed "to create a Division of Physical Education which would include the department of men's and women's physical education and the department of intercollegiate athletics. The coaches of the major sports would hold faculty appointments." Howard Jones, the athletic director and football coach since 1917, "objected strenuously to these arrangements."[6]

Troubles with Jones revealed problems in the Iowa athletic structure. Jones had been a football star at Yale from 1905 to 1907, and had coached at Syracuse, Yale, Ohio State, and Yale again before going into business. In 1917 he became the coach at Iowa.[7] He was highly successful, winning the Big Ten championship in 1921 and tying with Michigan for the same in 1922. Early in 1923 Byron Lambert, the faculty representative, wrote to Jessup about a "little unpleasantness" at a meeting of the athletic board that Lambert chaired. Among other things, Jones had charged Lambert with not working in harmony with him or his office. The whole thing was a surprise to Lambert, but since Jones felt as he did, Lambert thought it his duty to step aside. From certain things Jones said, Lambert felt that Jones held him personally responsible for the board's desire to combine the departments of athletics and physical education under a man other than Jones. The situation was delicate, but it could be relieved by allowing Lambert to resign from the board and appoint another member as chair.[8] Lambert continued to consider the suggestion that the board in control of athletics be placed over the Department of Physical Education, but he doubted the wisdom of such a move. It would increase the complexity of the work of the board and might involve it in problems beyond the scope of a senate committee. This would be especially the case unless someone was placed in charge of the whole work as professor of athletics and physical education. Lambert thought that they should first secure that person and then consider the advisory duties of the board with regard to physical education. Iowa should get an outstanding man in charge of all the work of athletics and physical education.[9]

Early in January 1924 Jones was ready to resign as coach and athletic director for personal and professional reasons, but Jessup and the athletic board were eager to retain him. Jones wanted a new contract with very favorable terms, but on

January 12, before the negotiations concluded, Jones accepted an offer to coach at Trinity College, later Duke University.[10] With Jones's departure likely, Lambert wrote to Jessup on January 11, 1924, that the departure would help the Iowa athletic situation. It was becoming evident that some radical reorganization would be necessary before athletics in general would be on the same plane as at some other conference schools. Lambert's dealing with faculty representatives in conference meetings and in visits to conference schools caused him to worry whether Iowa was living up to its possibilities. Lambert had tried to outline an organization capable of doing work as great or greater than, say, Illinois or Michigan, but he could not see where Jones would fit in except as a football coach, and Jones did not wish to give up as athletic director. "We all of course deeply deplore his going," Lambert added, "and especially under the circumstances that have arisen, but . . . we are now able to go ahead on plans that will greatly enlarge our possibilities for a great broadening of athletic activities, and a strengthening rather than a weakening in all departments."[11]

On January 15 Lambert informed Jones that he had asked President Jessup to release him at once from the board in control of athletics, and Jessup assented. Lambert wrote to Jones without delay about his request, since it would no doubt influence Jones's decision to remain at Iowa. The statement Jones gave to the press led people to believe that change of climate and part-time work were the reasons Jones decided to leave. "But today your friends are telling me that my presence on the Board has been given as the real reason that you cannot keep your contract with the University." Lambert added that since he had first tendered his resignation and was then influenced to remain "by the seemingly earnest expressions of yourself and the other members of the Board, I can only say that now it is really a pleasure to give way to your wishes. I trust that your reputation for fairness, honesty, and good sportsmanship will not be questioned and that nothing now stands in the way of your fulfillment of your contract."[12]

Lambert reported quite general agreement among Jones's best friends at Iowa that he had a one-track mind; his interests were to an extreme extent only in football. He was not an administrator, but until recently he would not listen to any suggestion that he give up this part of his duties.[13] (Jones was at Duke one year, and from 1925 to 1940, as coach at the University of Southern California, his teams won five victories in the Rose Bowl.)

Paul Belting at Iowa

In 1924 President Jessup appointed Paul E. Belting as director of physical education and chair of the athletic council. With this appointment Jessup looked forward to an improvement in Iowa's athletic status in the Big Ten. Belting, a varsity football player at Illinois in 1910 and 1911, had been the principal in three

Paul Belting, a former varsity football player at Illinois, became the athletic director at Iowa in 1924. Soon thereafter alumni boosters, convinced that he did not sufficiently support their interests, demanded his removal, and Belting was forced to resign. Source: University of Iowa Archives.

different high schools and had earned an AM (1918) and a PhD (1919) at Columbia University before becoming a professor of physical education at Illinois. Jessup placed full responsibility for intercollegiate athletics and physical education in Belting's hands, and he notified the faculty committee that its function would now be advisory and that it would be known as the athletic council. This appointment incensed the board, leaving its members in doubt about their responsibilities and concerned about faculty control of athletics.[14]

With Jones's resignation, Iowa needed another football coach, one with a reputation. Hawkeye officials sought Knute Rockne's advice about a good replacement. Although he was noncommittal, Rockne always felt that he was underpaid and was amenable to offers. Iowa officials quietly approached him.[15] Because he had reached an impasse with Notre Dame, he told the Iowa people that with the right offer, he was available. Rockne visited Iowa City on March 10–12 to meet with the board in control of athletics. Later, Belting met Rockne in Chicago. Rockne said he would accept an offer. The result was a written agreement for Rockne to become head coach at Iowa on the right terms, provided the matter received no publicity, which might prompt a counter offer from Notre Dame. A South Bend newspaper learned on March 20 that Rockne said he would accept an Iowa offer, and on March 23 the *Chicago Tribune* startled readers with an article under the headline "Events Point to Rockne as Iowa Coach in 1925."[16] Iowa authorities had visited Rockne in South

Bend and the deal was in effect closed. Rockne, it was known, would like to break into the conference, and Iowa had plenty of excellent gridiron material.[17]

The arrangement never materialized. Archival documents at Notre Dame suggest that Rockne used the Iowa offer as leverage in his power struggle at Notre Dame. A. D. McDonald, a Notre Dame alumnus who led a campaign to keep Rockne at Notre Dame, persuaded the administrators to consider Rockne's "reasonable requests." As a result, on March 25 the president of Notre Dame signed Rockne to a contract to employ him for ten academic years of ten months a year at an annual salary of $10,000. Rockne then announced to the press that the Iowa offer was a "rumor" that misled people to believe that he thought of going to another school next fall.[18]

Failing to attract Rockne, Belting appointed Burton Ingwersen, a former football player at the University of Illinois, as the new football coach. With the approval of the State Board of Education, Belting vigorously developed the physical facilities for the athletic program, building a field house and a stadium. The stadium was dedicated in the fall of 1929. Nevertheless, the coaches and the alumni boosters bitterly criticized Belting as not sufficiently supportive of their interests and charging that he had "a singular flair for antagonizing people." Belting became the target of widespread criticism and there was no compensating athletic success to neutralize the vituperative resentment that came from all over the state demanding his removal. Jessup seemed deaf to the criticisms of Belting.[19]

In December 1927 Griffith wrote to Jessup about football matters at Iowa. "Some Iowa alumni" had told Griffith that certain newspapers and Iowa alumni thought that Ingwersen was not competent to coach the football team, and they had started a movement to oust him. Others believed that Ingwersen was a good football coach, but that Belting and Walter R. Fieseler (the medical supervisor in the Division of Physical Education) had interfered with him to the extent that he had been unable to produce the desired results. They were trying to force Belting to resign. Griffith replied to these critics that consideration for individuals should be eliminated. His chief consideration was for the University of Iowa. He was concerned "lest a few sports writers and certain emotional and hysterical alumni and a few disappointed gamblers should make enough disturbance to affect the smooth running of Iowa's athletics." Most alumni, Griffith declared, were not qualified to select an efficient football coach and were more to blame for the situation at the university than the men at the head of athletics. In the early 1920s, Griffith knew, Iowa alumni had raised a sum of money that was used in getting athletes, that Aubrey Devine and other football heroes were employed to travel about the state soliciting athletic funds, and that the money was used illegitimately. Belting and Ingwersen had refused to permit this practice. They were now paying the penalty. Griffith sent Belting a copy of his letter.[20]

In January 1928 Griffith informed Belting that five men, whom he named, were making efforts to gain control of Iowa's athletics. One of them wanted to know if there was a conference rule "against having alumni representatives on the Conference university boards of control." A conference rule, Griffith replied, provided that no conference institution could belong to the conference unless the faculty had full and complete control. Griffith rejoiced that Jessup had "resisted the efforts of these meddlers" and had served notice that he administers the affairs of university "and will not turn the control of athletics over to them." As events would prove, Griffith was badly mistaken about Jessup.

Jessup, a very flexible president, finally yielded to the demands for Belting's removal. The two men discussed various possibilities, and on April 26, 1929, Belting submitted his resignation. Three days later Belting related the event to Stagg. Jessup had called Belting into his office and advised him to resign. "Suppose I refuse to resign?" Belting replied. "Well, then, I will have to take steps for your dismissal," Jessup said. He had based his request wholly on Belting's not being popular, which Belting said was the case because he wanted to live up to conference rules, and there were men in his department—he identified George T. Bresnahan, the assistant director in the Division of Physical Education and the track-and-field coach—who wished to use athletic funds to meet the expenses of athletes, as was done during the Howard Jones administration. Bresnahan, disappointed because he was not made the director of physical education when Jones departed, was using an athletic fund to pay athletes, whom Belting named. When Stagg expressed indignation over Belting's forced resignation, Belting quoted a man who described Jessup as one who placed policy above principle.[21]

On May 11 Griffith and Belting met with Stagg at the University of Chicago. Belting related that when he returned to Iowa City after his conference with Stagg, Jessup undertook to bribe him to remain at Iowa, fearing that Belting would "squeal on some of Iowa's athletic immoralities." Jessup had offered to pay him $5,000 to remain in a nominal position in connection with physical education. Moreover, Jessup had asked Belting to speak at a meeting of the athletic council, but then refused to let him talk. Belting responded by telling Jessup that "he was yellow, that he did not have any back bones." Jessup replied that Belting was angry and could not think straight. Jessup had announced that Belting had accepted a position in the physical education department before Belting had considered the matter. Belting refused to accept the position; he found it impossible to continue on the staff in any capacity.[22]

As Belting related, Jessup appointed Edward H. Lauer, the director of the extension department, as director of physical education and athletics, and he appointed Bresnahan as director of intercollegiate athletics. Belting showed Stagg a list of athletes who had given notes to the university, which were never expected to be paid. The athletes had either signed the notes or their names had been signed for them, with the understanding that they would not be forced to pay them. The total in the list of the notes amounted to more than $6,000.[23]

According to Belting, the whole state had been organized against him. Jessup had made a trade in which Belting was to be sacrificed in order to get the appropriation bill for the state passed. Jessup had called Belting in immediately after Jessup returned from the state legislature and told Belting that he would have to resign. The appropriation was then secured. Griffith named several men who had been active in raising a slush fund for Iowa and in seeking Belting's scalp. The Iowa alumni in Chicago, probably aroused by Jessup, planned an informal dinner on May 24 to meet Lauer and Bresnahan. Stagg declined an invitation to attend.[24]

A New Conference?

After Belting departed, Griffith and Stagg asked Huff to meet them on May 13 in Griffith's office. They discussed Big Ten athletics. Then Huff stated that he was depressed about the recruiting situation. The only way out, he thought, was to form a smaller conference that managed their athletics in the right way. As charter members, Huff suggested Chicago, Illinois, Michigan, Minnesota, and Ohio State. Although the conspirators were sorry and hesitant about doing away with the Western Conference, they agreed that, in intercollegiate athletics, at least three university presidents—Edward C. Elliott of Purdue, Walter Dill Scott of Northwestern, and Walter A. Jessup of Iowa—were men of policy, not principle. They could not be trusted to support "clean athletics." Huff and Griffith "were satisfied" that the situation at Indiana was bad; there the alumni were in the saddle. "Pres. [William Lowe] Bryan was a fine old man with the right ideals and principals [sic]," but he had not dominated the situation. According to Griffith, Zora G. Clevenger, the Indiana athletic director, was "disturbed" about Indiana; it hurt him to see the way the alumni were handling matters. He wanted another job. Both Huff and Griffith said that Nelson H. Kellogg, the Purdue athletic director, was also looking for a job. He felt he would not be able to last because "Pres. Elliott was a weak sister and a certain group of alumni who were plotting with Coach [James] Phelan for his scalp and are also using money in getting athletes, were in the saddle."[25]

Griffith raised the question of his relationship to the new conference, should it be formed. He had received an invitation to fill a similar position with the Pacific Coast Conference, but he did not wish to leave the Big Ten. Both Huff and Stagg said that they wanted him "to go with us."[26]

The question of Wisconsin's position arose. Because Wisconsin was a fine institution with a creditable record, Huff suggested that after those present had formed a conference with five members, they might "go to Wisconsin, tell them our reasons for not inviting them, and see how they reacted. If they would agree to go with us on high grounds, we might let them in."[27]

The universities not invited into the new conference would continue the Western Conference under the old name, Stagg thought, and would probably invite Notre Dame, Michigan State, and Marquette to join them. This group would not detract from the strength of the new conference because the leaders of the present conference would be with the new grouping.[28]

Finally, Huff and Stagg agreed that Huff would call a meeting of the athletic directors who would be involved in the new conference to see whether they could find a way to preserve the existing conference or to form a new one on the lines suggested. Huff arranged for a meeting on Sunday May 19.[29]

Meanwhile, Griffith outlined for Huff and Stagg his thinking about the directors' attempt to curtail the recruiting and subsidizing of conference athletes. Because the conference is loosely organized, he wrote, and because of "the makeup of certain groups in the Conference," its power and strength might be questioned. (The meaning of "the makeup of certain groups" is not clear.) "Many have reason to believe that the conference as a body will not take a definite stand on principles," he wrote. "The directors and football coaches almost unanimously agree that the recruiting situation has become worse since the four-year football schedule was adopted." The directors, he noted, were supposed to make up another long-term schedule in a few days. If nothing were done at that time, conditions would go from bad to worse. Belting was willing to go before the directors and faculty representatives and furnish definite proof that Iowa had not observed the conference rule as applied to recruiting and subsidizing of athletes. It may be true that other conference institutions had likewise failed to observe these rules, but it would be difficult to prove the points with the same finality that Belting could prove in relation to Iowa. Before taking action, Griffith continued, it would be "sporting" to have a joint meeting of the athletic directors and the faculty representatives at which Paul Belting and Louis Pelzer, the Iowa representative, would submit the facts. "We would be wrong in assuming that the conference will not act properly if given the chance. Then we might go further and suggest that some action might be taken at a subsequent meeting in relation to other conference members."[30]

As planned, Huff called a meeting for May 19. In addition to Huff, the athletic directors present were Stagg of Chicago, Yost of Michigan, Luehring of Minnesota, and St. John of Ohio State. They discussed recruiting in the conference, with each director telling what he knew and what steps to take to remedy the problem. Huff presented his idea of having the universities present withdraw from the conference and form a new body, possibly taking in Wisconsin later, with promises of good behavior. The plan was discussed at great length. St. John, fearful of the result of such an upheaval, advised against it. Yost was lukewarm. For sentimental reasons Stagg hoped the conference could continue. It had set the standard for more than seventy other athletic conferences and had the prestige of being "the most progressive intercollegiate body in the country." Stagg presented some evidence given to him by the auditor at the University of Iowa and by Willis W. Mercer, an Iowa City businessman, about a slush fund and notes for loans that athletes signed but did not pay. The men also discussed a new plan. The conference directors had previously agreed to meet on May 23 to draw up a football schedule for 1931 and 1932. Stagg said that when the directors met that day, one of them should move to postpone the arranging of a two-year schedule until later and move to postpone the games already scheduled for 1930. The directors agreed to follow the proposal. Meanwhile, each of them should convince their faculty representative of the need to take disciplinary action on Iowa.[31]

Two days before a scheduled conference meeting, the athletic directors of all the conference universities except Iowa met secretly in Chicago. The five directors who had previously agreed to postpone the drawing up of football schedules for 1931 and 1932 now took steps to prevent any other director from disrupting this plan. Fielding Yost "counseled" George Little, the Wisconsin director, to implement the plan previously agreed on. Little prefaced his motion with remarks about the athletic situation at Wisconsin, where "the minority faculty group" were defeated when they tried to raise a higher standard for athletic eligibility and not to have so much emphasis placed on the intercollegiate athletic program. Was Little playing to his audience? Did the directors relish such a comment? We do not know. Those present decided that a committee (Huff, Stagg, and Griffith) should prepare a statement about the reasons for postponing the scheduling of football games for 1931 and 1932. The committee also went over data on the University of Iowa that Griffith had prepared. Belting was called in to verify the evidence. The men agreed that each committee member should speak at the conference session the next day. In the evening, Yost, Griffith, and Stagg met with Huff and read over Griffith's memorandum on athletic conditions at Iowa, which they hoped to present to the conference. Earlier, Griffith had seen Paige (Minnesota), who had said that if the athletic directors brought charges against Iowa at the conference meeting, he would ask for the appointment of a committee to hear them. (One might reasonably suspect that Paige was not eager to punish a conference member who transgressed.) On May 24 Stagg read Griffith's memorandum to Vice President Frederic Woodward and Dean C. W. Boucher, who were to represent Chicago at the conference the next day. When Stagg read the statement that the registrar at the University of Iowa could not certify the scholastic eligibility of athletes because the task had been taken out of his hands, Woodward exclaimed, "Oh, my God," and then apologized for his exclamation. Stagg told Woodward that Northwestern, Purdue, and Indiana probably were about equally as bad as Iowa, and that the presidents of Northwestern and Purdue in particular were men of policy, not principle, in intercollegiate athletics. "Isn't it possible," Woodward asked, "for us to find three or four institutions who believe in the conduct of athletics like we do who would be willing to withdraw with us from the Conference and compete together?"[32]

Iowa and Its Transgressions

The directors and Griffith had planned well. At the conference session on May 25, things went according to the script. Huff, Stagg, and Griffith each spoke, a faculty committee consisting of James Paige, Thomas French, and George Goodenough was appointed, and it met with Huff, Stagg, and Griffith. At one point, according to Stagg, it seemed as if the committee would not take any action. But the committee concluded that Iowa had violated a conference rule, and it recommended that the conference sever athletic relations with the University of Iowa effective on January 1, 1930. The faculty committee acted accordingly. Because of the secrecy with which everything had been done, the deed hit the athletic world like an explosion. But, said Stagg, it would save the conference; it would frighten several conference universities into good behavior, strengthen the athletic directors who wanted to do the right thing, and stir up faculty and presidential authorities to better supervision. The effect of the action would reverberate throughout the United States and probably result in similar upheavals in other conferences.[33]

The conference did not make public the charges and the evidence on which it based its decision. "By the standards of a later day," the historian Stow Persons wrote, "the procedure of the conference in taking this drastic step was casual in the extreme. The university was given no opportunity to respond to charges; nor was the suspension accompanied by a statement of the university's offenses." The decision was like that of a referee in a football game who invokes a penalty without explaining to the player the basis for his decision. Leaving Iowa City, Belting went to the conference office in Chicago and allegedly gave Griffith an account of the situation at Iowa favorable to himself and damaging to his enemies.[34]

On May 26 Thomas E. French (Ohio State) visited Frederick G. Higbee in Iowa City regarding the former's text on engineering drawing. French had been present when the conference suspended Iowa; Higbee was head of the Department of Engineering Drawing, a member of the board in control of athletics, and secretary of the alumni association of the University of Iowa. Jessup asked Higbee to bring French to his house. He wanted to learn what the severing of athletic relations was about. In their conversations, the following facts were brought out. First, the conference had been investigating alleged infractions of conference regulations for some time. Three institutions had been found about equally guilty. Iowa was chosen for disciplinary action because more documentary evidence against it was available. Second, the infractions consisted of illegal and irregular recruiting practices, the subsidizing of athletes, the certification as eligible, and the playing of athletes who were scholastically and otherwise ineligible under conference rules. Third, Griffith had warned Jessup by letter that Iowa practiced irregularities in their conduct of intercollegiate athletics. Fourth, when asked why Iowa was not given an opportunity to be heard before action was taken, French mentioned the letter of warning and said that before a vote was taken, Pelzer, the Iowa representative, was asked if he wished to be heard. Pelzer replied, "This is something you just have to take on the chin." Fifth, faculty control of intercollegiate athletics was gravely in doubt. No one in the conference knew Lauer, French said, while Bresnahan was unfavorably known for recruiting. Both the Lauer appointment, described as a "stuffed shirt appointment," and the Bresnahan appointment reinforced the belief that faculty control at Iowa did not exist. Sixth, when pressed for the background of this belief, French stated that the whole Iowa picture gave the impression that alumni pressure was so severe that President Jessup had yielded to it. And seventh, when asked what Iowa should do to get reinstated, French replied that the first step would be to have a conference with Commissioner Griffith, become acquainted with all the charges in detail, correct the irregularities and violations, and ask for reinstatement.[35]

Two days later in Iowa City, Griffith met with Jessup in the morning and with the athletic council in the afternoon. He gave them the facts regarding the diversion of athletic association monies to the alumni account regarding the fund operated in Iowa City and relative to the connection between the university business office and the men who administered the alumni fund. As individuals but not as a group, they admitted that these things were true. Griffith told both parties that the alumni who had been fighting the administration for five years announced several years ago that they were going to put Bresnahan in as director of athletics, and when he was appointed, it seemed to substantiate the belief that this group of alumni was dictating Iowa's athletic policy. Griffith told Jessup that at least two of the "recalcitrant alumni" had boasted that they took the matter to the legislature, and that the legislature had forced Jessup to appoint Bresnahan as director of athletics. Jessup denied the charge. He knew of the statement that if Iowa could demonstrate that it had substantial faculty control, it could easily gain reinstatement. This could be accomplished in three days if Iowa wished. Griffith had refused to give any details to the press, but he gave them to Jessup and the council. Iowa would do everything it could to see that these matters were not given publicity because university officials were involved. Griffith believed that the faculty conference based its action not so much on charges that individual athletes had been paid but rather on the fact that a fund existed, that the treasurer and auditor knew this, and that they worked with the men who administered the fund. The press would attempt to make it appear that the conference acted hastily without definite information. For that reason no one was willing to divulge the charges. The *Tribune*, Griffith added, had sent Westbrook Pegler to come out here and "write cynical articles belittling the Conference."[36]

After this meeting, Jessup asked Griffith for the details that caused the conference to sever athletic relations with Iowa. Griffith replied that in the meeting he had presented general charges regarding the recruiting and subsidizing of athletes. Since some of the men present knew about these matters, he would not back up his statements with evidence unless the council so desired. A motion asking Griffith to submit the proof did not pass. Griffith did send Jessup a report of the evidence on which the conference acted. First, prior to 1924 the faculty board had authorized the diversion of monies accruing from the sale of student yearbooks to the alumni fund to be used to subsidize athletes. Jessup and Pelzer had told Griffith that they knew about this arrangement, and so many council members knew the facts regarding this matter that Griffith did not deem it necessary to submit additional proof. When Belting went to Iowa, Griffith said, he was told that it was customary for the athletic board to turn over a certain amount of money yearly to the alumni fund. Belting had refused to do so. Second, a fund had been in operation in Iowa City for several years; the money in it had been used to aid athletes. Griffith had reported the case of Tom Stidham, an athlete. An Iowa alumnus had given him transportation to Iowa City, where Mr. Goltman of the Iowa Supply Company met him and took him to the Kappa Sigma fraternity house, where he met Dr. White and Mr. Williams.[37] They offered Stidham $75 a month. He said he expected $100. So he was paid $100 a month in checks signed by Mr. Williams. Williams reportedly made arrangements at the business office for Stidham's fees and tuition. Stidham did not sign any notes or pay any money at the university treasurer's office. Mr. (William H.) Bates, the university treasurer and a member of the Athletic Council, was present when Griffith presented this charge. He did not deny its validity.

For years, Griffith added, a small group of Iowa alumni had been attacking Jessup and the athletic administration. They had recently claimed that the legislature had insisted that George T. Bresnahan be placed at the head of athletics. That this group of alumni wished to dominate Iowa athletics could have been the root of Iowa's trouble. Some men in the conference felt that "sovereignty" resided in this small group of alumni, not in the university officials.[38] In summary, it was generally believed that at one time athletic association money had been diverted to an alumni fund, that an athletic fund controlled by alumni and business men had been in operation in Iowa City for a number of years, and that the university business office had allowed coaches and business men to suggest that certain athletes have their tuition fees waived, and that individuals in some cases had paid for certain athletes' fees, such payments being made directly to the university business office. Some of the men in the recent meeting of the council said that they knew the first two charges were true and that the third charge also was possibly true.[39]

After meeting with Griffith in Iowa City, the athletic council drafted a petition requesting the Western Conference to reconsider its action and asking the support of alumni in carrying out in letter and spirit the rules and regulations of the Western Conference. The petition made no mention of an alumni athletic fund ("slush fund") in Iowa City that was rumored to exist. The athletic council dodged all discussion of the Big Ten ruling against Iowa and promised faculty control of athletics. Louis Pelzer, the chairman of the council and Iowa's faculty representative, wired the petition for re-admission to the conference committee.[40]

A few days later, the faculty representatives, except for Iowa, favored having the conference immediately reconsider Iowa's case. Griffith demurred. He had received telephone calls from men who felt that "recalcitrant alumni" had openly boasted for years that they were going to see to it that Bresnahan was made director of intercollegiate athletics, and when his appointment was announced they took it as prima facie evidence that they had gained their point. When Griffith told his callers that Lauer was in complete control, they were not convinced. Bresnahan had been active in recruiting athletes, they said, and would not cooperate fully with them in their efforts. Griffith had not and would not give to the press any detailed information regarding the charges, but since at least thirty men knew the details, it was unreasonable to believe that the story would not ultimately get out. Tremendous pressure was being brought to bear upon Goodenough (Illinois), who chaired the eligibility committee. He was the only person who had any right to speak for the conference.[41]

Since the faculty conference refused to release information about the Iowa scandal, the press gleefully filled the gap. Days after Griffith met with the Athletic Council in Iowa City, Westbrook Pegler reported the issues in the *Chicago Tribune*. He rehearsed the details of Iowa's transgressions, adding that Jessup and university officials not only refused to answer the charges but refused to acknowledge them. Jessup evaded all questions bearing on the particulars of the complaint. Jessup admitted doing no wrong but promised to do wrong no more.[42]

Since the Big Ten faculty representatives had no doubt as to the truth of the charge that Iowa subsidized athletes, Pegler wrote, the case was one in which a convicted defendant appealed for mitigation of the sentence and promised to reform. Iowa's only answer to the accusations could be expressed as a plea of "I don't know what you are talking about, but I won't do it anymore." Jessup's assurances that faculty control of athletics would be exercised henceforth would not be accepted because Iowa purported to have enforced faculty control all along.

Belting had resisted the practices alleged in the complaint. Lauer replaced him. He was described as a man with no practical knowledge of what it was all about. Bresnahan's appointment as director of intercollegiate athletics was viewed as a repudiation of the principles that Belting stood for. The Big Ten authorities believed that Bresnahan would be the athletic director in all but title. One condition of reinstatement would be to get rid of Bresnahan or relieve him of authority in athletic affairs. The faculty committee had seen in print the data which they were eager to keep secret. "Goodenough said that the difference between the Iowa trouble and similar evasions at other Big Ten schools was the difference between a broken leg and a stubbed toe."[43] Pegler may have been a cynic, but he understood the dynamics of conference athletics. Iowa was a public university, as were eight of the universities in the Western Conference. The public had a legitimate interest in the Iowa situation.

Confronted by the crisis, Jessup asked Rufus Fitzgerald, the director of the Iowa student union, to investigate. Fitzgerald reported in early June. He found the minor charges to be substantially correct. Jessup had known that alumni contributed to a "loan" fund from which athletes could borrow for incidental expenses, but he took no steps to prevent it, thinking it sufficient to disavow university involvement. Fitzgerald also discovered that Belting had transferred $1,703 of athletic department money to a trustee fund for the purpose of making loans to athletes. This was a major offense. The university sought to place the blame on Belting while exonerating the student athletes who had borrowed from the illegal fund. The university promised to clean house and sought reinstatement.[44]

Lauer was made director of physical education and of intercollegiate athletics after Bresnahan was eased out of this appointment. Lauer found it difficult to clean house because Belting had apparently stripped his office of its current records. Lauer verified that the certification of the eligibility of athletes for Big Ten competition was a "rubber stamp" procedure. Pelzer, the chairman of the athletic board, seemed to approve all lists submitted to him without verification. Lauer also verified that a member of the physical education staff had allowed credit in a summer session course to a high school coach in return for the "delivery" of an outstanding high school athlete. The coach had registered for but not attended classes in the course. Lauer affirmed that Belting had withdrawn money from athletic funds and deposited it with a local bank with instructions to loan the money only to men whom Belting certified. Lauer made efforts to discover proof of the ineligibility of athletes as charged by the conference, he collected information about a "slush fund" for subsidizing athletes that an Iowa City business man managed, and he planned to present a statement to the conference claiming a house cleaning and asking for Iowa's reinstatement.[45]

In late May Chauncey S. Boucher (Chicago) informed Goodenough that he had conferred with Acting President Woodward of the University of Chicago about Goodenough's view that the conference should not consider repeal of its decision until Iowa had shown "by actions rather than by resolutions a change of heart." Boucher and Woodward agreed. If Iowa were reinstated to good standing without having acknowledged wrongdoing and without guaranteeing a thorough housecleaning and proper conduct in the future, "the Western Conference would deserve to be regarded by the public as worse than a joke."[46]

In early June, before Iowa completed its study of possible violations of conference regulations, Jessup, Lauer, and Pelzer met in Chicago at Jessup's request with a conference committee (Paige, French, and Goodenough) to consider reinstatement. Jessup, wrote Pegler, "was a little too willing to let bygones be bygones." He blamed Belting for most of the subsidizing and proselyting that occurred at Iowa. In fact, Belting had fought against these practices, for which his enemies sought his ouster. At the same time, Belting was not entirely pure, as Fitzgerald's inquiry discovered. When "Roly Poly Goodenough, stern faced Jimmy Paige, and the ponderous French" found Iowa's repentance inadequate, Pegler wrote, the witnesses departed, whereupon Lauer, "the little black haired man," invited twenty reporters into the conference room. A vigorous inquisition followed. Jessup, Lauer, and Pelzer left for home thinking that Iowa would be reinstated about the first of the new year. But there was "great moral indignation among the elders and deacons of the conference." One member of the conference committee (Paige fits the description) declared that Iowa had broken faith with the conference, and Iowa must be punished. He and another member of the committee would insist that Iowa be left out of the conference for at least a year.[47]

The conflict between the Big Ten and Iowa had not yet run its course. It led Westbrook Pegler to write that the Big Ten came through its recent fever "somewhat diminished as to prestige, as well as in numbers." Personal spites, friendships, and ambitions had been served, and it became quite apparent that not many men who supervised athletics in the conference actually cherished the system of laws to which they subscribed. Iowa had been suspended for being caught, but Iowa went by the code of the racketeer and did not blow the whistle on Northwestern, Michigan, Purdue, Indiana, or Ohio State, although there had been surly mutterings about these universities. "In their distrust of one another," the Big Ten voted not to seek "to impose on the impecunious athletic student certain conditions which, if enforced, would place him at a disadvantage." Pegler saw "no moral reason why Ohio State, for example, should not solicit an Iowa [athlete]," and "the rule against subsidies would deny a poor athlete a kind of assistance" available to, Pegler noted, a saxophone player in nightclubs. The law against subsidization was only one of those laws that was passed for purposes of fine moral pretense. It was still easy to recruit and subsidize an athlete; Pegler described how easily this could be done. "The most depressing thing about the row over Iowa's recruiting and subsidizing has been the selfish evasiveness of the men who purport to set

[an] example for the young heroes of the campus. Not many of them live up to the rules willingly and none of them has had the candor to denounce them."[48] Pegler was a trenchant critic. His truth was not Griffith's truth.

During the summer the Iowa athletic scandal was quiescent, but the idea of forming a new conference blossomed. Stagg, mulling over the prospect, listed twelve principles on which to base a group of five or six universities. Among the principles to govern the new creation, Stagg included the following: mutual trust and confidence and absolute frankness between the members, each conference university would have a duty to reprimand or expel any coach who did not live up to the highest principles of fair dealing with other members, and alumni were to be asked not to help secure athletes. A professed idealist, Stagg simply did not understand the harsh realities of intercollegiate athletics.[49]

Meanwhile, according to Griffith, Iowa did not think that the conference would go through with its action. He had gained respect for Lauer, but Lauer was on trial, and it would be unpleasant for him to disqualify some of the athletes who had been helped financially. Since the last conference meeting, one member university had taken their traveling recruiter off the road, another had gotten rid of an alumni secretary who was unduly active, a third had discontinued the practice of having an alumnus in town run an employment bureau for athletes, and a fourth had decided to do away with a contact man. The conference was well on its way to the goal of athletic departments remaining as inactive in soliciting and aiding athletes as were academic departments in these respects. "If we can work this out satisfactorily," Griffith wrote, "it will be the greatest achievement the Conference has made to the Nation's athletics."[50]

Griffith in Pursuit

In September the Iowa athletic board announced that it would present material in support of its petition for reinstatement at the conference meeting in December. The board had named a committee to supervise strict enforcement of conference eligibility requirements for athletes, and it had named Clement C. Williams, dean of the College of Engineering and the new chairman of the board, as Iowa's faculty representative.[51]

In early October Griffith observed that the Iowans had not been as active in securing new "athletic material" during the summer as they had been formerly. Where they promised help they had instructed the boys to keep silent. And yet someone wrote to the athletes who presumably were given financial assistance last year, advising them that the old arrangements would still hold. Practically all of these men were now at Iowa. Twenty-six of them registered a week late, on the Friday preceding the game with Carroll College on September 28. "I am advised each had a roll of bills of the same denomination." The certification of scholastic eligibility of athletes that had formerly been taken out of the hands of the registrar had again been delegated to him, who, according to reports, was strict and honest. Griffith had received information that two and possibly three Iowa football men had played professional football before entering the university and also after matriculation. If these men violated the rule, Lauer would be placed in a rather embarrassing position. Although Iowa had largely refrained from recruiting new material, the Iowa authorities had kept the old crowd of athletes because if any of them were declared ineligible, they would perhaps tell a story embarrassing to university people. "Some Iowans feel that if they can keep the old crowd they will win some conference games and secure public support and sympathy." Griffith guessed that Iowa would not disqualify any men who were helped financially last year and presumably were being assisted financially this year. The trouble was in securing proof.[52]

Griffith had gathered information regarding Iowa men who had been helped financially. At Lauer's request he listed the names of thirteen athletes who had been helped financially, the amount of money given them, and the men who recruited and paid them. Walter R. Fieseler, an associate in surgery in the medical school, was the most prominent of many men in Iowa who had recruited and financed the athletes.[53]

In mid-October Griffith related some news about Iowa to his confidant Stagg. Griffith had been told that Judge McKinley of the Superior Court of Cook County, the president of the Iowa Alumni Club in Chicago, in an address to the Iowa-Illinois alumni group on October 17, said that he did not know why Iowa was disciplined. The alumni should run athletics instead of the faculty, he added, and the alumni were not for Ingwersen. Griffith did not believe that Williams, the new Iowa faculty representative, would have much power. Griffith had sent Lauer a list of the amounts of money supposedly given to various athletes, but he could not name the persons from whom he obtained the information. The Iowans had taken the attitude that unless "we" could prove that these men have been helped, Iowa would consider them eligible. Iowa planned to present its case to the conference in December, basing their claims for readmission on the grounds that they have established faculty control in athletics, had abolished the remitting of tuition for athletes, and had the situation in hand.[54]

Griffith probably underestimated the influence of Judge McKinley in Iowa affairs. Michael L. McKinley, who was born in Clayton County, Iowa, in 1872, graduated from the University of Iowa in 1895. He moved to Chicago, was admitted to the Illinois bar, practiced law in Chicago, was a member of the 43rd and 44th Illinois General Assemblies, and in 1911 became a judge of the Superior Court of Cook County. McKinley founded the Iowa Alumni Club of Chicago, and he gave devoted service to his alma mater. For example, he paid the travel expenses of many prospective students to visit the University of Iowa, he found summer jobs for Iowa students, he helped Iowa graduates find employment, and he established four full scholarships to the University of Iowa, funded through the Iowa Alumni Club of Chicago. Presumably much of this aid went to athletes. When the Big Ten censured Iowa, "Judge McKinley stepped in forcefully, rallied the alumni, demanded institutional changes, and saw them through."[55] The alumni were a force that President Jessup could not easily ignore. Nor could other conference presidents who put policy above principle.

In late November, the press reported, Iowa announced that it would keep secret its course of action at the December meeting.[56] University officials, students, and townspeople predicted that Iowa would be restored to good standing. The university was now "guarding more vigilantly the scholastic eligibility of its athletes." The athletic board had been "reorganized to assure faculty control." The university had "investigated all charges against individual athletes and . . . disqualified those against whom accusations were substantiated." The practice of "student notes" and the avoidance of paying tuition had been discontinued. The alumni athletic fund had been abolished.[57]

Griffith wanted the conference faculty committee to decide two questions. Should action similar to that regarding Iowa be taken against any of the other conference institutions because of illegitimate recruiting and subsidizing athletes? And should Iowa's petition for reinstatement be granted? Griffith had prepared a report on recruiting in the conference that he sent to Paige and French. It appeared to Griffith that Iowa had the support and sympathy of the newspapers and the general public, and that Iowa was intent on blaming a few individuals for the Iowa predicament. This was unjust and unfair to the individuals concerned. Griffith hoped that those who cast the final vote would not be swayed by public opinion.[58]

As the Hawkeyes awaited a verdict, they observed that only a majority vote— five of the nine conference schools—would be necessary to repeal the edict severing athletic relations. Illinois and Chicago were regarded as opposed to reinstatement. Michigan and Ohio State were regarded as doubtful. Iowa counted on Northwestern, Wisconsin, Minnesota, Indiana, and Purdue.[59] University of Iowa officials believed that they had done everything in their power to meet the faculty committee's requirements, but they insisted that Iowa be taken back on an equal footing with the other conference members or the school would prefer to remain on the outside.

The conviction was growing that it would be unfortunate for both Iowa and the Big Ten to refuse Iowa's bid. Alumni said that they would "not hesitate to make public the evidence they had against other conference schools if Iowa's plea

[was] turned down." Williams, the head of the Iowa athletic board, thought that Northwestern, Wisconsin, Indiana, Purdue, and Minnesota would favor Iowa, and probably Ohio State also. Chicago, Illinois, and Michigan were doubtful. In view of the Carnegie Report, "the conference would be hypocritical if it continued Iowa's suspension." Iowans said that Iowa was "no more guilty" than other conference members. "As long as Iowa remained a practice game for the Big Ten football leaders, nothing was said" about conditions in Iowa. But when Iowa counted in the "championship race, some Big Ten leaders decided it was time to do something." A former mayor of Iowa City, the president of the Iowa Alumni Association, and the alleged administrator of the so-called slush fund which figured in the ouster proceedings, said that they had enough evidence about athletic irregularities to "rock the conference" if Iowa was denied readmission.[60]

On December 3 Lewis Omer, an athletic coach at Carthage College, wrote Stagg about his experience with Iowa men. Carthage had an excellent halfback, a sophomore. The previous summer two Iowa students and Bresnahan had called at the swimming pool where this boy worked and offered him employment at Iowa that would pay all his expenses except books. Bresnahan sent the students (one was Carl A. Pignatelli, who earned a letter in football in 1929) to talk to the Carthage athlete. Bresnahan may have been technically honest, Omer wrote, but he violated the spirit of the rule and was "inethical." "IF IOWA IS LET BACK," Omer declared, "JUST SET BACK THE CLOCK OF ATHLETIC PROGRESS TWENTY YEARS IN THE BIG TEN."[61]

On the eve of the December conference session, Iowa authorities submitted to the faculty representatives and Commissioner Griffith a petition that asked for re-admittance to the conference. The charges against Iowa related to the recruiting of athletes, proselyting, diversion of funds, eligibility, athletic funds, notes of athletes, and excessive billing. The petition stated that six of the alleged abuses that led to the suspension had been corrected, and three were denied or defended as ethical under the conference code. The *Chicago Tribune* reported events in detail, and Griffith analyzed the petition critically.[62]

At the meeting on December 6 all ten member universities were represented. Early in the session the conference considered the Iowa case. The faculty committee agreed that the conference would furnish the press a copy of whatever information it wished to release, and no other information would be given out. Williams then presented the Iowa petition, prefaced by an explanation of the possible causes that led to questionable practices at the institution and a brief description of the internal organization of the university. Since the athletic directors had been invited to meet with the faculty representatives that day, a question arose as to whether the directors should hear and discuss the Iowa brief. The faculty committee agreed not to discuss this matter with the directors at that time, but to invite them to meet with the conference for the presentation of routine matters. On May 29, by mail ballot, the conference had asked the members of the Big Ten which of three options in the Iowa case was desired. (The three options are not a matter of record.) The chair of the session then announced that the members unanimously favored the third option—in other words, that the conference committee meet with Louis Pelzer, a former Iowa representative, and Lauer, the athletic director, and report to the conference.[63] Events superseded this approach.

The next day the faculty representatives, the athletic directors, and Griffith informally discussed the Iowa situation for nearly two hours. The conference then went into executive session. Having agreed to ask the judgment of the athletic directors in regard to Iowa, they invited Fielding Yost, the chairman of the committee of directors, to appear. "In the judgment of the Athletic Directors," Yost declared, "the Iowa situation is not yet satisfactory. It is our further judgment that Iowa be permitted, if she so desires, to renew her petition at the annual meeting in December 1930." Aigler moved that the Iowa petition be denied and that at some future time Iowa might petition for a resumption of relations. He then moved a long substitute resolution that said Iowa had made "earnest and definite steps to correct the evils which led to the May action," but the conference was of the opinion that steps remained to be taken, and that the petition of Iowa be denied. The motion carried unanimously, and the conference named Aigler to prepare a statement for the press on the action. A note in the conference records explained that adoption of the resolution did not mean that Iowa ceased to be a member of the conference on January 1, 1930, nor did it mean that Iowa was then suspended. The action meant that the resolution of May 25, 1929, severing athletic relations with Iowa effective on January 1, 1930, became operative on that date.[64] This seems to be a distinction without a difference.

Edward H. Lauer, the Iowa athletic director, left a valuable memorandum on the December meeting described. When he tried to show what had been done to bring the Iowa practices in accord with the conference regulations, the only hostility came from Yost, who argued that some of the Iowa athletes must have received improper financial aid. He did not refer to the Belting Fund. Huff was not convinced that Iowa had set her house in order. He cited details that troubled him: there had been no radical change in the board, Bresnahan was still on the staff, and no athletes had been declared ineligible. The next day, when the directors and faculty representatives met jointly, it became evident that Paige, Yost, and Griffith had agreed that the Belting Fund was the vulnerable point in Iowa's position. Huff brought up the matter of Bresnahan, Stagg brought up the personnel of the athletic board, and Yost brought up eligibility. The general opinion was that conditions at Iowa were very bad, "so bad that it seemed inconceivable that no athletes should be found guiltless." When the directors were excused from the meeting and were about to leave,

Yost asked if the faculty representatives desired to receive from the directors their formal judgment. The chairman said no such action had been taken, whereupon Aigler moved that such a request be made of the directors. The motion prevailed and the directors retired. "It was very evident," Lauer wrote, "that this motion was forced through by Mr. Yost and that Mr. Aigler acted on his instigation." The directors withdrew to another room (Lauer was asked not to join them), where they voted unanimously that athletic conditions at Iowa were not yet satisfactory. The directors went beyond their mandate, said Lauer, and recommended that the ban be continued. This action was transmitted to the faculty committee.[65]

In Iowa City, officials and students felt that the conference had done Iowa an injustice. Rush C. Butler, a Chicago attorney and alumnus member of the Iowa athletic board, declared, "There isn't a university in America with a cleaner athletic system than the one now in operation at the University of Iowa." "The Big Ten faculty committee," Butler charged, "had adopted an arbitrary attitude and was all wrong in its action and unreasonable" demands. Butler praised Jessup, describing him as "without censure for what had happened." He viewed Belting as "the cause of the entire affair." The Iowa university community, alumni, and local residents were equally unhappy with the Big Ten decision.[66]

Rush L. Butler was a Chicago lawyer and graduate of the University of Iowa. As a member of the Iowa athletic board, he saw no problem with whatever was done to promote athletics at Iowa. Source: University of Iowa Archives.

In December the conference had declared that Iowa had to take further steps before the school could rejoin the Big Ten. What steps? The minutes do not say. Would Iowa resign from the Big Ten or remain in the conference? Paige, the leader of the faculty fight on Iowa's re-admittance, excoriated the so-called "Belting loan fund." That fund was Yost's chief point of attack on Iowa. Williams and Lauer refused to yield to Paige's demand that all athletes who had received loans from the fund be declared ineligible. The conference committee called the fund a violation of its rules, and added that "Iowa's refusal to bar athletic recipients of loans" was "proof that Iowa hadn't reformed." The elimination of the loan fund was one of the main steps Iowa had to take before being readmitted to the Big Ten. In a long session on December 11, the Iowa athletic board decided that Iowa should remain in the Big Ten. It concluded that the attitude of the conference on the loan fund was justified, and it declared twenty-two athletes ineligible. The athletic board also voted to ask the Big Ten to send a committee to Iowa City to determine whether Iowa should reinstate these athletes. But the athletic board refused to recognize "the right of the conference to dictate who should or should not coach at Iowa." "This," the *Tribune* reported, "was a slap at . . . several athletic directors and faculty men" who had intimated that Bresnahan was "persona non grata" in this capacity.[67]

A special meeting of the conference was scheduled for February 1, 1930. Because some of the representatives had announced that the conference would then rescind the action taken in May 1929 with respect to Iowa, Griffith, to preempt them, sent Stagg, Huff, and Yost a "constructed story" based on bits of evidence about Iowa's continued violations of the rules. In the December meeting the Iowa delegate admitted that certain abuses had taken place under the former athletic director and had placed the responsibility on Belting; Iowa had not admitted that any athletes had been assisted since last May from unofficial funds or by unofficial employment committees. In 1928–29, Griffith continued, 169 athletes were given assistance at Iowa by the official employment bureau and the official scholarship and loan fund committees. He went on to name 22 athletes who were reported as having received little or no help last year from official sources, but "chances are" that many of them were assisted by the Work Fund committee. Thirteen of the twenty-two athletes had earned their letters in the 1929 football season. Griffith reported these matters to the Committee of Three prior to their visit to Iowa City. He suggested that Stagg, Huff, and Yost destroy his letter after reading it.[68]

In the February meeting the chairman reviewed matters leading to the calling of the special meeting, and French, the new chairman of the eligibility committee, described in detail the activities of the committee on a recent visit to Iowa. A general discussion of the Iowa situation followed. Griffith supplied such information as had become available to him and then withdrew. After further discussion the faculty committee adopted a resolution saying that the conference was "satisfied that the athletic authorities at the University of Iowa have re-established the principles of faculty control and are earnestly endeavoring to correct the conditions which led to the suspension of athletic relations, and whereas, although there was reason to suspect that certain forces outside the administration are still resorting to improper methods of aiding athletes, the Conference has confidence in the ability and determination of the Iowa authorities to ascertain the facts and to deal effectively with such abuses as might be found to exist." Therefore, athletic relations with Iowa were resumed, "effective at once." After further discussion, the conference agreed to inform the University of Iowa that "it would be inadvisable to apply for the reinstatement to eligibility of those athletes disqualified on December 11."[69]

The reinstatement of Iowa to full standing was not acclaimed in Iowa City. The public and the newspapers were critical of the conduct of athletics at the university. The athletic board was unpopular, the director of athletics was unpopular, athletic schedules for 1930 had been drawn up (of Big Ten teams, Iowa scheduled only Purdue), athletics was in bad shape financially, and many good athletes had been disqualified for competition.

Shortly after the meeting Griffith acutely analyzed the conference's decision. It would have been better, he thought, if the vote on Iowa had been delayed, but in light of certain developments it was well that the vote came out as it did. Iowa punished the men who benefited from the "Trust Fund" but not those who benefited from the "Mercer Fund" or the "Fieseler Work Fund." They placed full responsibility for the establishment of the "Trust Fund" on Belting. Their position appeared to be: some undesirable things happened under Belting; we dismissed him and thereby corrected matters; none of the present members of the athletic board or other administrative officials have had anything to do with recruiting and subsidizing practices at Iowa; therefore athletics at Iowa are now in good hands. By making it appear that Iowa's petition was denied in December solely because of the "Trust Fund" matter and disqualifying the men, they drew attention to the "Belting Fund." Shortly after they disqualified these boys the conference restored Iowa to her former status, thus making it appear that Iowa's only mistake was having employed a director who countenanced the establishment of the "Trust Fund." "We know that there were other more serious things than this trust fund," Griffith said, "but the public had been led to believe that this was not true." Iowa had made an adroit move. It would have been better for athletics in general and for the conference in particular, Griffith believed, had punishment been meted out to those who were subsidized by Mercer and Fieseler. With the matter concluded, Griffith made the following observations: the illegal recruiting and subsidizing of athletes had been temporarily checked;

the conference had demonstrated that it could and would punish any institution that was not strong enough to handle its own athletic affairs; no one believed, as they had last May, that Iowa would be better off outside than in the conference; and college athletics throughout the country had been in a bad way because of widespread recruiting and subsidizing practices. The conference was the first to recognize and to take measures to stop the evil. Conference action preceded the Carnegie Report and the action taken by other groups. "Thus this organization, as always, leads in establishing proper athletic policies and procedures."[70]

In March, when told that he would be asked to meet with the Iowa Board of Control, Griffith said he was unwilling to meet with them until he had "secured tangible proof of Iowa's misdeeds." That proof now secured, he was willing to go to Iowa City at any time. If the Iowans would not accept his proof and continued to insist that no wrong influences were at work after the May 25, 1929, meeting, the only recourse was to present the case before a board of arbiters or a court of law.[71]

Griffith was convinced that in the 1929 football season Iowa athletes had been assisted improperly and that outside influences were still at work. The Iowa athletic authorities resented the reference to outside influences and asked for proof of the charge. Griffith took steps to collect reliable evidence, and he sent a statement of some of the information he had obtained to Vice President Woodward of the University of Chicago. Griffith would be glad to meet any members of the Iowa Board of Control and lay the results of his investigation before them, but he would not ask any of his witnesses to appear in Iowa City. Iowa officials were blaming Griffith for Iowa's predicament.[72]

Griffith's statement of the evidence he had collected about Iowa's continued offenses contained five points. First, in the fall of 1929 Charlie Sessions of Davenport, Iowa, took $1,000 to Iowa City, where he was active in making arrangements for taking care of some of the athletes in connection with their tuition indebtedness. Second, Hi Jennings, an Iowa City insurance man, and two other local business men arranged matters with the endorsers and the men who signed the notes. Willis Glasgow, the 1929 team captain, signed one of the notes. Jennings interviewed five athletes, who are named, in his office, took them to the First National Bank, and arranged for them to sign the notes and receive the money needed to pay their back and current tuitions. Third, Seward Leeka was directed to board at Dewey's Restaurant in the fall of 1929 and was assured that he would not be asked to pay for his board. He took some of his meals at Sigma Chi fraternity house, where he resided and for which he signed a note to the fraternity. Assured that his meals at both places would be provided free, he found that he was expected to pay for his board at the fraternity house. The expenses that concerned him included $263 for a note at the bank, $115 for a note with Sigma Chi for board and room in 1928–29, $32.85 for board and room in 1929–30, $40 for a note for tuition in 1927, and $35 for tuition in 1927. Regarding the $40 note, Leeka understood that that obligation was to be taken care of out of the Iowa City "Slush Fund." Fourth, a list of students existed that indicated the amount of tuition past due for each one with remarks concerning their capacity to take care of the obligations themselves. Certain athletes were listed in groups along with the name of a business man who had possibly sponsored them. Fifth, Mr. Dewey stated that in the fall of 1929 he had twenty-eight University of Iowa students working in his restaurant, and he frequently carried the men for considerable time without exacting payment for their board indebtedness. Lauer, the athletic director, and Williams, the faculty representative, had explained in the December meeting that certain Iowa City business men had in the past been reimbursed from money in the "Work Fund" when such merchants ostensibly employed more athletes than they could legitimately pay for services rendered.[73]

On May 9, 1930, Griffith had a conversation with Lauer, the athletic director, and Williams, the faculty representative. He explained that he had made no more effort to ascertain whether Iowa had been guilty of illegitimate recruiting and subsidizing than he had to ascertain if the other nine conference universities had been guilty of the same practices. But the information given him about Iowa was so convincing that when he met with the faculty conference in February and was asked if outside influence had been operating at Iowa, he replied that it had been. After Williams had demanded proof, Griffith sent trained investigators out to Iowa to get at the facts. Griffith provided details about athletes and their notes and tuition found on a slip of paper belonging to Mr. Sessions of Davenport. Griffith offered more incriminating evidence. Griffith's investigators were willing to appear before Lauer, Williams, and the faculty conference for questioning at any time.[74]

Years later Griffith described how he proved that Iowa had subsidized athletes. After the penalty was imposed on Iowa, a conference committee had been ready to recommend that the restriction against Iowa be lifted. However, the members of the committee asked Griffith if he thought that Iowa had discontinued the practice of giving aid to athletes. Griffith was sure that the practice was being followed. The Iowa men demanded proof for the allegation that they had not yet cleaned house. Paige (Minnesota) told Griffith that he had to substantiate or withdraw his statement. So Griffith employed an undercover man who secured evidence that would stand up in a court of law. One Iowa athlete had said that Judge McKinley had offered to pay his way if he would go to Iowa. If the judge learned this, Griffith believed, quite likely he would sue Griffith. Then Griffith would have to retract the statement or reveal its source. He had promised the men that they would not be involved.[75]

At the conference meeting on May 23, 1930, Iowa presented a list of eight men declared ineligible in December 1929 and petitioned that they be restored to eligibility. The conference unanimously denied the petition. Aigler then moved and the faculty committee adopted a resolution in which the conference expressed its appreciation of the "thorough, effective and impartial work done by Commissioner Griffith in investigating, sometimes under trying conditions, the situation in the various member institutions regarding recruiting and subsidizing."[76] The tribute was greatly deserved.

The controversy precipitated by the Iowa athletic scandal was the darkest moment to date in the history of the Big Ten. The evidence revealed that faculty control of athletics was a sham. Cheating in order to win was rampant. Jessup, members of the athletic board of control, the athletic director, the faculty representative, and the registrar were all complicit in promoting and defending corruption. Iowa officials demonstrated a willingness to defend their university despite evidence that manifestly indicted it. An additional complication was the role of influential alumni who ardently defended their alma mater and eagerly criticized university officials who did not march to the beat of their drum. Iowa's perfidy was egregious. Its censure revealed that other conference members were almost equally guilty. Indiana, Northwestern, and Purdue were cited to illustrate the point. With delinquency so widespread, the Big Ten was weakened and damaged. Griffith was zealous in his determination to get the facts about the situation. He realized the extent to which the corruption in Iowa City weakened the conference, but, an inveterate booster, he declared that the conference led in establishing proper athletic policies and procedures.

CHAPTER 13

Cross Currents

The Great God Football ruled the nation's higher education when Abraham Flexner declared that American universities "are all mad on the subject of competitive and intercollegiate athletics—too timid to tell their respective alumni that excessive interest in intercollegiate athletics is proof of the cultural mediocrity of the college graduate, and a source of continuous demoralization to successive college classes." The colleges could not quickly improve the secondary schools, but with "intelligence and courage" they could tell the world that their problem is "complicated by giving loose rein to the athletic orgy in order to amuse and placate a populace, largely consisting of their own graduates. There is not a college or university in America which has the courage to place athletics where every one perfectly well knows they belong. On the contrary . . . proportionately more money is spent on college athletics than on any legitimate college activity." The football coach is better known to the student body and the general public than the president, and professors are, on the average, less highly remunerated. "Does the college or university have to endure this? Of course not. But it does more than endure: it advertises."[1]

In mid-February 1931, as the Iowa athletic scandal played out and Abraham Flexner fulminated, Commissioner Griffith alerted conference officials to a possible threat from the North Central Association of Colleges and Schools. The NCA, which had been organized in February 1895, was a membership organization of colleges, universities, and schools in the nineteen states between the Alleghenies and the Rockies and north of the Mason-Dixon line. Within this area were two hundred and seventy-nine colleges and thirty-nine athletic conferences. Most of the NCA officials were from small colleges. The NCA's Commission on Higher Education maintained scholastic standards by means of accreditation. If the NCA refused to accredit a college or university, students who transferred from that institution could not have their academic credits accepted at accredited schools. Historically, the Intercollegiate Conference (Big Ten) and the North Central Association had been in harmony with respect to the regulation of intercollegiate athletics. In 1926 the NCA's Commission on Higher Education established a Committee on Athletics. Its members were H. M. Gage, the president of Coe College, George F. Zook, the president of the University of Akron, and Commissioner John L. Griffith. In 1930 Griffith resigned and T. Nelson Metcalf of Iowa State College replaced him.[2] We know nothing about the reason for Griffith's resignation. He may have thought that it involved a conflict of interest.

From 1927 to 1930 NCA policy held that an athletic conference should adopt and administer North Central standards in order to be accredited. The Western Conference pledged cooperation with the NCA. Even so, some NCA members looked with disfavor on intercollegiate athletics, and others said that the NCA should not surrender its educational standards to agencies that attempted to administer college athletics.[3]

In February 1931 John Griffith informed the presidents, faculty representatives, and athletic directors of the conference colleges about two concerns. First, was the conference performing its work as it might reasonably be expected to do? Critics, including university presidents, had called attention to weaknesses in the conference. Some NCA investigators had said that "the Conference had failed and the N.C.A. was taking over the work that previously had been done by the men of this Conference." Conference men whose opinions carried weight had suggested that the conference was disintegrating, and since conference leadership was not sufficiently vigorous or powerful in controlling athletics, the NCA would not accept its leadership. Second, did the NCA or any similar national organization have the right to send paid investigators to conference universities for the purpose of deciding whether they merited punishment. "Those who feel that this Conference has failed," Griffith wrote, "certainly must have some other suggestion than that of asking an outside organization to do our work for us."[4]

Griffith also informed conference officials that paid investigators, men employed by the NCA athletic committee with funds provided by the Carnegie Corporation, were about to collect evidence about intercollegiate athletics at the conference colleges. The NCA's board of review would consider the evidence at the NCA's annual meeting in March.[5]

In early March men employed by the NCA Committee on Athletics began investigating athletics in Western Conference universities, including Chicago, Minnesota, Northwestern, and Ohio State. They spent six days at Northwestern looking over files and correspondence to which they were given free access. But when the sleuths declared that athletic conferences were no longer useful, Northwestern informed them that they were no longer welcome. Desiring advice about how to proceed, President Walter Dill Scott of Northwestern asked for a meeting of the conference.[6]

Shortly after this episode, Merle C. Prunty, the president of the North Central Association, avowed that the NCA would not take "any backward steps affecting the administration of athletics in its member schools and colleges." The NCA leadership was "firmly set in its decision" that their colleges should "remain educational institutions and not surrender educational standards to those agencies ... attempting to administer college athletics."[7]

Days later Griffith said to Big Ten athletic officials, "If the N.C.A. Athletic Committee recommends to the N.C.A. Board of Review that Northwestern be disciplined for consulting the conference regarding certain angles of this controversial question, then it will be clear that the NCA Athletic Committee is disposed to make a show of its power and authority." Griffith declared that there was a great deal of dynamite in intercollegiate football. "If the Board of Review of the N.C.A. were to bring in an adverse report relative to athletic conditions in any Conference institution it is safe to predict that the wild forces of man might bring about a repetition of this deplorable Iowa situation. It is a debatable question as to whether it is safe to permit other organizations in addition to the Conference to hold lighted matches near the fuse which is set in this keg of dynamite."[8]

The skirmish between the two organizations neared a climax at the annual NCA meeting in March. President Gage of the athletic committee declared that the NCA "did not wish to investigate any Big Ten school unless the door for such an investigation was open." At Northwestern, the NCA had "received a very courteous letter asking that the investigation be temporarily suspended until [officials] could discuss the situation" with other Big Ten members. The two organizations had the same ideas on high school and college sports and should help each other "preserve that order of things."[9] President Scott informed the assembly that the Western Conference was capable of conducting its athletics without the NCA's aid. The convention withheld its vote on placing the college on its accredited list of colleges and universities. According to the *Chicago Tribune*, "if a breach were to occur between the two groups, responsibility would rest not upon the athletic directors nor upon the faculty representatives but upon the presidents themselves."[10] The reference was to the presidents of the conference universities.

In late March Dean James B. Edmonson of the University of Michigan, the new NCA president, said that Northwestern would automatically sever relations with the NCA should it persist in refusing to submit its triennial report to the athletic department of the NCA.[11]

In mid-April, when the faculty representatives met to determine the attitude of the conference "with regard to inspections of athletic situations in the member

institutions by the North Central Association of Colleges and Secondary Schools,"
W. K. Smart (Northwestern) explained the circumstances attending the recent
investigation at Northwestern and the reasons Northwestern felt the matter to
be of moment to the conference. A general discussion followed, after which the
faculty representatives adjourned to meet in a joint session with the presidents
and the athletic directors of the conference universities.[12]

The presidents (except Illinois and Indiana), the faculty representatives, the
athletic directors, and Griffith then gathered at the University Club in Chicago,
and for six hours they discussed the problem that had come to a head when
Northwestern refused to permit NCA investigators to complete their inquiry
into athletic conditions at that university. Because of Northwestern's stand, the
NCA had withheld its vote on placing the school on its accredited list of colleges
and universities. Northwestern now sought the support of the other conference
members in its conflict with the NCA.

In early May, committees representing the Western Conference and the NCA
met in Chicago. The Big Ten committee consisted of three university presidents—
Walter Dill Scott (Northwestern), Alexander G. Ruthven (Michigan), and Emory
Elliott (Purdue). The NCA committee also consisted of three presidents—Gage
of Coe College, Lotus D. Coffman of Minnesota, and Edmondson of the North
Central Association. These men discussed the question of North Central supervision of Big Ten athletics. Gage indicated that the NCA would not insist on such
control. Scott believed that in the future the two groups would be able to cooperate. No official action could be taken, however, until the annual NCA meeting
in March 1932.[13]

In January 1932 representatives of fifteen athletic conferences in the North
Central territory, the NCA Athletic Committee, the NCA investigators, and NCA
officers met in Chicago. Presidents Scott, Ruthven, and Elliott, faculty representatives Aigler and Long, and the Big Ten commissioner also attended. Griffith
viewed the meeting as "packed": with few exceptions the speakers were identified
with the NCA Athletic Committee. Scott suggested that it was safer to entrust the
administration of athletics to the thirty-odd conferences in the North Central territory than to the NCA. Ruthven said that he had not gained any information of
value from the meeting, and Elliott suggested the advisability of the NCA making
public each year reports similar to those compiled by the conference relative to
scholarships, loans, and so on. From what he heard, Griffith gained two impres-
sions. One was that the NCA aspired to be a conference of conferences; as such,
it would largely duplicate the work of the NCAA. The other was that the men
in the meeting believed that the NCA athletic committee and its investigators
could work miracles. The NCA yoke was easy, it was argued, and their burden
was light.[14]

In March the Big Ten and the NCA committees agreed on nine carefully worded propositions as a definition of the responsibilities and relationships of the two organizations. Briefly stated, they were as follows: the two groups should work in harmony without either becoming subordinate to the other; all conference members would be required to observe NCA standards; the Committee on Athletics should call a meeting of athletic conferences for the purpose of defining the scope and procedures to follow in inquiring into the athletic policies and conditions of higher institutions; the NCA should send a representative to attend occasional meetings of intercollegiate athletic conferences; the NCA had the right to make periodic inquiries into athletics in accredited higher institutions holding membership in an approved athletic conference; the reports on athletic conditions prepared by NCA men should be referred to the athletic conference concerned for its information; the NCA should deal directly with a higher institution that was found guilty of violating the athletic standards of the association; the special committees of the NCA should submit these minutes to the executive committee of the NCA with the request that steps be taken to insure the preparation of a series of proposals embodying the agreements set forth in these minutes; and these proposals should be submitted at an early date to the Western Intercollegiate Athletic Conference.[15]

President Gage, the chairman of the NCA Committee on Athletics, reported on the January meeting. The NCA, being primarily occupied with educational matters, he wrote, was interested in the administration of athletics only in so far as athletics affected educational programs. The conferences were concerned with diverse matters that were not within the sphere of the NCA. The NCA was interested in matters of an academic-athletic character—for example, the educational qualifications of coaches, academic standards for all students, including athletes, proper proportion of time for athletics, the character and credit of courses in coaching, proper emphasis on intercollegiate athletics on the part of the institutional administration, educational byproducts of athletics (gambling, character building), and recruiting and subsidizing athletes. The NCA, Gage added, had minimum standards of athletic administration compatible with membership in the association. It would deal with any institution within its area that was not a member of a recognized conference in matters pertaining to its minimum requirements. For institutions within a recognized conference, the NCA administered its own devices for inspection in ascertainment of facts. Should it find the minimum requirements not being met by an institution, the matter might be officially brought before the recognized conference concerned by agreement with the conference. If the conference should not succeed in having the discrepancy satisfactorily adjusted, the NCA would take such final action as might be deemed advisable. The NCA should deal with its member institutions rather than with member conferences.[16]

Gage called attention to an important aspect of intercollegiate athletics—the NCA's Standard 5, which read, "Coaches should be regularly constituted members of the faculty, fully responsible to the administration." The NCA had adopted it in 1928. The standard had been criticized: calling a coach a faculty member did not make him so in training and professional attitude. Nevertheless, application of the standard contemplated an ideal situation in which the coach and the intercollegiate athletic program were part of the whole educational opportunity of the institution.[17]

In concluding, Gage declared that NCA approval of an athletic conference meant that the NCA would so far as possible work through the conference without relieving the conference from direct responsibility to the North Central for fulfillment of North Central standards. Further, the North Central Association depended on conferences for recognition of North Central decisions in making a schedule of games.[18]

The contretemps between the Big Ten and the NCA was evidence of a growing conflict over the control of intercollegiate athletics in the conference institutions. Perceptive observers had been well aware of problems in the Western Conference before the faculty committee imposed sanctions on Iowa. That event strengthened critics of the conference—in particular, NCA members who valued academic pursuits over athletic pursuits. Although the NCA was prepared to impose its academic standards on the Big Ten, nothing seemed to have changed as a result of the dispute between the two organizations.

Charity Games and Football Receipts

Commissioner John Griffith viewed himself as a constructive rather than a destructive person, and he believed that the nation's system of competitive intercollegiate and interscholastic athletics shaped the best qualities of the American people—individualism, democracy, capitalism, and the free enterprise system. "The best school of Americanism today," he observed, "is that presided over by our school and college coaches who believe in their country." The greatest problem was keeping the game on an amateur basis. "If the time ever comes when the philosophy of the play fields is rejected, then our whole free enterprise system will crumble, and the United States will go the way of other nations that have flourished for a brief time and then passed out."[19]

Confronted with an economic depression, many people called on the colleges to play football games for charity. In September 1931 Griffith observed that an effort would be made to force the conference to participate in some way in a charity football game, and, in the event two or more teams were tied, in a championship game.[20] At a special joint meeting of faculty representatives and athletic directors to consider the matter, it was proposed that the conference suspend the eight-game rule and the postseason-game rule for 1931 and permit each conference institution to play an extra game. After considerable discussion, the members decided that net receipts from the charity games would be allocated to the states represented in the conference based on population and then turned over to the governor's commissions of the various states.[21]

On Thanksgiving Day a four-team football meet was held on Stagg Field. In the first thirty-minute game, Illinois and Indiana fought to a scoreless tie. It was the ninth game in the season for both teams. In the next contest, Chicago defeated Iowa 7–0. It was the Maroon's tenth game in the season and the Hawkeyes' ninth. In the final event, Indiana trounced Chicago 4–0 before eight thousand spectators. The game brought in $18,000, of which $13,000 went to charity. On the following Saturday, a charity-game extravaganza took place. Six conference teams paired off in three different venues. In Ann Arbor, Michigan beat Wisconsin 16–0 before ten thousand people, whose contributions netted $20,000. It was the tenth game in the season for both squads. In Minneapolis, Minnesota defeated Ohio State 17–7 before a crowd of twenty-five thousand, a game that brought in $46,000. The contest was the tenth in the season for the Gophers and the ninth for the Buckeyes. In Chicago, Purdue defeated Northwestern 7–0 before thirty-five thousand onlookers and netted $75,000 for charity. The day's proceeds were added to the $13,000 yielded by the round robin, making the total raised by the Big Ten games $154,000, of which $141,000 would go to the unemployed relief fund in the seven states represented by the Western Conference.[22]

Football receipts, robust in the 1920s, declined in the early 1930s, as shown in table 13.1.

Table 13.1.   Football Receipts in the Conference Universities, 1930, 1931, and 1932

University	1930	1931	1932
Chicago	$ 161,987.98	$ 79,408.17	$ 61,055.92
Illinois	$ 326,988.29	$ 130,280.80	$ 56,952.87
Indiana	$ 82,192.61	$ 84,427.31	$ 34,191.37
Iowa	$ 58,675.66	$ 62,344.67	$ 28,834.41
Michigan	$ 438,924.07	$ 249,351.25	$188,684.84
Minnesota	$ 244,461.45	$ 213,880.97	$122,320.19
Northwestern	$ 334,676.08	$ 286,055.97	$22,089.62
Ohio State	$ 232,670.91	$ 226,875.62	$85,078.45
Purdue	$ 134,898.76	$ 70,773.65	$91,288.10
Wisconsin	$ 198,971.69	$ 146,430.99	$ 82,893.31
Total	**$ 2,217,447.50**	**$ 1,549,329.40**	**$975,389.08**

Despite the hard times, the conference carried on. At Iowa, as a result of its scandal, the athletic authorities had difficulty in scheduling football games. In both 1930 and 1931 the Hawkeyes played eight games, several with small colleges or distant opponents. In December 1931 the conference denied a request from Iowa to schedule a postseason game with Iowa State College. Meanwhile, the Northwestern football team tied with Michigan for the Big Ten championship in 1930. A year later the Wildcats tied with Michigan and Purdue for the same honor. Their success caught the attention of officials in Pasadena, who invited Northwestern to play in the Rose Bowl on January 1, 1932. The conference denied the request.[23]

Internal Tensions

In May 1932 the conference held a joint session with the athletic directors in Evanston.[24] In the program, Paige (Minnesota) spoke on the "History and Accomplishments of the Conference," Stagg (Chicago) on the "Functions and Responsibilities of an Athletic Director," Alfred C. Callen (Illinois) on "A Conference Representative's Opinion of the Function of an Athletic Director," Nelson Kellogg (Purdue) on "An Athletic Director's Opinion of the Functions of a Conference Representative," Griffith on "The Commissioner's View," and Aigler (Michigan) on "The Future of the Conference." After the talks, Long (Northwestern), Lauer (Iowa), and Clevenger (Indiana) led a discussion. One might well have likened the event to a Moral Rearmament confessional session, but such was not the case.[25]

The abstracts of four talks illuminate internal conference dynamics. According to Callen, the athletic director should be in sympathy with the rules, regulations, and ideals of the conference, and should recognize an educational duty to administer intercollegiate athletics in accordance with the spirit and letter of the rules.

Griffith spoke on the relation of academic and athletic goals. Those who cling to the traditional idea that an institution of higher learning exists solely to minister to the mind are increasingly out of touch with the trend of social changes. Deploring the influence of organized minorities in college athletic administration, he said, "Athletic sovereignty resides in those who can impose their will on the constitutional authorities or who exercise the power to employ or discharge the football coach." (This fuzzy utterance probably refers to alumni associations and their field secretaries.) The Depression had not had a deleterious effect on football but had led to the curtailment of the minor sports programs. The cost of maintaining football in a peak year in the conference universities was approximately $500,000, while the profit from the games played in the fall of 1931 was $1.5 million. "Those who a few years ago were advocating the curtailment of football receipts as a mean of promoting interests in intramural athletics are like the congressman who would handicap the rich as a means of enriching the poor." Vintage Griffith.[26]

Aigler analyzed faculty control, which he called the basic constitutional provision of the conference. (This is an odd statement, especially for a law professor: the conference had no constitution.) The faculty control contemplated was not a control vested in men who hold faculty rank. The history of the conference indicated that "faculty" means the academic interests of the school. This leads to the conclusion that the legislative power of the conference must be vested in a group of men, not merely faculty in rank, but representative of the academic sides of the ten institutions. Thus room must be found in the conference for both the faculty representatives and the athletic directors. It might be difficult to state accurately the dividing line between the functions of the two groups. It seemed clear that the faculty representatives must exercise the legislative power while the athletic directors act as the administrative agents. With mutual understanding actuating the members of these two groups, there was no occasion to worry about harmonious relations in the future. (One might fairly ask to what extent the faculty representatives represented faculty opinion as opposed to a narrow segment of the faculty.)[27]

Nelson Kellogg gave a long, passionate, and weighty address. He had had experience at Michigan, Iowa, and Purdue as an athlete and a director, and had had close personal ties with some conference leaders. He viewed the reason for the meeting as a desire for unity between two groups interested in the same affairs during a time of stress. In the past a feeling of antagonism between the faculty representatives and the directors had arisen. It was possible for the directors and the representatives of each school to live together in peace and harmony, but when the two groups met separately, they developed a group consciousness that might make one antagonistic to the other. A lack of understanding of the history of the conference contributed to the confusion over the functions and duties of the two bodies. When the conference was organized and control given to the faculty or faculty representatives, there were practically no stable administrations in the athletic departments. Now every conference athletic department had a stable organization with a permanent head with faculty rank. It might be well to realize that some functions should belong to the faculty representatives and others to the athletic directors. The faculty should make and enforce the rules, but the athletic directors should be consulted while the rules were in the formative stage. The schedules of the teams in the major sports should be subject to faculty approval so that schedules would not take the teams from their school work an undue amount of time. Each faculty representative should represent the faculty of his institution at the conference meetings and the conference to the faculty.

All the routine details of carrying on intercollegiate sport should be within the province of the directors.[28]

According to Kellogg, a certain amount of hard feeling had developed among the athletic directors by the manner of conducting the annual fall meeting. The faculty representatives met, did their business, summoned the directors to hear what they had to say, and then dismissed them. The procedure seemed productive of ill will. There was a tendency on the part of certain faculty representatives to feel that while the athletic directors had faculty rank, there was a marked distinction between the academic and the athletic staff. What was needed was for both the faculty representatives and the athletic directors to recognize the rights and prerogatives of the other parties. The directors were as much a part of the institution as the faculty. More joint meetings were needed at which the athletic directors could be freely consulted.[29]

Kellogg raised a vital question about the structure of the conference. And yet the question needed more careful definition. True, the faculty representatives were allegedly the voice of the faculty in the governance of conference athletics. Each representative was responsible to his university, not to the athletic director. But the faculty representatives were almost invariably identified with athletic sports. The directors and the coaches tended to press for more games, more practice time, and better athletes. The faculty representatives had to decide when and where to draw the line. Some tension was inevitable. The question was not about the proper relationship between faculty representatives and athletic directors, but rather about the relationship between the academic and the athletic purposes of a university.

About the time these tensions surfaced, Henry S. Pritchett recalled that the Carnegie Report had "made clear" that in American colleges "organized athletics, and particularly football, had ceased to be . . . played for sport's sake." It had "been transformed into shows for the public, through which the colleges received huge sums in gate receipts. . . . [T]rying to keep college football pure and undefiled . . . [ran counter] to human nature." The football player, he wrote, worked hard and was "inclined to feel . . . entitled to some of the swag." At this point the bootlegging alumnus was ready to subsidize the young athlete. How could one deal with the situation? One way was "to denature football as a money-making enterprise . . . cut out the professional coach, give up gate receipts," and make football a game. A second way was to "substitute some other sport" that would bring in as much revenue "while not exacting the toll in young lives and lowered college ideals for which football [was] in large measure responsible." Commercialized football shaped the lives of young men who come under its influence. "Boys start in the secondary school as candidates for football glory. They are steered into a football career in college, showered with demoralizing publicity, and . . . catch "but a faint vision of the intellectual life for which the college is supposed to stand (and sometimes does)."[30]

"The practical problem," Pritchett noted, was "to rescue these boys from the football regime and substitute something else which would bring the college just as much money. One sport fulfilled all these conditions—the noble sport of horse racing. It is a better money maker than football, an event on which old grads and undergrads could bet, and the whole audience could understand it.

Some people might ask what need has a university to make money out of football. No great European university had ever made a cent out of it. But this was beside the point. American universities contained an assortment of schools and colleges that attract students, and they desire to obtain large sums of money to maintain an athletic regime so that their boys might be induced to play games they would apparently not otherwise play. Hence the need for football. Horse racing was an admirable substitute. It would bring in as much or more money, give the boys time to study, and save the lives of a number of athletes every year. "Let that noble animal lift from the shoulders of mankind a load which becomes year by year more difficult to carry."[31] Was Pritchett's proposal persiflage? Or was he deadly serious?

In any case, intercollegiate football was firmly entrenched in American higher education. Developments at Chapel Hill illustrated the point. In 1935 Frank P. Graham, president of the consolidated University of North Carolina, launched his campaign to curb the rampant abuses in the football program and was soundly defeated.[32]

The Conference at Work

The faculty representative met as necessary to formulate conference policies and to settle disputes. Much of the work was done by standing committees. The Committee on Eligibility tried to define and maintain the eligibility of a student to represent his college in athletic contests. The Committee on Officials was designed to prevent referees from influencing the outcome of games.[33] In 1935 the conference ruled that a person could not officiate in both pro football and intercollegiate football games. In December the conference appointed new members to the committee—Weaver (Wisconsin) as chair, Rottschaefer (Minnesota), and Griffith—and made it a rotative rather than an elective body. Under rotation, a faculty representative served one year while Griffith served continuously. The following February a conference member moved to restore the rotative feature, but the motion was lost.[34] Since Griffith served continuously, he was the most influential member of the committee.[35]

The Training Table

The evening meal for football players had long been a matter of concern in the Big Ten. In 1908 the rule that prohibited a training table had helped prompt Michigan to withdraw from the conference. The ban on this perquisite was apparently intended to be permanent. In March 1933, however, the coaches and the athletic directors asked the conference authorities to consider the evening meal favorably. Nothing came of the request.[36] In 1934, though, Coach Zuppke, speaking for the coaches with the approval of the directors, recommended that each conference member might, if it desired, provide thirty-five men with evening meals at the expense of the athletic department every evening except Saturday and Sunday from the opening of the university in the fall to the end of the football season. The faculty committee unanimously disapproved of the request and reaffirmed its regulation, "There shall be no training table or training quarters for any athletic team."[37]

In May 1935 a motion to reconsider the prohibition was voted on and lost.[38] The following December the conference again denied the directors' request that the colleges be allowed to furnish an evening meal.[39] Two years later the directors, by 8 to 1, requested the faculty committee to reconsider the rule that prohibited athletic departments from providing evening meals for eligible football players on Monday, Tuesday, Wednesday, and Thursday during the football season. The conference deferred action on the recommendation until the following May.[40]

On that occasion the issue resurfaced with the proposal that athletic managements be authorized to furnish an evening meal on Mondays through Thursdays from the opening of college to the close of the football season to football players eligible for intercollegiate competition. This was understood to be an experiment; a joint committee of athletic directors and faculty representatives was to work out the details. In the vote on the measure Indiana, Iowa, Michigan, Northwestern, Ohio, Purdue, and Wisconsin were in favor, while Chicago, Illinois, and Minnesota were opposed. Since this was new legislation, it went to the faculties for approval.[41]

After the faculties had acted, the conference put the measure on its second passage under the White Resolution. It passed and became part of the rules. The conference appointed a joint committee—two faculty representatives and two athletic directors—to work out the details.[42] The Committee on the Evening Meal reported in May 1939, and the conference agreed on three regulations to govern the program. First, the number of men was to be restricted to fifty-five eligible football players. Second, discussions of and instructions in football were not to be carried on during the meal. And third, the term "meal" was understood as a meal for a group taken together, with the food of proper kind, quantity, and quality and properly served. This did not mean that the eligible athletes might eat at different places and that boardinghouse keepers and fraternities might be reimbursed. This new legislation was to go to the faculties.[43]

So the training table was restored. What accounts for the change? Perhaps the faculty representatives simply lacked the strength (or the will) to resist the relentless pressure of the directors. Or perhaps new conditions called for new responses. Intercollegiate football was not yet professional, it was only semi-professional. In any case, the directors responded to the situation as they saw it.

Meanwhile, the recruitment and subsidization of athletes increasingly threatened the Big Ten. In these matters, Griffith observed, there would always be a few who would attempt to cheat. For the previous few years the conference had had the matter in hand. His own statements belied the point, although the "pernicious recruiters" had been less active than formerly. During the Depression, athletic departments had helped needy athletes secure employment, but the employment bureaus had come to function solely in the interests of athletes. If they continued, the universities would be guilty of offering athletes jobs as inducements.[44]

Griffith sent the reports he received concerning this problem to a Committee on the Violation of Conference Regulations. Appointed in the spring of 1929, this committee was most likely a response to the exposure of corrupt practices at Iowa.[45] Like a grand jury, it received and considered charges of the violation of rules by its members. The athletic directors pledged to report through the commissioner's office rumors regarding possible infraction of conference rules. Copies of these reports, without the identity of the author, were sent to the athletic director and the faculty representative of the institution involved and to the infractions committee (Paige (chair), French, and Aigler). When the college in question reported its findings, the faculty committee decided how to proceed. Initially, most of the infractions identified were minor, but in one case a conference member dismissed a coach who was guilty of flagrant violation of conference regulations.[46]

In 1931 the committee proposed to add a new section to the conference rule on Compensation and Prizes. The addition, which dealt with subsidization, read as follows: "No student who, prior to the completion of one year of residence and one full year of work in a conference university has been (1) the beneficiary of a university loan fund however administered, or (2) the beneficiary of a remission of tuition, or (3) the recipient of a scholarship, unless such loan or remission or scholarship was made or awarded by or under the supervision of the university as a recognition of superior scholastic achievement, shall be eligible to represent such university in intercollegiate athletics." This being new legislation, it was to go to the faculties for approval. Aigler also proposed a revision that aimed at curbing delinquency in studies. The conference adopted the proposal, with the understanding that it was to be regarded as new legislation.[47]

The Committee on Infractions reported at the annual meeting. Beginning in the mid-1930s the committee consisted of Richart (Illinois), chair, Marshall (Purdue), and Moenkhaus (Indiana). Correspondence between the members and Griffith is revealing. Griffith sent the athletic directors bulletins on recruiting and subsidizing.[48] In 1936 he asked the directors to find out who was recruiting freshman athletes and what inducements they were offering.[49] In order to get a frank discussion, Griffith promised athletes that he would not embarrass them in any way, but if someone demanded proof, he would have to break his promise or get evidence some other way, as he had done in Iowa.[50]

Alumni, coaches, and athletic directors were eager to attract outstanding high school athletes. Griffith asked the directors to report on the aid given to freshmen athletes in their institutions. Their responses showed that in 1937 many were offered aid. The numbers were Chicago (6), Illinois (17), Indiana (13), Iowa (6), Michigan (11), Minnesota (7), Northwestern (20), Ohio State (3), Purdue (20), and Wisconsin (8). The aid, given to men identified only by number, took many forms. At Iowa, for example, an alumnus said he would take care of Athlete #4. At Michigan, Coach Kipke offered Athlete #11 a "scholarship and enough jobs to get through, although a poor student." At Northwestern the alumni secretary offered Athlete #4 a job, a high school teacher tried to induce Athlete #7 to go to Northwestern, and "Tug" Wilson offered Athlete #5 all expenses and a job on Saturday for $5 per day.[51]

In the summer of 1937 Griffith learned that recruiters from Pittsburgh, Pennsylvania, Florida, and Tennessee had visited Charles Maag, who had just graduated from high school in Sandusky, Ohio, and made him offers. In May, Kipke, the Michigan coach, had called Maag out of class and assured him that he would have no difficulty with finances if he attended Michigan.[52]

Writing anonymously, a correspondent related that Bernie Bierman, the Minnesota football coach, had come to Bemidji, Minnesota, for a high-school banquet, and "seeing a big, husky chap with the build of a Nagurski" proceeded to recruit him. The boy had been on the high-school team, but his folks were poor farmers, and he had never dreamed of going to college. Bierman gave him a job on the campus for the summer and employed him when he entered the General College. The writer, a member of the boy's class, knew that Danowsky, McCormick, and Galloway, also at Minnesota, were railroaded through high school by a coach who was assisted by his brother-in-law, the principal. Students in the school were ordered to "help these dumbbells with their homework." The coach and his assistant gave them undeserved high marks to offset low marks from other teachers. The coach led the athletes to believe that coaches would bid for their services, but the Big Ten and private schools had turned them down as deficient for college admission. So they enrolled at Minnesota and bragged that it did not matter whether they were good scholastically. "It is a crime," the writer added, "when selfish High coaches do a stunt like that to the youth of the land, but why are University coaches . . . allowed to get away with it."[53]

In September 1937 Griffith learned that Purdue had a training table for first-string football men who dined together every night, the cost of the meal being paid from the receipts of the spring football game. He passed this rumor along. Purdue's acting athletic director explained that a fraternity group was making it possible for some of the boys to have a hot evening meal, which might have been an infraction of the Big Ten rule on the subject. The parties concerned were acting in good faith, with a desire to be of service not only to their fraternity brothers but also to the football squad. "We have requested," the athletic director added, "that the practice be discontinued."[54]

In another case, a man informed Griffith that either Northwestern or Purdue had entertained David Miller. Griffith asked the infractions committee how to respond. If Purdue or Northwestern alumni paid the expenses of the boy to Chicago, Lafayette, or Evanston, was that a violation of a conference rule or of the spirit of the rule? "This young man has never been on the Purdue campus," Marshall, the Purdue member of the infractions committee, replied. He was a guest at a banquet given by Purdue alumni for prominent athletic possibilities and others. The university had nothing to do with the affair. "My informant . . . was quite frank about saying that the young man would be here soon, brought here by an alumnus. . . . This is possibly a violation of the spirit of our rules, but I can not think that we have anything to go on in the matter of infractions of Conference Regulations."[55]

In December 1938 the conference discontinued its Committee on Infractions.[56] Perhaps its findings were too devastating. In any case, recruitment and subsidizing continued.

Griffith was fully aware that conference coaches knew the names of outstanding high-school athletes and importuned them to attend their university. They promised them jobs while the alumni guaranteed them summer employment.[57] And yet he blithely admired how much the philosophy of the playing fields affected "our American philosophy of life." For many years he had been convinced that "our games on the whole exert an influence for good." Swelling with pride, he sent the faculty representatives, athletic directors, and coaches excerpts from his editorials in his *Athletic Journal* in the 1920s. If ever valuable, the editorials were dated. Big Ten Intercollegiate athletics had since gone from order to disorder.[58]

Conflict at Wisconsin

The athletic situation at the University of Wisconsin that came before the conference in 1936 had deep roots. The football team, lackluster since 1927, had caused acute financial pressures. In 1932 a legislative committee began investigating the Wisconsin athletic program, and a faculty committee appointed in 1930 reported. The Brown Committee, as it was known, warned of the growing professionalism of college football and over-coaching, which it attributed to the pressure of the alumni and the general public for a winner or a new coach. The committee recommended the restructuring of the athletic council, pruning it to seven persons, including three faculty members. The council owed its existence to and derived its powers from the faculty under the authority of the regents. At the next faculty meeting, J. F. A. Pyre, the chairman of the Athletic Council, recommended that intercollegiate athletics be administered as a separate department, distinct from the department of physical education, and that there be a director of intercollegiate athletics responsible to the University faculty through the Athletic Council.[59]

Two days later, on January 20, the board of regents accepted the resignations of the head football coach and the director of physical education. The board was still unhappy over the state of Wisconsin athletics. Regent Daniel H. Grady, an ardent Badger sports fan, presented a resolution calling for the replacement of the athletic council with an athletic board, a move that would assure direct regent involvement in athletics. The board of regents decided to defer action on the Grady resolution until their next meeting. Meanwhile, the Wisconsin legislature had passed a joint resolution expressing the state's "great disappointment" that the performance of the university's athletic teams did not match its academic stature. On March 9, Regent Grady succeeded in replacing the athletic council with an athletic board to consist of four faculty members, two representatives of the alumni association (rather than one), and the president of the student athletic board. The new board would also have two advisory members without vote—a regent and the university's business manager.

Arthur Hove, UW historian, writes, "A major reason for the regents' dissatisfaction with the old Athletic Council was its reluctance to nominate Clarence W. Spears as the new football coach. Spears, the head football coach at the University of Oregon, was the favored candidate of influential alumni and key regents." He bargained hard and won a "ten-month salary of $10,000 and moving expenses from Eugene, Oregon." Arriving in April 1932, "he was received like a conquering gladiator." The board was committed to "a revival of Badger athletic fortunes." It was "no credit to a university to build a great team," President Glenn Frank declared, if it did "no more than attract . . . the support of a sport-mad crowd that was not interested in the total purposes of the institution."[60]

"Whether the . . . new Athletic Board met the Big Ten requirement for faculty control of intercollegiate athletics was questionable," Hove notes, but in Depression times the faculty was "not ready for a showdown with the regents." Coach Spears did well in his first season (6-1-1), but then his teams spiraled downward (2-5-1, 4-4-0, and 1-7-0), and "he did not work well with colleagues," especially with Walter E. Meanwell in the athletic department. As events unfolded, the faculty became ready to remind the Board of Regents of the faculty's key role in intercollegiate athletics. At a special faculty meeting on February 10, 1936, the chairman of the University Committee read a proposed statement that declared that the control and administration of intercollegiate athletics was the responsibility of the faculty. The faculty members present unanimously endorsed the statement. "The showdown . . . came at a regents' meeting on February 14–15, when the Athletic Board recommended that [Spears] be fired . . . [and] that Meanwell be retained as athletic director." The regents rejected the recommendations and voted to let both Spears and Meanwell go. Declaring that the regents' action "made a mockery of faculty control, . . . the faculty members of the Athletic Board resigned, joined by the president of the [student athletic board]."[61]

Griffith kept abreast of Wisconsin events, and he commented on the conflict before it ran its course. The alumni members of the board of control, he wrote, usually two men from Milwaukee and Chicago, suggested some time earlier that the board fire football coach Glenn Thistlethwaite and hire Spears. "When Arlie Mucks went out to sign up Spears he promised that they would make him director. These alumni men and some of the Regents were responsible for this deal. The faculty does not want Doc [Thistlethwaite] as director." They were willing to let him stay as coach until the trouble occurred. "When the team won only one of its games these fellows . . . started blaming Meanwell for Spears' disastrous season. It is really a fight for power. The alumni and some of the Regents against the Faculty Committee."[62]

In mid-February the Intercollegiate Conference delegated Dean George A. Works, the faculty representative of the University of Chicago, and Bland A. Stradley of Ohio State to investigate a situation that had been widely reported in the national press. They arrived "the very day of the regents meeting" and reported to the conference what they found. On February 19, when the faculty representatives met, they heard from John Callahan, the Superintendent of Public Instruction in Wisconsin and a member of the board of regents, who was present by invitation. The conference then approved a preliminary statement that said "no one would seriously deny" that the board has "plenary control over the affairs of [their institutions], [but] it was equally clear that the Conference has jurisdiction to determine whether member institutions comply with requirements for continued membership therein. . . . [F]aculty control of intercollegiate athletics is a prime requirement for membership [in the conference]," and such membership "implies a definite compact with the other members that [control of athletic affairs] is delegated to the faculties." The statement further declared that "a persistent . . . course of action in repudiating duly expressed faculty sentiment could only mean that the faculty . . . does not have that measure of control demanded by the basic law of the Conference. . . . [A]thletic control involves more than the power to determine rules of eligibility, . . . schedules, and conditions of practice and participation; it must include a considerable measure of control over the selection of personnel of the staff in active charge. The evidence at hand establishes more than a reasonable doubt that Wisconsin now has that degree of faculty control required of [conference members]."[63]

Accordingly, the conference resolved that "the University of Wisconsin shall be declared suspended from membership in the conference beginning July 1, 1936," unless "the faculty in the meantime [notified] the conference that they consider themselves in control of their athletic affairs." In addition, the conference created a committee consisting of Works (Chicago), chair, Aigler (Michigan), and French (Ohio State) to act on its behalf "in receiving any communications from representatives of the University of Wisconsin and with power on behalf of the Conference to make any further studies or to participate in any conferences with such Representatives of the University of Wisconsin." The conference agreed to release the statement and the resolutions to the press.[64] The regents denied the Big Ten the "right to dictate," but Wisconsin faced suspension unless faculty control was re-established.[65]

On March 10 the conference ultimatum led the regents to accept the principle of faculty control of athletics embodied in the February 10 faculty declaration. The reconstituted athletic board was chaired by William F. Lorenz of the medical school, and at a special meeting on March 13 the faculty adopted a resolution declaring that the faculty of the University of Wisconsin considered itself in control of the athletic affairs of the institution.[66]

On May 22 the special committee appointed to act for the conference on the athletic situation at Wisconsin noted that the Wisconsin faculty had reconstituted its athletic board and established its powers, and that on May 4, the faculty considered itself in control of the athletic affairs of the university. The conference accepted this action as satisfying the requirement laid down by the conference on February 29, 1936, and it lifted its sanction.[67]

Shortly after the imbroglio at Madison, Glenn Frank, the president of the University of Wisconsin, wrote an article in which he argued that "football honestly administered, played by intelligent young men, under clean and competent leadership, can be made as effective an instrument of moral and intellectual discipline as any enterprise the American university fosters." He offered a creed of sportsmanship for young athletes "as definite and dominant as the creeds of religion drafted by the church fathers." Frank stated the ideal case.[68]

The Rose Bowl

The Western Conference had a history with the Rose Bowl. On January 1, 1902, the Michigan Wolverines had played Stanford in the Pasadena spectacle. The following November the faculty representatives declared that Michigan's participation was not in accord with the rule that all games should be played on the grounds of a conference school. In December 1920, after the Rose Bowl had won a national reputation, the conference allowed Ohio State to play in the game the following January, but the permission was not to be a precedent. In June 1921 the conference declared that disapproval of postseason games was now a rule. Soon thereafter Iowa anticipated an invitation to play in Pasadena, but the conference declared that appearance in a postseason game would violate the rule made in 1921. Accordingly, when Northwestern was invited to play in the Rose Bowl game in 1932, the faculty committee denied the request. In 1933 the athletic directors recommended an amendment of the postseason game rule so that it would be possible for a conference university team to accept an invitation to take part with reasonable frequency in the Rose Bowl game. The faculty committee decreed that the rule regarding postseason games would remain in place.[69]

Intercollegiate football won an increasingly devoted following between the two world wars. The Big Ten Conference remained the preeminent organization of its type, but several regional athletic conferences had gained a measure of acclaim over the years. In such a climate, entrepreneurs established venues designed to stage championship games between leading conference teams on a festival day. The Orange Bowl in Miami, Florida, became operative on January 1, 1935, the same day that the Sugar Bowl in New Orleans was the site for a championship game. The Sun Bowl in El Paso, Texas, was the venue for another championship game on December 31, 1935. And in 1937 the Cotton Bowl in Dallas, Texas, joined in.

Coaches, athletic directors, and fans witnessed these festivals, and in October 1938 William B. Owens described the possibilities of such an encounter in a letter to Ralph W. Aigler. Owens was a professor of law at Stanford, the Stanford representative to the Pacific Coast Conference, and the president of the NCAA. Aigler was a professor of law at Michigan and the Michigan representative to the Western Conference.[70]

The Pacific Coast Conference (PCC) was formed in 1915. Its charter members were the universities of California (Berkeley), Washington, Oregon, and Oregon Agricultural College (later Oregon State College). Six colleges later joined the conference: Washington State College (1917), Stanford University (1918), and the universities of Idaho (1922), Southern California (1922), Montana (1924), and California, Los Angeles (1928). The PCC employed a paid commissioner. Tensions between California and the Northwest schools troubled the conference, which had a formal code of conduct, a system of reporting athletic eligibility, and a history of being strict about standards. In 1924 the PCC suspended Southern California from the conference.[71]

Owens wrote that he was disturbed by "certain factors" that would inevitably affect Stanford and the other schools in what he called the Pacific Coast Intercollegiate Athletic Conference unless a solution to the problem was found. The

Rose Bowl game was here to stay; it had to be dealt with as part of intercollegiate athletics. The history and tradition of the game, its location in a center of a sports-minded population with college alumni from all over the country made certain a large "gate" no matter what teams played in the bowl games. The Rose Bowl was a lure to the colleges that did not stand for the best in athletics. It led them to practice many of the evils that others had been trying to eradicate. For the better schools to allow the others to play in the Rose Bowl was not good for intercollegiate athletics. To prevent such an outcome, the Pacific Coast Conference (PCC) had assumed the management and conduct of the game. During the previous summer many of the problems had been ironed out, placing the game in collegiate hands. The Tournament Committee was to receive a stipulated rental, with provision made for amortizing the cost of enlarging the bowl.[72]

Despite collegiate control, the game was connected with a civic enterprise, the Tournament of Roses, which condemned it in the minds of some college administrators. The future of the game depended on whether the better schools controlled or abandoned it. If the PCA were to stand aside, the game would fall into the hands of the institutions on the coast that did not reflect the best in athletics, and they would compete with similar institutions from other parts of the country. Other "bowl" games springing up intensified the objections. A football game would be played in Pasadena on New Year's Day. Who would control it? Owens proposed that the PAC and the Western Conference control the game and make it a force for good in intercollegiate athletics. Failure to do so would intensify the evils by permitting the game to fall into other hands.[73]

At present, the hope that some institutions had of playing in the Rose Bowl led some eastern and southern schools to do "heavy proselyting" in the Big Ten area. Good men were being drawn from the Western Conference area to these schools "to the detriment of educational interests of the boys themselves and the injury of sport generally." If the two conferences took over the Rose Bowl game, they would strengthen themselves and promote the interests of intercollegiate athletics. While a team selected by each conference would meet, the game would not constitute a "national championship." From the share of the team participating in the game, each conference could deduct a sum to pay the expenses of the conference, and all member institutions would share in the financial return.[74]

Owens countered the feeling that participation in the game would unduly prolong the football season by stipulating that there would be no formal practice by the teams participating from the end of the season until shortly before the game, which "would enable the players to devote their time to their studies until the Christmas holidays." The proposed arrangement could be tried for three years.[75]

Aigler submitted Owens's letter to the faculty representatives and suggested an exchange of views on the subject. Omera Long (Northwestern) recalled that "several conference members had received invitations to take part in the Rose Bowl game, and that one or two such games were authorized by special vote years ago. But for some time the conference had turned down the invitations for valid reasons, such as no more than eight games in our schedule, ending the football season on the Saturday before Thanksgiving, and no postseason games in any sports." The difficulties mentioned by Owens "were no doubt real," Long added, "but they were not of our making." The PAC might have control of certain features, but the Tournament Committee determined large items of expenses and fixed charges, and it shared equally with the two competing schools in the net receipts up to $100,000, with a sliding scale above this amount. "This still leaves the commercial element as a silent (?) partner in the set-up. . . . The argument about proselyting athletes from our territory was a two-edged sword. . . . We would likely increase rather than lessen our own troubles in this respect." The national championship aspect might not be in the mind of the Pacific Coast promoters, but the newspapers would serve that up "to their own taste" regardless of good intentions in the conference. The Pacific Coast could solve their own difficulties without our changing "a sound, traditional position. We ought to protect our students as students and we ought not to raise a larger target for the opponents of football to shoot at."[76]

Frank Richart, the Illinois faculty representative, wrote that the university's faculty athletic committee, which he chaired, did not favor the proposal. It would prolong the football season, "which left the athlete very little time to catch up on studies which are almost certainly slighted during the football season." Participation would lead to invitations to play in other "bowl" games and would break down resistance to postseason games in other sports as well. The committee thought that the PAC did not absolutely control the management and conduct of the game. For various reasons, a Big Ten team would always be playing under a physical handicap. If the Big Ten made an agreement with the PAC and the Tournament Committee, the public would assume that it was done for the money involved. In sum, the advantages of entering such an agreement seemed doubtful. The committee was against the proposal.[77]

Aigler was inclined to be critical of the proposal. Had it not been that Bill Owens was a man of high standing, Aigler doubted whether he would have presented it to the faculty committee. "Owens's standing was such that we ought to examine the plan as asked. If a majority of the conference were to favor any such plan, we should, as Richart suggested, incorporate limitations. The teams on the Pacific Coast competed under much more liberal conditions than ours did. Their rules of eligibility were not as severe, and they did not have the same attitude toward recruiting and subsidizing as we have. The competition would be in many respects unfair, and we would stand to lose a lot of prestige by going into the plan." Moreover, Aigler wanted to put a stop to the annual track meet between the Pacific Coast Conference and the Western Conference. "I have gone so far as to say that, while the Michigan disposition is to be fully cooperative with the other nine institutions [in the Big Ten], if this East-West meet is to go on, it will have to be staged without Michigan's active help."[78]

Nevertheless, the idea of a Rose Bowl game between a Western Conference team and a Pacific Coast Conference team excited many. The financial rewards were attractive. At the time the Rose Bowl Committee received one-third of the receipts, the competing universities the remainder. But the multiplication of bowl games had weakened the claim that the Rose Bowl game was the outstanding postseason contest. In the fall of 1938, there was a great deal of publicity about prolonging the football season in order to permit postseason games. The teams for the 1939 Rose Bowl contest had already been chosen. Looking forward to 1940, several Big Ten athletic directors, including Illinois's Wendell Wilson, favored a reciprocal arrangement between the Pacific Coast and the Western conferences. When the faculty committee met in early December they unanimously reaffirmed the conference ruling that the season was to end the Saturday before Thanksgiving Day.[79]

The Rose Bowl continued to be a magnet. In 1940 the athletic directors recommended that Big Ten teams be permitted to play in Pasadena. Aigler moved to reject the proposal, and his motion carried unanimously. The decision was costly. The visiting team's share of the Pasadena game receipts was roughly $100,000. In the same session, a request came for a postseason football game in Ann Arbor between the Michigan and Minnesota teams with the proceeds to go to the Detroit Red Cross. The conference voted to adhere to the existing regulation concerning post-season football games.[80] Thus the conference courageously reaffirmed its opposition to postseason games.

This decision was in accord with precedent and made the conference look good. However, a closer look at intercollegiate football revealed that the great American amateur sport had long been corrupted by a vicious professionalism. "In the seventy years of its existence," John R. Tunis wrote, "football has made liars out of college presidents, chiselers out of athletic directors, professional sports promoters out of head coaches, and bums out of 'amateur' players." These things were no secret in 1939. Nevertheless, Commissioner Griffith charged that "those who have indicted college football invariably fail to name the institutions that have allegedly adopted illegal practices, have practiced hypocrisy, and been animated by the lust for profits." Thus challenged, Tunis named the guilty institutions and players, based on their written and signed statements.[81]

Tunis began by listing the pickings of a Big Ten head coach whose salary as football coach was $8,200; with additional salary as professor of physical education and as vice president of a local cleaning company, income from lectures and writing, and royalties, his total "pickings" was $23,500. At that time the annual salary of the president of the University of Illinois was $16,000.[82]

The terms "amateur" and "professional" mean nothing in intercollegiate football today, wrote Tunis, who went on to classify the colleges. One group of sixty-seven named colleges were chiefly interested in the main purposes of education and did not pay their athletes. Another group of twenty-four colleges, including Indiana and Minnesota, paid only one or two key men, often though not invariably by the alumni. "The president usually knows this, but the chief business of college presidents is not to allow the right hand to know what the graduates are doing." In a third group of thirty-three colleges, among which were Michigan, Northwestern, Ohio State, Purdue, and Wisconsin, many squad-members were assisted in one way or another. Of the Big Ten universities, only Chicago, Illinois, and Iowa were not on any Tunis list. Finally, Tunis listed the colleges where the profit motive was important, sometimes decisive, and admittedly so. This group included the Southeastern Conference, the Southwest Conference, the Southern Intercollegiate Athletic Association, and the Southern Conference.[83]

In describing what football players received for their efforts, Tunis discussed five Big Ten schools: Wisconsin, Ohio State, Northwestern, Michigan, and Purdue.[84]

"Why do the colleges indulge in a racket like football?" Tunis asked. "To begin with, it's a habit and habits are hard to break." There was no easy way of escape, for many of the colleges owed huge sums on athletic plants. Moreover, a winning team helped keep the graduates happy. Football was good advertising. "Even if the college president were courageous, which the majority are not, he would open himself to terrific pressure if he took steps to drop the game." So football stays. It was easy to pretend that the problem was a minor one, but intercollegiate football affects millions of students everywhere. "It reaches down to the high schools and has an influence on our educational system from the top to the bottom. Football determines the conduct of college presidents, deans, and administrative officers. It has become an unsavory racket, and as such has no justifiable place on a college campus."[85]

In 1945, the conference yielded to continuing pressure and agreed to participate in the Rose Bowl game. The commercialization of Big Ten intercollegiate athletics had triumphed.

CHAPTER 14

Closing Out Half a Century

In the late 1930s the Big Ten operated in a challenging political, economic, and cultural climate. The Great Depression and the European dictators were the background of the 1936 presidential campaign. Griffith served on a national committee to put Alf Landon into the White House, but Roosevelt won in a landslide. In a postelection effusion, Griffith lamented that the American people now believed in an omnipotent and providential state. The free enterprise system was being discarded in favor of the totalitarian idea. In a system of state capitalism, athletics in colleges would be dependent on state support or state dictation.[1] Griffith became increasingly shrill about the threat to unfettered capitalism. To the proposal that someone should limit how much athletic coaches might earn, he replied that this peculiar un-American philosophy was given impetus by Karl Marx years ago and had been promulgated by people who believed in leveling down.[2]

The nation, Griffith believed, was gradually moving toward a corporate state. This would lead to a demand that the government control the nation's athletics. The conference should set an example of wise, honest, and efficient administration of athletics. People generally believed that the conference had held fast to its principles and had served the interests of the players and nonplayers alike. We should do everything possible to prevent the ultimate regimentation of our athletics.[3]

The Western Conference was widely recognized as the nation's premier intercollegiate athletic organization. Its eminence was based in part on the size of the student body in the member schools. In 1938 the five universities with the largest full-time enrollment were California, 24,809; Minnesota, 15,148; Columbia, 14,980; New York University, 14,257; and Illinois, 13,872. The full-time student enrollment in the other conference universities was Ohio State, 13,148; Michigan, 11,438; Wisconsin, 11,438; Purdue, 6,440; Chicago, 6,212; Indiana, 6,007; Northwestern, 5,933; and Iowa, 5,901.[4]

In late 1938 Griffith reported that total attendance at college football games in the fall was estimated at forty million. That large crowds enjoy football condemned it in some minds. "They fear that the presence of such folks might degrade the atmosphere of educational institutions and that spectators could spend their time to better advantage."[5] Griffith alerted the conference athletic directors to "the annual attack on college football," citing mass-circulation magazines to illustrate his point. "Some say that these destructive criticisms should be ignored. The attendance at games shows that the average citizen does not care whether or not our players are hired. What to do? Present the facts regarding those institutions in which athletics were properly administered and see that our own house is in order."

"There are persons in the Conference," Griffith acknowledged, "who violate the Conference rules regarding recruiting and subsidizing."[6] Indeed. On this matter the Big Ten was on a precipice and falling. Most of the complaints by coaches, alumni, and journalists regarding eligibility had to do with these matters. One unidentified coach said that the reason his team lost was that the commissioner did not have the courage to make the competing school conduct their athletics with no paid players. This coach had not complied with Griffith's request to turn in all the information he had on alleged illegitimate recruiting and subsidizing. Conference athletes were not being paid weekly or monthly salaries, Griffith believed, and no slush fund was in operation. The chief problem was colleges that offered to find athletes jobs as an inducement to enrollment.[7]

In 1937 a North Central College Association committee reported on recruitment and subsidization in athletic conferences in the Big Ten area.[8] The replies showed that the practice was more prevalent than before. In these practices the alumni were no less noxious than the coaches. There was more "shopping around" than previously. The press built up an athlete, who became conscious of his market value, aided by some high school principals and coaches, and the colleges courted such boys.[9]

Each year the conference universities sent the commissioner reports concerning scholarships, loans, and jobs for athletes, both on and off campus. The reports dealt only with men who actually competed in intercollegiate contests and freshmen numeral men. The reports for 1937–38 revealed the number of athletes in each institution who were recipients of aid as follows: Chicago (14), Illinois (36), Indiana (33), Iowa (31), Michigan (37), Minnesota (27), Northwestern (34), Ohio State (37), Purdue (44), and Wisconsin (39).[10]

In 1938, Big Ten football revenue was $1,898,607. Ohio State led, followed by Minnesota, Northwestern, and Michigan. Six universities received less than $200,000 from their teams.[11]

John A. Hannah, who became the president of Michigan State in 1940, viewed gridiron success as a means of transforming an agricultural school into a research university. He coveted a place in the Big Ten.[12] Over the years Michigan State had produced some strong football teams by subsidizing players. But Michigan overshadowed Michigan State, and Ann Arbor was unwilling to share its football glory and profits with the East Lansing upstart. Ralph Aigler (Michigan) impeded Hannah's effort to join the conference.[13]

When the conference met on May 22, 1937, the chairman reported that Michigan State had applied for membership. After discussing the matter, the members unanimously voted "that it was the sense of the Conference that it was inexpedient to increase the size of the Conference at this time." Aigler, present when the meeting was called to order, absented himself when the application was discussed and voted upon.[14]

The Big Ten and Pittsburgh

Football gained a hold at the University of Pittsburgh in the early twentieth century, and in 1915 Pitt aspired to pigskin supremacy with the hiring of Glenn S. "Pop" Warner as the head football coach. One of Warner's players was John Bain Sutherland. Born in Scotland, he came to America in 1907 at age eighteen, enrolled in Pitt in 1914, and became a famous end on Warner's winning teams. "Jock" Sutherland coached at Lafayette College from 1919 to 1923, returning to the campus after the football season each year to earn a degree at Pitt's School of Dentistry. In 1924 Sutherland succeeded Pop Warner as the head football coach at Pitt. From 1924 to 1937 the Pitt Panthers won the Eastern football championship seven times and played in the Rose Bowl four times.

In 1921 John G. Bowman became the chancellor of the university. Bowman and Sutherland came into conflict. Bowman devoted himself to raising money to build the Cathedral of Learning, while Sutherland built an athletic stadium. It was completed in 1925 at a cost of $2,500,000.

With the stadium it became necessary to schedule money games to pay off the debt. To do so it was necessary to recruit and subsidize athletes. From 1924 to 1936 the players were paid on an individual basis. The payment varied from $400 to $650, plus tuition and books, with no work required. From 1924 to 1939, the Pitt Panthers played nine games in nine seasons, ten games in six seasons, and eleven games in one season. Among their opponents were Nebraska (thirteen seasons), Notre Dame (seven seasons), Ohio State (four seasons), and Minnesota and Wisconsin (two seasons each).[15]

In 1937 the tension between the academic and athletic forces at Pitt became acute. W. Don Harrison, the athletic director, and Jock Sutherland had long been at odds. After a conflict over payment to athletes, Harrison resigned. With the Sutherland faction victorious, Chancellor Bowman called for an athletic policy against the subsidization of athletes and appointed Jimmy Hagan as the new athletic director. Determined to run his own show, Hagan required athletes to work for their monthly payment. Faced with such a Draconian measure, Sutherland and the Alumni Association's Athletic Council adopted a secret policy of subsidization.

Early in 1938 Chancellor Bowman instituted a program designed to insure that Pitt acted in accord with the best traditions of intercollegiate athletics. The Faculty Committee on Athletic Policy replaced the athletic council, whereupon athletes had to pay their tuition or work it out, the number of football games was reduced from nine to eight a season, football practice was to begin on September 10, and an athlete had to advance with his class.[16]

The faculty committee made a recommendation, which Chancellor Bowman delivered to the executive committee of the board of trustees on January 31, 1939, "that the University enter into cooperative agreement with the Western Conference, whereby the commissioner of the Western Conference would render that same service to the University of Pittsburgh as he does for the ten university [sic] comprising the Conference and the University would furnish him with the same type of information concerning the conduct of Athletics."[17]

The faculty committee requested that the trustees approve the proposal before final action was taken. The recommendation added that "a proposed arrangement for cooperation between the University and the ten Universities of the Western Conference be approved as proposed by the faculty committee on Athletic Policy."[18]

Then someone at Pitt turned to the Big Ten commissioner for help.[19] They asked Griffith if he would investigate their setup and request conference men to assist by passing through his office reports concerning Pittsburgh's athletic affairs. They would pay the cost of any work that he might do. Griffith was willing and would not accept any pay for his services, provided the men in the conference were willing. He asked Richart (Illinois) about the Pitt approach. Richart thought it would be "quite all right" for Griffith to investigate and to act as a clearinghouse on information for their benefit, assuming it would not interfere with his duties in the Big Ten. "A little missionary work here should be of a great deal of help to us in the Big Ten in building up public opinion in favor of sports on a strictly amateur basis."[20]

Omera Long (Northwestern) was more cautious. Some conference members were disturbed over Pittsburgh's claim that she was under the supervision of the Big Ten and that Griffith was their sponsor. Long was sorry that the news about Griffith's work with Pitt had not come before the faculty representatives before any such arrangement was agreed upon.[21]

Richart had assumed that Griffith was writing to all the faculty representatives. He had the impression that the investigation Griffith was to make was a temporary affair and that any further aid would be more or less confidential information. The impression one got from the newspapers was quite different. It seemed probable that "Pittsburgh hopes to get some benefit of the name and prestige of the Big Ten without assuming any of the responsibilities of such connection." Pitt was not obligated to act on information Griffith might supply or to follow Big Ten rules. For that reason Griffith's connection with Pittsburgh might be undesirable even though the intention was perfectly good. Any permanent connection with Pitt should be put before the faculty representatives for their approval. There has been no reason for the assumption that Pitt's overture was a preliminary to get-ting Pittsburgh into the Big Ten.[22]

The hiring of Griffith threatened to end winning football at Pitt, and it led to heated protest by Pitt alumni and students.[23] Griffith denied any conference al-liance with Pitt and claimed that no Pitt officials had approached him regarding membership in the conference.

In May 1939 a Big Ten conference committee discussed the Pitt situation and decided that "in the matter of the relation of this Conference to other confer-ences, it was agreed that Professor Aigler might act as the representative of this Conference in conferring with such other conferences as might invite him."[24]

Griffith developed good working relations with Hagan, the Pitt athletic direc-tor. They concluded that there might be merit in Pitt joining the Western Confer-ence. In February 1941 Griffith asked St. John, the Ohio State athletic director, to join in a confidential meeting in Pittsburgh to facilitate Pitt's planning. St. John probably helped the Panthers schedule football games with Western Conference members for the next several years.[25]

In December 1944, when the faculty representatives met in Chicago, the usual order of business was changed to permit a hearing requested by members of the Pittsburgh faculty. R. E. Sherrill and H. L. Mitchell then gave some information about the athletic organization and policies at Pitt. When they left, the business meeting was resumed.[26] It is highly likely that Sherrill and Mitchell pleaded Pitt's case to become a member of the Big Ten conference.

Sic Transit Gloria Chicago

Harper and Stagg had been united in their determination to win a reputation for the University of Chicago by means of football. Stagg relentlessly promoted both himself and his Maroons. Harper backed him. After Harper died, Stagg continued to demand special consideration for himself and his football team. For years he met little restraint from the administration or the faculty. Football enthusiasts within the university sided with Stagg, while critics of football or Stagg were discretely silent. For years Chicago had been successful on the gridiron, winning the Big Ten football championship in 1899, 1905, 1907, 1908, 1913, and 1924. Victories spread the university's name and brought in large gate receipts. In this milieu, Ernest H. Wilkins went unheard.

The year 1924 was a turning point for both Stagg and Chicago football. The Maroons began an irreversible decline. For many reasons the pool of players was thin. As a result, the Maroons were no longer able to compete with other conference teams on a reasonably equal basis. Stagg remained the football coach, but from 1925 to 1932 he had a record of 25-39-5. During the 1928 season, a Chicago home game with Iowa attracted thirty thousand spectators, while on the same day a conference game at Evanston drew fifty thousand spectators, and a Navy–Notre Dame game at Soldier Field attracted about 120,000 fans. Continually decreasing attendance meant reduced revenue. In 1924 Chicago's football receipts had been $233,577. In 1932 they were $61,055.

In 1929 Robert Maynard Hutchins became the president of the University of Chicago. One of three sons of a Presbyterian minister, Hutchins had grown up in Oberlin, Ohio, where his father taught homiletics. An excellent student, Hutchins

Robert Maynard Hutchins, the incoming president of the University of Chicago, is pictured here with Frederick Woodward, university vice president, and Harold H. Swift, chairman of the board of trustees. Source: University of Chicago, Special Collections Research Center.

worked his way through Yale. After a brief stint with the Yale alumni office, Hutchins taught in the Yale law school and became its dean at the age of twenty-nine. He was thirty when he arrived in Chicago as the new president. A brilliant and independent thinker, Hutchins did not share his father's religious faith, but he was a latter-day Puritan who relentlessly searched for fundamental truth.[27]

The university was reconstructing its undergraduate academic program when Hutchins arrived. Both the ferment of change and football's declining fortunes put Stagg's future at risk. In a preemptive strike three years before his seventieth birthday, Stagg wrote to Hutchins in an effort to ensure his future at Chicago. His "audacious plan [was to] 'retire' from the faculty but be given the new position of 'Director or Chairman of Intercollegiate Athletics.'" Hutchins, in a delayed response, "suggested instead two public relations positions . . . one working with high schools and alumni; the other, as university representative to intercollegiate athletic meetings." Stagg took eight months to reply, and then turned down the offers.[28]

Hutchins hired T. Nelson Metcalf as the new athletic director. An Oberlin family friend who had been a student, coach, and physical educator at Oberlin before going to Iowa State as athletic director, Metcalf arrived in 1933. Stagg retired after the 1932 football season and went to the College of the Pacific in Stockton, California. As the new football coach, Metcalf hired Clark D. Shaughnessy, a tackle on the 1912 Minnesota team who had coached for years at Tulane. From 1933 to 1939 his record with the Maroons was 17-34-3.[29]

Metcalf's views on intercollegiate athletics were unlike those that prevailed in Chicago before his arrival. He did not want athletics to interfere with academic work. He believed in "light schedules, playing only natural rivals, short practice periods, and a minimum of absence from classes." Metcalf viewed "recruiting and subsidizing players as the 'greatest evil' in collegiate athletics." Hutchins most likely shared these views.[30]

In theory and in practice, the university faculty and the senate should have been able to eliminate football, which was located in an academic department, the Board of Physical Culture and Athletics. In fact, however, football was a volatile substance, to be dealt with by the board of trustees. When Hutchins and Metcalf presented their case for terminating football to the board, all of the trustees voted in favor except Harold H. Swift, the president of the board. For years Swift had recruited athletes, especially from California. Now he fell in line with the board.

In 1938 Hutchins stated his views on football and the culture of which it was a part in the Saturday Evening Post. The reason nobody has done anything about the "overemphasis on athletics" for almost fifty years, he wrote, is that "nobody wants to give up gate receipts." "Money is the cause of athleticism in the American colleges." Hutchins distinguished between athletics and athleticism. Athletics are fine; colleges should provide students with opportunity for physical education. Athleticism is "sports promotion . . . carried on for the monetary profit of the colleges through the entertainment of the public." Athleticism confuses the public about the primary purpose of higher education. Colleges are dedicated to the development of the mind.

Hutchins went on to analyze some athletic myths (myths that Griffith purveyed, although Hutchins did not name him). Apologists for athleticism say that "biceps are a substitute for brains," that "athletic colleges are a bulwark against Communism," that "gate receipts are used to build laboratories" and pay for some sports on the campus. These myths have a certain plausibility, Hutchins admitted, but these supposed advantages are tinged with the "color of money," which casts "a mercenary shadow" over "every relaxation of standards." "Young people who are more interested in their bodies than their minds should not go to college. . . . [A]thleticism gives the student a mistaken notion of the qualities that make for leadership in later life. . . . [I]t focuses . . . on doing good for the boys who least need it—those eligible for intercollegiate competition." "The alleged connection between athletic experience and moral principles," he continued, "was highly dubious." "The cheers that rock the stadium have a rapid depreciation rate."[31]

Hutchins traced a vicious circle in intercollegiate athletics. An athlete is "made to feel that his primary function in college is to win football games. The coach demands it, . . . the alumni demand it," but "the prestige that winning teams confer upon a university, and the profits that are alleged to accompany prestige, are the most serious obstacle to reform." "The myth that donors . . . are impressed by football victories collapses on examination." Athleticism is bad for the colleges and universities, he asserted: "They want to be educational institutions but they can't. . . . A college should not be interested in a fullback who is a half-wit. Recruiting, subsidizing, and the double educational standard cannot exist without the knowledge and tacit approval, at least, of the colleges and universities themselves. Certain institutions encourage susceptible professors to be nice to athletes now admitted by paying them for serving as 'faculty representatives' on the college athletic board."[32]

Pressing his point, Hutchins declared that "if colleges and universities were to commend themselves to the public chiefly through their athletic accomplishments," they should choose as president a sports promoter. "To make big money in athletics you have to spend big money. . . . Subsidizing is expensive. . . . The myth that football receipts support research, education, or other sports had been exploded," Hutchins said. He cited the 1925 AAUP report, which "expressed the hope that colleges would publish the cost of their stadiums." The reason the costs could not be paid off was that the stadiums were "built for only one sport, football," and pro football was "attracting larger and larger crowds and may ultimately do for college football what pro baseball has done for college baseball."[33]

What, Hutchins asked, is the cure for athleticism? "Take the money out of athletics." Hutchins suggested that a group of prestigious colleges and universities, which he named, do certain things to promote change. "Reduce admission to games to ten cents, . . . give athletic directors and coaches some kind of tenure," broaden the base of athletic participation by urging students "to play for fun and health," and "emphasize games which students will play in later life." "In a word: more athletics, less athleticism," he asserted. If the prestigious colleges and universities he named took the recommended steps, other schools would not be able to ignore the example. The public "has been taught to accept football. It can . . . be taught to accept education. . . . The task of the colleges and universities is to show the country a substitute for athleticism"—in other words, light and learning. "The colleges and universities, which taught the country football, can teach the country that the effort to discover truth, to transmit the wisdom of the race, and to preserve civilization is exciting and perhaps important too."[34]

John Griffith had always been quick to rebut criticism of Big Ten athletics, but a direct reply to Hutchins would not be prudent. Six months later, however, Griffith castigated Hutchins in the *Athletic Journal* without naming him. "Today the competitive system [in athletics] is being attacked. . . . It is significant that the collectivists in our own country are invariably opposed to what they choose to call 'Athleticism.' This is natural because they do not believe in competition."[35]

In December 1939, after the football season, Chicago terminated its football program and asked for release from its gridiron commitments. This was a turning point in the history of the conference. Chicago did not cease to participate in other intercollegiate conference sports at this time. In 1946, however, Chicago withdrew from the conference.

Circling the Wagons

Shortly after the Chicago trustees voted to discontinue football, an anonymous spokesman who claimed to speak for the trustees said that no school could play football of Big Ten caliber without violating the conference rules on recruiting and subsidization. Hutchins had set a high scholarship standard for the University and had come out against proselyting. Confronted with Chicago terminating football and the anonymous charge, the presidents of the other Big Ten universities rallied around intercollegiate football.

Clarence A. Dykstra (Wisconsin), Edward E. Elliott (Purdue), Franklin B. Snyder (Northwestern), Herman B. Wells (Indiana), Eugene A. Gilmore (Iowa), Alexander G. Ruthven (Michigan), William McPherson and James L. Morrill (Ohio State), and Arthur C. Willard (Illinois) responded to Hutchins with variations on the theme that intercollegiate football had an integral place in education, a strong effect on the spirit of an institution, and it built character.

Tom Harmon had an illustrious career playing football at Michigan. In this picture Harmon is punting from his own end zone in a game with Minnesota in 1940. Source: University of Michigan, Bentley Historical Library.

On January 12, as the Big Ten presidents circled their wagons, Hutchins gave an address, "Football and College Life," on the Midway campus. On the whole, Hutchins said, the game has been "a major handicap to education" in the United States. It has done much to "originate and disseminate . . . the popular conceptions of what a university is—a kindergarten and a country club. . . . [T]he advantages of football are not unique to that game." The other Big Ten universities, he asserted, are much larger than the University of Chicago, and "an estimated 50 percent of football players in the Big Ten are students in schools of physical education." The *Chicago Tribune*'s assessment was that Hutchins's address scored "a rhetorical touchdown for his side," giving "a brilliant exhibition of grammatical broken field running" that elicited "thunderous cheers" from an overflow student audience.[36] His address did not go unnoticed. Fielding Yost, the Michigan athletic director, replied that thirty-five thousand schools and one thousand colleges in America sponsored football. Hutchins was the one who was out of step.[37]

The most valuable comment on Chicago's elimination of football and on the presidents' reaction to the decision was an editorial in the *Chicago Defender*, an African-American newspaper. "One might be charitable towards morons and imbeciles who measure the worth and standing of an academic institution by the victories recorded on the gridiron," wrote the editor. "But when university presidents enthusiastically marshal their logic in the defense of a game whose value, even in the realm of physical education, is doubtful, the intelligent public cannot fail to question the intellectual honesty and integrity of such educators. None of the heads of the Big Ten schools came to the rescue of . . . Hutchins, [who] stood alone in his contention that the game . . . is not indispensable to the academic health and tone of an institution of higher learning. [Hutchins] might have added . . . that it is not conducive to good scholarship and institutional development. . . . What then, is the argument in favor of college football? . . . [M]any silly sentimentalities . . . are advanced by the devotees of the game, [but] in reality there are but two possible arguments, and they are dubious." To the contention that "football advertises the institution," the editor said, "one might say that an academic institution . . . advertises itself by the quality of its scholars and byproducts. The great centers of learning in Europe . . . have no football teams. Yet there are no empty seats . . . in any of those halls of learning." It is contended that football brings additional revenues. "What is generally meant . . . is money raised for football equipment, for travelling expenses of the team, for the coaching staff and for paying off unnecessary debts incidental to the erection of a pretentious stadium. If advertising and additional revenues could not be secured through any other method, it would be cheaper and more dignified to hire a professional team or to engage frankly in open subsidy of all the players. There can be no sound logical ground on which to criticize" Hutchins' recent decision. "He is running an academic institution, and not an advertising school."[38]

The War and the Ferment of Change

In May 1941, with Europe at war, the conference offered its cooperation with Major Ted Banks, the officer in charge of the U. S. Army's athletic program. The Big Ten appointed a committee to consider the extent to which the conference might be useful in "the present emergency."[39] In September the commanding officer of Camp Grant, located just south of Rockford, Illinois, requested that their service team be permitted to compete in football with the B teams of the conference universities.[40]

In a special March meeting after Pearl Harbor, the conference agreed to waive certain rules for the duration of the war and six months thereafter. In addition, the conference waived certain rules for 1942 to permit the playing of ten football games, at least two to be with service teams. Games were to be permitted one week before and one week after the current football season. In addition, the conference agreed to waive a regulation so freshman teams could compete in all sports with freshman teams from other colleges, with service teams, and with varsity teams from other colleges, provided that in football the number of such games be limited to three, and that such games were not to be played until after a conditioning period of four weeks.[41]

The following May, on request from the directors and in consideration of the lengthening of the football schedule to permit games with service teams, another regulation was waived for the 1942 season so that the date for the opening of football practice might be either three weeks before the opening game of the season or on the opening day of classes, whichever was earlier (but not before September 1).[42]

The athletic directors steadily pushed for expansion of the football program. In 1943, noting that many football candidates would be new students who lacked the benefit of spring practice, the directors recommended that football practice be permitted for four weeks during the 1943 summer. Only the fourth week would involve body contact. A motion to eliminate all body-contact practice failed, after which the original motion passed, with three dissenting votes. Moreover, because the football schedule had been lengthened to permit games with service teams, the directors again recommended and the faculty committee waived a regulation for the 1943 season so that football practice could be held either three weeks before the opening game of the season or September 1, whichever was earlier. These suspensions of regulations due to the war emergency were to be considered temporary, not as new legislation.[43]

Historically, the conference had circumscribed competition with nonconference schools and had banned freshmen from participating on varsity athletic teams. In December 1935 the athletic directors recommended and the conference agreed to allow conference competition in all sports except football with institutions that did not observe the freshman rule. The waiver was to be final.[44] A year later, when some conference schools reportedly had been inviting freshmen to report for football practice, the conference declared that the practice was inconsistent with the spirit of the freshman rule. No freshmen should be invited to report for practice, and football squad activities should not be permitted until the opening of the regular school year.[45]

Under the impact of war, however, the conference revised the rule in order to permit freshman teams to compete in all sports with freshman teams from other colleges, with service teams, and with varsity teams of other colleges, provided that in case of football the number of games be limited to three, and that such games were not to be allowed until after a four-week conditioning period in the first part of the semester or quarter, and that the residence requirement of one academic year be waived to permit freshmen to compete as described.[46]

In the early twentieth century, the Western Conference had opposed postseason games and championship teams as inimical to academic values. In December 1944 Aigler introduced the subject of championships in football and some other sports. It might be desirable, he suggested, to have a procedure whereby the conference could select the championship team in all sports rather than leave the decision to journalists. The faculty committee referred the matter to the directors, with the request that they report back on the desirability of the proposal.[47] The conference was allowing the press to force its hand.

As the war wound down, the Big Ten neared the end of its first half-century. John Griffith died in his office at the Hotel Sherman on December 7, 1944. The athletic directors had just renewed his contract for five years. The *Chicago Tribune* acclaimed Griffith as "an arbiter of disputes, policy director, and calm adviser" whose policies were copied in other sections of the country. "In recent years," the paper reported, "he had become interested in the suppression of subversive practices. He was the national vice president of the Paul Reveres, an organization designed 'to promote patriotism, to advance Americanism and to combat radicalism.'"[48] In the early voting for football's man of the year sponsored by the Football Writers Association, Griffith ranked second of the five nominees. He outpolled General H. H. "Hap" Arnold, the commandant of the Army Air Force during the war.[49]

Kenneth Wilson, the Northwestern athletic director, temporarily replaced Griffith. In January the directors and faculty representatives agreed to invest the commissioner's office with more authority, to begin conference meetings with a joint executive session to outline problems, and to have the commissioner sit in at meetings of the faculty representatives. Reportedly, the commissioner's salary would be increased from $10,000 to $15,000.[50]

Guy Mackey, the Purdue athletic director, reported that Herbert O. "Fritz" Crisler was the unanimous choice of the directors for conference commissioner. Crisler had played football at Chicago from 1919 to 1921, had been an assistant coach there from 1922 to 1929, the head coach at Minnesota from 1930 to 1931 and at Princeton from 1932 to 1937. He became the head football coach at Michigan in 1938, had an excellent record, and was in that position in 1945. After a long discussion, the directors agreed to tender Crisler a six-year contract at $15,000 for the first three years and at $17,500 for the next three years, with a suitable retirement policy.[51]

Crisler declined the offer. He remained the head football coach at Michigan until 1947 and then became the athletic director at Ann Arbor. So the directors named "Tug" Wilson for the position. He had graduated from the University of Illinois in 1920 with a BS in agriculture. As an undergraduate he was a member of the varsity football, basketball, and track teams and had competed in the discus throw in the 1920 Summer Olympics. He had been the athletic director at Drake University from 1925 to 1945 and was now in the same position at Northwestern. His appointment was for a six-year term.[52]

In late November 1944 the faculty representatives met to consider Ohio State's request to participate in the Rose Bowl game on January 1, 1945. The Buckeyes had just won the Big Ten championship. As the faculty committee considered the matter, they discussed an earlier proposal that the Rose Bowl game be confined to members of "the two conferences" (the Western Conference and the Pacific Coast Conference), together with certain consequences if the Big Ten's post-season rule was maintained. "Mention was made of other post-season games, of which one was recently refused by Conference action and another by a member institution." A motion to waive a rule to permit Ohio State's football team to compete in the 1945 Rose Bowl game, if invited, lost by a vote of 7 to 3.[53] The Big Ten courageously held to its historic position: no postseason games.

In December, however, Aigler (Michigan) introduced in a conference meeting the subject of official championships in football and some other sports. In the past the faculty representatives had opposed such contests. It might be desirable, Aigler now suggested, to have a procedure by which the conference might select the championship team rather than leave the decision to the news writers. Once again the faculty representatives were allowing the press to force their hand. The faculty committee agreed to refer the awarding of official championships in all sports to the directors, with the request that they report as to the desirability of the proposal.[54] Times had changed. None could doubt that official championships were about to be permitted.

Meeting on or about March 1945, the faculty representatives discussed the Rose Bowl, the Pacific Coast Conference, and postseason games. Rottschaefer (Minnesota) generally opposed Rose Bowl and postseason games, primarily because of their commercial nature and the time when they were held. He noted that arguments in favor of participating in the event had been presented previously and had been turned down a year ago. Aigler made a long plea in favor of the Rose Bowl game, after which he moved that, as an exception to the present postseason regulation, the game be permitted. The motion was approved 6 to 3.[55] The exception soon became the rule. Thus the Big Ten accelerated the commercialization of intercollegiate football.

In December 1945 the Intercollegiate Conference celebrated its fiftieth anniversary. The festivities began with a meeting of the directors, football coaches, and faculty representatives in Chicago's Hotel Sherman. Commissioner Wilson reported on the work of his office.[56] A dinner meeting of the presidents of the conference universities, the faculty representatives, and the athletic directors was held at the University Club.[57] Here, in tracing the history of the Big Ten, Aigler observed that it was a meeting of the college presidents in 1895 that gave rise to the conference. He emphasized the underlying philosophy of the conference in terms of its basic rules, called attention to the problems confronting the members, and invited advice from the university administrators present. St. John, the senior athletic director, reviewed the growth of the organization with reference to the role of the directors. All present agreed that the Big Ten should reinstate its prewar standards as soon as possible. To do so, several presidents declared, would not be easy. The presidents had few suggestions to offer; such, in their opinion, was the responsibility of the faculty representatives and the directors. Several presidents declared that the future of the conference was safe "as long as the caliber and integrity of the men immediately responsible for its administration were maintained."[58] This fatuous remark was perhaps appropriate for the occasion.

Meeting on December 8, the faculty representatives voted to continue the nine-game football schedule, provided that six were conference games and two were home games. The football season was to begin no earlier than the last Saturday of September and to close no later than the Saturday preceding the last Thursday in November. This rule was to become effective in the 1947 season. The representatives voted to eliminate summer football practice but to permit a five-week preseason practice.[59]

With this meeting the Big Ten ended its first half-century. The end came with neither a bang nor a whimper, but one could wonder about the future of the conference. President Angell of Yale had recently observed that the 1929 Carnegie Report had led many institutions to conduct an overdue housecleaning, but retrogression had set in. After describing the worst features of football, Angell posed questions that had to be dealt with by anyone who believed in the worth of university education and appreciated the values inherent in football. First, was football to be kept a game or was it to be run "as a business and for advertising purposes"? Second, if it was to be a game, was it "to be played by amateurs or by hired men"? And third, if by amateurs, "was the training to be given by educated men with high character or by men whose preponderant interest was in holding their lucrative jobs by producing winning teams at whatever cost"?[60] Angell's observations were appropriate, but by this time the answers to his questions were obvious.

The Western Conference had changed dramatically since its founding. One might well ask how it would balance the competing claims of higher education and intercollegiate athletics as it went forward. Sufficient unto the day would be the evil thereof.

Postscript: A Look Forward

Some of the main developments in the Big Ten since 1945 deserve notice here. Most significant was the creation of a football structure of fourteen members divided along geographical lines that preserved historic rivalries. Each of its two divisions contained seven members. The East Division included Indiana, Maryland, Michigan, Michigan State, Ohio State, Penn State, and Rutgers. The West Division included Illinois, Iowa, Minnesota, Nebraska, Northwestern, Purdue, and Wisconsin. All schools in the East Division were in the eastern time zone and all schools in the West Division were in the central time zone with the exception of Purdue. James E. Delany, the Big Ten commissioner, designed the new configuration to tap into the lucrative East Coast football market, especially Rutgers and Maryland.

The football division alignments were to begin in 2014, and the nine-game conference schedules were to start in 2016. Each school was to play the other six schools in its division plus two teams from the other division in the transitional years in which the schools would still be playing eight-game schedules. Beginning in 2016 each school would play three teams from the other division as part of its nine-game schedule. The cross-division games were to include one protected matchup on an annual basis between Indiana and Purdue.

Rutgers might be hopelessly outmatched in football competition with Michigan, but the game was viewed as a financial win-win for both the conference and the school. As long as Rutgers was determined to participate in big-time athletics, it was better off in the Big Ten, where it received millions of dollars annually in conference revenue, than not in the conference. In Rutgers's first year in the conference, the Big Ten Network (BTN) added eight million homes in the New York City area and experienced a higher-than-expected rise in advertising revenue. Without Rutgers and Maryland, it was not clear that the Big Ten could have supported rights deals with ESPN, Fox Sports, and CBS Sports worth $250 million annually.

The Big Ten Network, a joint venture between Fox Sports and the Big Ten Conference, was the first successful collegiate television network to be partially owned by a conference.

Mark Silverman, the president of the Big Ten Network, holds a BA in economics from the University of California, Los Angeles, and an MBA from the University of Michigan. He began his media career at the Walt Disney Company.

Large crowds and television revenue from big games promised to enrich the universities whose football teams provided the spectacle. In 2011, for example, the University of Michigan football team played the Ohio State football team before 114,132 people, and Michigan faced Nebraska before 113,718 fans. A year later

Michigan engaged Michigan State before 113,833 spectators. In 2013, attendance at a Michigan-Ohio State contest was 113,518, and in 2014 Michigan played Penn State before 113,085 spectators.[61] One might wonder how much, if any, of the revenue from these games went to educational purposes. In any case, the purpose universities are intended to serve—to educate students for useful pursuits—seemed to be lost, and few cared.[62]

Closely related to the developments described is another feature of the times. In an earlier age young men went to college for an education and played football as a diversion. Now high-school students with an athletic reputation shop around for the university that offers them the best "package." Once admitted, they are described as "student-athlete," an oxymoron coined by the NCAA.

Once upon a time the football season culminated each year with two of the nation's best football teams playing in the Rose Bowl on January 1. Now multiple forces have combined to give the public some forty bowl games beginning on December 17 and ending on January 9 with the so-called National Championship between the winners of the Peach Bowl and the Fiesta Bowl (both of these games will have been played on December 31), scheduled for January 9. Four bowl games—the Outback, Cotton, Rose, and Sugar—will have been played on January 2.[63]

As events played out, it becomes clear that President Angell had accurately envisioned some of the worst things that might happen in intercollegiate football. Football had become less a game than a business, run for revenue, not for education. Moreover, football was played increasingly by men who were neither entirely amateur nor entirely hired. And football coaching was given by men whose preponderant interest was holding their lucrative jobs at whatever cost.[64]

Epilogue

The American university is unique among the universities of the world in combining academic programs and commercialized athletics under the same roof. In other parts of the world the university is for higher learning, and for that alone. Students may participate in athletic sports if they wish, but in extramural venues. Since the United States contains many of the best universities in the world, a question arises as to the relation between commercialized intercollegiate athletics, the American university, and American intellectual and cultural life.

College football had become a thuggish and savage enterprise by 1895, when the presidents of seven midwestern universities agreed that the game had to be reformed or abolished. Convinced that football was too good to abandon, they decided to retain and reform it. Their action led to the formation of the Intercollegiate Conference of Faculty Representatives (the Western Conference, later the Big Ten). The conference was committed to two principles. One was faculty control of intercollegiate athletics. Such athletics were to be subordinate to the higher learning. Another was amateur athletics. This code, an English import, held that gentlemen play for love of the game. The code was ill suited to America.

In its early years, the Western Conference set a worthy standard. When Michigan athletic authorities insisted on having their own way, the conference showed courage in not yielding to a dissident member.

Before the world war, the Western Conference supported a balance between academic values and athletic pursuits in the member universities. The result was a few football games each season, no postseason games, and no championship games. By the end of the war, the conference had imposed reasonable order on intercollegiate athletics.

From 1920 to 1945 the Big Ten went from order to disorder. John L. Griffith, the commissioner, who viewed universities as agencies for socializing rather than educating students, fought a losing battle against the recruitment and subsidization of athletes. The Big Ten censured Iowa for athletic transgressions not because it was the only conference member that flouted the rules but because the case against Iowa could most easily be documented. Griffith was admirably zealous in the pursuit of Hawkeye transgressions and transgressors.

Nevertheless, multiple forces undermined faculty control of intercollegiate athletics. In theory, faculty representatives were the voice of the faculty in athletic affairs, but in practice presidents chose for this position a faculty member known for devotion to athletic sports. Beholden to many constituencies, university presidents were reluctant to deal with football problems. "I am convinced that the faculty representatives with all their sincerity have little or no real power," one faculty representative wrote. "The coaches, business managers, and athletic directors tolerate us, and the sports writers are frankly contemptuous. The proselyting and subsidizing of promising material is going on without interruption." The situation was aggravated by the falling off of patronage and the desperate need for funds, the observer added, which could be secured only by putting out high-powered teams. "There is no use trying to deceive ourselves any longer; the situation has passed beyond our control; and I am convinced that it is because of the very definite and universal commercialization of the sport. . . . The faculty representatives are no doubt sincere, but they are helpless in the matter, and I have come to the conclusion that they are butting their heads against a stone wall.[1] This account, from a faculty representative in the Southwest Conference, applied equally well to the Big Ten.

Many of the twenty best universities in the world are located in the United States, and most of them have football teams. So what does it matter if academic and athletic pursuits are part of the same institution? It matters because the intense devotion to intercollegiate football gives a large portion of the American people within and beyond university precincts a mistaken notion of the purpose that universities are designed to serve. And it also matters because intercollegiate football is a model for interscholastic football. Together, intercollegiate football and interscholastic football go far to shape American culture. John R. Tunis understood this relationship. Having watched intercollegiate sport become a "training ground for a jungle society," he believed that "interscholastic sports was taking the same highway."[2] Studies reveal that American secondary schools lag behind those in other parts of the world.[3] One reason for the discrepancy is the emphasis on competitive athletic sports in both secondary and higher education in the United States. J. F. A. Pyre, the Wisconsin faculty representative, understood this connection. He once declared that "the heaviest count against intercollegiate sports [was] that they have combined with social disruptions and other frivolous pursuits to throw into shade those voluntary intellectual interests whose honors were once the most coveted parts of an undergraduate career."[4]

In writing history, the historian must make judgments, not simply provide a chronicle of the past. For years the Big Ten was courageous in upholding its rules and in opposing postseason games, all with a view to upholding academic values. But in time, corruption became widespread, and intercollegiate athletics became commercialized. The result was a strange perversion of the true spirit of university life.

Conference Rules

The Rules Proposed by the Presidents' Conference, 1895

1. Each college and university which has not already done so shall appoint a committee on college athletics which shall take general supervision of all athletic matters in the respective college or university, and which shall have all responsibility of enforcing the college or university rules regarding athletics and all intercollegiate sports.

2. No one shall participate in any game or athletic sport unless he be a bona fide student doing full work in a regular or special course as defined in the curriculum of his college; and no person who has participated in any match game as a member of any college team shall be permitted to participate in any game as a member of another college team until he has been a matriculate in said college under the above conditions for a period of six months. This rule shall not apply to students who, having graduated at one college, shall enter another college for professional or graduate study.

3. No person shall be admitted to any intercollegiate contest who receives any gift, remuneration, or pay for his services on the college team.

4. Any student of any institution who shall be pursuing a regularly prescribed resident graduate course within such institution, whether for an advanced degree or in one of its professional schools, may be permitted to play for a period of the minimum number of years required for securing a graduate or professional degree for which he is a candidate.

5. No person who has been employed in training a college team for intercollegiate contests shall be allowed to participate in any intercollegiate contest as a member of any team which he has trained, and no professional athlete and no person who has ever been a member of a professional team shall play at any intercollegiate contest.
6. No student shall play in any game under an assumed name.
7. No student shall be permitted to participate in any intercollegiate contest who is found by the faculty to be delinquent in his studies.
8. All games shall be played on grounds either owned or under the immediate control of one or both of the colleges participating in the contest, and all games shall be played under student management and not under the patronage or control of any other corporation, association, or private individual.
9. The elections of managers and captains of teams in each college shall be subject to the approval of its committee on athletics.
10. College teams shall not engage in games with professional teams nor with those representing so-called athletic clubs.
11. Before every collegiate contest a list of men proposing to play shall be presented by each team or teams to the other or others, certifying that all the members are entitled to play under the rules adopted, such certificate to be signed by the registrar or the secretary of the college or university. It shall be the duty of the captains to enforce this rule.
12. We call upon the expert managers of foot-ball teams to so revise the rules as to reduce the liability of injury to a minimum.[1]

The Intercollegiate Rules Recommended by the Conference, November 1896

1. No one shall participate in any intercollegiate game or athletic sport unless he be a bona fide student doing full work in a regular or special course, as defined in the curriculum of his college; and no person who has participated in any intercollegiate game as a member of any college team, shall be permitted to participate in any game as a member of another college team until he has been a matriculate in such college under the above conditions for a period of one year, or has obtained a college academic degree.
2. No person shall be admitted to any intercollegiate contest who receives any gift, remuneration, or pay for his services on the college team.
3. No student shall play upon the teams of any college or colleges for more than four years in the aggregate unless he shall have secured a degree, in which case he may play two additional years, provided he be a candidate for a second degree.

4. No student shall participate in any intercollegiate contest who has ever used or is using his knowledge of athletics or his athletic skill for gain. This rule shall be operative after October 1, 1896. No person who receives any compensation from the university for services rendered by way of regular instruction shall be allowed to play on any team. This rule shall take effect December 1st, 1896.
5. No student shall play in any game under an assumed name.
6. No student shall be permitted to participate in any intercollegiate contest who is found by the faculty to be delinquent in his studies.
7. All intercollegiate games shall be played on grounds either owned by or under the immediate control of one or both of the colleges participating in the contest, and all intercollegiate games shall be played under student or college management, and not under the control of any corporation or association or private individual.
8. The election of managers and captains of teams in each college shall be subject to the approval of its committee on athletics.
9. College football teams shall play only with teams representing educational institutions.
10. Before every intercollegiate contest the respective chairman of the athletic committees of the institutions concerned shall submit to each other a certified list of players, eligible, under the rules adopted, to participate in such contest. It shall be the duty of the captains of the respective teams to exclude all players from the contest save those certified.
11. Athletic committees shall require each candidate for a team to represent the university in intercollegiate contests to subscribe to a statement that he is eligible under the letter and spirit of the rules adopted.
12. No person having been a member of any college athletic team during any year, and having been in attendance less than one college year, shall be permitted to play in any intercollegiate contest thereafter until he shall have been in attendance six consecutive calendar months.

The Intercollegiate Athletic Rules in Force as of November 1901

1. No one shall participate in any intercollegiate sport unless he be a bona fide student doing full work in a regular or special course as defined in the curriculum of his college; and no person who has participated as a college student in any intercollegiate game as a member of any college team and who has not afterward obtained a college academic degree, shall be permitted to participate in any game as a member of any other college team until he has been a matriculate in such college, under the above conditions, for a period of one year and until after the close of the

succeeding season devoted to the sport in which he last participated; and in the institutions represented in this conference preparatory students shall not be eligible to membership on the college teams.

2. No person shall be admitted to any intercollegiate contest who receives any gift, remuneration or pay for his services on the college team.

3. No student shall participate in baseball, football and track athletics upon the teams of any college or colleges for more than four years in the aggregate, and any member of a college team who plays during any part of an intercollegiate football (or baseball) game, does thereby participate in that sport for a year.

4. No student shall participate in any intercollegiate contest who has ever used or is using his knowledge of athletics or his athletic skill for gain. No person who receives any compensation from the University for services rendered by the way of regular instruction, shall be allowed to play on any team.

5. No student shall play in any game under an assumed name.

6. No student shall be permitted to participate in any intercollegiate contest who is found by the faculty to be delinquent in his studies.

7. All intercollegiate games shall be played on grounds either owned by or under immediate control of one or both of the colleges participating in the contest, and all intercollegiate games shall be played under student or college management, and not under the control of any corporation or association or private individual.

8. The election of managers and captains of teams in each college shall be subject to the approval of its committee on athletics.

9. College football teams shall play only with teams representing educational institutions.

10. Before every intercollegiate contest the respective chairmen of the athletic committees of the institutions concerned shall submit to each other a certified list of the players eligible under the rules adopted, to participate in said contest. It shall be the duties of the captains of the respective teams to exclude all players from the contest except those certified.

11. Athletic committees shall require each candidate for a team to represent the university in intercollegiate contests, to subscribe to a statement that he is eligible under the letter and spirit of the rules adopted.

12. No person having been a member of any college athletic team during any year, and having been in attendance less than one college half year, shall be permitted to play in any intercollegiate contest thereafter until he shall have been in attendance six consecutive calendar months.

Faculty Representatives

Over the years, many faculty members represented their universities in the conference. Several were closely identified with athletics, while a few were from academic departments and unwilling to devote time to intercollegiate athletics. The conference members were eager to establish their institutional reputation.

The conference was based on the idea of faculty control of intercollegiate athletics. In theory, a faculty spokesman represented the faculty, but in practice the president named an athletic devotee for the position. The conference was like a government's legislature in which the members were not only from the same political party but from one of its factions as well.

The Western Conference consisted of one faculty member from each conference university. Most of them served briefly, and the fluid nature of the group limited their effectiveness. Those who served for years had an advantage in shaping policy to promote their university and the conference, goals that were not always compatible. Some biographical information on a few conference stalwarts follows.

Albion Small served as Chicago's faculty representative from 1912 to 1924. Born in Maine in 1854, he graduated from Colby College, attended the Newton Theological Seminary, and was ordained as a Baptist minister. He went to Germany to study the social sciences, returned briefly to the Colby faculty, and earned a doctorate at Johns Hopkins University. In 1892 Small became the head of the sociology department at the University of Chicago and later was the dean of the

Graduate School of Arts and Sciences. Small was both an athletics enthusiast and a strong proponent of academic values.

George A. Goodenough became the Illinois faculty representative in 1907. A native of Michigan, he earned a bachelor's degree at the Michigan Agricultural College and a master's at Illinois. Initially an assistant professor of mechanical engineering at Illinois, in 1911 he became a professor of thermodynamics. Goodenough served on many conference committees and was for years the chairman of the Committee on Eligibility. His long and devoted service made him an influential and respected representative. Goodenough died in 1929.

Arthur G. Smith was briefly the Iowa representative when the conference was born. He assumed this post again in 1904 and held it for many years. Born in Indiana, in 1890 he was the quarterback and captain of the Iowa football team. He graduated from Iowa in 1891 (PhB), received an AM (1894) at Cornell, and pursued graduate study at Göttingen and Cambridge. He was the chairman of the Board in Control of Athletics from its founding to 1909 and the leading force in building up athletics in the university. In 1911 he became a professor and head of the department of mathematics and astronomy at Iowa. With brief interruptions, Smith was the Iowa representative until 1914.

Alfred H. Pattengill, the Michigan delegate beginning in 1898, graduated from Michigan in 1868, joined the faculty in 1869, and became a professor of Greek in 1889. Not a scholar, he was the chairman of the Board in Control of Athletics for more than a decade. He was sympathetic with the undergraduate view of intercollegiate sport. Pattengill died suddenly in 1906. In 1917 Ralph W. Aigler became the university's delegate. Born in Bellevue, Ohio, in 1885, he received his law degree from Michigan in 1907, briefly practiced law in Chicago, and in 1910 joined the Michigan law faculty as a full professor. A renowned expert on property law, Aigler served as a visiting professor at many leading American universities. He was the chairman of Michigan's Faculty Board in Control of Athletics from 1917 to 1942 and the representative to the conference for more than three decades. Aigler guarded Michigan's interest, often in collaboration with Fielding Yost, and was not eager to share Michigan's prestige with Michigan State.

James Paige became the Minnesota representative in 1907 and served in that capacity for a quarter-century. He was born in St. Louis, Missouri, where his father was a Presbyterian minister and the editor of a Presbyterian newspaper. James graduated from Phillips Andover Academy in 1884 and went to Princeton. He followed a brother to Minneapolis, and for a year he read law in his brothers' office. In 1889 he entered the Minnesota law school, graduated in 1890, joined the law faculty, and in 1896 became a professor of law. He published books dealing with criminal law, domestic relations, torts, commercial paper, partnership, and agency. In 1906 President Cyrus Northrup named Paige as a member of the athletic association, and a year later he became Minnesota's faculty representative. A flinty Calvinist, Paige was "so inflexibly dedicated to what he considered to be right that his mind became a gladiatorial arena in which virtue had constantly to be defended against the assault of the savages."[1] He zealously promoted Minnesota's interest.

Henry S. White, the Northwestern representative in 1899 and 1900, deserves to be remembered. Born in Cazenovia, New York, he graduated in 1882 from Wesleyan University (Connecticut) and was an instructor there for three years. He then went to Göttingen, where he earned a doctorate in 1891, and returned to Wesleyan as an assistant professor in mathematics. In 1892 he went to Northwestern. A prolific author and a distinguished mathematician, White became the Henry S. Noyes Professor of Pure Mathematics in 1894. He is the father of the White Resolution, which went far to slow down and shape the conduct of conference business.

Omera F. Long is best remembered as the Northwestern representative. In 1902 he became the chairman of the Faculty Athletic Committee and the faculty representative, and he attended most of the conference sessions until 1906. Long became the Northwestern representative again in the 1920s and served in this capacity for many more years. Born in Millersburg, Kentucky, Long graduated from Kentucky Wesleyan College in 1890 and taught in secondary schools for a time. He received a doctorate in the classics from the Johns Hopkins University and became an instructor at Northwestern. Not a scholar, he was a booster of intercollegiate athletics and the chairman of the Faculty Athletic Committee from 1902 until his retirement.

Thomas E. French became the Ohio State representative in 1912, the year the university became a conference member. He was the head of the Department of Engineering Drawing and a member of several prestigious campus committees. He became the president of the Board in Control of Athletics when it was organized in 1912 and was an active and influential faculty representative well into the 1920s.

Three worthies represented Purdue in early conference history. Winthrop E. Stone, who earned a doctorate at Göttingen in 1888, joined the Purdue faculty in 1889. He represented Purdue in 1896 and from 1900 to 1921 served as the president of Purdue. Clarence A. Waldo, a professor of mathematics, represented Purdue from 1897 to 1902. He was the conference arbitrator for several years. Thomas F. Moran became the Purdue delegate in 1901. He received a bachelor's degree (1887) from the University of Michigan and was admitted to the Michigan bar that year. For a time Moran was the superintendent of schools at Elk River, Minnesota. In 1895 he earned a doctorate from the Johns Hopkins University and joined the Purdue faculty as a professor of history and head of the department of history and economics. Moran was a member of several professional organizations and the author of several books and articles. He was the chairman of Purdue's Committee on Athletic Affairs and Purdue's representative for twenty-six years. He strove to balance academic values and intercollegiate athletics.

Edward A. Birge was the Wisconsin emissary in 1896, 1898, and 1899. He had earned a Harvard doctorate (1878) as a limnologist, and taught the premedical studies at Madison. Birge was the acting president of the university from 1900 to 1906. Max Mason, a former Wisconsin football player and later the president of the University of Chicago, was the Wisconsin delegate in 1915. James Francis Augustus Pyre succeeded Mason and served as the representative until 1932. Pyre was born in 1871 of Wisconsin farming stock. He earned a bachelor's degree (1892) and a doctorate (1897) at Wisconsin. As an undergraduate he was a leader in debate and oratory, dramatics, and athletics. A tackle on the football team in 1891, 1894, and 1896, he also stroked the varsity crew. Pyre joined the English department faculty and attained professorial status in 1909. He was a productive scholar, a member of the athletic council, and its chairman for years.

Notes

Prologue

1. For a concise discussion of the "muscular Christian" ideal, see Chandler, Cronin, and Vamplew, *Sport and Physical Education*, 147.

2. Watson, Weir, and Friend, "Development of Muscular Christianity," 2.

3. Holt, *Sport and the British*, 98.

4. Smith, *Sports and Freedom*, 136–37.

5. Ibid.

6. Eliot, *Annual Reports*, 12–14.

7. Ibid., 12–22.

8. Powel, *Walter Camp*, is an "authorized biography"; Jardins, *Walter Camp*, is comprehensive, critical, discerning, and timely.

9. Qtd. in Bergin, *The Game*, 58.

10. Oriard, *Reading Football*, 35–56; Westby and Sack, "Commercialization and Rationalization."

11. Powel, *Walter Camp*, appendix A, 209–32, lists his selections from 1889 to 1924.

12. Oriard, *Reading Football*, 150–63.

13. The older literature on the subject includes Stearns, *Be a Man*; Mangan and Walvin, *Manliness and Morality*, 1–4; Rotundo, *American Manhood*, 222–46; Rotundo, "Body and Soul," 23–38. The more recent literature includes Bederman, *Manliness and Civilization*, which is something of a sprawl, and Putney, *Muscular Christianity*, is enormously helpful.

14. Pope, *New American Sport History*, 123–24.

15. Ibid., 125–26, 129–30.

16. Stagg and Stout, *Touchdown!*, 48.

17. Ibid., 130–31.

18. Lester, *Stagg's University*, 66.
19. Curti and Carstensen, *University of Wisconsin*, 1:387.
20. Bernstein, *Football*, 30.
21. Topping, *Century and Beyond*, 140.
22. Stagg and Stout, *Touchdown!*, 148.
23. Lester, *Stagg's University*, 19.
24. Stagg and Stout, *Touchdown!*, 155–58; Lester, *Stagg's University*, 199.
25. Stagg and Lester differ on the record for the year. I follow Stagg's figures.
26. Stagg and Stout, *Touchdown!*, 159.

Chapter 1. The Beginning of the Big Ten

1. "Chicago Conference of College Presidents," *IC Minutes*. See also Voltmer, *Brief History*, 4, and Roberts, *Big Nine*, 25.

2. *IC Minutes*, 3–4; Voltmer, *Brief History*, 6–7. "Boys Must Not Slug: College Presidents Interested in Football Rules," *Chicago Tribune*, January 12, 1895 (which lists ten rules). On Draper's vote, see Barton, "College Conference," 46.

3. *IC Minutes*, February 8, 1896 (also, *Proceedings*, 5–13). The entire text is in appendix 1.

4. *IC Minutes*, n.d. (following the Intercollegiate Rules); RS 4/1/1, Faculty Record, May 4, 1896, 3:318–19, University of Illinois Archives; Barton, "College Conference," 49. See also "Rules of the Inter-Collegiate Athletic Conference," in University of Illinois, *Regulations for the Government of Athletics* (Urbana, 1896), 15–17. Secretaries compiled the rules and regulations of the conference periodically (for example, 1907, 1908, 1913); third revision, *A Digest of the Proceedings of the Intercollegiate Conference of Faculty Representatives, 1895–1920* ([1920]). Both this *Digest* (1920) and the *Proceedings* (1901) are in RS 28/1/805, box 1, folder "Minutes of the Intercollegiate Conference, 1895–1933," University of Illinois Archives.

5. *IC Minutes*, November 27, 1896.
6. Ibid., following November 27, 1896.
7. Ibid., "Madison Conference of College Presidents," 25–26.
8. Ibid., 25–32. Powell, "Development and Influence," 15–26, discusses the Madison Conference without shedding any light on its significance.
9. *IC Minutes*, November 26, 1897.
10. Smith, *Sports and Freedom*, 141–42; see also Smith, "Preludes to the NCAA."
11. Smith, *Sports and Freedom*, 142–43.
12. Ibid., 143.
13. Ibid.
14. Ibid. See also Smith, *Pay for Play*, 30–33.
15. Needham, "College Athlete," 260n.
16. *IC Minutes*, December 1, 1899; Young, *Arrogance and Scheming*, 151–52.
17. Burns, *Being Catholic, Being American*, 3–172; Schlereth, *University of Notre Dame*, 1–122; Sperber, *Shake Down the Thunder*, 3–26.
18. *IC Minutes*, February 23, 1901; "'Big Nine' Stands Firm," *Chicago Tribune*, February 24, 1901 (quotation).

19. Burns, *Being Catholic, Being American*, 78–86; Gleason, "American Catholic Higher Education," 35–36; Sperber, *Shake Down the Thunder*, 18.

20. *IC Minutes*, November 30, 1900.

21. Ibid., November 29, 1901. The White Resolution, introduced on November 30, 1900, was discussed on February 23, 1901, before being passed.

22. "Constitution and By-Laws" appears in *Proceedings*, 1–8 (separately paginated).

23. *IC Minutes*, November 6, 1901.

24. Sargent, "History," 256–57.

25. Michelson and Newhouse, *Rose Bowl Football*, 30–37; Hendrickson, *Tournament of Roses*, 2–8, 11–13; Ours, *Bowl Games*, 1–4; "Rival Elevens for Pasadena," *Detroit Free Press*, December 31, 1901.

26. *IC Minutes*, November 28, 1902.

27. Ibid., December 1, 1905; "Football Gate Too Prominent," *Chicago Tribune*, December 2, 1905.

28. *IC Minutes*, January 19, 1906, 2–4.

29. Ibid., 4; Shaw, *Encyclopedic Survey*, 2:607, 609 (quotation).

30. *IC Minutes*, January 19, 1906, 4.

31. Jacobs, *Historical World*, 37–40; Bennett, *Frederick Jackson Turner*, 66.

32. Curti and Carstensen, *University of Wisconsin*, 2:536–38 (quotation at 538); Billington, *Frederick Jackson Turner*, 266–71; "Mystery Veils Football's Fate," *Chicago Tribune*, January 20, 1906, 8; "Deals Football Knockout Blow," *Chicago Tribune*, January 21, 1906.

33. *IC Minutes*, January 19, 1906.

34. "Mystery Veils Football's Fate," *Chicago Tribune*, January 20, 1906, 8.

35. *IC Minutes*, January 19, 1906.

36. Ibid. Pattengill either exaggerated or did not know Yost's salary.

37. Ibid., 8–10.

38. The Sampson report stops at this point.

39. *IC Minutes*, January 19, 1906, 11–12.

40. Ibid., January 20, 1906.

41. Ibid., January 19, 1906.

42. Ibid., January 19–20, 6–13.

43. Ibid.

44. "'Champion' Teams Things of Past," *Chicago Tribune*, January 22, 1906.

45. Ware, *Fifty Years of Football*, 17–18.

46. Behee, *Fielding Yost's Legacy*, 17–47.

47. Pierce, "Origin, Growth, and Function," 27–32. On the rules and the Rules Committee, see Nelson, *Anatomy of a Game*.

48. ICAAUS, "Proceedings of the First Annual Meeting . . . December 29, 1906," 3–37 (Stagg's comments at 23).

49. Ibid., 24–25.

50. Lucas, "Hegemonic Role."

51. ICAAUS, "Proceedings of the First Annual Meeting," 9, 13.

52. Stagg, "Reports."
53. Pierce, "Intercollegiate Athletic Association" (1910), 84–85.
54. Ibid., (1911), 75–76.
55. "President Ordered to China," 495.
56. Pierce, "Intercollegiate Athletic Association," (1910), 86.
57. Phillips, "Length of Intercollegiate Schedules."
58. Waldo, "Proper Control."
59. Hawkins, *Banding Together*.

Chapter 2. Michigan Withdraws from the Conference

1. "Deals Football Knockout Blow," *Chicago Tribune*, January 21, 1906.
2. RS 4/2/1, February 5, 1906, 2:131–33, University of Illinois Archives.
3. *IC Minutes*, March 10, 1906.
4. Ibid.; "Modify Football Views," *Chicago Tribune*, March 9, 1906; "Football Coach Necessary Evil," *Chicago Tribune*, March 10, 1906. Pattengill died in Ann Arbor on March 16, 1906.
5. *IC Minutes*, March 10, 1906.
6. RS 4/2/1, April 2, 1906, 2:141–43, University of Illinois Archives.
7. RS 4/2/1, June 1, 1906, 2:159, University of Illinois Archives.
8. *IC Minutes*, December 1, 1906; "May Partly Lift Football 'Lid,'" *Chicago Tribune*, December 1, 1906; "College Reforms to Be Continued," *Chicago Tribune*, December 2, 1906; "Athletic Changes Meet with Favor," *Chicago Tribune*, December 3, 1906; Scott and Shaw, "Michigan and the Conference," 38.
9. "Ratify 'Big Four' Move at Madison," *Chicago Tribune*, February 5, 1907; "Michigan Looks to the East," *Chicago Tribune*, February 19, 1907; "Wolverines Choose East," *Chicago Tribune*, March 17, 1907; Scott and Shaw, "Michigan and the Conference," 38–39.
10. "Athletic War on at Madison," *Chicago Tribune*, December 7, 1906; "Wisconsin Rejects Changes," *Chicago Tribune*, December 11, 1906.
11. RS 4/2/1, December 21, 1906, 2:172–73, University of Illinois Archives.
12. *IC Minutes*, January 12, 1907; "'Big Nine' Meet Today," *Chicago Tribune*, January 12, 1907; "'Big Nine' Keeps Athletic Lid On," *Chicago Tribune*, January 13, 1907.
13. "The Referee," *Chicago Tribune*, February 3, 1907; "Michigan Now at Parting of Ways," *Chicago Tribune*, February 4, 1907; "Academic Freedom," *Chicago Tribune*, February 21, 1907; "Lose in Big Nine Fight," *Chicago Tribune*, February 23, 1907; Shaw, "Michigan and the Conference," 39.
14. Stagg to Charles Baird, January 20, 1907, Stagg Papers, box 88, folder 5, Special Collections and Manuscript Library, University of Chicago.
15. Shaw, "Michigan and the Conference," 40.
16. Lane to Small, March 15, 1907, Stagg Papers, box 88, folder 4.
17. Bates to Small, March 22, 1907, Stagg Papers, box 88, folder 4.
18. Small to Bates, March 25, 1907, Stagg Papers, box 88, folder 4.
19. Ibid.
20. Ibid.
21. "Pass Up the Wolverine," *Chicago Tribune*, March 31, 1907.

22. Bates to Small, March 22, 1907, Stagg Papers, box 88, folder 4.
23. "College Athletics," *Chicago Tribune*, April 20, 1907.
24. Shaw, "Michigan and the Conference," 41.
25. *IC Minutes*, November 30, 1907; Shaw, "Michigan and the Conference," 40–41.
26. RS 4/2/1, 1:225 (December 9, 1907), University of Illinois Archives.
27. Stagg to Moran, December 24, 1907, Stagg Papers, box 85, folder 5.
28. *IC Minutes*, January 4, 1908.
29. "Michigan Hears of the Action," *Chicago Tribune*, April 14, 1907.
30. Waldo to Stagg, February 24, 1908, Stagg Papers, box 88, folder 4.
31. "Program for Monday Student Meeting," *Daily Illini*, January 19, 1908, 1; "Student Sentiment Favors Seven Games," *Daily Illini*, January 21, 1908, 1.
32. University of Illinois, Board of Trustees, *24th Report* (1908), 419.
33. RS 4/2/1, 1:236–37 (February 10, 1908), University of Illinois Archives.
34. *IC Minutes*, June 6, 1908.
35. Ibid.
36. Ibid.
37. Ibid.
38. Ibid.
39. Amos A. Stagg, "The Conference of December 3, 1910," Stagg Papers, box 88, folder 4.
40. Ibid.
41. Ibid.
42. A. A. Stagg, "Mr. Editor," n. d. Stagg Papers, box 88, folder 4. On Stagg's early career at the University of Chicago, see Lawson and Ingham, "Conflicting Ideologies."
43. Amos A. Stagg, "Memorandum concerning Meeting with President George E. Vincent of the University of Minnesota, Sunday, November 26, 1911," Stagg Papers, box 88, folder 6.
44. Amos A. Stagg, "Memorandum of the Meeting of the Conference December 2, 1911," Stagg Papers, box 88, folder 7.
45. Scott and Shaw, "Michigan and the Conference," 42–44.
46. Ibid., 43; Keene Gardiner, "Michigan Board May Be Changed," *Chicago Tribune*, March 24, 1913.
47. Gardiner, "Michigan Board"; "Sporting," *Chicago Tribune*, April 2, 1913.
48. University of Michigan, *Proceedings of the Board of Regents. Nov. 1910-July 1914*, May 29, 1913 meeting, 724.
49. Vincent to James, August 4, 1913; James to Vincent, August 6, 1913; Vincent to James, August 12, 1913, RS 2/5/3, box 37, folder "George E. Vincent," University of Illinois Archives.
50. Vincent to James, September 11, 1913, RS 2/5/3, box 39, folder Athletics, University of Illinois Archives.
51. Kinley to Vincent, September 13, 1913, RS 2/5/3, box 39, folder "Athletics," University of Illinois Archives.
52. Vincent to Kinley, September 15, 1913, RS 2/5/3, box 39, folder "Athletics," University of Illinois Archives.
53. "Report of the Committee on Intercollegiate Athletics to the Senate," September 20, 1913, RS 2/5/3, box 39, folder "Athletics," University of Illinois Archives.

54. George E. Vincent, "To the Presidents of the Conference Colleges," September 23, 1913, RS 2/5/3, box 39, folder "Athletics," University of Illinois Archives.

55. James to Vincent (letter and telegram), October 3, 1913; James to Judson, telegram, October 3, 1913, RS 2/5/3, box 39, folder "Athletics," University of Illinois Archives.

56. Vincent to James, October 6, 1913, RS 2/5/3, box 39, folder "Athletics," University of Illinois Archives.

57. Judson to James, October 6, 1913, RS 2/5/3, box 39, folder "Athletics," University of Illinois Archives.

58. University of Illinois, Board of Trustees, *27th Report* (1914), 656.

59. RS 4/2/1, 3:132–33 (October 6, 1913), University of Illinois Archives.

60. Stone to James, October 7, 1913, RS 2/5/3, box 39, folder "Athletics," University of Illinois Archives.

61. James sent the same letter to all the other presidents of conference institutions except for Indiana on October 11, 1913: RS 2/5/3, box 39, folder "Athletics," University of Illinois Archives.

62. Vincent to James, October 13, 1913, RS 2/5/3, box 39, folder "Athletics," University of Illinois Archives.

63. Judson to James, October 22, 1913, enclosing the resolutions of the Board of Trustees, RS 2/5/3, box 39, folder "Athletics," University of Illinois Archives.

Chapter 3. The Crisis over Amateurism

1. Pope, "Amateurism and American Sports Culture," 292–98.

2. Ibid., 303–4; Turrini, *End of Amateurism*, 9–15.

3. Huff, "Collegiate Baseball and Professionalism," 206–8; Huff, "Amateur Baseball Standing," 123–26.

4. Herbert J. Barton, *Alumni Quarterly* 2 (October 1908): 126–29.

5. *IC Minutes*, December 2, 1911.

6. "'Pro' Ball Law Unjust—Huff," *Chicago Tribune*, December 11, 1911; "In the Wake of the News," *Chicago Tribune*, December 12, 1911.

7. "Stagg Firm against the 'Pros'," *Chicago Tribune*, December 12, 1911.

8. *IC Minutes*, December 2, 1911, and January 26, 1912.

9. Ibid., January 26, 1912.

10. Ibid., January 27, 1912.

11. James's comments are in an untitled manuscript in RS 2/5/6, box 26, folder "Athletics," University of Illinois Archives.

12. Ibid. The untitled manuscript includes the statements by students and senate members alike.

13. RS 4/2/1, March 11, 1912, 3:5–6, University of Illinois Archives.

14. "Help Decide Illinois' Future at the Mass-Meeting Tonight; Will Discuss Withdrawal from Conference Tonight," *Daily Illini*, March 13, 1912, 1; "Conference Reform Is Sentiment of Enthusiastic Mass-Meeting," *Daily Illini*, March 14, 1912, 1–2.

15. "Illinois and the Western Conference: A Symposium," *Illinois Magazine* 3 (March 1912): 321–30.

16. "Meeting of the Presidents of the Universities Comprising the Intercollegiate Conference Athletic Association," Chicago, Illinois, March 19–20, 1912 (a typewritten document). Also in RS 2/5/3, box 27, folder ICAA, University of Illinois Archives.

17. Ibid.

18. Ibid. The Intercollegiate Conference Athletic Association is not the same as the Intercollegiate Conference of Faculty Representatives (Western Conference; later Big Ten). Many people, including President Harris, confused the two.

19. Ibid. Also: Kinley, "To the Members of the University Senate, April 4, 1912," and Kinley to James, April 6, 1912, RS 2/5/6, box 26, folder "Athletics," University of Illinois Archives.

20. James, "To the Students, Faculty, and Friends of the University of Illinois," in *Report on the Eligibility Rules in Intercollegiate Athletics, Adopted by the Senate of the University of Illinois, May 8, 1912*, 3–5, in RS 2/5/6, box 26, folder "Athletics."

21. Kinley to James, May 22, 1912, RS 2/5/6, box 26, folder "Athletics," University of Illinois Archives.

22. Senate Committee, "Athletics of the University of Illinois on Amateurism in Intercollegiate Athletics," in *Report on the Eligibility Rules*, 6–10, RS 2/5/3, box 26, folder "Athletics."

23. George A. Vincent to David Kinley, May 14, 1912, RS 2/5/3, box 27, folder "ICAA," University of Illinois Archives. Vincent marked his letter "*Personal* except so far as President James is concerned."

24. Harry Pratt Judson to James, April 17, 1913, RS 2/5/3, box 33, folder "Harry P. Judson," University of Illinois Archives.

25. Pollard, *Ohio State Athletics*, 107.

26. Ibid., 107–8; *IC Minutes*, April 6, 1912.

27. Knoll, *Prairie University*, 63; Israel, *Cornhuskers*, 46, 50; *IC Minutes*, December 6, 1930.

28. Hamilton, *Story of Marquette*, 37, 46, 113–19.

29. Schlereth, *University of Notre Dame*, 101–25; Sperber, *Shake Down the Thunder*, 1–16; *IC Minutes*, December 6, 1913.

30. Albion Small to My Dear Colleague, Saturday Eve Dec [6], 1913, Stagg Papers, box 87, folder 2, Special Collections and Manuscripts, University of Chicago.

31. Foster, "Indictment of Intercollegiate Athletics."

32. *IC Minutes*, June 8, 1917, and December 8 and 9, 1917.

33. Ibid., December 9, 1917.

34. Ibid., December 6, 1919.

35. Ibid., November 29 and 30, 1912.

36. Ibid., November 30, 1912.

37. Ibid., December 5, 1914.

38. Ibid.

39. Ibid., May 31, 1912.

40. Ibid.

41. Ibid., June 6, 1913.

42. Ibid., December 6, 1913, and December 5, 1914.

43. Ibid., June 6, 1914.

44. Ibid., June 6, 1914, June 5, 1915, and December 4, 1915.

45. Ibid., December 6, 1913.

46. Ibid., December 4, 1915, and June 2, 1916.

47. Ibid., December 7, 1918, and December 4, 1920.

48. Ibid., December 6, 1919, June 5, 1920, and June 4, 1921.

49. Ibid., December 5, 1914, and December 4, 1920.

50. Ibid., December 6, 1919, and June 5, 1920.

Chapter 4. The Conference and the War

1. *IC Minutes*, June 9, 1917.

2. Ibid., December 9, 1917.

3. Ibid., June 9, 1918.

4. Ibid., September 26, 1918; "Big Ten Turns Sport Contract over to War Department," *Chicago Tribune*, September 27, 1918.

5. Gruber, *Mars and Minerva*, 214–18. The Student Army Training Corps established both a collegiate and a vocational division. Only the former is discussed here. On the SATC, see also Levine, *American College*, 26–32.

6. Gruber, *Mars and Minerva*, 222; "President James," 536, 539.

7. Gruber, *Mars and Minerva*, 229.

8. *IC Minutes*, October 3, 1918, including exhibit "A" (a digest of French's report); "Report Ruling on Sport Today," *Chicago Tribune*, October 3, 1918.

9. "1918 Grid Game Rides over Its War Handicaps," *Chicago Tribune*, December 29, 1918.

10. *IC Minutes*, December 7, 1918; "Big Ten Men Will Arrange Future of Athletics Today," *Chicago Tribune*, December 7, 1918.

11. *IC Minutes*, June 9, 1918.

12. Ibid., December 7, 1918; "Big Ten Expands on Athletics for New Year of Peace," *Chicago Tribune*, December 8, 1918; *A Digest of the Proceedings of the Intercollegiate Conference of Faculty Representatives, 1895–1913* (1913), 21.

13. "Regime of S.A.T.C. Shows Colleges How to Better Athletics," *Chicago Tribune* December 11, 1918.

14. Cramer, *Newton D. Baker*, 98–102; Fosdick, *Chronicle of a Generation*, 142–54; Lewis, "World War I," 109–12; Pope, *Patriotic Games*, 145–50.

15. Fosdick, *Chronicle of a Generation*, 177–82.

16. *The Inter-Allied Games: Paris, 22nd June to 6th July 1919* (Paris: Games Committee, 1919).

17. "What the Draft Should Teach Us," 39.

18. Angell, "Reconstruction Program, 44–46 (full text, 44 to 54).

19. Ibid.

20. "'Big Ten' Coaches Select Officials for Grid Games," *Chicago Tribune*, March 23, 1918; "Big Ten Grid Coaches Order Time Out on Forward Pass Plays," *Chicago Tribune*, March 24, 1919.

21. "Big Ten Colleges Inaugurate Football Practice Today," *Chicago Tribune*, September 15, 1919.

22. *IC Minutes*, October 17, 1919; "Badgers Inquire Status of 4 Purple Players, Report," *Chicago Tribune*, October 17, 1919.

23. *IC Minutes,* June 5, 1920.

24. "Conference Coaches to Book More 'Big Ten' Contests," *Chicago Tribune,* November 20, 1919; "Illini and Harvard Gain Honors in Stirring Year," *Chicago Tribune,* November 24, 1919.

25. "Five Lose Lives in 'Grid' Games Season of 1919," *Chicago Tribune,* November 30, 1919.

26. "'Big Ten' to Take Action against Grid Pros Today," *Chicago Tribune,* December 6, 1919.

Chapter 5. The Big Ten in the Golden Age of Sports

1. Foster, "Intercollegiate Athletics and the War," 532–33; John W. Weeks, Secretary of War, as reported in "Physical Fitness," *Athletic Journal* 5 (September 1924): 14–15.

2. Dyreson, "Emergence of Consumer Culture," 267–79.

3. Holtzman, *No Cheering in the Press Box,* based on taped interviews with sportswriters, includes John R. Tunis, 260–72.

4. Tunis, "Gas and the Games," 12–13, 44.

5. Ward, "Football in the Middle West," 133–34, 135.

6. "Summer Ball in Little Nineteen Works Out Well," *Chicago Tribune,* April 28, 1921.

7. *IC Minutes,* December 4, 1920.

8. Hendrickson, *Tournament of Roses,* 39–40; Ours, *Bowl Games,* 8–11; *IC Minutes,* December 4, 1920, and June 4, 1921.

9. *IC Minutes,* December 2, 1921; Michelson and Newhouse, *Rose Bowl Football,* 48; Ours, *Bowl Games,* 12–13.

10. *IC Minutes,* June 4, 1921.

11. "Badgers Break with Buckeyes at Conference," *Daily Illini,* December 5, 1920, 1.

12. "Coach Richards Tells Why Ohio Is Not on Badger 1921 Schedule," *Daily Cardinal,* January 5, 1921, 1.

13. W. O. Thompson to E. A. Birge, March 5, 1921; Birge to Thompson, March 7, 1921; Thompson to Birge, March 9, 1921 (the quotation); Birge to Thompson, April 30, 1921. I owe these references to David Null of the University of Wisconsin Archives.

14. *IC Minutes,* June 4, 1921.

15. University of Illinois, *Annual Register* (1914–1915), 212; (1915–1916), 213; (1916–1917), 202; (1917–1918), 198; (1918–1919), 190; *Daily Illini,* July 26, 1917, October 20, 1919, 1; June 27, 1920, 11.

16. Huff to James, January 31, 1916; James to Huff, March 25, 1916, RS 2/5/3, box 88, folder "Huff," University of Illinois Archives.

17. RS 4/2/1, 5:114–16 (April 7, 1919), University of Illinois Archives; University of Illinois, Board of Trustees, *30th Report* (1920), 314–16; "Department of Coaching to Open at University," *Daily Illini,* June 14, 1919, 1.

18. University of Illinois, Board of Trustees, *30th Report* (1920), 315–16.

19. RS 2/5/3/ 810, Registrar's Report, Enrollment by Curriculum, University of Illinois Archives.

20. *Athletic Journal* 1 (April 1921), advertisement, reverse of title page (Chicago), 24 (Ithaca).

21. Murray Sperber, *Shake Down the Thunder*, 225–26.
22. *Athletic Journal* 3 (March 1923): 25; *Athletic Journal* 4 (May 1924): 20.
23. *IC Minutes*, December 2, 1921.
24. Ibid.
25. Ibid.
26. Ibid., December 3, 1921.
27. Ibid., June 2, 1922, exhibit "A."
28. Ibid.
29. "Committee J, College Athletics," 76–78.
30. Ibid., 78–79.
31. Ibid., 79.
32. Ibid., 79–80.
33. Tunis, "Great Sports Myth."
34. March, *Pro Football*, 86; Peterson, *Pigskin*, 13–16, 23–30.
35. Whitney, "Amateur Sport."
36. Maltby, *Origins and Early Development*, 45–47.
37. Ibid., 47–49.
38. Ibid., 56.
39. Ibid., 58–59.
40. McClellan, *Sunday Game*, 3–4.
41. March, *Pro Football*, 46–50; Peterson, *Pigskin*, 49–51; Jable, "Birth of Professional Football," 131–47; Carroll and PFRA Research, *Ohio League*, 1–96.
42. These data are compiled from the rosters and schedules of the teams in McClellan, *Sunday Game*, appendix A, 398–460.
43. Schobinger was a member of the 1912 U. S. Olympic Track and Field team and captain of the 1915 track team. McClellan, *Sunday Game*, 258, 285, 287, 288, 300, 345.
44. Camp, "Camp's All-America Eleven," 13, 26–27.
45. "At the Orpheum," *Daily Illini*, March 24, 1917, 6.
46. "Bart Macomber Signs Up with Ohio Professional Team," *Daily Illini*, October 9, 1917, 1; McClellan, *Sunday Game*, 30, 105, 107, 109–11, 167–68, 245, 352, 373, 441.
47. Milton G. Silver to *Illinois Alumni News*, January 15, 1972, Franklin B. Macomber Morgue File, University of Illinois Archives.
48. *IC Minutes*, December 9, 1916.
49. Ibid., December 9, 1917.
50. Ibid., June 9, 1917.
51. Ibid., December 6, 1919.
52. Ibid., December 6, 1919; A. A. Stagg to A. H. Sharp, March 1, 1920, Stagg Papers, box 87, folder 2.
53. *IC Minutes*, June 7, 1919, and December 6, 1919. Rule 5 (a) read: "No student shall participate in any intercollegiate contest who has ever used or is using his knowledge of athletics or his athletic or gymnastic skill for gain; or who has taken part in any athletic contest in which a money prize was offered, regardless of the disposition made of the same."
54. Ibid., June 5, 1920.

55. Ibid., December 4, 1920. Arthur Daley, "Professional Football," in Danzig and Brandwein, *Sports Golden Age*, 171–82, describes the emergence of professional football during the 1920s and asserts that by the end of the decade pro football had gained "maturity, respectability, solidity, popularity, and prosperity" (171).

56. "Coach Charges Hired Players Given Double X," *Daily Illini*, January 29, 1922, 1.

57. "Charge That Scouts Recruit Illini Stars Gets Laugh from 'G'," *Daily Illini*, January 29, 1922, 1.

58. "Taylorville Backer Airs Big Ten Charges," *Chicago Tribune*, February 2, 1922.

59. "Accused Football Men Have Alibis," *New York Times*, January 30, 1922; "Notre Dame Banishes Eight from Athletics," *Daily Illini*, January 31, 1922, 1; "Setting the Example," *Daily Illini*, February 1, 1922, 4.

60. "Illinois Bars Nine Athletes for 'Pro' Game," *Chicago Tribune*, January 28, 1922, 1; "Star Athletes under Ban," *New York Times*, January 28, 1922.

61. "Illinois Bars Nine Athletes."

62. "When College Players Play for Money," *Chicago Tribune*, January 31, 1922.

63. Amos Alonzo Stagg, "An Epoch Making Period in Conference Intercollegiate Athletics," August 12, 1922, 2. Stagg Papers, box 87, folder 3.

64. Stagg, "Epoch Making Period"; "Athletic Directors Attack Pro Menace," *New York Times*, February 8, 1922.

65. "Annual Meeting of the Athletic Directors of the Conference Colleges," March 1922, Stagg Papers, box 87, folder 2.

66. Stagg, "Epoch Making Period," 6.

67. Stagg, "Epoch Making Period," 7, 3.

68. "Minutes of the Meeting of the Conference Directors, June 1st, 1922," Stagg Papers, box 87, folder 2.

69. "Report of the Committee to select a Conference Commissioner," July 24, 1922, Stagg Papers, box 87, folder 2, Special Collections and Manuscripts, University of Chicago.

Chapter 6. The Commissioner and the Conference

1. RS 2/5/15, Griffith, John L. (appointment file), University of Illinois Archives, contains biographical information and the Huff–Griffith correspondence; Ritchey, *Drake University*, 126, 128, 180–81, 142–45, 148 (quotation); *University of Illinois Four Year Course in Athletic Coaching*, 23 (a pamphlet in RS 28/3/810, box 1, folder "1921," University of Illinois Archives). An expanded version of the pamphlet appears in the *University of Illinois Bulletin* 22, no. 19 (January 5, 1925), RS 28/3/810, box 1, folder "1925."

2. J. L. Griffith, "The War Department Commission on Training Camp Activities: Suggestions from the Field," *Proceedings of the Thirteenth Annual Convention of the National College Athletic Association*, 1918, 62–66.

3. On training camps in World War I, see Fosdick, *Chronicle of a Generation*, 142–86.

4. University of Illinois, Board of Trustees, *30th Report* (1920), 400, 477.

5. University of Illinois, Board of Trustees, *31st Report* (1922), 250.

6. "Campus Brevities," *Daily Illini*, October 25, 1919, 2, refers to "Major Griffith." I have found no other use of this title in Illinois documents while he was on the faculty. The

National Personnel Records Center of the Department of Defense reports that the record needed to determine Griffith's rank was lost in the July 1973 fire that destroyed millions of their records, including those of army veterans discharged between November 1, 1912, and December 31, 1939. Records Center to author, July 18, 2011.

7. "The Athletic Journal," *Athletic Journal* 1 (March 1921): 8; "A Coaching Magazine," *Athletic Journal* 2 (September 1921): 16–17.

8. John L. Griffith, "The Journal a Success," *Athletic Journal* 2 (January 1922), 16–17.

9. John L. Griffith, "Sportsmanship," *Athletic Journal* 3 (September 1922), 14–15.

10. "Augur Follows Murry on Ineligibility List," *Daily Illini*, November 3, 1922, 1.

11. E. A. Birge to George A. Goodenough, December 29, 1922, Birge Papers, RS 4/12/11, box 32, MI–MZ, University of Wisconsin Archives. My thanks to David Null for this reference.

12. A. A. Stagg, "College Men in Professional Football," dictated September 12, 1922, Stagg Papers, box 84, folder 10, Special Collections Research Center, University of Chicago.

13. *IC Minutes*, December 2, 1922.

14. Ibid.

15. Don Murry, who had participated in the Carlinville-Taylorville game, played professional football with the Racine Legion from 1922 to 1924 and with the Chicago Bears from 1925 to 1932.

16. "Football—The Frankenstein of Athletics," 52, 56, 58–59.

17. Faculty Athletic Adviser, "Commercialism in College Athletics."

18. John L. Griffith to The Directors of Athletics, September 20, 1925, Stagg Papers, box 84, folder 10.

19. Rooney, *Recruiting Game*, 80, 98, 102, 109, 120.

20. John L. Griffith, "Number of Players in Each Big Ten University from Outside the Particular State in which the University Is: 1924–1929," no date, Stagg Papers, box 86, folder 3.

21. *IC Minutes*, June 2, 1923.

22. Ibid., December 1, 1923.

23. Ibid., June 6, 1924.

24. Ibid., December 5, 1925.

25. John L. Griffith to The Directors of Athletics of the Western Conference, August 8, 1925; John L. Griffith to A. A. Stagg, August 17, 1925; John L. Griffith to The Directors of the Western Conference, August 20, 1925, Stagg Papers, box 84, folder 10.

26. John L. Griffith to A. A. Stagg, November 13, 1922, Stagg Papers, box 84, folder 5.

27. John L. Griffith to A. A. Stagg, March 7, 1924, Stagg Papers, box 84, folder 9.

28. Ibid.

29. John L. Griffith to The Directors of Athletics in the Intercollegiate Conference, n.d., Stagg Papers, box 88, folder 1.

30. Soderstrom, *Big House*, 126–28.

31. This description of Griffith's views on intercollegiate athletics in American higher education is based on his editorials in the *Athletic Journal* from 1922 to 1925.

32. David Kinley, "Are Intercollegiate Athletics Justifying Their Existence in State Universities," *Transactions and Proceedings of the National Association of State Universities in the*

United States of America, 14 (1916): 167–74. Kinley was a dean when he gave this address, but his views had not changed by the mid-1920s.

33. John L. Griffith to The Directors of Athletics in the Western Conference, November 4, 1926, Stagg Papers, box 84, folder 6.

34. John L. Griffith to The Directors of Athletics of the Western Conference, February 19, 1924, Stagg Papers, box 84, folders 8 and 10.

35. For Angell's confession of faith in matters athletic, see Angell, "Reconstruction Program," and Angell, "Familiar Problems."

36. Griffith to The Directors, February 15, 1924, Stagg Papers, box 84, folders 8 and 10.

37. Ibid.

38. Bryce, *University and Historical Addresses*, 229–45 (quotations at 241).

39. Meiklejohn, "What Are College Games For?" 665–68; "Griffith Defends Paid Coach in Sport," *New York Times*, November 27, 1924; John L. Griffith to The Directors of Athletics of the Western Conference, January 30, 1925, Stagg Papers, box 84, folder 10. See also Ingrassia, *Rise of Gridiron University*, 178–83.

40. Meiklejohn, "What Are College Games For?" 663–71; Angell, "Increasing the Intellectual Interests," 272–74.

41. Angell, "Increasing the Intellectual Interests," 274.

42. Griffith to The Directors, January 30, 1925.

43. St. John, "Future of Intercollegiate Sports."

Chapter 7. The Big Ten Stadiums

1. Dyreson and Trumpbour, *Rise of Stadiums*, 1–2; Trumpbour, *New Cathedrals*, 8–11; Perry, "Stadium and College Athletics," 576.

2. Smith, "Far More than Commercialism"; Perry, "Stadium and College Athletics," 573. Ingrassia, *Rise of Gridiron University*, 141–44, briefly describes the Harvard, Princeton, and Yale bowls.

3. Smith, "Far More than Commercialism," 35–41; Perry, "Stadium and College Athletics," 576, 578–83.

4. Tilton and O'Donnell, *History and Growth*, 101–2. On stadium building in America to 1914, see Perry, "Stadium and College Athletics," 571–86.

5. Stewart, *College Football Stadiums*.

6. Blickstein, *Bowls of Glory*, 82–95 (with excellent photographs).

7. Pollard, *History of the Ohio State University*, 234, 249, 251–52, 254, 255, 259; Pollard, *Ohio State Athletics*, 3, 23, 60, 65, 66, 67, 90, 114, 117–30.

8. Tunis, "This Football Madness," 47.

9. University of Illinois, Board of Trustees, *31st Report* (1920), December 14, 1920, 155–56.

10. Ekblaw to David Kinley, February 2, 1921, RS 2/5/6, 8:46, folder "Stadium," University of Illinois Archives.

11. Raphaelson, "How Money Talked," 235–36.

12. University of Illinois, Board of Trustees, *31st Report* (1921), 200 (March 8, 1921).

13. Ibid., 231 (June 13, 1921).

14. Ibid., 18 (August 1, 1921).

15. Brundage ('09, BS civil engineering) was a general contractor in Chicago and a former superintendent of construction for Holabird and Roche. Carr ('93, BS science) was a member of the board of trustees from 1915 to 1921. Since 1906 he had been president of the Dearborn Chemical Company.

16. "Report of Alumni Meeting," November 22, 1921, RS 2/6/1, box 66, folder "Stadium," University of Illinois Archives.

17. University of Illinois, Board of Trustees, *31st Report* (1922), 157–58 (February 8, 1922); Lindaman, "That Our Youth," 211.

18. University of Illinois, Board of Trustees, *31st Report* (1922), 170, 173–74 (March 14, 1922).

19. University of Illinois Archives, RS 2/6/1, box 121, folder "Stadium." See also the reverse side of a document, "Memory of These Illini Dead," in the same location. See also Soderstrom, *Big House*, 145–47.

20. David Kinley, "Address at Stadium Dedication," October 17, 1924, RS 2/6/1, box 121, folder "Stadium," University of Illinois Archives.

21. Lindaman, "Up! Up! Stadium," 108–9.

22. Ibid., 112.

23. The coaches were A. A. Stagg of Chicago, Robert Zuppke of Illinois, William Ingram of Indiana, Howard Jones of Iowa, Fielding Yost of Michigan, William Spaulding of Minnesota, Glenn Thistlewaite of Northwestern, and John J. Ryan of Wisconsin. Lindaman, "Up! Up! Stadium," 112.

24. Ibid., 112–13.

25. Ibid., 113.

26. Ibid., 114–15.

27. Kelly, *David Ross*, 1–108.

28. Kelly, *George Ade*, 187–98.

29. Lester, *Stagg's University*, 99, 126–30.

30. Williamson and Wild, *Northwestern University*, 93, 161, 172.

31. Pp. 219–20 and 230–32 (December 11, 1924); 249, 254–56, 272–75 (January 8, 1925).

32. Ibid., 273.

33. *Ann Arbor News*, December 17, 1924.

34. The preceding account of the building of the University of Michigan stadium draws on Soderstrom, *Big House*.

35. Kryk, *Natural Enemies*, 116–19.

36. Beyer, "Fifth District," 27–28.

Chapter 8. Red Grange and the Lure of Professional Football

1. My comments on Grange's academic standing are based on an evaluation of his official student record. Powel, *Walter Camp*, 230.

2. Ibid., 231. Following Camp's death in 1925, *Collier's* asked Grantland Rice to take over the selecting. Rice did it for a year. Then several other sports reporters joined him on a board that made the picks for the next twenty-one years. Rice, *Tumult and the Shouting*, 207.

3. Oriard, *King Football*, 126–28; Schoor, *Red Grange*, 74, 82 (quotation at 80).

4. Inabinett, *Grantland Rice*, 74–79.

5. Johnston, "Profiles." On another of Pyle's promotions, see Charles B. Kastner, *Bunion Derby: The 1928 "Footrace Across America"* (Albuquerque: University of New Mexico Press, 2007).

6. This is Grange's account in Whittingham, *What a Game They Played*, 18.

7. The immediately preceding paragraphs draw on Grange, *Red Grange Story*, 3–68, 89–94; Halas, *Halas by Halas*, 99–106; my study of Grange's academic record, Carroll, *Red Grange*, 11–76; and "'Red' Grange to Make Known Plans after Next Game," *New York Telegram*, November 18, 1925.

8. David Kinley to Harold E. Grange, November 14, 1925, Kinley Papers, RS 2/6/1, box 129, folder "Red Grange," University of Illinois Archives.

9. "Red Grange's Father Opposes Pro Game," *New York Times*, November 17, 1925; "'If Pro, Turn in Suit,' Zuppke Tells Grange," *New York Times*, November 18, 1925; "Grange Declares He Has Not Signed," *New York Times*, November 19, 1925.

10. Grange, *Red Grange Story*, 95–97; "Grantland Rice on Red Grange's Last Game," *New York Herald Tribune*, November 22, 1925, is included in *The Best of Grantland Rice*, selected by Dave Camerer (New York: Franklin Watts, 1963), 125–31.

11. Inabinett, *Grantland Rice*, 83; Grantland Rice, "The Sportlight," *New York Herald Tribune*, November 23, 1925, reprinted in *The Best of Grantland Rice*, 134–35.

12. David Kinley to Edward O. Keator, December 16, 1925, RS 2/6/1, box 129, folder "Red Grange," University of Illinois Archives.

13. "A Fallen Idol," *Wood River (Illinois) Journal*, ca. December 5, 1925, in the Kinley Papers, RS 2/6/1, box 129, folder "Red Grange," University of Illinois Archives.

14. Tunis, "All-American." Tunis described his profile as "not polite." Harold Ross, the editor of the *New Yorker*, then in its infancy, said of it, "Excellent piece; somewhat exciting." See Tunis, *Measure of Independence*, 159.

15. "'Pro' Football Is Coming in Favor," *New York Times*, November 22, 1925.

16. "Griffith Says Grange Will Cut Loose in Pro Football as He Did in College," *New York Times*, November 25, 1925.

17. Grange, *Red Grange Story*, 101–2.

18. Ibid., 102.

19. Grange's account in Whittingham, *What a Game They Played*, 20.

20. Grange's exhibition tours are described in Grange, *The Red Grange Story*, 98–121 (quote on 112), and in Carroll, *Red Grange*, 107–39.

21. "Football History," 29–30, 32, 33–39 (quotation at 30).

22. Carroll, *Red Grange*, 130–32, 142–43, 153–54.

23. Halas, *Halas by Halas*, 117–18.

24. Whittingham, *What a Game They Played*, 24–25.

25. Rice, "Pigskin Ballyhoo," 20.

26. C. E. Durst to David Kinley, November 6, 1925; Kinley to Durst, November 11, 1925, RS 2/6/1, box 129, folder "Red Grange," University of Illinois Archives. In 1950 the Illinois Republican party named Grange as one of three candidates for election to the university's

board of trustees. The Republican candidates won in the general election. Grange outpolled his running mates. He served three years of a six-year term and then resigned.

27. The sculptor was George W. Lundeen of Loveland, Colorado. He had a BA (1971) from Hastings College in Nebraska, an MFA (1973) from the University of Illinois, and had done postgraduate work at the Accademia di Belle Arti in Florence, Italy, in 1973–74.

28. Oriard, *King Football*, 234–35.

29. Harris, *King Football*, 100–108.

30. Griffith to the Athletic Directors, 1926.

31. Tunis, "Great God Football," 746.

32. Ibid. 742–52.

33. Ford, *Soldier Field*, 182–83; Noll and Zimbalist, *Sports, Jobs, and Taxes*, 330, 327.

Chapter 9. The Conference at Work

1. *IC Minutes*, December 7, 1924, and December 7, 1928.

2. Ibid., December 4, 1920.

3. Ibid., December 1–2, 1922.

4. Ibid., March 19, 1923.

5. Ibid., June 1, 1923.

6. Yost, "Administration," 115–18.

7. *IC Minutes*, March 14, 1925.

8. Ibid., June 6, 1925.

9. Ibid., December 4, 1925.

10. Ibid., March 13, 1926.

11. Ibid., May 28, 1926.

12. Ibid., November 26, 1926.

13. John L. Griffith, "Football Schedules," January 21, 1927, Stagg Papers, box 85, folder 5.

14. *IC Minutes*, May 27, 1927.

15. Ibid., December 2, 1927.

16. Ibid., May 25, 1929.

17. Ibid., May 26, 1928.

18. Ibid., December 7, 1928, and exhibit B.

19. Ibid., May 23, 1930.

20. Rule 12, "Attendance," dealt with migrant athletes.

21. *IC Minutes*, May 25, 1929, and exhibit A.

22. Ford, *Soldier Field*, 91.

23. *IC Minutes*, December 5, 1930.

24. Ibid., December 5, 1925.

25. Ibid., May 27, 1927.

26. Ibid., December 2, 1927.

27. Ibid., June 1, 1923.

28. Ibid., December 1, 1923.

29. Ibid., December 5, 1925.

30. Ibid., May 25, 1929.
31. Ibid., December 7, 1929.
32. Soderstrom, *Big House*, 96–97, 154–55, 224–26, 235–36.
33. Ibid., May 28, 1926.
34. Ibid., December 7–8, 1924, and March 15, 1925.
35. *Rules, Regulations and Opinions of the Intercollegiate Conference of Faculty Representatives* (1925).
36. Ibid., December 1, 1923.
37. Ibid., June 4, 1921, December 2, 1921, and exhibit A.
38. Ibid., December 2, 1927.
39. "A Digest of the Proceedings of the Intercollegiate Conference of Faculty Representatives, 1895–1920," 9–11; *IC Minutes*, June 4, 1921. The digest also lists colleges in Arkansas, California, Colorado, Idaho, Kansas, Kentucky, Missouri, Montana, Nebraska, Nevada, North Dakota, Oregon, South Dakota, Tennessee, Utah, Washington, and Wyoming, 10–12.
40. *IC Minutes*, December 2, 1921.
41. Ibid., December 2–3, 1922.
42. The *Digest of the Proceedings of the Intercollegiate Conference of Faculty Representatives, 1895–1920* listed the names of institutions that should be considered colleges for conference purposes.
43. *IC Minutes*, December 7, 1924, and exhibit B.
44. Ibid., November 30, 1912, and exhibit A.
45. Ibid., December 6, 1919.
46. Ibid., December 4, 1920.
47. Ibid., December 1, 1923.
48. Ibid., December 7, 1924.
49. Griffith to Stagg, February 7, 1925, Stagg Papers, box 85, folder 1, "Special Collections and Manuscripts," University of Chicago; *IC Minutes*, March 14, 1925.
50. "Western Conference Officiating," 36–37, 41.
51. *IC Minutes*, December 4, 1925.
52. Griffith to Stagg, January 21, 1927, Stagg Papers, box 85, folder 3.
53. *IC Minutes*, May 27, 1927.
54. Ibid., December 2, 1927.
55. Griffith, memorandum, December 14, 1927, Stagg Papers, box 85, folder 3.
56. O. F. Long, "Fourth District," *NCAA Proceedings* 24 (January 1, 1930): 40.
57. Murray Sperber, *Shake Down the Thunder*, 34, 44, 49, 90, 114–16.
58. Griffith to Rockne, February 6, 1925, Notre Dame Archives, UADR 12/80.
59. Rockne to Griffith, February 9, 1925, Notre Dame Archives, UADR 12/80.
60. Rockne to Griffith, March 17, 1925, Notre Dame Archives, UADR 12/80.
61. Rockne to Griffith, September 22, 1925; Griffith to Rockne, October 8, 1925, UADR 12/80.
62. Sperber, *Shake Down the Thunder*, 127–28, 139, 191–92, 312 (the quotation).
63. Griffith to Rockne, October 29, 1926, Notre Dame Archives, UADR, 12/80.
64. Rockne to Griffith, October 25, 1926, Notre Dame Archives, UADR, 12/80.

65. Griffith to Rockne, October 27, 1926, Griffith to Rockne, October 29, 1926, Griffith to Rockne, November 3, 1926, Notre Dame Archives, UADR, 12/80.

66. Ross, "Athletics."

67. Ibid., 45–46.

68. Ibid., 46.

69. Ibid., 47.

70. Ibid.

71. Ibid., 47–48.

72. As quoted in Austin, "Protecting Athletics," 260.

Chapter 10. The True Spirit of the University

1. Lester, *Stagg's University*, 126–27, 259n2.

2. Wilkins, "Relation of Intercollegiate Football," 81–88.

3. Wilkins, "Report by Committee G," 218–34.

4. Ibid., 218–22.

5. Ibid., 224–25.

6. Ibid., 225–26.

7. Ibid., 226–28.

8. Ibid., 228.

9. Ibid., 228–29.

10. Ibid., 229.

11. Ibid., 229–31.

12. Ibid., 231–33.

13. Ibid., 233–34.

14. "What the Editors Say," 40–46.

15. Wilkins, "Report by Committee G," 218–34.

16. Sanford, "Reply to Professor Wilkins' Report," 89–101. Steadman V. Sanford, a native Georgian, had been at the University of Georgia since 1903. He held only a bachelor's degree but had done some postgraduate study at the University of Berlin and at Oxford. He was dean of the Henry W. Grady School of Journalism from 1921 to 1927 and faculty chair of athletics, in which capacity he had worked hard to advance the role of athletics. See Thomas G. Dyer, *The University of Georgia: A Bicentennial History, 1785–1985* (Athens: University of Georgia Press, 1985), 206.

17. "Griffith Says Big Ten Will Not Tinker with Grid Card," *Chicago Tribune*, January 26, 1927, 17; "Big Ten Hits at College 'Pros' in Meeting Today," *Chicago Tribune*, January 28, 1927.

18. "Minutes of Special Committee of Sixty," RS 2/6/1–130, University of Illinois Archives, 5.

19. "Minutes of Special Committee of Sixty," 6–8; "Big Ten Puts Curb on Recruiting," *Chicago Tribune*, January 29, 1927.

20. "Minutes of Special Committee of Sixty," 8.

21. "University President's View of Athletics," 38, 40–41.

22. J. Frank Lindsey to A. A. Stagg, January 29, 1927, Stagg Papers, box 85, folder 5, University of Illinois Archives.

23. Wallace, "Hypocrisy of Football Reform," 570–71.

24. "Big Ten Draws 4 Year Grid Schedule," *Chicago Tribune*, January 27, 1927.

25. Sperber, *Shake Down the Thunder*, 207–8.

26. *IC Minutes*, May 28 and May 29, 1926.

27. Sperber, *Shake Down the Thunder*, 209.

28. *IC Minutes*, November 26, 1926.

29. Burns, *Being Catholic, Being American*, 194.

30. Ibid., 189–90.

31. Sperber, *Shake Down the Thunder*, 211.

32. Burns, *Being Catholic, Being American*, 174, 245, 246–47, 252–57.

33. Hayes, *Catholic Brain Trust*.

34. "Complete Statement of Net Income from Football of the Conference Universities, 1923–1929," and "Complete Total Receipts of All Big Ten Universities, 1923–1929, "Stagg Papers, box 84, folder 7, University of Illinois Archives.

35. Sperber, *Shake Down the Thunder*, 293.

36. *IC Minutes*, May 28, 1927.

37. Griffith to Stagg (Confidential), April 11, 1927, Stagg Papers, box 85, folder 5, University of Illinois Archives.

38. Griffith to Lindsey, April 13, 1927, Stagg Papers, box 85, folder 5, University of Illinois Archives.

39. Harris, *King Football*, chap. 3.

Chapter 11. The Carnegie Report

1. Pritchett, "Abuse of Intercollegiate Athletics."

2. Pritchett, "College Athletics."

3. Savage, Bentley, McGovern, and Smiley, *American College Athletics* 23. On the background to the report, see also Thelin, *Games Colleges Play*, 13–24.

4. Pritchett, "Preface," *American College Athletics* 23, xviii.

5. Ibid., xx.

6. Savage, Bentley, McGovern, and Smiley, *American College Athletics* 23:100.

7. Ibid.

8. Ibid., 121–22.

9. Ibid., 128–29.

10. Ibid., 133.

11. Ibid., 161–89, quotation at 189.

12. Ibid., 190–223, quotation at 199. Savage cited the rivalry between Michigan and Notre Dame as an example of wholesome extramural collegiate athletic rivalry. Nothing could be more wide of the mark. See Kryk, *Natural Enemies*.

13. Savage, Bentley, McGovern, and Smiley, *American College Athletics* 23:225.

14. Ibid., 228, 228n.

15. Ibid., 236, 236n.

16. Ibid., 238.

17. Ibid., 238 (quotation), 242–63.

18. Oriard, *Reading Football*, expands on this theme.

19. Savage, Bentley, McGovern, and Smiley, *American College Athletics*, 23:266–90 (quotation at 273).

20. Ibid., 291–311.

21. "You've Seen the Highlights—Now for Carnegie Side Lights," *Chicago Tribune*, October 25, 1929.

22. "Carnegie Probe Seems to Be a Waste of Time," *Chicago Tribune*, October 25, 1929.

23. John L. Griffith, "The Carnegie Report," *Athletic Journal* 10 (November 1929): 43–46.

24. See Watterson, *College Football*, 170–76, on the Carnegie Report and its critics.

25. The athletic directors were Z. G. Clevenger (Indiana), Kenneth L. Wilson (Northwestern), L. W. St. John (Ohio State), Noble Kizer (Purdue), H. O. Crisler (Michigan), and F. W. Leuhrig (Minnesota). Griffith was a member of the NCAA executive council. Stagg was chair of an NCAA committee. Iowa, under censure, was not represented, but Edward H. Lauer of Iowa was present.

26. Savage, "Aspects," 90–95.

27. "Kipke Addresses Illinois Coaching Men at Banquet," *Daily Illini*, January 11, 1930, 8.

28. Henry S. Pritchett, "Foreword," in Ryan, *Literature*, xi–xii.

29. "Ralph W. Aigler," Wikipedia.

30. Griffith, "Carnegie Reports," *Journal of Higher Education*, 325–30. Griffith mentions Ryan, *Literature of American*.

31. Ibid.

32. Flexner, *Henry S. Pritchett*, 121.

33. "Carnegie Report Asked," *New York Times*, November 20, 1936; "New Carnegie Investigation Is Considered," *Chicago Tribune*, November 21, 1936.

Chapter 12. The Big Ten Censures Iowa

1. "In the Wake of the News," *Chicago Tribune*, May 28, 1929. Schmidt, *Shaping College Football*, 181–88, briefly treats "the Iowa slush fund scandal."

2. *IC Minutes*, May 25, 1929. Among Big Ten schools, Purdue, Ohio State, Michigan, Northwestern, and Wisconsin were charged with running highly organized recruiting systems on and off campus. Schmidt, "1919 Iowa Football Scandal," 348.

3. *IC Minutes*, May 28, 1927.

4. *Rules Regulations and Opinions of the Intercollegiate Conference of Faculty Representatives*, revised 1925 (published by the conference), 12.

5. *IC Minutes* and exhibit B, May 25, 1929; "Big Ten Expels Iowa from Conference," *Chicago Tribune*, May 26, 1919.

6. Persons, *University of Iowa*, 96–97; Gerber, *Pictorial History*.

7. Rea, *Die-Hard Fan's Guide*, 52; Pollard, *Ohio State Athletics*, 68, 90, 91, 92.

8. Lambert to Jessup, February 2, 1923, University of Iowa Archives.

9. Lambert to Jessup, May 9, 1923, University of Iowa Archives.

10. Lamb and McGrane, *75 Years*, 81–84.

11. Lambert to Jessup, January 11, 1924, University of Iowa Archives.

12. Lambert to Jones, January 15, 1924, University of Iowa Archives.

13. Lambert to W. O. Finkbein, February 2, 1924, University of Iowa Archives.

14. F. G. Higbee, "Athletic Board Matters and the Reorganization of the Alumni Association," SUI Faculty Memoirs, University of Iowa Archives, LD 2568-3-89, 1.

15. "Page, Rockne Talked as New Hawk Coach," *Chicago Tribune*, March 3, 1924; Murray Sperber, *Shake Down the Thunder*, 154.

16. "Events Point to Rockne as Iowa Coach in 1925," *Chicago Tribune*, March 23, 1924.

17. Lamb and McGrane, *75 Years*, 85–88.

18. Sperber, *Shake Down the Thunder*, 154–55.

19. Higbee, "Athletic Board Matters," 2, University of Iowa Archives.

20. Griffith to President Walter A. Jessup, December 6, 1927, Stagg Papers, box 78, folder 7.

21. Amos Alonzo Stagg, "Resignation of Dr. P. E. Belting from the Directorship of the Department of Physical Education at Iowa," ca. April 29, 1929, Stagg Papers box 78, folder 6.

22. Amos Alonzo Stagg, "Resignation of Dr. P. E. Belting from the Directorship of the Department of Physical Education at the University of Iowa and Subsequent Events," ca. May 11, 1929, Stagg Papers, box 78, folder 6.

23. Ibid.

24. Ibid.

25. Ibid.

26. Ibid.

27. Ibid.

28. Ibid.

29. Ibid.

30. John L. Griffith to George Huff and A. A. Stagg, May 15, 1929, Stagg Papers, box 7, folder 6.

31. Amos Alonzo Stagg, "Meeting of the Athletic Directors of Illinois, Michigan, Minnesota, Ohio, and Chicago on Sunday, May 19, 1929," ca. May 20, 1929, Stagg Papers, box 78, folder 6.

32. Amos Alonzo Stagg, "Conference Athletic Directors' Meeting May 24th, 1929 at Morrison Hotel," ca. May 25, 1929, Stagg Papers, box 78, folder 6.

33. Amos Alonzo Stagg, "Meeting of the Intercollegiate Faculty Conference at the North Shore Hotel, Evanston, Saturday, May 25, 1929," ca. May 26, 1929, Stagg Papers, box 78, folder 6.

34. Persons, *University of Iowa*, 97.

35. Higbee, "Athletic Board Matters," 4–6, University of Iowa Archives; Griffith to Stagg, May 27, 1928, Stagg Papers, box 85, folder 8.

36. Griffith to G. A. Goodenough, May 29, 1929, Stagg Papers, box 78, folder 6.

37. Dr. White cannot be identified. Mr. Williams may be Rolland F. Williams, the head basketball coach.

38. Griffith to Jessup, May 31, 1929, Stagg Papers, box 78, folder 6; Higbee, "Athletic Board Matters," 6–8, University of Iowa Archives.

39. Griffith to Jessup, May 31, 1929, Stagg Papers, box 78, folder 6; Higbee, "Athletic Board Matters," 6–8, University of Iowa Archives.

40. "'Give Us New Hearing,' Iowa Plea to Big 10," *Chicago Tribune*, May 29, 1929.

41. "Big Ten Faculty Men Open Minded about Iowa's Plea," *Chicago Tribune*, May 29, 1929; Griffith to Jessup, May 29, 1929, Jessup Papers, RG 05-01-09, box 233, folder 87, 1928–1929, University of Iowa Archives.

42. "Reveal Why Iowa Was Ousted from Big Ten," *Chicago Tribune*, June 1, 1929; "Cite New Iowa Evidence," *Chicago Tribune*, June 2, 1929.

43. "Goodenough Talks: But Only in Parables," *Chicago Tribune*, June 2, 1929.

44. R. H. Fitzgerald to W. A. Jessup, June 3, 1929, Jessup Papers, RG 05-01-09, box 235, folder 87, 1928–1929, University of Iowa Archives; Persons, *University of Iowa*, 98.

45. Higbee, "Athletic Board Matters," 8–9, University of Iowa Archives.

46. C. S. Boucher to G. A. Goodenough, May 31, 1929, Stagg Papers, box 78, folder 6.

47. "Coach Plans Expose of Purdue Athletics: Attack on Belting Fails," *Chicago Tribune*, June 5, 1929; "Reporters Quiz Pres. Jessup: He Explains and Explains," *Chicago Tribune*, June 5, 1929.

48. "Big Ten Dotes on Rules That Only Exist to Be Broken," *Chicago Tribune*, June 8, 1929.

49. Amos Alonzo Stagg, "Principles Which Should Govern the New Conference of Five or Six Universities," July 24, 1929, Stagg Papers, box 78, folder 6.

50. Griffith to Yost, ca. July 20, 1929, Stagg Papers, box 78, folder 6.

51. "Iowa to Ask Big 10 Reinstatement Dec. 6," *Chicago Tribune*, September 25, 1929.

52. Griffith to Stagg, October 7, 1929, Stagg Papers, box 78, folder 6.

53. Griffith to Edward H. Lauer, October 7, 1929, Stagg Papers, box 78, folder 6.

54. Griffith to A. A. Stagg, October 18, 1929, Stagg Papers, box 78, folder 6.

55. "Sports," *Chicago Herald-American*, May 12, 1947 (a clipping in McKinley's vertical file in the University of Iowa Archives, kindly furnished to me by Denise K. Anderson of the University of Iowa Archives).

56. "Hawkeyes Keep Reinstatement Plans Secret," *Chicago Tribune*, November 27, 1929.

57. "Iowa's Friends Expect Big Ten Reinstatement," *Chicago Tribune*, November 30, 1929.

58. Griffith to A. A. Stagg, November 30, 1929, Stagg Papers, box 78, folder 6.

59. "Hawkeyes Await Verdict on Plea," *Chicago Tribune*, December 1, 1929.

60. "Hawkeye Alumni Give Their Views on Readmission," *Chicago Tribune*, December 1, 1929.

61. Lewis Omer to A. A. Stagg, December 3, 1929, Stagg Papers, box 78, folder 6.

62. "Reveal Iowa's Plea for Readmittance," *Chicago Tribune*, December 4, 1929; Griffith to James Paige and Thomas E. French, December 4, 1929, Stagg Papers, box 78, folder 6.

63. *IC Minutes*, December 6, 1929; Irving Vaughan, "Iowa Asks Reinstatement in Big Ten Tonight," *Chicago Tribune*, December 6, 1929.

64. *IC Minutes* and Exhibit "B," December 7, 1929; Persons, *University of Iowa*, 98.

65. Edward H. Lauer, "Memorandum of the Meeting of the Big Ten at Chicago, [December 6–7, 1929], from the point of view of the Athletic Directors, Records of the Board in Control of Athletics, RG 28/02/05, series 2, "Minutes," box 2, vol. 1929–1934, 33, University of Iowa Archives.

66. "Iowa Alumnus Calls Big Ten Action Wrong," *Chicago Tribune*, December 8, 1929. Butler and Cornelius Lynde of Cassoday, Butler, Lamb, and Foster in Chicago were the

authors of *The Federal Trade Commission and the Regulation of Business under the Federal Trade Commission and Clayton Laws* (Chicago: Callaghan, 1915).

67. "Iowa Bows to Big Ten: Bars 22 Athletes," *Chicago Tribune*, December 12, 1929.

68. John L. Griffith to A. A. Stagg, George Huff, and Fielding Yost, January 31, 1930, Stagg Papers, box 28, folder 7. See Walsh, *Intercollegiate Football*, 208.

69. *IC Minutes*, February 1, 1930; "Big Ten Reinstates Hawkeyes," *Daily Illini*, February 2, 1930.

70. John L. Griffith to Vice President F. C. Woodward [sic], February 5, 1930, Stagg Papers, box 28, folder 7.

71. John L. Griffith to A. A. Stagg and George Huff, March 27, 1930, Stagg Papers, box 28, folder 7.

72. John L. Griffith to Vice President F. C. Woodward, March 31, 1930, Stagg Papers, box 28, folder 7.

73. John L. Griffith, untitled document, March 31, 1930, Stagg Papers, box 28, folder 7.

74. John L. Griffith, "A Resume of the Conversation with Mr. Lauer and Dean Williams, May 9, 1930," Stagg Papers, box 28, folder 7.

75. Griffith to E. J. Moenkhaus, William Marshall, and Frank A. Richart, July 13, 1937, 4/2/12, box 2, folder "Commissioner, 1936–37," University of Illinois Archives. Griffith was writing to the Committee on Infractions about violations of conference rules when he cited the parallel of the Iowa case.

76. *IC Minutes*, May 23, 1930.

Chapter 13. Cross Currents

1. Flexner, *Universities: American, English, German.*

2. John L. Griffith, "Memorandum to the Faculty Representatives and Athletic Directors," February 28, 1931, Stagg Papers, box 86, folder 3, Special Collections and Manuscripts, University of Chicago.

3. John L. Griffith to the Faculty Representatives and Athletic Directors, February 19, 1931, Stagg Papers, box 86, folder 3.

4. John L. Griffith, "Confidential Memorandum" (to the athletic directors), February 26, 1931 (first quotation), and John L. Griffith, "Memorandum to the Presidents, Faculty Representatives and Athletic Directors of the Intercollegiate Conference," February 23, 1931 (second quotation), both in Stagg Papers, box 86, folder 3.

5. Griffith to the Faculty Representatives and Athletic Directors, February 18, 1931, Stagg Papers, box 86, folder 3.

6. "Big Ten Nears Break with North Central Group," *Chicago Tribune*, March 4, 1931; "Big Ten Presidents to Discuss North Central Case," *Chicago Tribune*, March 5, 1931.

7. "North Central Head Sticks to Guns against the Big Ten," *Chicago Tribune*, March 10, 1931.

8. Griffith, to the Presidents, Faculty Representatives, and Athletic Directors of the Intercollegiate Conference, March 12, 1931, Stagg Papers, box 86, folder 3.

9. Howard Barry, "North Central Seeks Peace with Big Ten Schools," *Chicago Tribune*, March 18, 1931.

10. "North Central to Hear N. U. Head Today," *Chicago Tribune* March 19, 1931; "Who Is to Control Athletics in the Conference Universities?" *North Central Association Quarterly* 6 (June 1931): 195–98; "North Central Defers Ruling on Big Ten Sport," *Chicago Tribune,* March 20, 1931.

11. John L. Griffith, to the Presidents, Faculty Representatives, and Athletic Directors of the Intercollegiate Conference, March 30, 1931, Stagg Papers, box 86, folder 3.

12. *IC Minutes,* April 18, 1931.

13. "North Central, Big Ten Near End of Quarrel," *Chicago Tribune,* May 10, 1931.

14. John L. Griffith, "Memorandum" to the Faculty Representatives and Athletic Directors of the Conference," January 26, 1932, Stagg Papers, box 89, folder 2.

15. "Report of the Committee on Athletics," *North Central Association Quarterly* 7 (December 1932): 274–78. The report was made in March 1932.

16. Ibid.

17. Ibid.

18. Ibid., 278–83.

19. John L. Griffith, "The Football Situation," *Athletic Journal* 17 (October 1936): 20; John L. Griffith, "Enduring Attitudes," *Athletic Journal* 17 (October 1936): 21.

20. Griffith to the Faculty Representatives and Athletic Directors of the Conference, September 21, 1931, Stagg Papers, box 89, folder 1.

21. *IC Minutes,* September 30, 1931; Long, "Fourth District," *NCAA Proceedings* 26 (1931).

22. "Big Ten Football Nets $154,000 for Poor of 7 States," *Chicago Tribune,* November 29, 1931.

23. *IC Minutes,* December 4, 1931.

24. Those present were as follows: Chicago, Dean George A. Works and Director Stagg; Illinois, Professor Callen and Coach Zuppke; Indiana, Professor Moenkhaus and Director Clevenger; Iowa, Dean Williams and Director Lauer; Michigan, Professor Aigler, Director Yost, and Coach Cappon; Minnesota, Professor Paige and Director Crisler; Ohio State, Professor French and Director St. John; Purdue, Professor Marshall and Director Kellogg; Wisconsin, Professor Weaver, Acting Director Phillips, and Assistant Director Levis. Commissioner Griffith was also present.

25. *IC Minutes,* May 20–21, 1932.

26. Ibid.

27. Ibid.

28. Ibid.

29. Ibid.

30. Pritchett, "Substitute for Football."

31. Ibid.

32. Stone, "Graham Plan of 1935."

33. *IC Minutes,* December 8, 1933.

34. Ibid., February 29, 1936.

35. John L. Griffith, "Report of Commissioner Griffith on the State of Athletics in the Conference," December 6, 1934, *IC Minutes,* December 7–8, 1934, exhibit B.

36. *IC Minutes,* May 20, 1933.

37. Ibid., May 19, 1934; "Big Ten Votes Down Football Training Table," *Chicago Tribune*, May 20, 1934.

38. *IC Minutes*, May 25, 1935.

39. Ibid., December 7, 1935.

40. Minutes of Meetings of Directors of Athletics, December 3, 1937, RS 12/1/2, box 2, folder "Meetings of Athletic Directors, 1937–40," University of Illinois Archives; *IC Minutes*, December 4, 1937.

41. *IC Minutes*, May 21, 1938; "Vote to Modify Rule on Big Ten Training Tables," *Chicago Tribune*, May 22, 1938.

42. Richart to E. G. Schroeder, L. W. St. John, Harry A. Stuhldreyer, and W. F. Lorenz, January 11, 1939; Schroeder to Richart, April 22, 1939; Lorenz to Richart, April 24, 1939, RS 4/2/12, box 2, folder "Western Intercollegiate Conference, 1937–38," University of Illinois Archives.

43. *IC Minutes*, May 20, 1939.

44. John L. Griffith, "Report of Commissioner Griffith on the State of Athletics in the Conference," December 6, 1934; *IC Minutes*, December 6, 1934, exhibit B.

45. The date of the appointment of the committee is not a matter of record. The conference severed athletic relations with the University of Iowa on May 29, 1929. In 1936 Griffith described the appointment of the committee as taking place "in the spring of 1929."

46. *IC Minutes*, December 6, 1936, appendix II, "Report to the Faculty Conference Submitted by the Commissioner of Athletics of the Intercollegiate Conference," 15.

47. *IC Minutes*, December 4, 1931.

48. Griffith to Moenkhaus, Marshall, and Richart, May 17, 1937, sending Bulletin No. 8, RS 4/2/12, box 2, folder "Commissioner, 1936–37," University of Illinois Archives.

49. Griffith to The Directors of Athletics, November 18, 1936, RS 4/2/12, box 2, folder "Commissioner, 1936–37," University of Illinois Archives.

50. Griffith to Moenkhaus, Marshall, and Richart, July 13, 1937, RS 4/2/12, box 2, folder "Commissioner, 1936–37," University of Illinois Archives.

51. Griffith to Moenkhaus, Marshall, and Richart, August 10, 1937, with the "Tabulation of the Conference Members," RS 4/2/12, box 2, folder "Commissioner, 1936–37," University of Illinois Archives.

52. Griffith to Fielding Yost, July 27, 1937, RS 4/2/12, box 2, folder "Commissioner, 1936–37," University of Illinois Archives.

53. Disgusted Youngster to Major John L. Griffith, n.d.; Griffith to Moenkhaus, Marshall, and Richart, July 28, 1937. Forwarding the letter, Griffith wondered if one should pay attention to anonymous communications. If anyone transgresses, he added, the facts will ultimately come out. RS 4/2/12, box 2, folder "Commissioners, 1936–37," University of Illinois Archives.

54. Griffith to Robert Woodworth, September 23, 1937; R. C. Woodruff to Griffith, October 14, 1937, RS 4/2/12, box 2, folder "Committee on Infraction of Regulations, University of Illinois Archives."

55. Griffith to Marshall, Moenkhaus, and Richart, January 17, 1938; Marshall to Griffith, Moenkhaus, and Richart, January 10, 1938, RS 4/2/12, box 2, folder "Committee on Infraction of Regulations," University of Illinois Archives.

56. *IC Minutes*, December 3, 1938.

57. John L. Griffith, "The Commissioner's Report," *IC Minutes*, December 4, 1937, exhibit A.

58. Griffith to The Faculty Representatives, Athletic Directors and Football Coaches, August 30, 1937, RS 4/2/12, box 2, folder "Commissioner, 1936–37," University of Illinois Archives.

59. Cronon and Jenkins, *University of Wisconsin*, 253–69; Sellery, *Some Ferments at Wisconsin*, 73–84, describes events at Wisconsin on which my account relies.

60. Hove, *University of Wisconsin*, 261.

61. Ibid., 266–67.

62. Griffith to A. A. Stagg, February 5, 1936, Stagg Papers, box 89, folder 3.

63. *IC Minutes*, February 29, 1936.

64. Ibid.

65. "Regents Deny Big Ten Right to Dictate," *Chicago Tribune*, March 1, 1936; "Wisconsin Faces Suspension by Big Ten," *Chicago Tribune*, March 1, 1936.

66. Cronon and Jenkins, *University of Wisconsin*, 267–69.

67. *IC Minutes*, May 22, 1936.

68. Frank, "Football in the American University," 15–16.

69. *IC Minutes*, May 20, 1933.

70. Owens to Aigler, October 6, 1938, RS 4/2/12, box 2, folder "Western Intercollegiate Conference, 1938–39," University of Illinois Archives.

71. Ibid.

72. Ibid.

73. Ibid.

74. Ibid.

75. Ibid.

76. Long to Frank E. Richart, October 25, 1938, RS 4/2/12, box 2, folder "Western Intercollegiate Conference, 1938–39," University of Illinois Archives.

77. Richart to Aigler, November 8, 1938, RS 4/2/12, box 2, folder "Western Intercollegiate Conference, 1938–39," University of Illinois Archives.

78. Aigler to Richart, November 10, 1938, RS 4/2/12, box 2, folder "Western Intercollegiate Conference, 1938–39," University of Illinois Archives.

79. "Report Big Ten Will Vote on Rose Bowl Bid," *Chicago Tribune*, November 8, 1938; *IC Minutes*, December 3, 1938.

80. *IC Minutes*, December 6, 1940; Edward Prell, "Big Ten Votes to Retain Ban on Bowl Games," *Chicago Tribune*, December 8, 1940.

81. John R. Tunis, "What Price College Football?" *American Mercury* 48 (October 1939): 129. Tunis based his story on evidence on file in the *American Mercury* offices.

82. Ibid., 130.

83. Ibid., 131–32.

84. Ibid., 133, 134, 136, 137.

85. Ibid., 141–42.

Chapter 14. Closing Out Half a Century

1. John L. Griffith, "Looking Ahead," *Athletic Journal* 17 (June 1937): 22–23.

2. John L. Griffith, "Coaches Salaries," *Athletic Journal* 18 (April 1938): 23.

3. John L. Griffith, "To the Directors of Athletics of the Conference: Amateur Athletics in a Corporate State," July 26, 1938, RS 4/2/12, box 2, folder "Commissioner 1937–38," University of Illinois Archives.

4. Griffith to the Directors of Athletics of the Conference, January 10, 1939, RS 4/2/12, box 2, folder "Commissioner 1938–39," University of Illinois Archives. Griffith took these data from Raymond Walter, "Statistics of Registration in American Universities and Colleges, 1938," *School and Society* 48 (December 17, 1938): 765–86.

5. John L. Griffith, "Football Crowds," *Athletic Journal* 18 (December 1937): 20.

6. Griffith, "To the Directors of Athletics in the Conference," November 8, 1938, RS 4/2/12, box 2, folder "Commissioner 1937–38," University of Illinois Archives.

7. John L. Griffith, "Report to the Faculty Conference Submitted by the Commissioner of Athletics of the Intercollegiate Conference," *IC Minutes*, December 5, 1936, appendix II.

8. B. L. Stradley to Frank E. Richart, May 11, 1937, RS 4/2/12, box 2, folder "Commissioner, 1936–37," University of Illinois Archives.

9. North Central Association of Colleges and Secondary Education, "Report of the Committee on Physical Education and Athletics," 1937, RS 4/2/12, box 2, folder "Commissioner, 1936–1937," University of Illinois Archives.

10. "Summary of Scholarships, Loans and Jobs Held by Varsity Men During Season of 1937–1938," in RS 4/2/12, box 2, folder "Commissioner 1938–39," University of Illinois Archives.

11. "Football Takes Stand! Big Ten Football Revenue $1,898,607 in 1938," *Chicago Daily News*, January 24, 1939, as cited in Austin, "Protecting Athletics," 269n38.

12. Hannah, *Memoir*, 117.

13. Young, *Arrogance and Scheming in the Big Ten*, 51–112.

14. *IC Minutes*, May 22, 1937.

15. Wallace, "Test Case at Pitt," 14–15, 47–49, 51–52; Walsh, *College Football*, 643–44; Smith, *Pay for Play*, 78–81.

16. Board of Trustees Minutes, 1845–1954, UA 01/04/1938–1939, p. 44, safe 2, University of Pittsburgh Archives. I am indebted to Marianne Kasica, University Archivist, University of Pittsburgh, who kindly furnished the information in my text.

17. Ibid.

18. Ibid.

19. David Young, *Arrogance and Scheming in the Big Ten*, 167.

20. Griffith to Richart, January 12, 1939, RS 4/2/2/ box 2, folder "Commissioner 1938–39"; Richart to Griffith, January 17, 1939, ibid., University of Illinois Archives.

21. Long to Richart, February 21, 1939, RS 4/2/12, box 2, folder "Commissioner, 1938–39," University of Illinois Archives.

22. Richart to Long, February 22, 1939, RS 4/2/12, box 2, folder "Commissioner, 1938–39," University of Illinois Archives.

23. Wallace, "Football Laboratory Explodes," 20–21, 80, 82, 85–86.

24. *IC Minutes*, May 20, 1939.

25. Young, *Arrogance and Scheming*, 167. From 1940 to 1945, Penn played a total of sixteen football games with Western Conference teams as follows: Ohio State (6), Illinois (3), Indiana (3), Minnesota (2), Michigan (1), and Purdue (1).

26. *IC Minutes*, December 8, 1944.

27. Lester, *Stagg's University*, 150–52; McNeill, *Hutchins' University*, 18–24; Mayer, *Robert Maynard Hutchins*, 1–136; Lawson and Ingham, "Conflicting Ideologies," 48–60.

28. Lester, *Stagg's University*, 148.

29. T. Nelson Metcalf, "Memorandum to the Athletic Directors, Intercollegiate Conference," April 4, 1940, Stagg Papers, box 89, folder 5; Lester, *Stagg's University*.

30. Lester, *Stagg's University*, 153.

31. Hutchins, "Gate Receipts and Glory," 23, 73.

32. Ibid., 74.

33. Ibid., 74–76.

34. Ibid., 76–77.

35. John L. Griffith, "An American Type," *Athletic Journal* 19 (June 1939): 20–21 (quotation on 20).

36. "Football Shackles Nation's Education—Hutchins," *Chicago Tribune*, January 13, 1940.

37. "35,000 Schools Can't Be Wrong—Yost to Hutchins," *Chicago Tribune*, January 14, 1940.

38. "A Notable Decision," *Chicago Defender*, January 27, 1940.

39. *IC Minutes*, May 17, 1941.

40. Ibid., September 13, 1941.

41. Ibid., March 7, 1942.

42. Ibid., May 16, 1942.

43. Ibid., May 15, 1943.

44. Ibid., December 7, 1935.

45. Ibid., December 5, 1935.

46. Ibid., March 7, 1942.

47. Ibid., December 8, 1944.

48. "Maj. Griffith, Big Ten Commissioner, Dies," *Chicago Tribune*, December 8, 1944.

49. "5 Lead Poll for Football's Man of Year Award," *Chicago Tribune*, December 24, 1944.

50. "Big 10 Athletic Directors Hold Secret Confab," *Chicago Tribune*, January 8, 1945; *IC Minutes*, January 20, 1945; "Big Ten Chief When Named, to Get New Power," *Chicago Tribune*, January 21, 1945.

51. *IC Minutes*, January 20, 1945.

52. Ibid., February 9, 1944.

53. Ibid., November 26, 1944. The record gives no breakdown of the vote.

54. Ibid., December 8, 1944.

55. This paragraph is based on the handwritten, undated notes of a joint meeting of the faculty representatives and the athletic directors. The author may have been Frank A. Richart, the Illinois faculty representative, who was the secretary of conference meetings as late as March 1945. The document is in RS 4/2/12, box 2, folder "Notes 1945," University of Illinois Archives.

56. *IC Minutes,* December 6, 1945.

57. Ibid.

58. Ibid.

59. Ibid., December 8, 1945.

60. Angell, "Collegiate Sport Complex," 250–58.

61. Bentley Historical Library, "The Michigan Stadium Story: Michigan Stadium Attendance Story," http://bentley.umich.edu/athdept/stadium/index.html.

62. "Rutgers' Move to Big Ten Is a Win-Win Everywhere but the Field," *New York Times,* October 12, 2016.

63. *Chicago Tribune,* December 5, 2016, lists the matchups, sites, dates, and TV coverage of each of the bowl games.

64. *IC Minutes,* December 6, 1945.

Epilogue

1. D. A. Penick, University of Texas, quoting a faculty member of a Texas college in "Report on the Sixth District," *Proceedings of the 27th Annual Convention of the NCAA* [1932], 37.

2. Tunis, *Measure of Independence,* 255–59; Jacobs, "John R. Tunis," 51.

3. On this point see Ripley, *Smartest Kids in the World.*

4. Pyre, *Wisconsin,* 317.

Appendix 1

1. "Chicago Conference of College Presidents," in *Proceedings [of] The Intercollegiate Conference of Faculty Representatives of the Athletic Committees or Boards of Control of the Following Universities: Chicago, Illinois, Indiana, Iowa, Michigan, Minnesota, Northwestern, Purdue, Wisconsin* (Minneapolis: University Press, 1901), 3. The original minutes of the Intercollegiate Conference of Faculty Representatives are in the Big Ten Conference headquarters in Park Ridge, Illinois. On February 23, 1901, Frederick S. Jones, the Minnesota faculty representative, moved to print the conference minutes. The proceedings cited in this note accurately record the original minutes through 1900, as I verified by comparing the original documents and the printed copy. The proceedings contain some documents that were not in the original minutes when I examined them.

Appendix 2

1. This paragraph draws on a biographical sketch provided by Erik Moore of the University of Minnesota Archives, and on James Gray, *The University of Minnesota, 1851–1951* (Minneapolis: University of Minnesota Press, 1951), 551 (the quotation).

Bibliography

Adelman, Melvin L. "Academicians and American Athletes: A Decade of Progress." *Journal of Sport History* 10 (Spring 1983): 80–106.

———. "Academicians and Athletics: Historians' Views of American Sport." *Maryland Historian* 4 (Fall 1973): 123–37.

———. *A Sporting Time: New York City and the Rise of Modern Athletics, 1820–70*. Urbana: University of Illinois Press, 1986.

Allen, Edward F. *Keeping Our Fighters Fit for War and After*. New York: Century, 1918.

Angell, James R. "The Collegiate Sport Complex." In Angell, *American Education: Addresses and Articles*, 250–58. New Haven, Conn.: Yale University Press, 1937.

———. "The Familiar Problems of College Athletics." *NCAA Proceedings* 25 (1930): 94–110.

———. "The Reconstruction Program for Physical Education in the Colleges." *NCAA Proceedings* 13 (1918): 44–54.

Angell, Robert C. "Increasing the Intellectual Interests of Students." *Michigan Alumnus* 31 (October 12, 1924–September 20, 1925): 272–75.

Austin, Brad. "Protecting Athletics and the American Way: Defenses of Intercollegiate Athletics at Ohio State and across the Big Ten During the Great Depression." *Journal of Sport History* 27 (Summer 2000): 247–70.

Babcock, Robert W., ed. *Addresses and Records: Semi-Centennial Ceremonial*. Purdue University, May 1924. Indianapolis: Burford, 1928.

Baker, L. H. *Football: Facts and Figures*. New York: Farrar and Rinehart, 1945.

Barber, William J., Jr. *George Huff: A Short Biography*. Master's thesis in Physical Education, University of Illinois, 1951.

Barton, Herbert J. "The College Conference of the Middle West." *Educational Review* 27 (January 1904): 46.

Bederman, Gail. *Manliness and Civilization: A Cultural History of Gender and Race in the United States: 1880–1917*. Chicago: University of Chicago Press, 1995.

Behee, John R. *Fielding Yost's Legacy to the University of Michigan*. Ann Arbor: Lithocrafters, 1971.

Bennett, James D. *Frederick Jackson Turner*. Boston: Twayne, 1975.

Bergin, Thomas G. *The Game: The Harvard-Yale Football Rivalry, 1875–1983*. New Haven, Conn.: Yale University Press, 1984.

Bernstein, Mark F. *Football: The Ivy League Origins of an American Obsession*. Philadelphia: University of Pennsylvania Press, 2001.

Betts, John R. *America's Sporting Heritage: 1850–1920*. Reading, Mass.: Addison-Wesley, 1974.

Beyer, S. W. "Fifth District." *NCAA Proceedings* 21 (1926): 27–28.

The Big Ten Records Book, 1968–1969. [Chicago]: Big Ten Service Bureau, 1969.

Billington, Ray Allen. *Frederick Jackson Turner: Historian, Scholar, Teacher*. New York: Oxford University Press, 1973.

Blickstein, Steve. *Bowls of Glory: Fields of Dreams: Great Stadiums and Ballparks of North America*. Encino, Calif.: Cherbo, 1995.

Bok, Derek. *Universities in the Market Place: The Commercialization of Higher Education*. Princeton, N.J.: Princeton University Press, 2003.

Bole, Ronald E. *An Economic Analysis of the Factors Influencing Football Attendance at the University of Illinois, 1926–1968*. PhD diss., University of Illinois, 1970.

Bond, William Scott. "The Intercollegiate Conference and the University of Michigan." *Wisconsin Alumni Magazine* 9 (May 1908): 318–23. Reprinted from the *Chicago Alumni Magazine*, April 1908.

Boyle, Robert H. *Sport: Mirror of American Life*. Boston: Little, Brown, 1963.

Boyles, Bob, and Paul Guido. *Fifty Years of College Football: A Modern History of America's Most Colorful Sport*. Washington, Del.: Sideline Commissions, 2006.

Brichford, Maynard. *Bob Zuppke: The Life and Football Legacy of the Illinois Coach*. Jefferson, N.C.: McFarland, 2008.

Bryce, James. *University and Historical Addresses: Delivered during a Residence in the United States as Ambassador of Great Britain*. New York: Macmillan, 1913.

Bundgaard, Axel. *Muscle and Manliness: The Rise of Sport in American Boarding Schools*. Syracuse, N.Y.: Syracuse University Press, 2005.

Burns, Robert E. *Being Catholic, Being American: The Notre Dame Story, 1842–1934*. Notre Dame, Ind.: University of Notre Dame Press, 1999.

Byers, Walter. *Unsportsmanlike Conduct: Exploiting College Athletes*. Ann Arbor: University of Michigan Press, 1995.

Cady, Edwin H. *The Big Game: College Sports and American Life*. Knoxville: University of Tennessee Press, 1978.

A Call to Action: Reconnecting College Sports and Higher Education. Report of the Knight Foundation Commission on Intercollegiate Athletics. June 2001.

Camp, Walter. *American Football*. New York: Harper and Brothers, 1891.

———. "Camp's All-America Eleven." *Collier's* 56 (December 18, 1915): 13, 26–27.

———. *Football Facts and Figures*. New York: Harper and Brothers, 1894.

———. *Walter Camp's Book of College Sports*. New York: Century, 1893.

Carlson, Kenneth. *College Football Scorebook*. 3rd ed. Lynwood, Wash.: Rain Belt, 1988.

Carroll, Bob, and Joe Horrigan. *Football Legends of All Time*. Lincolnwood, Ill.: Publications International, 1997.

Carroll, Bob, and PFRA Research. *The Ohio League, 1910–1919*. Canton, Ohio: PFRA, 1997.

Carroll, John M. *Red Grange and the Rise of Modern Football*. Urbana: University of Illinois Press, 1999.

Carter, Paul A. *Another Part of the Twenties*. New York: Columbia University Press, 1977.

Carter, W. Burlette. "The Age of Innocence: The First 25 Years of the National Collegiate Athletic Association, 1906 to 1931." *Vanderbilt Journal of Entertainment and Technology Law* 8 (Spring 2006): 211–91.

———. "Responding to the Perversion of *In Loco Parentis*: Using a Nonprofit Organization to Support Student-Athletes." *Indiana Law Review* 35 (2002): 851–923.

Chandler, Tim, Mike Cronin, and Wray Vamplew. *Sport and Physical Education: The Key Concepts*. 2nd ed. New York: Routledge.

Chidsey, Donald B. *John the Great: The Times and Life of a Remarkable American, John L. Sullivan*. Garden City, N.Y.: Doubleday/Doran, 1942.

Chu, Donald, Jeffrey O. Segrave, and Beverly J. Becker, eds. *Sport and Higher Education*. Champaign, Ill.: Human Kinetics, 1985.

Church, Seymour R. *Base Ball: The History, Statistics and Romance of the American National Game from Its Inception to the Present Time*. Princeton, N.J.: Pyne, 1902.

Clark, Thomas D. *Indiana University: Midwestern Pioneer*. Vol. 1: The Early Years. Bloomington: Indiana University Press, 1970.

———. *Indiana University: Midwestern Pioneer*. Vol. 2: In Mid-Passage. Bloomington: Indiana University Press, 1973.

Clotfelter, Charles T. *Big-Time Sports in American Universities*. Cambridge: Cambridge University Press, 2011.

Coffman, Edward M. *The War to End All Wars: The American Military Experience in World War I*. New York: Oxford University Press, 1968.

Cohane, Tim. *The Yale Football Story*. New York: Putnam's, 1951.

"Committee J, College Athletics." American Association of University Professors *Bulletin* 11 (January 1925).

Considine, Bob. *The Unreconstructed Amateur: A Pictorial Biography of Amos Alonzo Stagg*. San Francisco: Stagg Foundation, 1962.

Cope, Alexis. *History of the Ohio State University*. Edited by Thomas C. Mendenhall. Vol. 1: 1870–1910. Columbus: Ohio State University Press, 1920.

Coulter, Stanley. "Thomas Francis Moran: An Appreciation." *Indiana Magazine of History* 25 (March 1929): 47–51.

Cowley, W. H. "Athletics in American Colleges." *Journal of Higher Education* 1 (January 1930): 29–35.

Cramer, C. H. *Newton D. Baker: A Biography*. Cleveland: World Publishing, 1961.

Crowley, Joseph N. *In the Arena: The NCAA's First Century*. Indianapolis: NCAA, 2006.

Crunden, Robert M. *Ministers of Reform: The Progressives' Achievement in American Civilization, 1889–1920*. New York: Basic, 1982.

Curti, Merle, and Vernon Carstensen. *The University of Wisconsin: A History, 1848–1925*. 2 vols. Madison: University of Wisconsin Press, 1949.

Danzig, Allison. *The History of American Football: Its Great Teams, Players, and Coaches*. Englewood Cliffs, N.J.: Prentice Hall, 1956.

———. *Oh, How They Played the Game: The Early Days of Football and the Heroes Who Made It Great*. New York: Macmillan, 1971.

Danzig, Allison, and Peter Brandwein, eds. *Sport's Golden Age: A Close-Up of the Fabulous Twenties*. New York: Harper and Brothers, 1948.

Davis, Jeff. *Papa Bear: The Life and Legacy of George Halas*. New York: McGraw Hill, 2005.

Davis, Parke H. *Football: The American Intercollegiate Game*. New York: Scribner's, 1911.

Des Jardins, Julie. *Walter Camp: Football and the Modern Man*. New York: Oxford University Press, 2015.

Dibble, R. P. *John L. Sullivan: An Intimate Narrative*. Boston: Little, Brown, 1925.

Doyle, Andrew. "Foolish and Useless Sport: The Southern Evangelical Crusade against Intercollegiate Football." *Journal of Sport History* 24 (Fall 1997): 317–40.

Duderstadt, James J. *Intercollegiate Athletics and the American University: A University President's Perspective*. Ann Arbor: University of Michigan Press, 2000.

Dulles, Foster R. *America Learns to Play: A History of Popular Recreation, 1607–1940*. New York: Appleton-Century, 1940.

Durant, John, and Otto Bettmann. *Pictorial History of American Sports: From Colonial Times to the Present*. Rev. ed. New York: Barnes, 1952.

Dyreson, Mark. "The Emergence of Consumer Culture and the Transformation of Physical Culture: American Sport in the 1920s." *Journal of Sport History* 16 (Winter 1989): 261–81.

———. *Making the American Team: Sport, Culture and the Olympic Experience*. Urbana: University of Illinois Press, 1998.

———. "Regulating the Body and the Body Politic: American Sport, Bourgeois Culture, and the Language of Progress, 1880–1920." In *The New American Sport History: Recent Approaches and Perspectives*, edited by S. W. Pope, 121–44. Urbana: University of Illinois Press, 1997.

Dyreson, Mark, and Robert Trumpbour, eds. *The Rise of Stadiums in the Modern United States: Cathedrals of Sport*. London: Routledge, 2010.

Edwards, R. H., J. M. Artman, and Galen M. Fisher. *Undergraduates: A Study of Morale in Twenty-Three American Colleges and Universities*. Garden City, N.Y.: Doubleday/Doran, 1928.

Eliot, Charles W. *Annual Reports of the President and Treasurer of Harvard College, 1892–93*. Cambridge: The University, 1894.

Eubanks, Lon. *The Fighting Illini: A Story of Illinois Football*. Huntsville, Ala.: Strode, 1976.

Faculty Athletic Adviser. "Commercialism in College Athletics." *School and Society* 15 (June 24, 1922): 681–86, and 16 (1 July 1922): 7–11.

Falla, Jack. *NCAA: The Voice of College Sports: A Diamond Anniversary History, 1906–1981*. Mission, Kan.: NCAA, 1981.

Farr, Finis. *Fair Enough: The Life of Westbrook Pegler*. New Rochelle, N.Y.: Arlington House, 1975.

Finn, Mike, and Chad Leistikow. *Hawkeye Legends, Lists and Lore*. Champaign, Ill.: Sports Publishing, 1998.

Flath, Arnold W. *A History of Relations between the National Collegiate Athletic Association and the Amateur Athletic Union of the United States (1905–1963)*. Champaign, Ill.: Stipes, [1964].

Flexner, Abraham. *Henry S. Pritchett: A Biography*. New York: Columbia University Press, 1943.

———. *Universities: American, English, German*. New York: Oxford University Press, 1930.

"Football History as Made by the Illinois Iceman." *Literary Digest* 87 (December 26, 1925): 29–39.

"Football—The Frankenstein of Athletics." *Literary Digest* 79 (December 1, 1923): 52–59.

Ford, Liam T. A. *Soldier Field: A Stadium and Its City*. Chicago: University of Chicago Press, 2009.

Fosdick, Raymond B. *Chronicle of a Generation: An Autobiography*. New York: Harper and Brothers, 1958.

Foster, William T. "An Indictment of Intercollegiate Athletics." *Atlantic Monthly* 116 (November 1915): 577–88.

———. "Intercollegiate Athletics and the War." National Education Association of the United States, *Addresses and Proceedings of the Fifty-Fifth Annual Meeting, 1917*. Washington, D.C.: 1917.

Fountain, Charles. *Sportswriter: The Life and Times of Grantland Rice*. New York: Oxford University Press, 1993.

Fox, Stephen. *Big Leagues: Professional Baseball, Football, and Basketball in National Memory*. New York: Morrow, 1994.

Frank, Glenn. "Football in the American University." *Athletic Journal* 17 (February 1937): 15–16.

Frey, James, ed. *The Governance of Intercollegiate Athletics*. West Point, N.Y.: Leisure, 1982.

Gems, Gerald R. *For Pride, Profit, and Patriarchy: Football and the Incorporation to American Cultural Values*. Lanham, Md.: Scarecrow, 2000.

———, ed. *Sports in North America: A Documentary History*. Vol. 5: Sports Organized, 1880–1900. Gulf Breeze, Fla.: Academic International, 1996.

———. *The Windy City Wars: Labor, Leisure, and Sport in the Making of Chicago*. Lanham, Md.: Scarecrow, 1997.

Gerber, John C. *A Pictorial History of the University of Iowa*. Expanded Ed. Iowa City: University of Iowa Press, 2005.

Gleason, Philip. "American Catholic Higher Education: A Historical Perspective." In *The Shape of Catholic Higher Education*, ed. Robert Hassenger, 15–53. Chicago: University of Chicago Press, 1967.

Goerler, Raimund E. *The Ohio State University: An Illustrated History*. Columbus: Ohio State University Press, 2011.

Gorn, Elliott J., ed. *Sports in Chicago*. Urbana: University of Illinois Press, 2008.

Gorn, Elliott J., and Warren Goldstein. *A Brief History of American Sports*. Urbana: University of Illinois Press, 1993.

Grange, Harold E. *The Red Grange Story as Told to Ira Morton*. New York: Putnam, 1953.

Gray, James. *The University of Minnesota, 1851–1951*. Minneapolis: University of Minnesota Press, 1951.

Griffith, John L. "The Carnegie Reports." *Journal of Higher Education* 1 (June 1930): 325–29.

Gruber, Carol S. *Mars and Minerva: World War I and the Uses of the Higher Learning in America*. Baton Rouge: Louisiana State University Press, 1975.

Gruensfelder, Melvin H. *A History of the Origin and Development of the Southeastern Conference*. Master's thesis, University of Illinois, Urbana, 1964.

Guiliano, Jennifer. *Indian Spectacle: College Mascots and the Anxiety of Modern America*. New Brunswick, N.J.: Rutgers University Press, 2015.

Gulick, Luther H. "Amateurism." *NCAA Proceedings* 2 (1907): 40–46.

Gurr, Charles S. *The Personal Equation: A Biography of Steadman Vincent Sanford*. Athens: University of Georgia Press, 1999.

Guttman, Allen. *The Games Must Go On: Avery Brundage and the Olympic Movement*. New York: Columbia University Press, 1984.

Halas, George. *Halas by Halas: The Autobiography of George Halas*. With Gwen Morgan and Arthur Veysey. New York: McGraw-Hill, 1979.

Hamilton, Raphael N. *The Story of Marquette University: An Object Lesson in the Development of Catholic Higher Education*. Milwaukee: Marquette University Press, 1953.

Hanford, George H. *A Report to the American Council on Education on An Inquiry into the Need for and the Feasibility of a National Study of Intercollegiate Athletics*. Washington, D.C.: American Council on Education, 1974.

Hannah, John A. *A Memoir*. East Lansing: Michigan State University Press, 1980.

Harding, Samuel B., ed. *Indiana University, 1820–1904. Historical Sketch: Development of the Course of Instruction*. Bibliography. Bloomington: Indiana University, 1904.

Harris, Reed. *King Football: The Vulgarization of the American College*. New York: Vanguard, 1932.

Hart-Nibbrig, N., and Clement Cottingham. *The Political Economy of College Sports*. Lexington, Mass.: Lexington, 1986.

Hawkins, Hugh. *Banding Together: The Rise of National Associations in American Higher Education, 1887–1950*. Baltimore, Md.: Johns Hopkins University Press, 1992.

———. *Between Harvard and America: The Educational Leadership of Charles W. Eliot*. New York: Oxford University Press, 1972.

Hayes, Patrick J. *A Catholic Brain Trust: The History of the Catholic Commission on Intellectual and Cultural Affairs, 1945–1965*. Notre Dame, Ind.: University of Notre Dame Press, 2011.

Hendrickson, Joe. *Tournament of Roses: The First 100 Years*. Los Angeles: Knapp, 1989.

Hepburn, William M., and Louis M. Sears. *Purdue University: Fifty Years of Progress*. Indianapolis: Hollenbeck, 1925.

Herring, Donald G. *Forty Years of Football*. New York: Carlyle, 1940.

Hill, Dean. *Football Thru the Years*. New York: Gridiron, 1940.

Holt, Richard. *Sport and the British: A Modern History*. Oxford: Clarendon, 1990.

Holtzman, Jerome, ed. *No Cheering in the Press Box*. New York: Holt, Rinehart, and Winston, 1973.

Hooper, Osman C. *History of Ohio State University*. Vol. 2: 1910–1925. Columbus: Ohio State University Press.

Hopkins, Ernest M. "The Place of Athletics in an Educational Program." *NCAA Proceedings* 20 (1925): 1–9.

Hove, Arthur. *The University of Wisconsin: A Pictorial History*. Madison: University of Wisconsin Press, 1991.

Huff, George A. "Amateur Baseball Standing." *Alumni Quarterly* 2 (October 1908): 123–26.

———. "Collegiate Baseball and Professionalism," *Illio '09*, 206–8.

Hurd, Richard M. *A History of Yale Athletics, 1840–1888*. New Haven, Conn.: Hurd, 1888.

Hutchins, Robert M. "Gate Receipts and Glory." *Saturday Evening Post*, December 3, 1938, 23, 73–76.

Hyman, Mervin D., and Gordon S. White Jr. *Big Ten Football: Its Life and Times, Great Coaches, Players and Games*. New York: Macmillan, 1977.

IC Minutes (Intercollegiate Conference Minutes). The minutes of the Intercollegiate Conference of Faculty Representatives are in the Big Ten Conference headquarters in Park Ridge, Illinois. The *Proceedings of the Intercollegiate Conference of Faculty Representatives of the Athletic Committees or Boards of Control of the Following Universities: Chicago, Illinois, Indiana, Iowa, Michigan, Minnesota, Northwestern, Purdue, Wisconsin* (Minneapolis: University Press, 1901) contain the minutes through 1900.

Inabinett, Mark. *Grantland Rice and His Heroes: The Sportswriter as Mythmaker in the 1920s*. Knoxville: University of Tennessee Press, 1994.

Indiana University, 1820–1920: Centennial Memorial Volume. Bloomington: Indiana University, 1921.

Ingrassia, Brian M. "Public Influence inside the College Walls: Progressive Era Universities, Social Scientists, and Intercollegiate Football Reform." *Journal of the Gilded Age and Progressive Era* 10 (January 2011): 59–88.

———. *The Rise of Gridiron University: Higher Education's Uneasy Alliance with Big-Time Football*. Lawrence: University of Kansas Press, 2012.

The Inter-Allied Games: Paris, 22nd June to 6th July 1919. Paris: Games Committee, 1919.

Israel, David. *The Cornhuskers: Nebraska Football*. Chicago: Regnery, 1975.

Jable, J. Thomas. "The Birth of Professional Football: Pittsburgh Athletic Clubs Ring in Professionals in 1892." *Western Pennsylvania Historical Magazine* 62 (April 1979): 131–47.

Jacobs, Wilbur R. *The Historical World of Frederick Jackson Turner with Selections from His Correspondence*. New Haven, Conn.: Yale University Press, 1968.

Jacobs, William Jay. "John R. Tunis: A Commitment to Values." *Horn Book* 43 (February 1967): 51.

Johnston, Alva. "Profiles: C. C. Pyle, Cash and Cary." *New Yorker*, December 8, 1928, 31–33.

Kaye, Ivan N. *Good Clean Violence: A History of College Football*. Philadelphia: Lippincott, 1973.

Kelly, Fred C. *David Ross, Modern Pioneer: A Biography*. New York: Knopf, 1946.

———. *George Ade: Warmhearted Satirist*. Indianapolis: Bobbs-Merrill, 1947.

Kemp, James E. "The Proper Function of Athletics in Colleges and Universities." *American Physical Education Review* 13 (February 1908): 91–97.

Kennedy, Charles W. *College Athletics*. Princeton, N.J.: Princeton University Press, 1925.

———. *Sport and Sportsmanship*. Princeton, N.J.: Princeton University Press, 1931.

Knight Commission on Intercollegiate Athletics. *A Call to Action: Reconnecting College Sports and Higher Education.* June 2001. Available at http://www.knightcommission.org/images/pdfs/2001_knight_report.pdf.

———. *Keeping Faith with the Student Athlete: A New Model for Intercollegiate Athletics.* March 1991. Available at http://www.knightcommission.org/images/pdfs/1991-93_kcia_report.pdf.

Knoll, Robert E. *Prairie University: A History of the University of Nebraska.* Lincoln: University of Nebraska Press and the Alumni Association of the University of Nebraska, 1995.

Kryk, John. *Natural Enemies: The Notre Dame-Michigan Football Feud.* Kansas City, Mo.: Andrews and McMeel, 1994.

Lamb, Dick, and Bert McGrane. *75 Years with the Fighting Hawkeyes.* Dubuque, Iowa: Brown, 1994.

Larson, Melissa. *The Pictorial History of College Football.* New York: Gallery, 1989.

Lawrence, Paul R. *Unsportsmanlike Conduct: The National Collegiate Athletic Association and the Business of College Football.* New York: Praeger, 1987.

Lawson, Hal A., and Alan G. Ingham. "Conflicting Ideologies Concerning the University and Intercollegiate Athletics: Harper and Hutchins at Chicago, 1892–1940." *Journal of Sport History* 7 (Winter 1980): 37–67.

Lester, Robin. *Stagg's University: The Rise, Decline, and Fall of Big-Time Football at Chicago.* Urbana: University of Illinois Press, 1995.

Levine, David O. *The American College and the Culture of Aspiration, 1915–1940.* Ithaca, N.Y.: Cornell University Press, 1986.

Lewis, Guy. "World War I and the Emergence of Sport for the Masses." *Maryland Historian* 4 (Fall 1973): 109–22.

Lindaman, Matthew. "'That Our Youth May Have Strength in Spirit, Mind, and Body': The Conception and Construction of Illinois Memorial Stadium." *Journal of Illinois History* 7 (Autumn 2004): 201–20.

———. "Up! Up! Stadium: Planning and Building a War Memorial." *Minnesota History* 62 (Fall 2010): 107–16.

Littlewood, Thomas B. *Arch: A Promoter, Not a Poet: The Story of Arch Ward.* Ames: Iowa State Press, 1990.

Long, O. F. "Fourth District." *NCAA Proceedings* 24 (January 1, 1930).

———. "Fourth District." *NCAA Proceedings* 26 (1931).

Lucas, Charles P. "Commercializing Amateur Athletics." *World To-Day* 10 (March 1906): 281–85.

Lucas, John. "The Hegemonic Rule of the Amateur Athletic Union 1888–1914: James Edward Sullivan as Prime Mover." *International Journal of the History of Sport* 11 (December 1994): 355–71.

Lucas, John A., and Ronald A. Smith. *Saga of American Sport.* Philadelphia: Lea and Febiger, 1978.

MacCambridge, Michael. *America's Game: The Epic Story of How Pro Football Captured a Nation.* New York: Random House, 2004.

March, Harry A. *Pro Football: Its "Ups" and "Downs": A Light-Hearted History of the Post Graduate Game.* Albany, N.Y.: Lyon, 1934.

McCallum, John D. *Big Eight Football*. New York: Scribner's, 1979.

———. *Big Ten Football since 1895*. Radnor, Penn.: Chilton, 1976.

———. *Ivy League Football since 1872*. New York: Stein and Day, 1977.

McCallum, John, and Charles H. Pearson. *College Football U.S.A., 1869–1972*. New York: Hall of Fame/McGraw-Hill, 1972.

McCaskey, Patrick. *Bear with Me: A Family History of George Halas and the Chicago Bears*. With Mike Sandrolini. Chicago: Triumph, 2009.

McClellan, Keith. *The Sunday Game: At the Dawn of Professional Football*. Akron, Ohio: University of Akron Press, 1998.

McNeill, William H. *Hutchins' University: A Memoir of the University of Chicago, 1929–1950*. Chicago: University of Chicago Press, 1991.

Maltby, Marc S. *The Origins and Early Development of Professional Football*. New York: Garland, 1997.

Mallette, Bruce I., and Richard D. Howard, eds. *Monitoring and Assessing Intercollegiate Athletics*. San Francisco: Jossey-Bass, 1992.

Mangan, J. A., and James Walvin, eds. *Manliness and Morality: Middle-Class Masculinity in Britain and America, 1800–1940*. Manchester: Manchester University Press, 1987.

March, Harry A. *Pro Football: Its "Ups" and "Downs": A Light-Hearted History of the Post Graduate Game*. Albany, N.Y.: Lyon, 1934.

Mayer, Milton. *Robert Maynard Hutchins: A Memoir*. Berkeley: University of California Press, 1993.

Meiklejohn, Alexander. "What Are College Games For?" *Atlantic Monthly*, November 1922, 663–71.

Menke, Frank D. *The Encyclopedia of Sports*. 4th rev. ed. New York: Barnes, 1969.

Mennell, James. "The Service Football Program of World War I: Its Impact on the Popularity of the Game." *Journal of Sport History* 16 (Winter 1989): 248–60.

Michelson, Herb, and Dave Newhouse. *Rose Bowl Football since 1902*. New York: Stein and Day, 1977.

Michener, James A. *Sports in America*. New York: Random House, 1976.

Miller, John J. *The Big Scrum: How Teddy Roosevelt Saved Football*. New York: Harper, 2011.

Miller, Patrick B. "The Manly, the Moral, and the Proficient: College Sport in the New South." *Journal of Sport History* 24 (Fall, 1997): 285–316.

Miller, Richard I. *The Truth about Big-Time Football*. New York: Sloane, 1953.

Moore, John H. "Football's Ugly Decades, 1893–1913." *Smithsonian Journal of History* 2 (Fall 1967): 49–68.

Moran, Thomas F. "Courtesy and Sportsmanship in Intercollegiate Athletics." *American Physical Education Review* 15 (February 1910): 118–24.

Myers, Burton D. *History of Indiana University*. Vol. 2, 1902–1937: The Bryan Administration. Bloomington: Indiana University, 1952.

Needham, Henry Beach. "The College Athlete: His Amateur Code: Its Evasion and Administration." Part II: "'Summer Ball,' the Gate-Money Evil, and 'Unnecessary Roughness' in Football." *McClure's* 25 (July 1905): 206–73.

———. "The College Athlete: How Commercialism Is Making Him a Professional." Part I: "Recruiting and Subsidizing." *McClure's Magazine* 25 (June 1905): 115–28.

Nelson, David M. *The Anatomy of a Game: Football, the Rules, and the Men Who Made the Game.* Newark: University of Delaware Press, 1994.

Noll, Roger G., and Andrew Zimbalist, eds. *Sports, Jobs, and Taxes: The Economic Impact of Sports Teams and Stadiums.* Washington, D.C.: Brookings Institution Press, 1997.

O'Hanlon, Timothy P. "Interscholastic Athletics, 1900–1940: Shaping Citizens for Unequal Roles in the Modern Industrial State." PhD diss., University of Illinois, 1979.

Oriard, Michael. *Brand NFL: Making and Selling America's Favorite Sport.* Chapel Hill: University of North Carolina Press, 2007.

———. *The End of Autumn.* Urbana: University of Illinois Press, 2009.

———. "In the Beginning Was the Rule." In *The New American Sport History: Recent Approaches and Perspective,* edited by S. W. Pope, 88–120. Urbana: University of Illinois Press, 1997).

———. *King Football: Sports and Spectacle in the Golden Age of Radio and Newsreels, Movies and Magazines, the Weekly and the Daily Press.* Chapel Hill: University of North Carolina Press, 2001.

———. *Reading Football: How the Popular Press Created an American Spectacle.* Chapel Hill: University of North Carolina Press, 1995.

Ours, Robert M. *Bowl Games: College Football's Greatest Tradition.* Yardley, Penn.: Westholme, 2004.

———. *College Football Almanac.* New York: Barnes and Noble, 1984.

Pack, Philip Clarkston. *100 Years of Athletics: The University of Michigan, 1837–1937.* Ann Arbor: The "M" Club and the Michigan Athletic Managers' Club, 1937.

Page, Joseph S. *Football Championships before the Super Bowl: A Year-by-Year History, 1926–1965.* Jefferson, N.C.: McFarland, 2011.

Park, Roberta. "Biological Thought, Athletics and the Formation of a 'Man of Character,' 1800–1940." In *Manliness and Morality: Middle-Class Masculinity in Britain and America, 1800–1940,* edited by J. A. Mangan and James Walvin, 7–34. Manchester: Manchester University Press, 1987.

———. "From Football to Rugby—and Back: The University of California-Stanford University Response to the 'Football Crisis of 1905.'" *Journal of Sport History* 11 (Winter 1984): 5–40.

Paulison, Walter. *The Tale of the Wildcats: A Centennial History of Northwestern University Athletics.* Chicago: N Men's Club/Northwestern University Club of Chicago/Northwestern University Alumni Association, 1951.

Peckham, Howard H. *The Making of the University of Michigan, 1817–1967.* Ann Arbor: University of Michigan Press, 1967.

Pendergast, Tom. "'Horatio Alger Doesn't Work Here Any More': Masculinity and American Magazines, 1919–1940," *American Studies* 38 (Spring 1997): 55–77.

Perrin, Tom. *Football: A College History.* Jefferson, N.C.: McFarland, 1987.

Perry, Charles M. *Henry Philip Tappan: Philosopher and University President.* Ann Arbor: University of Michigan Press, 1933.

Perry, Lawrence. "The Stadium and College Athletics." *Scribner's* 56 (November 1914): 576.

Perry, Will. *The Wolverines: A Story of Michigan Football.* Huntsville, Ala.: Strode, 1974.

Persons, Stow. *The University of Iowa in the Twentieth Century: An Institutional History.* Iowa City: University of Iowa Press, 1990.

Peterson, James A. *Grange of Illinois.* Chicago: Hinckley and Schmitt, 1954.

Peterson, Robert W. *Pigskin: The Early Years of Pro Football.* New York: Oxford University Press, 1997.

Phillips, Paul C. "Length of Intercollegiate Schedules." *American Physical Education Review* 13 (February 1908): 105–12.

A Pictorial History of Northwestern University, 1851–1951. Evanston: Northwestern University Press, 1951.

Pierce. Bessie L. *A History of Chicago.* Vol. 3: The Rise of a Modern City, 1871–1893. New York: Knopf, 1957.

Pierce, Palmer, E. "The Intercollegiate Athletic Association of the United States." *American Physical Education Review,* 15 (February 1910): 84+.

———. "The Intercollegiate Athletic Association of the United States." *American Physical Education Review,* 16 (February 1911): 75–78.

———. "The Intercollegiate Athletic Association of the United States." *NCAA Proceedings* 1 (1906): 3–37.

———. "The International Athletic Association of the United States: Its Origin, Growth, and Function." *NCAA Proceedings* 2 (1907): 27–32.

Pilat, Oliver. *Pegler: Angry Man of the Press.* Boston: Beacon, 1963.

Plant, Marcus L. "The Board in Control of Intercollegiate Athletics." In *The University of Michigan: An Encyclopedic Survey,* edited by Walter A. Donnelly and Wilfred B. Shaw, 4:1959–67. 4 vols. Ann Arbor: University of Michigan Press, 1958.

Pollard, James E. *History of the Ohio State University: The Story of Its First Seventy-Five Years, 1873–1948.* Columbus: Ohio State University Press, 1952.

———. *Ohio State Athletics: 1879–1959.* Columbus: Ohio State Athletic Department, 1959.

Poole, Gary A. *The Galloping Ghost: Red Grange, An American Football Legend.* Boston: Houghton Mifflin, 2008.

Pope, Edwin. *Football's Greatest Coaches.* Atlanta: Tupper and Love, 1935.

Pope, S. W. "Amateurism and American Sports Culture: The Invention of an Athletic Tradition in the United States, 1870–1900." *International Journal of the History of Sport* 13 (December 1996): 290–309.

———, ed. *The New American Sport History: Recent Approaches and Perspectives.* Urbana: University of Illinois Press, 1997.

———. *Patriotic Games: Sporting Traditions in the American Imagination, 1876–1926.* New York: Oxford University Press, 1997.

Porter, David L., ed. *Biographical Dictionary of American Sports: Football.* New York: Greenwood, 1987.

Powel, Harford, Jr. *Walter Camp, the Father of American Football.* Boston: Little, Brown, 1926.

Powell, John T. "The Development and Influence of Faculty Representatives in the Control of Intercollegiate Sport within the Intercollegiate Conference of Faculty Representatives from Its Inception in January 1895 to July 1963." PhD diss. Physical Education, University of Illinois, 1964.

Presbrey, Frank, and James H. Moffatt, comp. and eds. *Athletics at Princeton: A History*. New York: Presbrey, 1901.

"President James and the Land Grant College." *Outlook* 112 (8 March 1916): 536, 539.

"President of Collegiate National Athletic Association Ordered to China." *American Physical Education Review* 17 (June 1912): 495–512.

Pritchett, Henry S. "The Abuse of Intercollegiate Athletics." In *Eighteenth Annual Report of the President and of the Treasurer*, Carnegie Foundation for the Advancement of Teaching, 33–39. New York: The Foundation, 1923.

———. "College Athletics." In *Twentieth Annual Report of the President and of the Treasurer*, The Carnegie Foundation for the Advancement of Teaching, 132–36. New York: The Foundation, 1925).

———. "Preface." In Savage et al., *American College Athletics* Bulletin 23.

———. "A Substitute for Football." *Atlantic Monthly* 150 (September 1932): 44–48.

Proceedings of the Intercollegiate Conference of Faculty Representatives of the Athletic Committees or Boards of Control of the Following Universities: Chicago, Illinois, Indiana, Iowa, Michigan, Minnesota, Northwestern, Purdue, Wisconsin. Minneapolis: University Press, 1901. Cited as *Proceedings*. The minutes of the Intercollegiate Conference of Faculty Representatives are in the Big Ten Conference headquarters in Park Ridge, Illinois. The *Proceedings* contain the minutes through 1900 and some other documents.

Pruter, Robert. *The Rise of American High School Sports and the Search for Control, 1880–1930*. Syracuse: Syracuse University Press, 2013.

Pullen, Carol F. *A History of Intercollegiate Football at the University of Illinois*. Master's thesis in Physical Education, University of Illinois, 1957.

Putney, Clifford. *Muscular Christianity: Manhood and Sports in Protestant America, 1880–1920*. Cambridge: Harvard University Press, 2001.

Pyre, J. F. A. *Wisconsin*. New York: Oxford University Press, 1920.

Rader, Benjamin G. *American Sports: From the Age of Folk Games to the Age of Spectators*. Englewood Cliffs, N.J.: Prentice-Hall, 1983.

Raphaelson, Sampson. "How Money Talke—$700,000 of It—To the Everlasting Glory of Illinois." *Alumni Quarterly and Fortnightly Notes* 6 (May 15, 1921): 235–36.

Ratermann, Dale. *The Big Ten: A Century of Excellence*. Champaign, Ill.: Sagamore, 1996.

Rea, Mark. *The Die-Hard Fan's Guide to Buckeye Football*. Washington, D.C.: Regnery, 2009.

Reid, Bill. *Big-Time Football at Harvard, 1905: The Diary of Coach Bill Reid*. Edited by Ronald A. Smith. Urbana: University of Illinois Press, 1994.

"Report by Committee G, Intercollegiate Football." *Bulletin of the American Association of University Professors* 12, no. 4 (April 1920): 218–34.

Rice, Grantland. "The Pigskin Ballyhoo." *Collier's* September 18, 1926.

———. *The Tumult and the Shouting: My Life in Sport*. New York: Barnes, 1954.

Richards, Gregory B., and Melissa H. Larson. *Big-10 Football*. Greenwich, Conn.: Bison, 1987.

Reiff, Guy G. "The Establishment of the National Intercollegiate Football Rules Committee," *Physical Educator* 19 (December 1962): 135–38.

Riess, Steven A. *The American Sporting Experience: A Historical Anthology of Sport in America*. New York: Leisure, 1984.

———. *City Games: The Evolution of American Urban Society and the Rise of Sports*. Urbana: University of Illinois Press, 1989.

———. *Sport in Industrial America, 1850–1920*. Wheeling, Ill.: Harlan Davidson, 1995.

———. *Touching Base: Professional Baseball and American Culture in the Progressive Era*. Rev. ed. Urbana: University of Illinois Press, 1999.

Riess, Steven A., and Gerald R. Gems, eds. *The Chicago Sports Reader: 100 Years of Sports in the Windy City*. Urbana: University of Illinois Press, 2009.

Ripley, Amanda. *The Smartest Kids in the World: And How They Got That Way*. New York: Simon and Shuster, 2013.

Ritchey, Charles J. *Drake University through Seventy-Five Years, 1881–1956*. Des Moines, Iowa: Drake University, 1956.

Roberts, Howard. *The Big Nine: The Story of Football in the Western Conference*. New York: Putnam's, 1948.

———. *The Story of Pro Football*. New York: Rand McNally, 1953.

Rooney, John F., Jr. *The Recruiting Game: Toward a New System of Intercollegiate Sports*. 2nd ed. Lincoln: University of Nebraska Press, 1987.

Ross, David E. "Athletics." *Proceedings of the Association of Governing Boards of State Universities and Allied Institutions* (October 30, 1931): 44–49.

Rotundo, E. Anthony. *American Manhood: Transformations from the Revolution to the Modern Era*. New York: Basic, 1993.

———. "Body and Soul: Changing Ideals of American Middle-Class Manhood, 1770–1920." *Journal of Social History* 16 (Summer 1983): 23–38.

Rudolph, Frederick. *The American College and University: A History*. New York: Knopf, 1962.

Ryan, W. Carson, Jr., *The Literature of American School and College Athletics*. Bulletin 24. New York: Carnegie Foundation for the Advancement of Teaching, 1929.

Sack, Allen L., and Ellen J. Staurowsky. *College Athletes for Hire: The Evolution and Legacy of NCAA's Amateur Myth*. Westport, Conn.: Praeger, 1998.

Sanford, S. V. "A Reply to Professor Wilkins' Report on 'Intercollegiate Football.'" *NCAA Proceedings* 21 (1926): 89–102.

Sargent, Dudley A. "Competition in College Athletics." *NCAA Proceedings* 4 (1909): 49–55.

———. "History of the Administration of Intercollegiate Athletics in the United States." *American Physical Education Review* 15 (April 1910): 252–63.

Savage, Howard J. "Aspects of the Relation of Education to College Sport." *NCAA Proceedings* 24 (January 1, 1930), 90–95.

Savage, Howard J., Howard Bentley, John T. McGovern, and Dean F. Smiley. *American College Athletics*. Bulletin 23. New York: Carnegie Foundation for the Advancement of Teaching, 1929.

Savage, Howard J., John T. McGovern, and Harold W. Bentley. *Current Developments in American College Sport*. New York: Carnegie Foundation for the Advancement of Teaching, 1931.

Sawyer, R. McLaran. *Centennial History of the University of Nebraska*. Vol. 2: The Modern University, 1920–1969. Lincoln, Neb.: Centennial, 1973.

Schlereth, Thomas J. *The University of Notre Dame: A Portrait of Its History and Campus*. Notre Dame, Ind.: University of Notre Dame Press, 1976.

Schmidt, Raymond. "The 1929 Iowa Football Scandal: Paying Tribute to the Carnegie Report?" *Journal of Sport History* 34 (Fall 2007): 343–51.
———. *Shaping College Football: The Transformation of an American Sport, 1919–1930.* Syracuse: Syracuse University Press, 2007.
Schoor, Gene. *Red Grange: Football's Greatest Halfback.* With Henry Gilfond. New York: Julian Messner, 1952.
Scott, Walter Dill, and Wilfred B. Shaw. "Michigan and the Conference: A Ten-Year Argument over the University's Athletic Relations." *Michigan Alumnus* 54, no. 10 (December 6, 1947): 34–48.
———. *The University of Michigan.* New York: Harcourt, Brace, and How, 1920.
———, ed., *The University of Michigan: An Encyclopedic Survey.* 4 vols. Ann Arbor: University of Michigan Press, 1951.
Schwartz, Robert A. "Tappan, Henry Philip." In *American National Biography*, edited by John A. Garraty and Mark C. Carnes, 21:315–16. New York: Oxford University Press, 1999.
Sellery, G. C. *Some Ferments at Wisconsin, 1901–1947: Memories and Reflections.* Madison: University of Wisconsin Press for the University of Wisconsin Library, 1960.
Smith, Ronald A. "Far More than Commercialism: Stadium Building from Harvard's Innovations to Stanford's 'Dirt Bowl.'" In Dryeson and Trumpbour, *Rise of Stadiums,* 35–41.
———. "History of Amateurism in Men's Intercollegiate Athletics: The Continuance of a 19th-Century Anachronism in America." *Quest* 45 (1993): 430–47.
———. *Pay for Play: A History of Big-Time Athletic Reform.* Urbana: University of Illinois Press, 2011.
———. "Preludes to the NCAA: Early Failures of Faculty Intercollegiate Athletic Control." *Research Quarterly for Exercise and Sport* 54 (1983): 372–82.
———. *Sports and Freedom: The Rise of Big-Time College Athletics.* New York: Oxford University Press, 1988.
Soderstrom, Robert M. *The Big House: Fielding H. Yost and the Building of Michigan Stadium.* Ann Arbor: Huron River, 2005.
Solberg, Winton U. *The University of Illinois, 1867–1894: An Intellectual and Cultural History.* Urbana, University of Illinois Press, 1968.
———. *The University of Illinois, 1894–1904: The Shaping of the University.* Urbana: University of Illinois Press, 2000.
Spalding's Athletic Library. *Athletic Almanac, 1920.* New York: American Sports Publishing, 1920.
Sperber, Murray. *College Sports, Inc.* New York: Holt, 1990.
———. *Onward to Victory: The Crises that Shaped College Sports.* New York: Holt, 1998.
———. *Shake Down the Thunder: The Creation of Notre Dame Football.* New York: Holt, 1993.
Stagg, A. A. "Reports from the District Representatives of the Intercollegiate Athletic Association." *American Physical Education Review* 14 (February 1909): 114–15.
Stagg, Amos Alonzo, and Wesley W. Stout. *Touchdown!* New York: Longmans, Green, 1927.
Stearns, Peter N. *Be a Man: Males in Modern Society.* New York: Holmes and Meier, 1979.
Stewart, Alva W. *College Football Stadiums: An Illustrated Guide to NCAA Division 1-A.* Jefferson, N.C.: McFarland, 2000.

St. John, L. W. "The Future of Intercollegiate Sports and the Use of Large Gate Receipts." *American Physical Education Review* 28 (1923): 260–66.

Stone, Richard. "The Graham Plan of 1935: An Aborted Crusade to De-emphasize College Athletics." *North Carolina Historical Review* 64 (July 1987): 274–93.

Stone, Winthrop E. *President of Purdue University, 1900–1921: A Memorial.* Lafayette: 1922.

Storr, Richard J. *Harper's University: The Beginnings; A History of the University of Chicago.* Chicago: University of Chicago Press, 1966.

Sumner, Jim L. "John Franklin Crowell, Methodism, and the Football Controversy at Trinity College, 1887–1894." *Journal of Sport History* 17 (Spring 1990): 5–20.

Taylor, Michael. *Contesting Constructed Indian-ness: The Intersection of the Frontier, Masculinity, and Whiteness in Native American Mascot Representations.* Lanham, Md.: Lexington, 2013.

Telander, Rick. *The Hundred Yard Lie: The Corruption of College Football and What We Can Do to Stop It.* New York: Simon and Shuster, 1989.

Thelin, John R. *The Cultivation of Ivy: A Saga of the College in America.* Cambridge: Schenkman, 1976.

————. *Games Colleges Play: Scandal and Reform in Intercollegiate Athletics.* Baltimore, Md.: Johns Hopkins University Press, 1994.

Thomas, Michael J., comp. *College Football: Big Ten Style; A Comprehensive Report of Every Football Game Ever Played by Big Ten Teams through January 1, 2000.* Chicago: College Football Report, 2000.

Tilton, Leon D., and Thomas E. O'Donnell. *History and Growth and Development of the Campus Plan of the University of Illinois.* Urbana: University of Illinois Press, 1930.

Toma, J. Douglas. *Football U.: Spectator Sports in the Life of the American University.* Ann Arbor: University of Michigan Press, 2003.

Topping, Robert W. *A Century and Beyond: The History of Purdue University.* West Lafayette, Ind.: Purdue University Press, 1988.

Treat, Roger, *The Encyclopedia of Football.* 14th rev. ed. New York: Barnes, 1976.

Trumpbour, Robert C. *The New Cathedrals: Politics and Media in the History of Stadium Construction.* Syracuse, N.Y.: Syracuse University Press, 2007.

Tunis, John R., "All-American." *New Yorker*, October 31, 1925, 11–12.

————. "Gas and the Games." *Saturday Evening Post* 202 (January 25, 1930): 12–13, 44.

————. "The Great God Football." *Harper's* 137 (November 1928): 742–52.

————. "The Great Sports Myth." *Harper's* 156 (March 1928): 122–431. A shorter version is in John R. Tunis, *Sports: Heroics and Hysterics* (New York: John Day Co., 1928), 16–35.

————. *A Measure of Independence: An Autobiography.* New York: Atheneum, 1964.

————. "This Football Madness." *Collier's* 74 (November 29, 1924): 28, 47.

————. "What Price College Football?" *American Mercury* 48 (October 1939): 129–42.

Turrini, Joseph M. *The End of Amateurism in American Track and Field.* Urbana: University of Illinois Press, 2010.

"A University President's View of Athletics." *Athletic Journal* 6 (December 1925): 38–41.

Vass, George. *George Halas and the Chicago Bears.* Chicago: Regnery, 1971.

Voltmer, Carl D. *A Brief History of the Intercollegiate Conference of Faculty Representatives with Special Consideration of Athletic Problems.* New York, 1935.

Waldo, Clarence A. "The Proper Control of College Athletic Sports." *American Physical Education Review* 14 (February 1909): 83–90.

Waldorf, John. *NCAA Football Rules Committee Chronology of 100 Years, 1876 to 1976*. Shawnee Mission, Kan.: NCAA, 1975.

Wallace, Francis. "The Football Laboratory Explodes: The Climax in the Test Case at Pitt." *Saturday Evening Post* 212 (November 4, 1939): 20–21, 80, 82, 85–86.

———. "The Hypocrisy of Football Reform." *Scribner's* 82 (November 1927): 568–73.

———. "Test Case at Pitt: The Facts about College Football Play for Pay." *Saturday Evening Post* 212 (October 28, 1939): 14–15, 47–49, 51–52.

Walsh, Christy, ed. *College Football and All America Review*. Culver City, Calif.: Murray and Gee, 1949.

Walsh, Christy, and Glen Whittle, eds. *Intercollegiate Football: A Complete Pictorial and Statistical Review from 1869 to 1934*. New York: Doubleday/Doran, 1934.

Ward, Arch. "Football in the Middle West." In Danzig and Brandwein, *Sports Golden Age*, 131–44.

Ward, Estelle F. *The Story of Northwestern University*. New York: Dodd, Mead, 1924.

Ware, Frederick. *Fifty Years of Football: A Condensed History of the Game at the University of Nebraska*. Omaha, Neb.: Omaha World-Herald, 1940.

Warnock, Arthur R. "The Position of Illinois in the Western Conference." *Alumni Quarterly* 6 (April 1912): 104–14.

Watson, Nick J., Stuart Weir, and Stephen Friend. "The Development of Muscular Christianity in Victorian Britain and Beyond." *Journal of Religion and Society* 7 (2005): 1–21.

Watterson, John S. *College Football: History, Spectacle, Controversy*. Baltimore, Md.: Johns Hopkins University Press, 2000.

———. "The Football Crisis of 1909–1910: The Response of the Eastern 'Big Three.'" *Journal of Sport History* 8 (Spring 1981): 33–49.

———. "The Gridiron Crisis of 1905: Was It Really a Crisis?" *Journal of Sport History* 27 (Summer 2000): 291–98.

———. "Inventing Modern Football." *American Heritage* 39 (September/October 1988): 102–6, 109–11, 113.

Weeks, James. "Football as a Metaphor for War." *American Heritage* 39 (September/October 1988): 113.

Westby, David L., and Allen Sack. "The Commercialization and Functional Rationalization of College Football: Its Origins." *Journal of Higher Education* 47 (November/December 1976): 625–47.

"Western Conference Officiating Procedure and Interpretations." *Athletic Journal* 6 (October 1925): 36–41.

Weyand, A. M. *American Football, Its History and Development*. New York: Appleton, 1926.

"What the Draft Should Teach Us." *Literary Digest* 62 (August 2, 1919): 39.

"What the Editors Say About Athletics." *Athletic Journal* 6 (June 1926): 40–46.

Whitney, Caspar W. "Amateur Sport." *Harper's Weekly* 39 (December 23, 1895): 1123–24, and 40 (December 28, 1895): 1257–58.

Whittingham, Richard. *The Chicago Bears: An Illustrated History*. Chicago: Rand McNally, 1979.

———. *Saturday Afternoon: College Football and the Men Who Made the Day*. New York: Workman, 1985.

———. *What a Game They Played: Stories of the Early Days of Football by Those Who Were There*. New York: Harper and Row, 1984.

Wiggins, David K., ed. *Sport in America: From Wicked Amusement to National Obsession*. Champaign, Ill.: Human Kinetics, 1995.

Wilkins, Ernest H. "Intercollegiate Football: Report by Committee G." American Association of University Professors *Bulletin* 12 (April 1926): 218–34.

———. "The Relation of Intercollegiate Football to the Purpose of the American College." *NCAA Proceedings* 21 (New York, 1926): 81–88.

Williamson, Harold F., and Payson S. Wild. *Northwestern University: A History, 1850–1975*. Evanston, Ill.: Northwestern University, 1976.

Wilson, Kenneth L. "Tug," and Jerry Brondfield. *The Big Ten*. Englewood Cliffs, N.J.: Prentice Hall, 1967.

Wilson, Robert A. *A History of the Administration of Intercollegiate Athletics at the University of Illinois*. Master's thesis, University of Illinois, 1948.

Wood, Bob. *Big Ten Country: A Journey through One Football Season*. New York: William Morrow, 1989.

Wylie, Theophilus A. *Indiana University: Its History from 1820, When Founded, to 1890*. Indianapolis: Burford, 1890.

Yost, Fielding H. "Administration of Intercollegiate and Interscholastic Games." *American Physical Education Review* 30 (March 1925): 115–18.

———. *Football for Player and Spectator*. Ann Arbor: University Publishing, 1905.

Young, David J. *Arrogance and Scheming in the Big Ten: Michigan State's Quest for Membership and Michigan's Powerful Opposition*. Lansing, Mich.: DJY, 2011.

Zimbalist, Andrew. *Unpaid Professionals: Commercialism and Conflict in Big-Time College Sports*. Princeton, N.J.: Princeton University Press, 1999.

Index

WINTON U. SOLBERG is professor emeritus of history at the University of Illinois at Urbana-Champaign. His many books include *The University of Illinois, 1894–1904: The Shaping of the University* and *Redeem the Time: The Puritan Sabbath in Early America.*

University of Illinois Press
1325 South Oak Street
Champaign, IL 61820-6903
www.press.uillinois.edu